A SOCIAL HISTORY
OF THE
BRITISH OVERSEAS

THE BRITISH
IN THE
FAR EAST

A SOCIAL HISTORY
OF THE
BRITISH OVERSEAS

EDITED BY
PETER QUENNELL

THE BRITISH
IN THE
FAR EAST

George Woodcock

ATHENEUM

New York

1969

CONTENTS

Preface   xiii
Introduction   xv

PART I   THE EMPIRE MAKERS
1   The Traders   3
2   The Mariners   20
3   The Men of War   33
4   The Administrators   51
5   The Adventurers   71
6   Men and the Land   88
7   Spokesmen of the Imperial Deity   98

PART II   THE BRITISH COMMUNITIES
8   The Way to the East   113
9   The Ways of Government   126
10   The Cities   134
11   Shanghai and other Places   150
12   Private Houses   162
13   The Social World   185
14   The Life of the Mind   204

PART III   IMPERIAL TWILIGHT
15   The Catastrophe   221
16   The Final Phase   233
     Select Bibliography   246
     Index   251

ILLUSTRATIONS

THE CHINA TRADE (*between pp. 12 and 13*)

Portrait of Sir Jamsetjee Jejeebhoy Bt., by George Chinnery (*Jardine Matheson*)

Canton harbour, from a nineteenth-century engraving (*Mansell Collection*)

Watercolour by W. Alexander of an English ship on the Canton river (*India Office Library*)

A map of China made by John Neuhoff

Watercolour of a Chinese market-place (*India Office Library*)

Children's toys made in China for the export trade (*India Office Library*)

Interior of a house, painted to show the range of goods made in China (*India Office Library*)

Sketches by Alexander (*India Office Library*)

Portrait of William Jardine by George Chinnery (*Jardine Matheson*)

Portrait of James Matheson by George Chinnery (*Jardine Matheson*)

The Jardine residence at Macao, painted by George Chinnery (*Jardine Matheson*)

Print of the steamship, *Falcon* (*Jardine Matheson*)

Samples of wallpaper and silk from China (*Jardine Matheson*)

THE MARINERS AND MEN OF WAR (*between pp. 28 and 29*)

The Coxswain of the Commodore's barge at Batavia by Alexander (*India Office Library*)

Sketch of Bantam by Alexander (*India Office Library*)

Jardine's clipper brig, *Lanrick*, off Singapore in 1850 (*Jardine Matheson*)

The S.S. *Chusan* (*P & O Line*)

Engraving of an engagement near Peking in 1860 (*Mansell Collection*)

The British guard of Customs Volunteers in Peking

Englishmen being rowed by Chinese boatmen (*India Office Library*)

Armed anti-pirate guard (*Paul Popper*)

The pirate queen, Wa Lao Choi San (*Paul Popper*)

The P & O's *Canton* and H.M.S. *Columbine* (*P & O Line*)

Execution of pirates at Kowloon (*Press Association*)
Junks (*Overseas Missionary Fellowship*)

THE RULERS (*between pp. 68 and 69*)

Portrait of Lord Macartney (*India Office Library*)
Sketch of the Chinese Emperor, Tchien Lung, by Alexander (*India Office Library*)
Watercolour portrait of the Emperor (*India Office Library*)
Scientific instruments from the Planetarium (*India Office Library*)
Agate sceptre of peace presented to Sir George Staunton (*India Office Library*)
Sketch of the son of Sir George Staunton, by Alexander (*India Office Library*)
The embassy crossing the Whang-ho river (*India Office Library*)
A mandarin carrying the Emperor's official letter (*India Office Library*)
Chinese soldiers by a fort (*India Office Library*)
The garden of a temple at Lewchew (*India Office Library*)
Evening parade at Manilla (*India Office Library*)
The race-course at Happy Valley, Hong Kong (*Jardine Matheson*)
A Chinese law-court (*Mansell Collection*)
The cangue in use (*Radio Times Hulton Picture Library*)
Three women prisoners yoked together in Shanghai, 1907 (*India Office Library*)
Statue of Sir Stamford Raffles, Singapore (*Press Association*)
Sir Rutherford Alcock (*Mansell Collection*)
Meeting of the British commissioner and the village headman at Weihaiwei in 1898 (*India Office Library*)
Celebrations at the Royal Wellington Barracks in 1897 (*India Office Library*)
Shantung at the time of Edward VII's coronation (*India Office Library*)
General Mei and his watch (*India Office Library*)
Customs post between Hong Kong and China (*India Office Library*)
The British and Chinese commissioners at Starling Islet, Hong Kong (*India Office Library*)
British and Chinese officials at Sham Chin, Hong Kong (*India Office Library*)
Scene at a Japanese court in 1863 (*Radio Times Hulton Picture Library*)

ADVENTURERS, MINERS AND PLANTERS (*between pp. 92 and 93*)

Sir James Brooke (*Mansell Collection*)
Illustrations of a Javan chief from Sir Stamford Raffles' *History of Java* (*India Office Library*)
Painting of a slave by Alexander (*India Office Library*)
J. Clunies Ross (*Mansell Collection*)
Alfred Russel Wallace (*Mansell Collection*)
Painting of Malayan slaves by Alexander (*India Office Library*)
Tomb of Caroli Cathcart (*India Office Library*)

Englishmen embarking on the lake of Taal (*India Office Library*)
Chinese pig-farm (*India Office Library*)
Junk-farming (*India Office Library*)
The verandah of Dent and Co's residence at Macao (*Jardine Matheson*)
A neglected rubber plantation
Open-cast tin mining near Kuala Lumpur (*Doreen Leigh*)
A well-tended rubber estate at Penang
Overseeing clearing and planting

SPOKESMEN OF THE IMPERIAL DEITY (*between pp. 108 and 109*)

Trinity Church, Shanghai (*India Office Library*)
Title-page from 'China's Millions' (*Overseas Missionary Fellowship*)
St George's Church, Penang (*Press Association*)
Cathedral of the Immaculate Conception at Hong Kong (*India Office Library*)
The parade at Hong Kong in 1857 (*Mansell Collection*)
Father Nani, Roman Catholic missionary (*Press Association*)
Three veteran missionaries (*Overseas Missionary Fellowship*)
A member of the China Inland Mission in 1904 (*Overseas Missionary Fellowship*)
The hospital of the China Inland Mission at Sui-Ting Fu (*Overseas Missionary Fellowship*)
Callisthenic display at Chefoo (*Overseas Missionary Fellowship*)
Boiling and testing opium, 1881 (*Mansell Collection*)
Opium smokers in 1874 (*Mansell Collection*)

DAYS OF PERIL – THE BOXER REBELLION (*between pp. 124 and 125*)

The Empress dowager of China, 1900 (*Press Association*)
Cartoon from an English journal (*Mansell Collection*)
Print of the Rebellion, from a Chinese newspaper (*Mansell Collection*)
Li-Hung-Chang (*Press Association*)
British legation under seige during the Boxer Rebellion (*Mansell Collection*)
The approach to the British legation in Peking (*Mansell Collection*)
Lady Macdonald (*Mansell Collection*)
Royal Marine artillery detachment embarking from Portsmouth (*Mansell Collection*)
Peking in flames (*Mansell Collection*)
Fortifications at Peking (*Mansell Collection*)
Foreign troops in the Forbidden City (*Press Association*)

THE CITIES (*between pp. 148 and 149*)

Sketch of Batavia by Alexander (*India Office Library*)
View of Whampoa harbour, Canton, by Thomas Daniel (*Jardine Matheson*)

View of the Canton river (*Jardine Matheson*)
Factories at Canton, 1830 (*Jardine Matheson*)
Macao harbour (*Paul Popper*)
The square in Macao, by Chinnery (*Jardine Matheson*)
The Bund at Ningpo (*Paul Popper*)
The administrative buildings at Penang (*India Office Library*)
Offices of the Federal Rubber Stamp Co., Penang (*India Office Library*)
The roadstead at Singapore (*Mansell Collection*)
Flints Buildings, Singapore
Japanese print of a European merchant's house in Yokohama (*Jardine Matheson*)
The port, Yokohama (*Paul Popper*)
The Bund at Yokohama in 1900 (*Jardine Matheson*)
The Bund at Yokohama (*Jardine Matheson*)
Hong in nineteenth-century Shanghai (*Jardine Matheson*)
Modern hongs in Shanghai (*India Office Library*)
Refuse cart in Kuala Lumpur (*India Office Library*)
Open-fronted shops in Kuala Lumpur (*India Office Library*)
Hong Kong, with the Cathedral (*Jardine Matheson*)
Boats at Deep Bay, Hong Kong (*India Office Library*)
Street scene in Hong Kong (*Paul Popper*)
Queen's Square, Hong Kong (*Paul Popper*)
Kowloon Railway station, Hong Kong (*Paul Popper*)
Holt's Wharf, Kowloon (*Paul Popper*)
Hong Kong branch of the Hong Kong-Shanghai Bank (*Jardine Matheson*)
Home of a wealthy Chinese merchant in Hong Kong (*Press Association*)
The house of Aw Boon Haw, Singapore (*Press Association*)

SOCIAL WORLD (*between pp. 196 and 197*)

Horse-race meeting in Shanghai, 1879 (*Mansell Collection*)
Sketches of actors by Alexander (*India Office Library*)
Caricature of J. M. Fabris by R. W. Bradell
Scene from *The Mikado*
Caricature of A. Y. Gahagan by R. W. Bradell
Performance of *The Yeoman of the Guard*
Chinese group photograph (*Press Association*)
English formal group (*Mansell Collection*)
Sketches from *The Graphic* (*Mansell Collection*)
Trip in a Chinese house boat, 1889 (*Mansell Collection*)
Marble palace of Charlie Wun Ho (*Paul Popper*)
Street of gambling houses (*Paul Popper*)
Jungle picnics and rafting parties
Malaya, 1913
Party at the Kuala Lumpur Races, 1913

Kuala Lumpur Races
February meeting at Kuala Lumpur, 1923
Polo tournament, 1923
The 'Season' in the Far East
Band programme, Singapore, 1913
Voyage diary and passenger list of the S.S. *Warwickshire*
Balls held in Kuala Lumpur, 1913
Lake Club and St George's ball
Tea party on board ship in 1937
Cruise ship leaves Yokohama, 1937
Visit to the Great Wall of China (*India Office Library*)
On arrival at the Wall (*India Office Library*)
View of Hong Kong (*Paul Popper*)

IMPERIAL NOON AND TWILIGHT (*between pp. 236 and 237*)

Family group (*Mansell Collection*)
Shanghai, the Garden Bridge and Soochow Creek (*Overseas Missionary Fellowship*)
Shanghai; the public gardens and river (*Overseas Missionary Fellowship*)
Ipoh, Perak (*Press Association*)
Visit of the Prince of Wales to North Borneo, 1922
Reception for the Prince of Wales at Sarawak
Raffles Hotel, Singapore (*Press Association*)
View of Singapore (*Press Association*)
Waterfront at Singapore, 1953 (*Radio Times Hulton Picture Library*)
Surrender ceremony at the end of the Second World War
Flats for artisans in Malacca

ACKNOWLEDGEMENT

The author and publishers would like to thank all those mentioned above who have lent illustrations for the book. In particular, they are grateful to Messrs Jardine Matheson, and to Mrs Gatcliffe and friends, and the India Office Library for their unfailing help.

Picture research by Jacquemine Charrott-Lodwidge

Preface

During my childhood, the periodic reappearance of a middle-aged uncle from the Far East, where he worked as branch-manager of a large Anglo-Oriental bank, first in the Philippines, then in Japan, and finally in what is now Malaysia, was always an event to which I looked forward. He was a stout, pink, fastidious personage; and he brought with him, not only a collection of interesting and unexpected gifts – a Chinese puppet that nodded its head, a flame-shaped Malayan short sword and the miniature model of a Japanese rickshaw that ran on tiny golden wheels – but a pervasive air of ease and dignity. I remember his acute distress when he was obliged to carry his own bag between the station and our house. At home, he reminded us, he was attended by a posse of devoted servants; and he often spoke of the social amusements he shared with fellow members of the British colony – picnics, dinner-parties, elaborate pierrot shows and the operettas in the style of Gilbert and Sullivan that he himself composed and staged.

Years later, when I was travelling to Tokyo, I passed briefly through some of the Eastern cities that had formed the harmonious background of my uncle's life. There I saw other bank-managers, equally pink and bland, holding court with their middle-class wives among good-mannered native boys. I saw their pretty gardens and their solid ugly bungalows; and at Shanghai I witnessed a magnificent demonstration of the imperial power that lay behind them. A British warship, beautifully dressed and beflagged, came sweeping up the River Whangpoo. A band was playing on the scrubbed white deck, everything about the vessel and its crew was exquisitely trim and elegant; and, as it passed, raising a tremendous wake, the dingy Chinese junks, clustered along the shore, rocked and bowed and bobbed at anchor.

That was in 1930; and since those days both the affluent commercial structure, in which my uncle performed his modest rôle, and the imperial system that supported it have almost vanished from the Far East. Relics of Empire remain; but, like Hong Kong, they are closely beleaguered outposts; and Mr Woodcock's book deals with an important historical period, of which the generation that is now emerging has very little first-hand knowledge. The Roman Empire lasted long; its decline and collapse were very gradual. The British Empire ended with startling suddenness. 'To many a young Englishman who went east in 1930', writes Mr Woodcock, 'it must have seemed that the empire would never end, as though the lordly relation in which his race stood to the native peoples of the Far East would continue into the indefinite vagueness of the future'.

How did the prospect change? Was it as the result of emergent nationalism – which the Far East, of course, had originally imported from the West? Or did the whole idea of Europe's 'manifest destiny', once the inspiration of her soldiers and traders, contain a damning moral flaw, which would presently undermine her influence? Mr Woodcock does not minimise either the harm that Europeans did to the East, or the enormous benefits that they conferred. He has created a gigantic panorama, and filled in every corner of it with some fascinating piece of human detail. Though his scope is vast, his eye for personalities is extraordinarily keen and sure, whether he is writing of the great Sir Stamford Raffles, who founded Singapore in 1819, or Sergeant Pennefather, who embraced the Moslem faith and commanded a ragged army of Arab and Indian mercenaries, which fought and died amid the jungles of Selangor. One was a mighty architect; the other, no doubt, an unprincipled ruffian. But each plays his characteristic part in the story Mr Woodcock tells.

PETER QUENNELL

Introduction

Eastward from Malaya the last vestiges of colonialism are those communities which cling like limpets to the shore of a militantly anti-imperialist China; Portuguese-held Macao and British-held Hong Kong, survivors respectively of the oldest and the most powerful European empires in the Far East. Their presence is appropriate and symbolic. For centuries, the roads of empire were the roads to China. The lure of Cathay and its largely legendary wealth drew Columbus and Cabot over the Atlantic and – as a magnificent irrelevance – led to the founding of the great modern countries of the western hemisphere. The same lure drew Magellan round the Horn, and a vast company of other explorers to lose their ways and often their lives in the frozen maze where – unconquered until the present century – the North-West Passage traces its impracticable course. It was on the road to Cathay that the Portuguese, the Dutch and the British in turn established their greatest imperial holdings in India and south-east Asia, but these gifts came to them almost as consolations for the difficulties they encountered in establishing effective trade relations with a China which, until the 1840s, remained as difficult to penetrate as it is again today.

I deal with the social history of the British as founders and custodians of empire in the region which, as one sails eastward, begins with Malaya, the land whose special position in the trade of the Far East has been recognized since classical antiquity. Before the days of steam, it was important to sailors as the point where the two monsoon systems of the Indian Ocean and the South China Sea converged; it became the natural meeting place for traders from India and China, the two wealthiest countries of Asia, and from the spice-rich Indonesian archipelago.

Projecting in a great spearhead from the land mass of south-east Asia, and extended by the island barriers of Sumatra and Java, Malaya not merely divides the seas of Asia and geographically terminates what

Europeans describe as the Far East. It is also the point where two cultural traditions merge before drawing apart. The customs of its Malay population combine primitive tribal elements with traditions derived from long periods of Indian and later Moslem domination. But almost half its population is now Chinese. Not only do these overseas Chinese remind one of the millennia of trade between Malaya and China, with the inevitable transmission of cultural influences; they also preserve many of those traditions of an older China which have already been destroyed on the Communist mainland.

East of Malaya the China Seas are bounded by the island shores of Indonesia, the Philippines and the lesser archipelagos that terminate to the north in Japan. Long before the Portuguese in 1511 seized Malacca and penetrated this great region, Chinese influences were potent there. From island to island, the cumbersome junks had found their way, engaging in trade, granting local rulers the recognition of the Son of Heaven, and depositing communities of mercantile Chinese who lived in self-preserving isolation and yet influenced the tribal or partly Hinduized societies they encountered. In Japan, in Annam and Tonking, in Thailand and Cambodia, there arose independent cultures largely shaped by Confucian political concepts and Chinese classical literature. Over some of these countries, as over Tibet, China maintained and even at times enforced its claims to suzerainty. Around the wilder shores of the islands, the political influence was slight and the cultural influence shallow, but it was never completely absent. Its absence would, indeed, have been surprising, since in prehistoric times the whole of the Malay archipelago, including the Philippines, as well as the mainland of south-east Asia, was populated by tribes from southern China who brought with them diluted elements of the early proto-civilizations of the Middle Kingdom.

The China Seas were thus appropriately named. They formed an area in which China had for long been culturally powerful and in which, during the almost forgotten expansionist phases of Chinese imperialism, its political strength had been great. To win commercial domination over this area and eventually over a decadent China became the aim of Europeans between the sixteenth and early twentieth centuries. During the nineteenth century the lead in pursuing this aim was assumed by the British. It led them, unwillingly but inevitably, towards the parallel goal of political domination. In this process, until the emergence of Japan as an unexpected factor in the power spectrum of the China Seas, the relations between the Chinese and the British were of crucial importance to the future of the region. They were relations marked by a peculiar ambivalence. Officially, China resisted – with diminishing firmness and effectiveness – the attempts of Europeans and Americans even to establish commercial relations with her subjects;

this situation resulted in much officially encouraged xenophobia, and in a series of wars, beginning with the so-called Opium War of 1840, which eventually destroyed the Manchu dynasty and opened China to western trade and to western cultural influences. But the resisting traditionalists were not representative of all Chinese; there were others – and secretly many officials were among them – whose dislike of the red-haired foreign devils was less active than their attachment to trade. The collaboration of the Chinese merchant class was in fact indispensable to the kind of imperial society which the British created in the Far East. When the British founded cities, whether in Malaya or on the coasts of China, it was the Chinese who populated them, and the whole trading system that bound Penang and Singapore, Shanghai and Hong Kong, and even Yokohama and Kobe, with the City of London, was given life by the capillary network of small Chinese traders and compradors – or middlemen – who collaborated with the British merchant houses that controlled the China trade.

In the end, of course, there was a great deal more to the British empire in the Far East than the China trade alone. As in every other continent of the world, it became a territorial as well as a commercial empire. The administrator, the planter, the miner, the missionary and the adventurer eventually took their places beside the merchant and the seaman. But in the strict sense it never became a colonial empire, since it received no colonists. Once, in 1785, a certain Captain Thomas Forrest proposed to the East India Company the colonization of the hills of Penang. 'The fittest from Great Britain to Colonize and Multiply in these Islands are the Highlanders from Scotland,' he remarked, 'but let them not embark on the Thames, let them carry their simplicity with them.' No British settlers carried their simplicity to Penang or anywhere else in the China Seas. Either the climate, as in Malaya and Borneo, or the existing density of population, as in China and Japan, prevented any attempt to import people from Britain who would exploit the land with their own labour or serve as an immigrant working class. In consequence no homogeneous British society of the kind that grew up in the white dominions ever developed in the Far East. As in India, the British ruled there as a dominant race over countries and communities in which they remained a minuscule and socially isolated minority. They were sustained, at least until the disastrous days of the Japanese invasions after Pearl Harbour, by a sense of their own superiority which they contrived to communicate to their subject peoples, and by an attitude towards native races – even towards the civilized Chinese – that combined in varying degrees contempt and affection.

Over a few of the British – no more than an individual here and there – the Far East wielded a charm so potent that they never wished to depart, and, as Maurice Collis has said, 'would rather be buried in a palm-grove within sound of the surf and mourned by their progeny of half-bred sons, than face English cold, English haste and English women'. But for the vast majority of those who survived the climate and the tropical sicknesses of a pre-prophylactic era, their terms in the east were deliberately temporary. For a few years, sometimes mounting to decades, they made their money as merchants or carried out their duties as administrators: but, however long the time, England lay at the end, with all its disillusionments, and the places where they lived beside the China Seas never seemed home until they receded into nostalgic memory. These China Hands, and Malaya Hands, and Borneo Hands, did not even become, like the conquistadors in Latin America, a ruling class rooted to the alien soil they had won; they remained, like Roman proconsuls, the transient representatives of a distant imperial power.

This feeling of impermanence which most of them shared imposed on the societies they created the limitations of scope that distinguished them from genuinely colonial settlements. While the English in Canada and Australia created over the generations their own political customs and social patterns, even their own cultures shaped by the dramatic spaciousness of their environments, one searches in vain among the communities of the British in the Far East for such manifestations of developing independence. Scattered from Penang in the south-west to Yokohama in the north-east, they showed a remarkable similarity in social organization, in attitudes, in ways of living; it was only the lesser details of life that were likely to vary from country to country and to be influenced by local environments.

Like most expatriate ruling communities, those we shall encounter were especially lacking in manifestations of creativity, whether literary, artistic or scientific. The writers who most eloquently recorded their ways of life, such as Joseph Conrad, Somerset Maugham and Anthony Burgess, were among their most temporary inhabitants. This, of course, was another manifestation of the impossibility of real individuality in the little Englands of the China Seas. Acutely conscious of the importance of *esprit de corps* among a dominant minority, they distrusted any departure from the established norms of behaviour; even missionaries, if they identified themselves too closely with their converts, became suspect, and the artist and the social critic were doubly so. The few eccentrics who survived in such societies were likely to become recluses on distant plantations or adventurous wanderers in the hinterlands, sometimes, like Alfred Russel Wallace in the wilds of Sarawak, drawing inspiration out of their isolation.

The social rigidity of the British Far Eastern communities existed in paradoxical combination with a political flexibility which resulted in a great variety of relationships with the native peoples around the China Seas. The pattern of political and commercial domination which eventually emerged can, however, only be understood in the historical context of British and other European penetration into the region. Even during the late Middle Ages the Far East was not unknown to Europeans. Marco Polo was only one of a number of travellers, mainly Italians, who made the journey to China either overland through central Asia or by sea from the Persian Gulf; they included those whose curiosity had mercantile motives and those, like Friar John of Montecorvino, who wished to proselytize the heathen. But if the accounts of these travellers had made China known to European rulers and merchants by the beginning of the fifteenth century, the problem still remained of finding a way there that would circumvent the land route through the hostile Moslem lands of the Near East. Vasco da Gama pioneered one route in 1498 when he reached India via the Cape of Good Hope; Magellan found another when he sailed round Cape Horn in 1520, and, despite the centuries of effort to discover a north-west passage around what is now Canada and a north-east passage around Russia, these remained, until the Suez Canal was opened in 1869, the only possible routes between Europe and the Far East. By establishing themselves on the Malabar coast and by capturing Malacca in 1511, the Portuguese sought to control the western entry to the China Seas and to make the whole of east Asia a trading province. With the Spaniards dominating the western coasts of America from California to Tierra del Fuego, and since 1570 established in the Philippines, the intent was clearly to turn the whole Pacific into an Iberian sea.

Neither the Spanish nor the Portuguese were in fact able to exclude the ships belonging to the rising sea powers of England and Holland. The first Englishman to enter the China Seas was Sir Francis Drake, coming westward round the Horn and making the first British commercial transaction in the Far East when in 1579 he landed at Ternate in the Moluccas and traded with the Sultan for six tons of cloves. Eight years later Thomas Cavendish followed Drake over the same westerly route and landed on Java in 1587. In the meantime another Englishman, travelling by land and by native coastal craft, had reached Malaya and Siam. This was Robert Fitch, who in 1583 left England with a party of merchants under the auspices of the Turkey Company to explore the overland route to the east. They sailed by the *Tiger* to Aleppo, thus providing a topical line for Shakespeare to use in *Macbeth*, and travelled over the desert to Basra. Four of them, including Fitch, went on to India. Fitch alone continued to Burma, and, reaching Pegu, was the first Englishman to enter a Buddhist kingdom. He went over the mountains to Chiengmai in Siam, 'a very faire and great towne, with faire houses of stone, well peopled, the streets are very large, the men very well set and strong, with a cloth about them, bare headed and bare footed: for in all these countreys they weare no shoes. The women are much fairer than those of Pegu'. Fitch returned to Pegu and sailed down the coast to Malacca, 'where the Portugals have a castle which standeth nere the sea'. Having experienced the religious fanaticism of the Portuguese in Goa, he stayed only long enough to observe that: 'Hither come many ships from China and from the Malucos, Banda, Timor, and from many other Ilands of the Javas, which bring great store of spices and drugs, and diamants and other jewels'. He then returned, via Babylon, to London.

The observations of Drake, Fitch and Cavendish were not lost on the traders of London. In 1591 a group of merchants sent out a small fleet of three ships under the command of George Raymond and James Lancaster. After one ship had been lost at sea and another sent home filled with sick men, Lancaster reached Sumatra and Penang, where he raided Portuguese ships but did no trade. Returning via St Helena and the West Indies, he lost his ship by an absurd accident – it drifted away while he was collecting provisions on one of the islands – and was finally brought home by French privateers. Another expedition was sent out in 1596, bearing a letter in Latin from Queen Elizabeth to the Emperor of China. It travelled by the westward route and eventually all its men except one died of sickness or were killed by Spanish privateers. They never even reached Cape Horn.

By the time the first successful trading expedition sailed from London in 1601, British sailors had penetrated far into the China Seas as hands on Dutch vessels which were already beginning to threaten the Portuguese commercial hegemony of the region. One of these men, Will Adams, whose ship lost its way in the North Pacific, was the first Englishman to reach Japan.

The knowledge gained in the service of the Dutch stood the English in good stead during the 1601 expedition, which was organized by the Merchant Venturers of London, and consisted of five ships under the command of James Lancaster, with the Arctic voyager John Davis, formerly employed by the Dutch, as its pilot-major. Lancaster traded at Acheen in Sumatra, and before he returned to England established the first British trading factory in the Far East at Bantam on the island of Java.

By the time the next ships set out for the China Seas in 1604, the East India Company had been formed, under the title of 'The Governour and Company of Merchants of London trading into the East Indies'. The expedition took over the post at Bantam, but on attempting to extend its trade farther into the Indonesian archipelago encountered the stubborn and sometimes brutal opposition of the Dutch, who at this time were busily engaged in expelling the Portuguese from the Spice Islands and had no intention of dividing this rich prize with the English.

Sporadic trade continued for twenty years, and factories were established at various places, such as Jacarta, Macassar and Amboyna, with smaller posts scattered through the islands. But they proved precarious enterprises, and the British gave up any serious intent of extending their activities in the Indonesian archipelago after the Dutch in 1623 arrested the British factors or senior merchants at Amboyna on a false charge of treacherous plotting, tortured them mercilessly and finally executed ten of them; the incident gave Dryden the subject of his epic drama, *Amboyna*. The British retained their original post at Bantam until, before the end of the century, they were driven away from this last beach-head. Later they were to return in spectacular triumph to the archipelago when the whole of Java was captured by a massive military expedition in 1811 to keep it out of the hands of Napoleon, but the East India Company only retained control for a few years before returning it in 1818 to the Dutch overlords.

The East India Company did not restrict its efforts to the archipelago. In 1612 its men established factories at Patani and Ayuthia in Siam, at various places in Borneo and on Sumatra, and at Hirado in Japan; they even tried to trade far inland at Chiengmai on the borders of Burma and Siam. Within a decade these factories were abandoned. Japan embarked on an isolationist policy which kept her closed to foreign traders for more than two centuries.

Trading posts were later established briefly in Cambodia (1654) and Tonking (1672), and the Company returned to Ayuthia, the capital of Siam, in 1662, only to find its business prospects and its political influence bedevilled by the competition of French diplomats and English private traders (the famous 'interlopers' who at this period became a growing problem). Seventeenth-century penetration into Siam ended disastrously with a massacre of Englishmen at the port of Mergui in 1687, which was followed shortly afterwards by a general slaughter of foreigners in Ayuthia when Phaulkon, the Greek adventurer who had become the king's chief minister, was overthrown.

Finally, in 1685, the East India Company established itself at Bencoolen on the coast of Sumatra, where Fort Marlborough remained in its hands until, in 1824, it was handed to the Dutch in exchange for Malacca. By this time the Company had become deeply involved in India, and for a century Bencoolen remained its only continuous centre of trade with Malaya and the archipelago.

But China, which had been the original goal of the mariners who set out for the Far East at the end of the sixteenth century, was not forgotten, though the intent to establish trade there had temporarily been diverted by fruitless efforts to compete with the Dutch in the East Indies. In 1635 the Company decided to attempt direct trading with China, and in the same year the *London* was sent from England on a trial voyage. Its captain was instructed to trade for 'alum, China roots, porcelain, brass, green ginger, sugar, and sugar candy, or silk, silk stuffs, lignum, aloes, camphor, benzoin, gold, pearls, and curiosities'. No mention was made of the commodity which, as eighteenth-century Englishmen developed into a nation of tea-drinkers, was to become the most sought-after product of China.

When the *London* dropped anchor off Macao, the East India factors found the Portuguese, who had been established there since 1557, unco-operative and the native merchants reluctant to trade; a pattern, often to be repeated, was initiated when the local mandarin who represented Chinese interests made it clear that he expected to be bribed. The *London* did not try to trade at any port under direct Chinese control.

Two years afterwards, however, the attempt was made, with a show of violence which also was to find its echoes in later Anglo-Chinese relations. In spite of the charter which gave the East India Company a monopoly in the China Seas, Charles I in 1635 gave a licence to Sir William Courteenes to trade with China and in 1636 Captain John Weddell set off under this licence with a flotilla of six ships. Disregarding the warnings of the Portuguese, he sailed up the Pearl River to Canton, bombarded one of the river forts, captured some Chinese craft, and in the end made such a nuisance of himself that he was allowed to buy ginger and sugar. But the Chinese authorities had a last characteristic word in the quarrel, for the merchants whom Weddell sent into Canton to complete the purchases were detained until he had signed a document admitting that he had done wrong to enter Canton and that he would never attempt it again.

This obstructive attitude to all traders except the Portuguese in Macao and the Russians to the north was sustained by the Chinese almost to the end of the seventeenth century. The English tried to trade through Portuguese intermediaries, particularly after Charles II's marriage to Catherine of Braganza; they also established factories at Amoy and Ningpo. But none of these efforts was very successful. Portuguese cooperation was minimal and the factories were soon suppressed. At last, in 1699, the East India Company's ship *Macclesfield* was allowed to trade peacefully at Canton, and others followed, until in 1757 the Chinese finally decided that regular commerce might be allowed through this port, which was given the monopoly of trade with all Europeans except the Russians. Trading could only be carried on with an approved guild of Chinese merchants, the Co Hong, and the restrictions under which the British factors and their staff were allowed to inhabit their little ghetto outside the walls of Canton were extremely onerous. Twice embassies from the King of England to the Emperor of China endeavoured to persuade the Celestial government to adopt a more liberal commercial policy. But the authorities in Peking sincerely believed that there was nothing their people needed from the outside world, and so Lord Macartney in 1793 and Lord Amherst in 1816 were dismissed with contempt, and their king, George III, was regarded as a barbarian vassal sending tribute to the Son of Heaven.

In spite of the difficulties it experienced in both China and the Indonesian archipelago, the East India Company considered the trade it did obtain worth the effort of establishing on the mainland of Malaya a series of beach-heads which would balance the Dutch settlements among the islands. In 1786 Penang was founded on an island obtained from the Sultan of Kedah; it was the first British territorial possession in the Far East. In 1795 Malacca was captured from the Dutch; though later returned to them, it was finally ceded to Britain in 1824 in exchange for Bencoolen. Most important, in 1819 Sir Stamford Raffles established the free port of Singapore, which soon became the commercial centre of the whole Malay world. In 1826 Penang, Malacca and Singapore were united in the Straits Settlements, subject to the government of India; only in 1867 did they become a separate crown colony.

The possession of these vital Malayan ports enabled the East India Company to foster its growing tea trade with China. At first the trade was dubiously profitable, because the merchants of the Co Hong were little interested in English manufactures; for their tea they demanded payment in silver. Eventually, however, one commodity was discovered which the Chinese desired avidly, even if they did not need it. This was opium. The Celestial government had forbidden its import, but the demand was so insistent that an illicit trade developed. The East India Company had a monopoly control over all the opium produced in India, but it did not wish to endanger its equally valuable monopoly of the tea trade by engaging in smuggling, no matter how profitable. Accordingly, it licensed private merchants, or 'country traders' – Englishmen, Parsees or Indian Jews – who bought the opium for silver, which paid for the company's tea purchases, and in turn sold it illegally and very profitably with the bought connivance of the local Chinese officials.

This system encouraged the development of aggressive and ruthless independent trading concerns, with considerable support in Britain among the many foes of the East India Company. When the Company's monopoly of the China trade ended in 1833, these independent traders came to the fore, demanding a relaxation of the Chinese restrictions on commerce. The Chinese authorities, far from yielding, precipitated a crisis by trying to suppress the opium trade. The Opium Wars followed, from 1840 to 1842. They were in fact less about opium than about free trade, and their result was the annexation of Hong Kong by Britain in 1841, and the Nanking Treaty of 1842 which named Shanghai, Canton, Ningpo, Foochow and Amoy as the first treaty ports. At these treaty ports the merchants lived in special districts where they enjoyed extra-territorial rights and virtual self-government, coming under the control of their own consuls and judges; the British were the dominant groups, in numbers and wealth alike. The Convention of Peking in 1860, following the so-called 'Arrow War' and the destruction of the Summer Palace at Peking by an Anglo-French army, resulted in the opening of further treaty ports and of the Yangtse River, while Britain added mainland Kowloon to its colony of Hong Kong. The British also gained at this time the right to reorganize and to appoint the head of the Chinese Maritime Customs which for eighty years remained virtually a British preserve. During the remainder of the nineteenth century every excuse was used by Britain and the other European powers to wring concessions from the Chinese. In 1898, for example, the British leased for their own use not only the port of Weiheiwai but also an area of 335 square miles of Chinese mainland, known as the New Territories, which was – and still is – administered by the colonial authorities of the neighbouring island of Hong Kong. This process culminated in the Boxer Rebellion of 1900, largely motivated by resentment of foreign encroachments; after its suppression the powers were allowed to set up a garrison in the very capital of the Celestial empire under the pretext of protecting their legations.

While, in these various ways, Britain had been taking the lead in securing enough political leverage in China to build a massive commercial empire, the territories farther west were being consolidated under direct imperial control. During the eighteenth century the East India Company had made a number of rather inept attempts to establish control over parts of Borneo. In 1840 the Byronic adventurer, James Brooke, arrived on the great island and succeeded where they had failed. After suppressing a revolt which threatened the rule of the Sultan of Brunei, he was named Raja of Sarawak. At first only a viceroy, he manoeuvred his little state into a position of independence, recognized by Britain in 1865. In 1846 Britain acquired as a crown colony the island of Labuan off the coast of Borneo; and in 1881 almost the whole remaining dominions of the Sultan of Brunei were purchased by the British North Borneo Company. In 1888 the British control over the whole region was formally proclaimed when North Borneo, Sarawak and Brunei all became protectorates.

Meanwhile a process of interference and consolidation began in the

Malay peninsula itself. With the spread of trade and the increasing numbers of Chinese tin miners working in the interior, the British government
decided that the endemic political disorder which characterized the native
states had become intolerable. In 1874 it intervened in the state of Perak,
where strife between Malays and Chinese, and between rival Chinese secret
societies, was bringing about a ruinous political and economic situation.
The Sultan was persuaded to accept a resident, or British political adviser,
who exercized a far-reaching control over the state's internal affairs. The
same year Selangor accepted a resident, and Pahang and Negri Sembilan
followed shortly afterwards; these four principalities became in 1895 the
Federated Malay States. In 1885 the state of Johore had accepted a separate
treaty of protection. The British hegemony over the Malay peninsula was
completed as late as 1909, when Siam transferred to Britain all its rights of
sovereignty over the states of Kelantan, Trengganu, Perlis and Kedah.

Farther north around the China Seas, though Manila was in British
hands for a short time in 1763, and though the leading English merchants of
the treaty ports maintained strong links there, the Philippines remained
outside the British sphere of interest, and when Spain's hold became loose,
they slipped into the hands of the United States.

In Japan, on the other hand, the American initiative, by which in 1854
Commodore Perry broke the long isolation imposed by the Tokugawa
Shoguns, was not allowed to pass unchallenged. British naval officers and
diplomats hastened to make their own terms, and in 1858 Lord Elgin concluded the treaty which established British rights in the ports opened to
foreign trade, of which the most important were Kanagawa and Hyogo,
later known as Yokohama and Kobe. Here, on seashores which the Japanese seem to have selected for their dismal ugliness, thriving new cities arose.
Because of the wealth and experience of her trading houses on the China
coast, Britain became, despite America's earlier start, the most important
commercial power in the Japanese concessions. As a result of the country's
rapid modernization, the system of treaty ports and extra-territorial rights
ended in Japan in 1899; with it passed away the last vestiges of foreign
political interference in Japanese affairs.

The first real fissure in the structure of the British empire in the Far East
appeared in 1927, when the British abandoned their concession at the treaty
ports of Hankow and Kiukiang in the face of military pressure from the
Chinese nationalists. This was followed by concessions to the Chinese in
the government of Shanghai, and, from 1937, even greater concessions to
the Japanese, whose military activities at this time forced the European
powers on to the defensive along the whole of the China coast. Then, in
1941 and 1942, when Britain was engaged in a life-and-death struggle in

Europe, a few months sufficed for every fragment of its empire in the Far East to fall into Japanese hands.

In 1945 the British returned, welcomed by native peoples who had found their fellow Asians worse rulers than the European empire-builders. But they came back only to liquidate the heritage of the past. In China the treaty rights were abandoned, extra-territoriality lapsed, the international settlements in the former treaty ports came under Chinese control, and Britain gave up her right, by virtually appointing the head of the vital Chinese Maritime Customs, to interfere directly in governmental affairs. If the British administrators did not return to Shanghai and the other ports, the merchants and the missionaries did, enjoying a brief heyday of gathering profits and souls until, in 1949, the Communists triumphed and, within a few years, all vestiges of foreign influence, political or commercial, were wiped from the face of China even more cleanly than they had been half a century before from the face of Japan.

In the territorial empire in the Far East the political order was quickly transformed. The Brooke dynasty in Sarawak and the Chartered Company in North Borneo gave up their sovereign rights in 1946, and these territories were temporarily transformed into crown colonies. The next stage was liberation. The new Federation of Malaya, which included Penang and Malacca as well as all the native states, attained independence in 1957; Singapore gained dominion status in 1958. Finally, in 1963, came the complete political breakaway from Britain when Sarawak, Sabah (the former North Borneo) and Singapore became independent by joining the Federation of Malaya in the new but short-lived country of Malaysia. Commercial interests and military obligations, which in the 1970s will come to an end, still bound these former colonies loosely to Britain. But as a political entity the British empire survived by the mid-1960s only in Hong Kong and the three hundred square miles of the Chinese mainland that are dependent on it.

Behind these historical facts one can see the changing pattern within which the British communities in the Far East developed. From the founding of the fort at Bantam in 1602 to the acquisition of Penang in 1786, the East India Company's aims in the Far East were entirely commercial. The British government was directly concerned only in so far as it began in the eighteenth century to provide naval protection for English ships in the east and particularly for the tea fleets from China.

The territorial empire was acquired in subsequent years slowly and reluctantly. Hong Kong was the first Far Eastern possession of the British crown, since until after the Indian Mutiny the Straits Settlements remained under Company control. Even at the height of Britain's power in the Far

East, its actual imperial possessions consisted only of the relatively small territories of the Straits Settlements, Hong Kong and Labuan. The protectorates in Malaya and Borneo were far larger in area, population and eventual productivity. They were also historically more curious, since they included in Sarawak the only native state to be governed successfully by a dynasty of English rajas, and in North Borneo the last territory to be ruled by a chartered company.

This miscellany of annexed, protected and leased territories which formed the territorial empire in the Far East was ultimately less important than the great commercial empire which lay beyond it, manifested in the chain of treaty ports. The ports remained Chinese territory, and the Peking government retained nominal control over its subjects who inhabited them. But the presence of British soldiers in the concessions, of British officials in the Chinese Maritime Customs, of British naval officers as advisers in the Chinese fleet, and of British gunboats protecting the trade on the Yangtse River, added up to an influence of a positive and formidable kind. Under the aegis of that influence traders penetrated into areas where there were no treaty ports; missionaries, scientists and geographers made their way into the remotest provinces of the Celestial empire, and a *condottiere* band of soldiers of fortune appeared who offered their mercenary services to the Chinese government and often, with commercial impartiality, to those who rebelled against it. Chinese Gordon, leading his Ever-Victorious Army against the Taiping rebels, was their ancestor; their truer representatives were flamboyant figures like One-Arm Sutton and Two-Gun Cohen. In their activities the fabric of empire shredded out into its most disreputable fringes. Many of them were disowned by its representatives. Yet they worked under its shadow, made its outposts their bases, and in their own way helped to keep alive its commercial and political influence.

One other country of the China Seas, unmentioned up to now, came under the powerful influence of Britain during the nineteenth century and contributed its own variations to the pattern of British Far Eastern communities. This was Siam, by the end of our period to become known as Thailand. As the French built up their influence in Indo-China and eventually took over the small kingdoms of Annam, Tonking, Cambodia and Laos, the British developed a natural interest in this independent kingdom which formed a buffer between French Indo-China and both Burma and Malaya. The interest was mutual, since Siam feared French encroachments to the east. Once, at least, Britain almost went to war with France over Siam. Siam became and remained until the beginning of the Second World War something less than a protectorate, but more than a sphere of influence. In 1909, as we have seen, Siam abandoned to Britain its suzerain power in

Malaya. British subjects enjoyed extra-territorial rights in its territory, and British consular courts operated as far inland as the northern city of Chiengmai. British commercial interests dominated the Siamese teak trade and Siamese coastal shipping. In the later nineteenth century, when King Chulalongkorn decided to call in foreign advisers to assist in running his government departments, the key posts, and particularly the important advisorships in Finance and Customs, were reserved for British nominees. Siam was never even nominally associated with the British empire; it remained nevertheless a necessary component in the imperial pattern in the Far East.

With the varieties of men who created that imperial pattern, and with their ways of life, the remainder of this book is concerned.

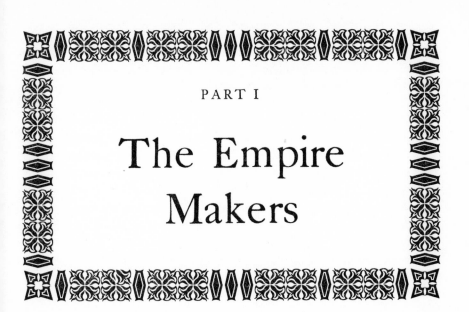

PART I

The Empire Makers

I

THE TRADERS

Merchants and mariners were the first Englishmen to sail down the coast of Malaya and into the China Seas; the first also to create minute British communities in the Far East. In the beginning it is difficult to discriminate between them. Drake, primarily a mariner, turned an honest or dishonest piece of silver whenever the opportunity arose, and trade suited his purpose as well as privateering or slaving. When the Merchant Venturers of London sent out the first successful trading expedition to the east in 1601, they had to choose for its commander a man who was experienced in seamanship, adroit in diplomacy, shrewd in trading. Once they had selected James Lancaster as general of the expedition, he was not only commander but also supercargo of his small fleet, assuming direction of its trading operations. By special patent from Queen Elizabeth he was also given power to punish and correct any of the four hundred people who sailed in the five ships under his command, and even, should the need arise, to declare martial law. Henry Middleton, commanding the second voyage in 1604, was specifically instructed by the East India Company not only to oversee all trading, but also to care for the training and moral welfare of the young men who were destined to set up commercial outposts in the East Indies.

As the Company established its factories in India and farther east, a division of functions came into being. The merchants who operated on shore and the captains who commanded the great ships known as East Indiamen assumed separate responsibilities, but the line of demarcation was never drawn with final sharpness. The captains of the East Indiamen still retained the privilege of private trading and it was not unknown even in later times for the two roles to be interchanged. Samuel White started in 1675 as a mate on one of the Company's ships, carried out trading operations in Madras, and later left the Company to take employment as master mariner to the King of Siam, combining trading and occasional piracy with his

3

duties as a sailor and later as *shahbander* or superintendent of the Siamese port of Mergui.

But even in the beginning there were certain members of each expedition who had no nautical training and who were destined to serve only as merchants. These men, usually of mercantile families, were recruited specifically to man the depots or factories in eastern countries where English goods – mainly cotton – were deposited to be traded for local products, such as pepper and other spices. Many such factors were hardly more than boys; in that age of long, hard voyages – it took Middleton seven months to reach Bantam in 1604 – and dangerous tropical living, youth was perhaps the most necessary of all qualifications for a trading life in the Far East. Even those who directed the expeditions were often surprisingly young; John Saris, for example, was thirty-two when he commanded the first English fleet to Japan in 1611, and most factors in the early days were a great deal younger than that.

They were not only young. They were also, inevitably, inexperienced. No Englishmen before them had settled down to trade on Asian islands among people whose customs and languages alike were almost completely unfamiliar. A little was known from the observations of English seamen who had sailed on Dutch ships; even so, the training which the prospective young merchants received must at first have been no more than perfunctory. Later, in 1610, the Company acquired the services of two Dutchmen, generally known as Peter Floris and Lucas Antheunis, who had worked in Dutch factories, and their advice was invaluable; by this time, in any case, there were already men who had survived their first spells in the East Indies and were able to use their acquired knowledge in building up a workable trading system. The first factors had none of this experience to draw upon. They were, in the most complete sense, pioneers, and they were to suffer all the mental and physical hardships to which pioneers are everywhere subject.

Of those who set off from England on the trading voyages, only a small proportion were destined to become factors. In 1601 there were four hundred men on board Lancaster's five ships, but most of these were seamen, for the heavy rate of sickness and death on seventeenth-century voyages in tropical waters demanded that out-going ships should, if anything, be overmanned. One factory, at Bantam, was actually established on the first voyage, and nine young men, under a chief factor named William Starkey, were left to man it.

Few of the earlier trading communities established by the East India Company in the region were any larger than Bantam. Hirado, the factory in Japan, was opened by seven merchants; three others joined them later. At

Ayuthia, in Siam, there were originally six merchants. Many small posts in the Indonesian archipelago were manned by two or three Englishmen. In 1609 Captain Keeling left thirteen merchants at Bantam, but only because this was considered a particularly important factory. At some factories a few Englishmen were employed in subsidiary or even menial capacities, and here tragic Amboyna was typical. In 1623 there were in all eighteen Englishmen on the island, ten in Amboyna itself and eight scattered in the three out-lying posts. Only twelve were factors; the rest included two clerks, a drunken barber-surgeon, a tailor and two servants. But the tone of the community was given by the factors; it was that middle-class tone which in later centuries distinguished the British empire in the Far East from its counterpart in India. The China Seas never provided the setting for those viceregal courts and massive military establishments in which aristocrats flourished. An occasional patrician might become involved in trade, like Sir Edward Michelbourne who in 1604 set sail with a special licence from James I to trade to China and the 'countries adjacent', and gave provocation to the Dutch and embarrassment to the East India Company by engaging in piracy off the coasts of Java. But such men were rare, and if the young factors had good connections they were usually with the richer merchants of the City; John Saris, for example, went home from Japan to marry the daughter of a former lord mayor. This middle-class tone dominated British society in the Far East to the end, partly because on the China coast and in the Straits Settlements the mercantile interest was always dominant and partly because the government services in this region rarely attracted the kind of upper-class young men who found appropriately dramatic careers in the Indian service.

But whatever their class, for many years the actual number of Englishmen resident in the China Seas was extremely small – a matter of scores rather than even hundreds. The English East India Company was far more sparing in staffing its Far Eastern posts than either its Dutch or its Portuguese rivals. While the Dutch in the early seventeenth century were turning their factories into military establishments, the English remained content for many years with unfortified and virtually defenceless warehouses run by handfuls of men. Not until the establishment of Fort Marlborough at Bencoolen towards the end of the century did their policy in this respect begin to change.

The factors lived in a kind of collegiate society, sharing a house which would sometimes be hired from the local sultan, occasionally be borrowed from the Dutch, as so unwisely at Amboyna, or, with growing frequency, built according to their specifications. The houses were constructed in an adaptation of the local style, of wood, raised on piles above the ground, and

5

thatched with palm-leaf. The house at Tonking, where the Company established itself in 1672, was doubtless typical. Captain William Dampier, who visited it in 1688, described it as 'a pretty handsome low-built house'.

There is a handsome dining-room in the middle, and at each end convenient apartments for the Merchants, Factors and Servants belonging to the Company to live in, and at each end of it there are smaller Houses for other uses, such as Kitchen, Store-houses, etc., running in a Line from the great House towards the River, Making two Wings, and a square Court open on to the River. In this square space, near the Banks of the River, there stands a Flag Staff, purposely for the hoysting of the English colours on all occasions.

There were strict injunctions, impressed upon the young factors on their voyage out, to avoid relationships with native women, and excessive drinking as well, but neither of these austerities appears to have been long observed. On the other hand, a great deal of attention was certainly paid to ceremonial, both in relations with the native rulers and among the factors and their servants. A little group of eight or ten traders obviously could not achieve the kind of pomp which attended James Lancaster when he appeared before the Sultan of Acheen, attended by thirty armed guards and bearing costly presents from Queen Elizabeth herself. Nevertheless, encounters with local princes were as formal as the circumstances allowed, and, to emphasize their difference from the Asians among whom they dwelt, the factors appeared, at least publicly, in heavy English clothes.

Ceremonial within the factory helped to create the routine of the merchants' lives in the loneliness of the islands. The day began with Anglican prayers, and on Sunday the flag of St George fluttered against the tropical skies. Meals were eaten in common: a light breakfast and supper, with heavy dinner at midday. The chief factor sat at the head of the table, with his assistants receding according to rank. The hierarchical structure of the factory was also reflected in the scale of salaries. At Hirado in Japan, Richard Cocks, the chief factor, received £150 a year, and Will Adams, invaluable as an interpreter and an intermediary with the shogun, £100, but the remaining factors were paid only £40. At Bantam in 1609 salaries ranged from £117 down to £6 paid to the lowest assistants; the expenses of the mess were, of course, met by the Company.

The hierarchical structure of the factories was not unlike that of a London merchant's establishment in the seventeenth century, but there was more to it than habit; it provided the necessary elements of discipline and stability. Personal frictions inevitably developed during the long periods of isolation from England. The factors at Bencoolen waited almost two years from Lancaster's departure at the beginning of 1603 to Middleton's arrival

6

in December 1604, without seeing a new English face; they received only one batch of mail, brought by a Dutch boat. Other posts saw no ships from home for as much as four years. There were few diversions, largely because the communities were so small; Richard Cocks, patiently following his hobby of gardening at Hirado (and incidentally introducing the potato into Japan), was an exception, and, in an age before the foundation of the Royal Society, very few of the Company's servants had developed the scientific and scholarly interests which their successors displayed in the eighteenth century. An outlet for energy was provided by trading trips to outlying villages and islands, but during the monsoons such journeys were impossible and the factors were thrown back on each other's all-too-familiar company. The injunctions against excessive drinking fell more and more into abeyance. Yet one finds surprisingly little evidence of serious internal disputes. Boredom and proximity may have frayed tempers near to breaking, but the breaking point rarely came because every member of these tiny groups of Englishmen, from the chief factor to the humblest assistant, was aware that their unity provided the only protection – and that often a very thin one – against the dangers they had to endure.

Some of these dangers were natural and in that age unavoidable. In Bombay it was said that two monsoons were the life of a man, and the first Englishmen in the archipelago were hardly better off than their contemporaries in India. Malaria, dysentery and typhoid were endemic, and epidemics of cholera and smallpox were frequent. Physicians and surgeons were rarely appointed to the early factories, and those who did practise were almost useless, since knowledge of tropical sicknesses was in its most rudimentary stage. One survived by good fortune rather than good treatment. A poignant report from Bencoolen in 1685 speaks for the trials Englishmen might endure at any time during the first two centuries of their life in the Far East.

All our servants are sick and dead, and at this minute there is not a cook to get victuals ready for those that sit at the Company's Table, and such have been our straits that we many times have fasted. The sick lie neglected, some cry for remedies, but none are to be had: those that could eat have none to cook them victuals, so that we now have no living to bury the dead, and if one is sick the other will not watch, for he says that better one than two die, so that people die and no notice taken thereof.

Bencoolen was noted for its high rate of sickness, and this letter was written at an exceptionally bad time, but no factory entirely escaped these tropical scourges and the chances of survival were so low as to make one wonder why the East India Company was never lacking in recruits. Perhaps this was in part due to the fact that it started its activities at a time when life in Europe itself was so often made precarious by epidemics of plague and cholera.

Other dangers were due to a combination of inexperience on the part of the East India Company's men and malice on the part of their neighbours. Because of their ignorance of Moslem customs, the first factors at Bantam aroused the hostility of the Malays, who attempted to burn down their houses. Native princes were rapacious, often treacherous, and factors were sometimes murdered at their orders. But their behaviour was frequently dictated by the Dutch, whose enmity, quite apart from its effect on trade, contributed greatly to the discomfort and danger in which the English factors lived.

It was virtually impossible to escape the Dutch. They operated in Siam, in Japan, in Cochin-China, as well as throughout the East Indies. Their fleet was at first so much larger than that of the English Company that its ships were sure to appear, sooner rather than later, at any island where the English attempted to set up a factory. They tried to frighten the local rulers into expelling their rivals; they bought pepper at uneconomically high prices which the English could not afford to meet; when these methods did not remove their rivals, they were ready for violence. This ranged from brawling, in which members of both sides were killed in sword play, to outright persecution. In 1616 the Dutch raided the English factory at Banda and made its factors prisoner. 'The Dutch,' reported one of its victims, 'caused crates and cages to be made in their ships and did put us therein, and carried us in them bound in iron from port to port amongst the Indians.' When ships of the East India Company interfered to protect their factories, they were eventually defeated by the Dutch, whose terroristic methods reached a climax at Amboyna. Mainly as a result of Dutch hostility, the early English trading communities in the Far East were like frontier posts on a troubled borderland. Those who inhabited them lived with an eye always to tomorrow, never to the day after, and consequently they developed only the most rudimentary of social organizations and only the most temporary of relationships with Asian peoples.

Bencoolen, on the other hand, founded two generations after the Company had abandoned its plans for large-scale trading in Java and the Moluccas, attained a longevity which its mediocre trading possibilities hardly justified, and during that time it developed into the largest and most complex British community of its time in the Far East. The Company had now ceased to be a mere association of merchants. To order and protect its interests in India, it had created armed forces of its own and an increasingly elaborate bureaucracy. Its factories were no longer mere trading posts; the more important

8

of them had become forts, in fact as well as name, and, though the Company had not yet begun to acquire its territorial empire in India, it already wielded a considerable political influence through its military strength and its trading arrangements with local rulers.

Bencoolen was modelled on the Company's Indian establishments. Fort Marlborough was intended as the centre from which a commercial hegemony could be exercized over a considerable area of western Sumatra; its dependencies eventually included some thirteen posts scattered over almost three hundred miles of coastline, with two garrisons, at Bencoolen and Bantal. It was ruled by a deputy governor, with a council of three, and some thirty other covenanted servants (factors, secretaries, accountants, storekeepers), together with five surgeons, a chaplain, and a considerable staff of writers (or clerks). A small military force completed the establishment. The officers and gunners were English; the rank and file consisted mainly of Eurasians and of Bugis recruited from the Celebes.

The merchants at Bencoolen observed all the ceremonial that attended the great company officials in Madras and Calcutta. When the deputy governor went riding he was preceded by mounted guards, the flag was carried behind him, and Bugis foot soldiers ran beside him. If he went on foot, four men armed with blunderbusses preceded him and a guard of Bugis brought up the rear. 'I have two servants,' said Joseph Collet who occupied this post in the early eighteenth century, 'and two slaves of my own, one of them a female too. . . . However to prevent scandal I keep her in another family where she works for me, ironing, etc., but never comes into my house.'

Collet was one of the more capable officers at Bencoolen. His successors, until Sir Stamford Raffles arrived a century later, were mostly incompetent and intemperate. Even Collet had cause to complain of his own council, whose members drank all night and brawled during the day. On one occasion, in his presence, the chief of council drew his sword on the second in council and slashed him across the face. Collet, indeed, was inclined to assign Drink as the main cause, not only of dispute but also of most of the deaths that took place in Bencoolen. The other leading cause, according to him, was Women. There were, he told his friends, only four white women in the settlement; one was a lunatic and kept confined in a dark room, another was a termagant whom he was sending away for her husband's protection, the third was a young widow 'as well shap'd as a Madagascar Cow', and the fourth 'a woman of the most indifferent personage but yet of consummate virtue'. It was the Asian women (imported Bengalis and native Malays) who in Collet's view were the great danger; 'a man that ventures on them seldom fails to get the Bencoolen fever'.

Bencoolen fever or not, many of the Company's servants did venture on the 'blacks', as Collet called them, and, perhaps because it was the only English settlement in an area of Dutch influence, Fort Marlborough adopted a much more tolerant attitude towards relationships between Europeans and native women, and towards their offspring, than was usual among the British in the Far East; visitors compared its morals to those of Batavia. As the eighteenth century advanced, this attitude was to have a great effect on the social life of Bencoolen, which became increasingly a Eurasian settlement. Some of the Eurasians were covenanted servants of the Company, occupying high positions in the Bencoolen hierarchy; others were writers, and over the years they developed a strong vested interest, so that young men sent out from England found it hard to progress in the service. 'Some had either quitted the place in disgust or returned to England,' Raffles discovered when he assumed control at Bencoolen in 1819, 'and the remainder are posted as assistants under the other description of servants, with an allowance of 150 dollars per month, a salary which in this place is most certainly not equal to the subsistence of a gentleman'.

Like the later British settlements in the Far East, Bencoolen had attracted, apart from the local Malays, a considerable population of Indians and Chinese who performed menial tasks and carried on petty trading, so that the English and the Eurasians were a small minority. The washermen and tailors were Bengalis. 'They are very extravagant in their charges,' remarked the naturalist Benjamin Hayne, who visited Bencoolen in 1812, 'and the servants of this class are exceedingly knavish. To make a common jacket the tailor charges four dollars, and for 100 pieces of linen, a washerman demands six dollars'.* There were also three hundred Malay and Negro slaves belonging to the Company, who were employed in the warehouses and on public works, and also as servants to the officials. When Raffles, the friend of Wilberforce, arrived, one of his first acts was to set them free.

Not all the Europeans living in Bencoolen at the beginning of the nineteenth century were servants of the East India Company, and here we must introduce a type of trader who had been increasing in numbers and importance since the middle of the seventeenth century. From the beginning of its operations the Company had been troubled by the problem of 'interlopers',

---

* The trade dollar of the east during the nineteenth century was equal to the American dollar, or roughly five to the pound sterling. In 1873 the American treasury actually issued special 'trade dollars' designed only for use in the Far East. Now the dollars in this region vary in value from place to place, though all have fallen in relation to the American dollar. The Malay dollar stands at three to the US dollar, and the Hong Kong at six.

or independent merchants who infringed on its monopoly. All attempts
to keep them out of the Indian Ocean and the China Seas proved in
the long run useless. Theoretically the Company had the right to forbid
the entry of unauthorized English subjects into the regions under its control, but it was impossible to police the seas; in the seventeenth century a
common way of evading the Company's rules was to sail a ship nominally
owned by an Ostend merchant, and therefore outside the Company's jurisdiction. Even the Company's most loyal servants began to traffic on their
own accounts, and eventually a blind eye was turned to such activities,
which made it possible to retain active men who might otherwise be
deterred by relatively low salaries. In the end a *modus vivendi* was worked
out by which the Company controlled trade between London and the east,
and the interlopers carried on what was known as 'the country trade' – the
local commerce between various Asian ports. Benjamin Hayne, who had been
accustomed to conditions in India, was surprised at the importance which
these free traders had assumed by 1812 at Bencoolen, and, though he was
amused by their pretensions, he looked favourably on their activity and
enterprise.

They are all in their own estimation [he recounts] gentlemen of consequence, and
live in hopes (as money in their opinion is the only qualification in England requi-
site for a great man) 'to spend some jolly days with the Prince Regent, the Duke
of York, and such other good company!' Their occupations chiefly consist in
trading to the interior of Sumatra, and to the eastern islands, which they hitherto
have supplied with opium, and with English and India goods, which were of late
much wanted by the Dutch. It is to be wished that there was a greater number of
the latter description of men on this island, as by nobody sooner than by them,
would the resources of the country be discovered, provided a reasonable latitude
and support were given them in trading, manufacturing and labouring as also
proper restraint laid on their behaviour towards the natives.

The times favoured the country traders. The Company found that its
growing territorial empire in India was more profitable than its minor trading ventures, and in the Far East it soon began to concentrate its attention
almost exclusively on the China tea trade. At the same time, trading mono-
polies were becoming increasingly unpopular in an England where opinion veered towards free trade, and it would have been as unwise politically
as it was difficult in practice to eliminate the private merchants. The country traders not only gathered around Company centres like Bencoolen and
(as we shall see) the factory at Canton, but also formed little settlements
of their own on islands with safe harbours, such as that on Junk Ceylon, off
the western coast of Siam, where Francis Light, the founder of Singapore, once lived with other merchants of his kind, and, like them, took a

mistress from among the Portuguese half-castes of the locality. When Penang was founded by the Company in 1786, a single private trader, James Scott, who was a close friend of Light, gained almost complete control over its commercial activities; in Singapore, created by Raffles thirty-three years later in the deliberate hope of making it a free entrepôt for the whole east, some twenty firms of British merchants established themselves within a decade.

But, striking as Singapore may have been as a sign of the vigour of pre-Victorian private enterprise, the China coast remained the main goal of the private merchants as of the East India Company itself, and, as we have observed, it was in Canton that their emergence assumed its most dramatic and least edifying aspects.

From the beginning, the life of the merchants in Canton, whether they were Company's servants or traded on their own account, was given a peculiar character by the restrictions which, in mingled fear and contempt of foreigners, the Chinese government imposed upon them. They lived within a restricted area about a quarter of a mile square, on the Pearl River outside the walls of Canton. Some thirteen long, narrow factories were crammed into this area. These were occupied by traders of various nationalities, but many found the conditions of trading too onerous and by the beginning of the 1830s only the English, the Americans, the Dutch and the French remained. By far the greatest share of the China tea trade fell into the hands of the English, and this was due mainly to the fact that they had the virtual monopoly of the good quality opium grown in India; the Americans had to be content with selling the greatly inferior Turkish opium. As I have already mentioned, the Company and the country traders complemented each other in effecting this exchange, the Company buying tea through the Co Hong according to the requirements of the Chinese government and paying for it with silver, obtained by the country traders through the illicit sale of opium which they bought by public auction from the Company in India. For European goods sold legally the market was disappointing; on the other hand the Company found a ready demand for certain exotic products, such as the sea otter skins bought by sea traders from the Indians at Nootka on Vancouver Island and used by the Chinese to trim their brocade robes.

The Company itself maintained the New English Factory at Canton, which was actually a large compound with a frontage of one hundred and forty feet and a depth of more than four hundred feet, containing warehouses, offices, a church, and public assembly rooms, as well as bedrooms, sitting rooms and dining rooms for the members of its staff. The staff

The China Trade

Sir Jamsetjee Jejeebhoy Bt. (1783–1859), a prominent Parsee country trader, with a flourishing agency in Canton. Through his initial help Jardine Matheson, one of the most important of the British companies trading in the Far East, was able to become established. (Painting by George Chinnery.)

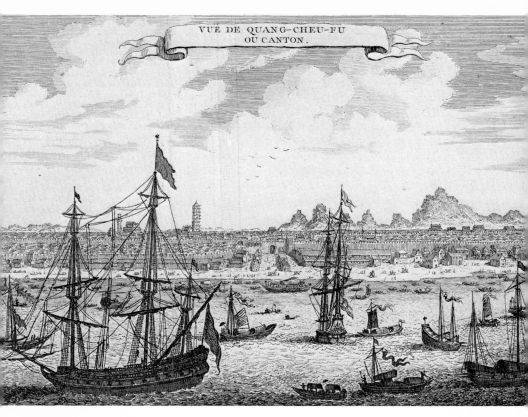

Canton harbour in the early nineteenth century with European trading vessels and Chinese junks.

An English ship, surrounded by junks, on the river at Canton. (Watercolour by Alexander.)

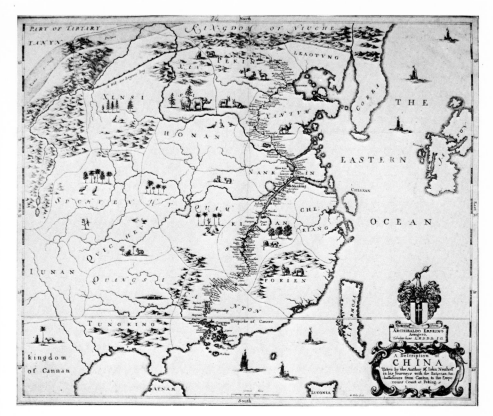

China, according to a map made by John Neuhoff 'in his Journeys with the Batavian Ambassadours from Canton, to the Emperours Court at Peking'.

A Chinese market-place, one of a series of early nineteenth-century watercolours painted in China for the English market.

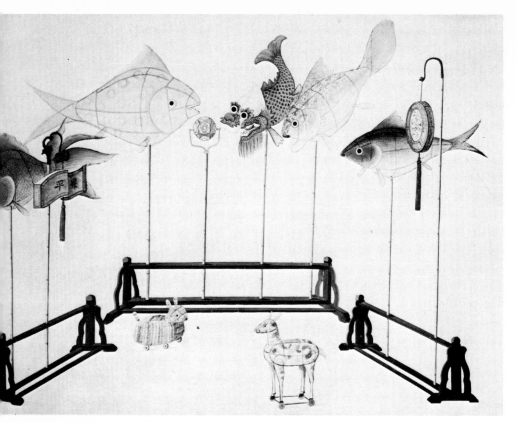

Childrens' toys made in China for export. Goods such as these formed an eye-catching, if unimportant, part of the growing trade with the Far East in Victorian times.

Chinese and an Englishman, sketches made by Alexander while attached to Lord Macartney's embassy to China, 1793.

(*opposite*) An interior of a house, painted to show the range of goods made in China and sent to England by the merchants of the treaty ports to gain orders for merchandise.

William Jardine: a portrait by George Chinnery.

James Matheson, Jardine's partner, was also portrayed by George Chinnery.

The Jardine residence at Macao, painted by Chinnery.

The *Falcon*, bought by Jardine Matheson and Co. from Lord Yarborough, was one of the first steamships in the Far East. Eventually the company had the engines removed and she was refitted as a clipper. This print was sent by the ship's commander to Alexander Matheson.

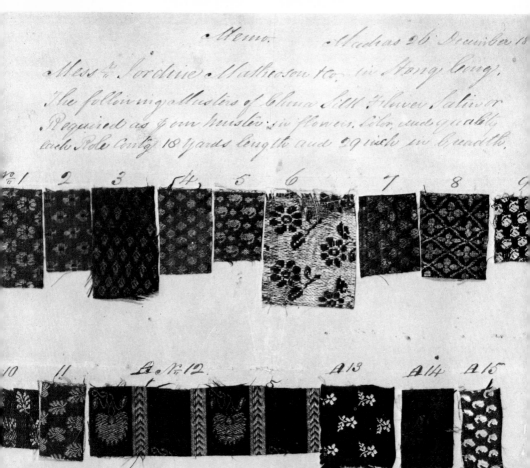

Samples of (*left*) wallpaper and (*below*) silk sent from China as part of Jardine Matheson's range of merchandise.

consisted of some twelve or fifteen supercargoes (the number varied from time to time), plus inspectors of teas, writers, surgeons and other lesser officials. A president – whom the Chinese gave the title of *taipan* – was in charge of the factory; he and the three senior supercargoes formed the select committee which sustained all relations with the Co Hong, the Chinese guild of merchants who acted as intermediaries between the Europeans and the mandarins; the latter did not condescend to maintain direct official communications with foreign merchants. Positions in Canton were eagerly sought after and were usually given to sons or protégés of the Company's directors; it was a great deal healthier for Europeans than India and the remuneration, by early nineteenth-century standards, was very high indeed. It took the form of a commission on all moneys passing through the factory, and, though no exact figures exist, it seems likely that the president received an average of about £8,000 a year, and the supercargoes a proportionately high payment; the inspector of teas received about £2,500 a year.

A few firms of country traders were allowed by the Company to occupy premises in the Canton factories abandoned by merchants of other nationalities. Most important among them was the firm of Jardine Matheson, run by two Scots, one a former surgeon and the other the son of a baronet. William Jardine and James Matheson represented the socially higher stratum among the country traders. Many were of humble and even somewhat disreputable antecedents. But, whatever their origins, the merchants of the 1830s differed little in their methods, and the patricians, Jardine and Matheson, had the reputation of being the toughest traders on the China coast, powerful in intrigue and disinclined to shrink from violence.

In all, counting servants and supernumeraries, between sixty and seventy Englishmen lived in the Canton factories during the period of the Company's ascendancy. They were allowed to stay there only for the five months of each winter shipping season, from September to March, when the year's tea crop was brought from the various sea and river ports of China to be traded in Canton. But this was the least annoying of the restrictions they endured. They were not allowed to bring their wives and families to Canton, or to import weapons into the factories, or to ride in sedan chairs, or to go for pleasure trips on the river. They could leave their tiny ghetto only three times a month, when they were allowed, in parties of no more than ten, to walk in the gardens on Honan Island. They could employ a strictly limited number of Cantonese servants. It was forbidden, under pain of death, to teach foreign devils Chinese. As a consequence, the world's most comic tongue, Pidgin English, was developed in Canton as a lingua franca for commerce.

Yet daily existence in Canton was not normally so tedious as these restrictions might suggest. Within the factory area a social life was established among the merchants of various nationalities, and the style of entertainment in the English factory was as splendid as that among the highest Company officials in Madras or Calcutta. The factory was a handsome building in a hybrid English-Chinese style of architecture, with what one visitor described as 'an elegant verandah, from which the views up and down the river are open and uninterrupted'. The great dining room was grandly furnished, with cut-glass chandeliers and Lawrence's portrait of George III, and the dinners, at which the supercargoes and their guests sat down with long-robed Chinese servants standing behind each chair, were worthy of the elaborate ceremonial with which they were served. William Hickey ate there, on an ordinary unfestive day, 'a capital dinner consisting of fish, flesh and fowl, all of the best, with a variety of well-dressed made dishes, being served up in two courses, followed by a superb dessert, the wines, claret, madeira, and hock, all excellent, and had as cold as ice'. When hunger had been satisfied, and the endless toasts drunk, the guest who did not desire more boisterous entertainment could browse in the only English library in the Far East (and, by all accounts, an excellent one).

Furthermore, though the mandarins held themselves aloof from the foreign merchants, and at most might condescend to be served a dinner without the company of their hosts, a great deal of social intercourse was maintained with the merchants of the Co Hong, who found means to circumvent the regulations and to entertain the Company's servants and the other merchants at their country houses. William Hickey gives a vivid description of a two-day entertainment of this kind provided in 1769 by a merchant the English called Pankeequa.

These fetes were given on the 1st and 2nd of October, the first of them being a dinner, dressed and served *à la mode Anglaise*, the chairman on that occasion using, and awkwardly enough, knives and forks, and in every respect conforming to the European fashion. The best wines of all sorts were amply supplied. In the evening a play was performed, the subject warlike, where most capital fighting was exhibited, with better dancing and music than I could have expected. In one of the scenes an English naval officer, in full uniform and fierce cocked hat, was introduced, who strutted across the stage, saying 'Maskee can do! God damn!' whereupon a loud and universal laugh ensued, the Chinese, quite in an ecstacy, crying out 'Truly have muchee like Englishman'.

The second day, on the contrary, everything was Chinese, all the European guests eating, or endeavouring to eat, with chopsticks, no knives or forks being at table. The entertainment was splendid, the victuals superiorly good, the Chinese loving high dishes and keeping the best of cooks. At night brilliant fireworks (in which they also excel) were let off in a garden magnificently lighted by coloured lamps, which we viewed from a temporary building erected for the occasion, and wherein there was exhibited sleight-of-hand tricks, tight- and slack-rope dancing, followed by one of the cleverest pantomimes I ever saw. This continued until a late hour, when we returned in company with several of the supercargoes to our factory, much gratified with the liberality and taste displayed by our Chinese host.

The East Indiamen were loaded, not at the factories, but some thirteen miles down river at Whampoa, and when the convoy was ready to sail for England, the merchants would close their establishments and make their way down river to Macao, where, on Portuguese soil, those who were married joined their families and the rest went into the palatial houses maintained by the company and the various private firms. The winter passed in a round of visits, balls, excursions, races and cricket matches, shared with the other contingent of merchants, who carried on their less reputable business at Lintin Island, in the Bay of Canton some twenty miles north-east of Macao.

Lintin had become the depot where – by private arrangement with the leading mandarins of Canton – the trade in smuggled Indian cotton goods and above all in opium was operated by the country traders, including those, like Jardine Matheson and their great rivals, Dent and Co., who also carried on an official trade at the Canton factories. The Chinese merchants carried the contraband away in fast rowing boats which could usually evade the dilatory war junks of the authorities.

The ambitions of the country traders are inseparable from the series of events which led to the Opium Wars of 1840-2 and later conflicts between Britain and China. The termination of the East India Company's monopoly of the China trade meant that the rich and legitimate commerce in tea became open to all comers, and immediately there was an influx of foreign merchants into the Canton factories. By 1839 the number of British subjects there had tripled, to more than two hundred, and a total of fifty-seven firms – mostly British – were operating. A new spirit of energy and enterprise permeated the trading community. Not content wth the legal facilities at Canton and the illegal ones on Lintin Island, they established what became known as 'the coast trade', a euphemism for aggressive smuggling; fast, well-armed boats prowled the coasts north and south of Canton, selling western manufactures, spices, and, of course, opium, in the ports where foreigners were theoretically forbidden to trade. The merchants justified their actions by a militant clamour for a freer trade on the Chinese as well as the British side; they wanted the restrictions on their movements to be abolished, the trading monopoly of the Co Hong to be terminated, and more ports to be opened; to further these aims they wielded a potent influence in political events on the China coast.

As a step towards achieving such changes, the British government attempted to replace the select committee of the East India Company with an official of their own, the chief superintendent of trade, who was empowered to carry on negotiations directly with the local mandarins. The Chinese refused to accept any arrangement which would acknowledge the equality of the barbarian King of England with the Son of Heaven in Peking, and in their turn exacerbated the situation by appointing a special commissioner with instructions to suppress the illegal opium trade. In an excess of zeal, this official kidnapped the foreign merchants by closing off the escape routes from the Canton factories, and as a ransom forced the handing over of the opium in their possession. Out of these events arose the Opium Wars of 1840-2.

The double defeat of China in these two wars resulted in the acquisition of Hong Kong, which fulfilled the merchants' demand for an island where they could be free from the threats and impositions of the Chinese authorities, and in the opening of the first five treaty ports. The firms already established in Canton were naturally the earliest to take advantage of these new opportunities. Hong Kong was favoured in the beginning as a convenient base for the illicit opium trade, but Shanghai soon proved the better centre for general commerce, and after the 1840s it rapidly assumed the lead among the mercantile communities of the China coast, which it maintained for a whole century until the 1940s brought a final end to the China trade.

Some of the patterns established in the Canton factories continued in the treaty ports. The most important merchants in Shanghai and along the whole coast were for many years Jardine Matheson and their old Canton rivals, Dent and Co., who were noted for their princely hospitality. Dents eventually went bankrupt, but Jardine Matheson still flourish, with their headquarters now in Hong Kong. As the opportunities for legitimate trade expanded, the larger houses became respectable, concentrating on tea and general merchandise, and acting as agents for London exporters. But the considerable number of medium and small traders who set up on the China coast during the mid-nineteenth century still relied largely on smuggling, and the trade in opium did not finally disappear until the dissolution, as late as 1917, of the Shanghai Opium Combine – an English concern tolerated by the British authorities until international opinion became too strong to allow its continuance. The larger houses maintained branches or agencies at all the treaty ports as well as in Hong Kong, and later, when Japan was opened to trade, the merchants from the China coast hastened to set up business there, mainly in Nagasaki and in the new settlements of Yokohama and Kobe.

The early establishments of these merchants were modelled fairly closely on those of the East India Company. Instead of being called factories, they went by the Chinese name of hongs, but for many years they followed the East India pattern of a compound containing a large building devoted to business transactions and to dwelling, with warehouses behind it. In the hongs the old collegiate way of living was continued. The partners or managers, called taipans like the East India Company presidents before them, and their assistants, the griffins (bearing the same name as the unbroken Mongolian ponies brought south for racing at Shanghai), lived in the spacious upper rooms of the hongs. In the larger hongs there were senior and junior messes, but in others taipans and griffins shared the same table and a kind of equality prevailed, rather like that among officers in an army mess. They were all young – even the taipans in the 1840s were rarely more than thirty; they were roughly of the same social milieu, middle class by origin and gentlemen – for the most part – by courtesy; the griffins were regarded as potential partners and were allowed and even encouraged to carry on a certain amount of trading on their own accounts. The clerical work was done mainly by Portuguese from Macao, and Chinese compradors were the intermediaries between the British hongs and the native merchants.

To trade effectively in the early days on the China coast, a merchant needed great resources in either capital or credit, since in the beginning there were no banking facilities. The first European banks were opened in Singapore in 1840, in Hong Kong in 1845, and in Shanghai not until 1850. A letter took six months to reach Europe, and a transaction between London and Shanghai might well take more than a year to complete. This meant that large stocks of trade goods had to be held, and only wealthy and established merchants or men in the confidence of English exporters could trade on any large scale. Smaller traders frequently had to rely on loans at high rates of interest from Chinese money-lenders and compradors.

The institution of the hong was transferred almost unchanged to Japan when trade started there in the early 1860s, but the methods of commerce were different and, in the beginning, more difficult, since Japanese ideas of propriety did not at first allow the display of eagerness to trade which came naturally to the Chinese merchants.

Instead of sending samples of substantial quantities, such as a thousand chests of tea or fifty bales of silk, and the owner or his broker coming to chaffer in the silk-room or the tea-room of the foreign merchant, the latter had to go the round of the Japanese shops to see what they had got. Early every morning the leading merchants might be seen booted to the thighs – for the rain was frequent and the roads unmade – trudging up and down the Japanese bazaar to see what novelties had come to hand. The more zealous would sometimes make a second round in the afternoon, in case there might be some late as well as some early worms to be picked up. The bodily fatigue and consumption of time involved in this process would have rendered a large business impossible. There were as yet no Japanese merchants properly so-called, and their endless parley resembled more the tenacious higgling of peasants than the negotiations of men of business.

(Alexander Michie, *The Englishman in China during the Victorian Era.*)

But methods changed, even in Japan, as the century continued and the country became rapidly more westernized.

The situation of the Far Eastern merchants and the nature of their establishments in both China and Japan also changed with growing momentum after 1860. The foundation in 1864, by a consortium of local merchants, of the Hongkong and Shanghai Banking Corporation provided a source of credit and a financial clearing house suited to the needs of the China trade. The Suez Canal was opened to steamships in 1869, and the telegraph reached both Hong Kong and Shanghai in 1870. The combination of rapid communication and quick sea transport meant that it was no longer necessary for European firms to maintain large stocks of goods. Warehouse space could be saved, and merchants' establishments gradually took on the aspect of office complexes rather than trading factories. Even more important, merchants could now trade on slighter reserves of capital or credit, and this enabled smaller enterprises to operate more easily. As time went on, the availability of private housing accommodation brought an end to the collective life of the early hongs, and the merchant houses ceased to exist as self-contained social microcosms.

With success and power, the original spirit of adventurousness did not desert the merchant community in the Far East. The great hongs might undergo such transformations that by the 1930s their successors in Shanghai, Hong Kong and Singapore were much like modern import and export corporations anywhere in the world. But Conrad's lone traders, operating in the islands and backwaters of the Malayan world, were not wholly fictional. The modern world was slow to penetrate the archipelago. The telegraph reached Sarawak only in 1900, thirty years after it reached Hong Kong, and the first bank opened there in 1924. The traditions of the original country merchants were maintained in these remoter regions until the beginning of the Second World War. The English traders, living in their bamboo houses thatched with grass, whom Wallace met on his naturalizing trips during the 1860s, survived for at least two generations, sometimes acting as agents for the big houses in Singapore, sometimes trading on their own accounts for the jungle products which Malays and Dyaks brought to their posts, and just as often involving themselves in shady partnerships, like the Labuan Trading Company which in the 1870s made its profits by running guns and other contraband into the Philippines. Disrespect for the laws of other nations, particularly when they were Asian nations, had been part of the British merchant's outlook since the events of the 1830s in Canton. However respectable the taipans might become, this attitude never completely vanished, and the British soldiers of fortune who operated in the Far East had their counterparts in the mercantile community.

One cannot complete any account of British merchants in the Far East without at least recognizing the presence and importance of the Chinese merchants on whom so much of the trade depended. The whole commercial system which was built up during the nineteenth century in Malaya, in the archipelago and on the China coast was in fact an elaborate symbiosis in which the British merchants provided Chinese merchants with a great western market and vice versa; without either side, trade would die immediately. The Chinese formed the majority in every new community the British established in the Far East, except in Japan. Most of those who emigrated to the new cities were, indeed, coolies or other menial workers, but the Chinese merchants were still far more numerous than their European counterparts and in many cases they were actually richer than the Englishmen with whom they dealt. It was they who carried out the indispensable functions of middlemen, who patiently collected small parcels of merchandize until they had assembled quantities worthy of the foreign merchant's attention, who kept alive the long chains of intermediaries with remote areas, and who, on many occasions, provided the capital or the credit which kept business going. Socially, relations might be tenuous and guarded, particularly after the arrival of the white women with their memsahib attitudes cast its special blight over the British communities, but commercially the Europeans and the Chinese were dependent on each other and, moreover, fully aware of it.

2

THE MARINERS

During three and a half centuries in which the British empire developed and declined in the Far East, the only effective land link to be constructed between Europe and the shores of the China Seas was the Trans-Siberian Railway. Completed late in our period, and intended largely as a means of building up Russian influence in Manchuria and northern China, it was of little use to the merchants of Britain. It is true that for many years the East India Company's mails were carried overland from Constantinople to Basra, so that news could reach India in three months and Singapore in four, instead of the six months it might take around the Cape of Good Hope. And in the mid-nineteenth century, before the opening of the Suez Canal, passengers were landed at Alexandria and taken overland to the Red Sea, thus saving the long journey around Africa. But few pieces of merchandize sent from Singapore or the China coast ever touched land on their way to England. Even the local transport of goods to the treaty ports and to centres like Hong Kong and Singapore for trans-shipment to London was done mainly by Chinese and Malay craft using the rivers and the channels between the islands, and, later, by the coastal steamers which competed with them. The introduction of air services and the building of railways has made little difference, except in the transportation of passengers; the railways merely feed the ports, and without ships the whole commercial life of the Far East would cease to exist.

As a result of this dependence on shipping, the early links between traders and mariners were never broken, and to this day the great merchant houses of the east are situated so that they look out over the harbours which sustain them. The East India Company and the country traders originally owned or controlled their own ships and the sailors were their employees. After the termination of the Company's monopoly in China, independent shipping lines began to appear – most important then as now the P.&O. – the Peninsular and Oriental Line, which began sailing to Singapore in 1845, and to Hong Kong and Shanghai shortly afterwards. With the advent of these lines, most of the merchants gave up as uneconomical the running of house fleets merely for their own trade. Even so, the links between the traders and the new shipping lines often remained very close. The established trading firms added to their functions those of agents for the freight shipping lines. Indeed, they often owned them, wholly or in part. In 1882, for example, Jardine Matheson made their private fleet the nucleus of the Indo-China Steam Navigation Company, and somewhat earlier, Butterfield and Swire had founded the China Navigation Company.

The mariners made a distinctive contribution to the lives of the British communities scattered around the China Seas. More than any other class they exemplified the mobility of this society, its temporary, unrooted nature. The captains of ships were – at least in the early days – among its notable patricians. The seamen provided its nearest approach to a European proletariat; out of their ranks emerged its shifting population of poor whites and also a high proportion of its adventurers.

As for the ships they sailed, these changed continually over the centuries. The splendid, massive East Indiamen of the Napoleonic period were followed by the swift opium clippers of the 1840s and the even swifter tea clippers of the 1850s, in which building for sail reached its height of elegance and functional appropriateness. In our own day their place has been taken by the steam freighters and the gigantic P.&O. liners, specially adapted for long voyages in tropical climates.

It was their appropriateness to the tasks they faced which distinguished all these types of ships from those in which British merchants and mariners first entered Asian waters. When James Lancaster sailed in 1601, neither his ship nor his men were in any way prepared for the voyages that lay before them. The ships were not built for Asian conditions, with which few Englishmen were yet familiar; they were bought at a price of £41,000 for the five of them, a mere fraction of the cost of a small modern freighter. The flagship, the *Red Dragon*, was of 600 tons burden, and the smallest of the five, the *Quest*, was only 130 tons. Such ships would seem lilliputian beside the vast tankers now produced in European and Japanese shipyards, but for a true comparison one must remember that when Frobisher set out in 1576 to discover the North-West Passage, his two ships were of 20 and 25 tons burden. By contemporary standards, the first British mariners to reach the Far East used the best craft available, and, despite the rigours which long tropical voyages then wreaked on ships as well as men, several of the vessels

21

which accompanied Lancaster sailed again with Middleton in 1604; the *Hector* even sailed with Captain Keeling in 1607.

The ships of Lancaster's fleet combined the functions of freighters, of floating warehouses from which direct trade could be carried out, and also of warships. When the conflict with the Dutch developed in the East Indies, Company's ships were in 1618 organized into a small battle fleet under Sir Thomas Dale, which at first fought successfully against the Dutch, though eventually it suffered defeat, losing twelve ships to the enemy, a disaster which made the East India Company decide, even before the massacre of Amboyna, to withdraw progressively from its posts in the archipelago. The crucial battle was possibly that in the harbour of Patani, where John Jourdain, the best of the East India Company's captains, was attacked with two of his ships by a superior Dutch force and shot – by accident, according to his enemies – after he had surrendered.

The commander, or 'general', of an early East Indian fleet had thus many responsibilities; he had to establish relations with local rulers, to trade, to set up factories, to act as chaplain and moral instructor, to assume the role of military commander in case of necessity. In consequence the task of navigation fell mainly into the hands of the pilot-master who, even if he had no knowledge of the seas he was entering, would be an experienced mariner with service in the Atlantic or even, like John Davis, in the Arctic. The crews were ordinary London seamen with no more experience and even less knowledge of tropical regions than their commanders. They would normally number between seventy and a hundred, according to the size of the ship. The *Clove*, when it reached Japan in 1613, carried – besides the seven factors landed at Hirado – a complement of seventy-four. Sixty-seven were English; the remaining seven were made up of a Spaniard and a Japanese, picked up on the voyage because their knowledge might be useful, and five Indians, precursors of those lascar seamen who were later to play such an important role in Far Eastern seafaring.

The hardships Lancaster's men endured on the first voyage of 1601 were prophetic of those which would afflict their successors until the end of the age of sail. The ships were loaded with supplies calculated to last twenty months, and set out with live cattle and what seemed like an abundance of fresh foods. But, as every traveller to the east was to discover, until the steamships began to travel quickly through the Suez Canal, most of the fresh foods were consumed long before the outward trip was completed, and the crew had to fall back on salt meat and ship's bread, with putrid Thames water as the principal drink. The inevitable consequences followed. Halfway down the coast of Africa they began to fall sick with scurvy, and, though Lancaster knew enough about the disease to treat his men with lemon juice, many died. The fleet had to wait at Table Bay until the crews could be revived with a diet of fresh meat and fruit bought from the local Negroes. Scurvy dogged all the early voyages. When Middleton's ships reached Bantam in 1604 there were hardly enough fit men to drop the anchors. The scourge continued until the early nineteenth century, partly because the diet of seamen continued to be monotonous and lacking in vitamins, and partly because of the scanty knowledge of anti-scorbutics; it was long, for example, before lime juice came into universal use on ships bound for the east, and as late as the end of the eighteenth century mariners' narratives tell of voyages in which almost the whole of a ship's crew would be incapacitated with scurvy. When Captain Bartlett reached St Helena on his way home in 1789, only four men of his whole crew were on their feet and Bartlett himself was at the wheel.

After the first exploratory voyages, the East India Company set up its own shipyard at Blackwall where ships were built according to its specifications, and during the Restoration period some of the largest ships of the period, up to 1,200 tons, were being launched for the India run. But it was only the smaller ships, at the time when the Company's interest in the Far East was at its lowest ebb, that supplied Bencoolen and the various shortlived posts which at this time were set up in Tonking, Siam and Borneo. When attention turned back to China in the mid-eighteenth century and regular trade was established at Canton, the Company no longer owned its fleet of East Indiamen. They were now built, still to its specifications, at the instance of middlemen – the owners – who hired them to the Company for six or at most eight runs to and from the east. The owner appointed the captain of the ship, or, to be more literal, sold him his commission. Otherwise the ship was operated strictly under the instructions and regulations of the Company.

The first of the East Indiamen to take part in the China trade were ships of about 750 tons burden and of a transitional form – narrow, deep-waisted ships, with high poops and forecastles, 'over built aloft, and too deep below for their breadth' as one contemporary critic remarked. Towards the end of the century trimmer and safer ships were built, with flush upper decks, and these craft, which ran in size up to 1,400 tons, formed the China fleet at the height of the Company's Canton trade during the early nineteenth century. They were the largest and best-built merchant vessels of their age, but, since they still retained heavy armaments, carrying up to forty-eight guns, they were also warships which could on occasion give a good account of themselves. At a distance, with their chequered paintwork, they looked so much like naval vessels that on one occasion in the Straits of Malacca a strong French naval squadron mistook a group of them for ships of the line and fled without risking an engagement.

East Indiamen not merely looked like naval vessels. They were also run with a strict naval discipline and a naval sense of hierarchy, which was hardly surprising, since their officers came from the same social milieu as the officers of His Majesty's fleet, and, indeed, often from the same families. It was the middle-middle class milieu typified by Jane Austen and her naval brothers, one of whom, Admiral Sir Francis Austen, was stationed in the China Seas during the 1840s.

The captain of an East Indiaman was dignified by the title of commander. He and his officers wore blue uniforms with black velvet cuffs and lapels, the rank being indicated discreetly by the gilt buttons on the cuffs. These officers and the petty officers were so numerous as to give a top-heavy appearance to the ship's company. Most merchant ships carried three or four mates; even a medium-sized East Indiaman carried six.

A ship of 650 tons and upwards carried, besides the six mates, surgeon and purser, a boatswain, gunner, carpenter, five midshipmen, a surgeon's mate, caulker, cooper, captain's cook, ship's cook, captain's steward, ship's steward, sailmaker, armourer, butcher, baker, poulterer, barber, and six quartermasters. These, with their respective mates and servants, together with fifty seamen, made up a total of about a hundred. In the 1200-ton ships the crew was larger by the addition of another twenty or thirty seamen.

(C. Northcote Parkinson, *Trade in the Eastern Seas* 1937)

In terms of privilege and of living conditions the gaps between the captain and his officers, and between the officers and the men were great indeed. The pay list of an East Indiaman gives a wholly deceptive picture of comparative equality. The captain's salary was £10 a month, that of the chief mate £5; an able seaman, at the same time, received £2.5.0 a month, and could consider himself well paid, since his counterpart in the navy received only £1.13.0.

Yet the post of commander on an East Indiaman was so much sought after that on occasion the purchase price would rise as high as £11,000. What made it so valuable were the two privileges accorded the captain; he received the fares of the passengers, and he was allowed to export 56 cubic feet of trade goods and to import 38 cubic feet. Thus he – and to a lesser extent his mates (who had much smaller allowances of space for trade goods) – were in fact merchants on a fairly respectable scale, particularly if they used the cargo space wisely, as did Captain William Mackintosh, who commanded the *Hindostan* during the 1790s, and invested a great deal of his capital in elaborate mechanical toys, called 'Singsongs', which the Chinese mandarins found intriguing. With these and other items, Mackintosh made £9,632 on a single outward voyage, and presumably, like other officers, invested his takings in Chinese goods which he sold for a second profit in London.

The commander of an East Indiaman was thus a man of wealth as well as standing, and he lived in the state which was usual among high officers of the East India Company. When his ship anchored at a Company's fort, he was entitled to a salute of thirteen guns, and when the China fleet gathered at Whampoa outside Canton the entertainment was so lavish that the two senior captains were between them allowed £800 by the Company to maintain a proper standard of hospitality to visiting Chinese officials. Even during the voyage the captain lived in relative luxury among his passengers in the isolation of the poop, attended by his own cook and his own steward.

In comparison, the crew lived as Spartanly as any ship's company of the time, swinging their hammocks on the gun deck, and eating the customary diet of salt meat, pease pudding, biscuits and grog, varied by beer on the way out, and rice on the way home. Because their diet was much inferior to that of the officers, they were more liable to scurvy and other sicknesses. Far into the nineteenth century the statistics of deaths in the ports of the Far East show that seamen were – with the sole exception of private soldiers – the worst sufferers among Europeans from tropical diseases.

Not the least of a seaman's trials was the threat of the press gang. Especially in wartime – which covered a good many of the years between 1757 and 1815 – the admirals in the China Seas regarded the East Indiamen as convenient reservoirs of manpower from which they could replenish the crews of naval vessels reduced by sickness. An East Indiaman might, with the cooperation of London crimps (who would not only recruit seamen but also hide them from the press gang), sail with a full crew from England. But on the return voyage, as the splendid convoy of fifteen or sixteen great East Indiamen, with perhaps thirty country ships and several escorting ships of the line and frigates, set its white sails towards India and England, death and impressment would have reduced the English sailors to a third of the full crew – usually the least able-bodied – and the rest would consist of lascars, Chinese and Portuguese half-breeds, all of them good seamen in fair weather, but of little use in a storm or a fight.

The ships of the country trade were much more numerous than the East Indiamen, but also somewhat smaller, so that, though there were twice as many at Canton each year, their aggregate tonnage was probably no greater than that of the East Indiamen. Up to the early nineteenth century, they were built in the shipyards of Bombay, Calcutta and Pegu by native craftsmen following European models. Since they were constructed of teak, which lasts long in tropical waters, some of them were more than a century old, and a fleet of country ships presented a veritable museum of shipping styles, from sham Portuguese caravels to imitations of the latest East Indiamen. They were owned by English or Parsee firms with offices in Bombay or Calcutta, and commanded always by British officers. Their crews were mainly lascars or Chinese. There were several reasons for the use of Asian crews, which is still practised by British merchant ships plying the eastern seas. Private traders could not afford the princely wastefulness of the East India Company and economized in both officers (there were rarely more than a captain and two mates) and men (lascars were, of course, paid much less than English seamen). Lascars and the Chinese crews, moreover, were not subject to impressment. And, even if the country traders had wished to employ English crews, these would have been almost impossible to recruit in the east, where the only Europeans available were likely to be deserters from other ships or men with no experience of the sea at all. This problem existed from the beginning, and Captain William Dampier in the 1680s made some comments on the subject which hold good for the whole period until the end of sailing ships. He told how a Captain Jones, having just acquired a new country ship in Sumatra, had to content himself with hiring a few English soldiers who had been serving as mercenaries to the King of Siam and possessed no sailing experience.

But here in the Indies [Dampier went on] our English are forc'd, for want of better, to make use of any Seamen such as they can get, and indeed our Merchants are often put hard to it for want of Seamen. Here are indeed Lascars or Indian seamen enough to be hired; and these they often make use of: yet they always covet an Englishman or 2 in a Vessel to assist them. Not but that these Lascars are some of them indifferent good sailors, and might do well enough: but an Englishman will be accounted more faithful, to be employed on matters of Moment; beside the more free Conversation that may be expected from them, during the Term of the Voyage. So that though oft-times their Englishmen are but ordinary Sailors, yet they are promoted to some Charge on which they could not be so capable anywhere but in the East Indies.

During the period of the Company's monopoly, some of the country ships sailed from Bombay with cargoes of cotton which were traded legally at Canton, or, later on, illegally at Lintin Island. In Calcutta opium played a large part in the trade, as did smuggling to the Dutch dominated East Indies. Both of these trades demanded swift, well-armed craft, and the boats which the sailed from Calcutta were usually even smaller than Bombay ships. The trade to the archipelago was carried out in ships of less than 200 tons, and that to the China coast in ships of 400 tons, one-third the capacity of the great slow-moving East Indiamen.

The captains were chosen for their daring, and were paid a commission on all trade transacted, so that many became rich men and merchants on their own account. Out of the opium ships developed the opium clippers and a tradition of speed maintained by the leading merchant houses of the China coast well into the age of steam. The first opium clipper was Jardine Matheson's *Red Rover*, built at Calcutta in 1829 in imitation of a New England-built American privateer. The *Red Rover* was a long, low, flush-decked ship of 254 tons, designed to sail into, as well as with, the monsoon, and capable of running between Calcutta and Lintin Island in eighteen days and of making three return trips within a trading season. Within a few years this firm and its rivals had established small fleets of such ships, manned by picked crews, whose speed not only gave them excellent powers of evasion, but also enabled the firm with the fastest ship – usually Jardine Matheson – to secure the most profitable deals by rapid transmission of both goods and information. Even after they had abandoned opium trading the great hongs of the China coast retained the habit of speed, and during the 1860s they maintained swift steamships which were used to intercept the mail steamers at Singapore and run the firms' letters quickly to Hong Kong and Shanghai, so that Jardine Matheson and Dent and Co. usually received their important dispatches from Europe two days ahead of the other merchants and were able to manipulate the market accordingly. All this, of course, ended with the coming of the telegraph in 1870.

Before the steamships finally triumphed, the sailing ship reached its apogee in the tea clippers, which graced the China Seas from 1850 to 1870. The most famous of them, the *Cutty Sark*, came at the end of the era, when steam communication had already made the clipper an obsolescent form of transport, though it was to be long into the twentieth century before the last of these most beautiful of ships finally left the seas. The tea clipper originated among the shipbuilders of Nova Scotia and New England. It was soon imitated by British – and particularly Scottish – shipbuilders, and, after the *Stornoway* was launched at Aberdeen in 1850, a whole succession of British-made clippers – of wood and later of iron or of wood on iron frameworks – began to leave the shipyards at Liverpool, Greenock and Glasgow, and ply between London and the Chinese treaty ports.

At the height of the clipper era, between 1864 and 1869, about forty of these ships sailed each season from the China ports. They carried the spring season crops of new tea, which were of the highest quality; the later, low quality crops followed by slower craft, including even, at this early period, the P.&O. mail steamers, with trans-shipment at Suez. The five main tea ports were Canton, Amoy, Foochow, Shanghai and Hankow. Hankow was disliked by clipper captains, because their ships had to be towed nine hundred miles up the Yangtse and frequently ran aground. Foochow was the most popular port because its teas were usually ready several weeks before those of the other centres and it was from Foochow that the clippers would race to gain the bonus paid to the ship first home with its cargo. The annual tea race acquired the excitement of a sporting event; the first sight of the clippers in the English Channel was awaited eagerly, and as soon as they came in view bets were laid on them, particularly in the City, where the first shipload of tea to arrive – no matter what its quality – fetched a particularly high price and was eagerly bought by the gracious livers of the day. The most famous race of all was that of 1866, when five clippers, ranging from the *Fiery Cross* of 695 tons to the *Ariel* of 852 tons, left Foochow within three days, and reached the Channel so close together that the *Ariel* passed the Downs ten minutes before the *Taiping;* the *Taiping* eventually reached its dock eighteen minutes before the *Ariel*, but only because its captain was fortunate enough to engage the first available tug. They had taken a hundred days, a little more than half the normal sailing time of an East Indiaman.

Such speed was possible only with magnificently designed ships and exceptional men. Among mariners, great prestige attached to the command of a good clipper, and there was never any difficulty in obtaining first-rate captains and mates, and crews of more than average quality. This was in spite of the fact that the owners – usually British shipping firms, since the China traders did not dabble in intercontinental shipping – could not offer the material inducements that had made the command of an East Indiaman such an enviable post. A clipper captain would earn £200 a year, with 25s a week board wages and comparatively few perquisities. A mate would earn £6 a month. The small, carefully picked crew – from thirty to forty men – earned scarcely more than the men on ordinary merchant ships. The only extra inducement was the bonus, up to £500, paid each year to the crew of the winning ship, but this was at best a sporting chance. Yet the crews of clippers were not crimped men and they had a special kind of *esprit de corps*, echoed in the seamen's shanties which first became popular on these ships, and demonstrated in the willingness with which their crews would enter into the spirit of the races and take a pride in the swiftness and good handling of their ships.

The last good year of the clippers was 1869. The next season – the first after the opening of the Suez Canal – they faced the competition of the steamships, which had crowded to the treaty ports and charged for taking the tea by the short route to England two-thirds the price of £7 a ton the

Mariners and Men of War

Coxswain of the Commodore's Barge, from the series of sketches made by
W. Alexander, while accompanying Lord Macartney's embassy to China in 1793.

the Cockswain of the Commodore's Barge
at Batavia

General Appearance of Bantam, taken on a th

Bantam on the island of Java, sketched by Alexander on a 'thick evening'.

Jardine's clipper brig *Lanrick* off Singapore in 1850. The ship was named after Lanrick Castle, the home of Mr Jardine.

The s.s. *Chusan*, a barque-rigged steamer, with which the P & O Line inaugurated their mail service to Australia in 1852. After the initial run, she ran between Singapore and Australia and, as a precaution, was well armed to withstand the attacks of pirates.

(*above*) Engraving of the king's dragoons fighting the Tartar cavalry at an engagement near Peking in 1860.

(*left*) Photograph of the British guard of Customs Volunteers in Peking in the 1890s.

Englishmen being rowed by Chinese boatmen.

Even in the present century, pirates on the Chinese rivers were so numerous that most boats had an armed anti-pirate guard, like these by the door leading to the second-class deck of a river steamer.

One of the pirate leaders, Wa Lao Choi San, the 'queen' of Bias Bay, here seen aboard her armed junk with two of her followers.

The P & O's *Canton* and H.M.S. *Columbine*, an English sailing warship, wrecking a number of pirate junks in the Canton river in 1849. The pirates in these waters were notorious and could easily escape from warships with sails if they were becalmed, as the *Columbine* had been.

(*above*) Justice for the pirates, if they were caught, was summary. An execution that took place in Kowloon.

(*left*) Junks were not only used for riverain work, but the larger ones were invaluable for local sea-borne trade. In 1848, one was even sailed from Canton to Gravesend, the journey taking 477 days.

merchants had in the past been paying to the clippers. The disappearance of the clippers from the tea trade did not mean the end of sailing ships in the China Seas, as readers of Conrad will know. For a long time they could still compete in handling slow freight, in trading around Malaya and among the islands of the archipelago, in the somewhat disreputable traffic of carrying Chinese coolies to South America.

The first steamships in the Far East were small boats constructed in India. The Company's steamship *Enterprise* brought the govenor-general to the Straits Settlements in 1829. In 1836 the *Jardine* was taken to Canton, where the merchants hoped to use her for a passenger service between Macao and Canton, but the Chinese authorities refused permission; taken to Singapore she stuck on a mud bank on her first trip (a 'steam picnic' for local celebrities) and caught fire on her second; her paddles were removed and she was demoted to a sailing vessel. On the other hand, the *Diana*, which reached Singapore from India in 1837, and the *Nemesis*, which in 1840 was the first steamship to round the Cape, did excellent service, the first in the East India Company's marine, and the second in the Navy, in dealing with Malay and Dyak pirates, who were demoralized by the sight of a ship advancing on them at full speed – without oars and belching smoke – in the midst of a dead calm.

Commercial steamships were introduced into the China Seas by the P.&O., whose Indian run from Suez began in 1840. In 1845 this was extended to Penang, Singapore and Hong Kong. It was a monthly service, and the line contracted with the Post Office to sail from Ceylon to Hong Kong, with two stops in the way, in 355 hours. The first ship on the run was the paddle-steamer, *Lady Mary Wood*, 566 gross tonnage, which reached Singapore on 4 August 1845. The mail she deposited there had been forty-one days on the way from London, less than half the time taken by the fastest of the tea clippers. In the following year the P.&O. service was extended to Shanghai, and shortly afterwards the steamer *Canton* was introduced to run a local service from Hong Kong to Canton and Macao. In 1852 the Australian run was instituted via Singapore, and in 1864 a further service linked Hong Kong with Yokohama. For more than a century, with a considerable diminution of traffic during the First World War, and a complete cessation during the Second, the P.&O. has remained the principal passenger line in the China Seas, where its most modern liners are luxury cruise ships sixty times larger than the *Lady Mary Wood*.

The P.&O. mail steamers carried not only passengers but also a certain amount of light cargo whose value justified the costs of trans-shipment in Egypt. Freight steamships as such did not appear in the China Seas until the 1860s, and the first regular European service around the Cape of Good

Hope was started in 1866 by Alfred Holt of Liverpool with his Blue Funnel Line. After the opening of the Suez Canal there was an immediate increase in the number of steamships plying in the Far East, new lines were founded in rapid succession, and a vast area of inland China was thrown open to sea-borne trade when freighters began to travel under their own power almost a thousand miles up the Yangtse to Hankow.

In some ways trade adapted itself slowly to the new form of transport. Well into the 1880s ships still raced – as in the days of sail – to bring home the first spring teas, which now reached London in little over a month. But soon the teas of Darjeeling were competing in the London market with those of China, and the attraction which the earliest consignment from Foochow had wielded over dealers and consumers alike gradually faded away. When the annual tea race came to an end, the freighters of the Far Eastern runs settled down to a prosaic routine of regular sailings, all the year round, unaffected by seasons of growth or winds of the monsoon. The British lines did not content themselves with the China trade. Malaya, of course, was a natural province for them, and they dominated the traffic with Siam, carrying, at the end of the nineteenth century, some three-quarters of its commerce.

From the 1860s the local steamship traffic proliferated as well, along the coasts of the China Seas and up the higher reaches of the Yangtse, for which river boats were specially designed and built in British shipyards. This coastal and river trade was at first dominated by the fleets of the large merchant houses, which, as we have seen, were later transformed into independent shipping lines. By the 1870s they had to face growing competition from ships coming from England and Germany through the Suez Canal to reap their share of the rich local trade. Nor were the Chinese traders backward in cultivating this field of profit. In 1874 they established the China Merchants Steam Navigation Company, while individual merchants in Hong Kong and Shanghai built up fleets of as many as a dozen small steamships, which they found well adapted to smuggling as well as to legitimate trade. On these Chinese owned ships the officers and engineers were usually British, and in time a considerable community of such mariners came to regard Shanghai as their home port; eventually they numbered than a thousand, not counting those who worked from Hong Kong.

In the era of steam, life on shipboard continued in many ways the traditions of sailing days, and in particular the division of the crews between British officers and engineers, and lascar or Chinese seamen remained untouched. There were of course the changes in duties which everywhere in the world followed the substitution of steam for sail, and, later, the substitution of oil fuel for coal; the stoker, that symbolic figure of human toil, appeared, sweated his time away and departed. But there were also changes which acquired a peculiar importance in the context of long eastern voyages. In particular the diet on shipboard improved because of the relative quickness of the voyages and of the coaling stops at which fresh food and water could be taken on board; this brought final elimination of scurvy as the mariner's special sickness, and a general improvement in health.

On shore the status of the seaman remained, as it always had been, anomalous. His occupation was essential to the very existence of British communities in the Far East, and yet he was always an outsider, disturbing and distrusted. Ships' captains were still highly regarded in the mercantile community and often retired from the sea to take up trade on their own account or to serve as harbour masters or master attendants of shipping, but the junior officers on merchant ships were less welcome and there were occasions when they were even barred from the clubs which the taipans frequented.

If the status of lesser ships' officers was ambiguous, like that of retailers and clerks, there was no doubt whatever that ordinary seamen were socially quite beyond the pale, regarded as uncouth beings who at best marred the image of the white man in the eyes of lesser races, and at worst broke the peace with extravagant abandon. We see them through the eyes of their merchant critics, mad drunk in the streets of seventeenth-century Hirado, fighting with the Dutch and robbing Japanese whores; drinking themselves unconscious a century later in the dives of Hog Lane behind the Canton factories, where the favourite tipple was a concoction of alcohol, tobacco juice, sugar and arsenic; rioting in Kowloon in 1839 and creating something near to a *casus belli* by killing a Chinese villager; and causing so much trouble in early Penang that Francis Light had to complain: 'The riots these people committed in striking and abusing and plundering the inhabitants made it necessary to establish a Police.' If the seamen abused and plundered, they received equivalent treatment from the hands of others. The Hog Laners picked their pockets and dumped them in the ditches; the disorderly-house keepers of Yokohama seized their clothes as security for drinks and sent them back half naked to their ships; and a committee of Singapore citizens in 1853 called attention to 'the low coffee houses and spirit shops in the outskirts of the town, where there is too much reason to fear the unwary sailor is stupefied by deleterious spirits, and unscrupulously robbed'. Excluded from the society of his fellow Europeans, the seaman gravitated to the shabby frontier of debauchery, one of the few borderlines on which, in those days, the races could mingle. When debauchery was not enough, he turned to adventure. Seamen jumped ship in Hong Kong to join the California Gold Rush, and in Shanghai to enrol as mercenaries on both sides in the Taiping rebellion, and they provided a shifting population of beachcombers and petty hoodlums who assisted in smuggling and on rare occasions took to piracy.

It was impossible for the British communities to ignore the presence of the seamen; there were too many of them. At times in the early days of Shanghai the sailors in port would outnumber the European residents ten to one, and as late as 1891 the Hong Kong census recorded fourteen hundred seamen, as against a resident European population of four thousand, two hundred. The respectable and stable part of the community viewed them with disapproval and even a certain fear, and, if they progressed from demands for Draconian laws to attempts at philanthropy, these were of a nature (involving the establishment of Sailors' Homes and Sailors' Hospitals) which merely emphasized the difference between the shifting and shiftless mariner and those who acceptably represented the civilization of white men in the Far East. As in all societies, the men who lived in houses rejected the wanderers; the Isaacs kept the Ishmaels from their doors.

3

THE MEN OF WAR

Military and naval defence, merging into various forms of police action, inevitably accompanied the British commercial presence in the China Seas; when presence moved nearer to dominance, the emphasis shifted from defence to aggression, so that long periods of small-scale garrison activity alternated with brief periods of military initiative, productive of commercial and political expansion.

This pattern belonged to the later period, from the 1780s onwards, when regular British military and naval forces began to move into the Malayan region and the China Seas. In the earliest days of British penetration into the Far East it is impossible to distinguish a real military class among those who took part in the expeditions to the East Indies, and equally impossible to detect any real awareness of the way in which military force should have been deployed in this area. Unlike the Dutch and the Portuguese, their principal competitors, the early English traders would not turn the first small posts they set up in the Malay archipelago into military establishments; they were at first factories, not forts. The traders appear to have relied on sea power, and when the flotillas of armed trading vessels which they assembled to counter Dutch aggressiveness were defeated, their posts became untenable. More than any other circumstance, the lack of an effective professional fighting force spelt an end to English trading in the East Indies during the greater part of the seventeenth century. The same military weakness made factories from Japan to Siam and Cambodia vulnerable to the caprices of local rulers, so that, until the foundation of Fort Marlborough at Bencoolen in the 1680s, no permanent British post was established east of India.

Bencoolen, which remained in British hands for almost one hundred and forty years and was lost not by conquest but by cession, owed its survival to the fact that by the end of the seventeenth century the East India Company had learned, from three generations of experience in India, the need to create a private army to defend its factories and its spheres of commercial influence.

'Here are six or seven garrisons under my command,' Governor Collet wrote home from Fort Marlborough in 1712. 'This and Bantal have forty or fifty guns each.' Yet all but two of Collet's 'garrisons' were small posts manned by a few men, and at Fort Marlborough and Bantal his forces were to be reckoned in the low hundreds. The soldiers were Bengalis or Bugis, with a few Portuguese half-castes, usually entrusted with sentry duty. Only the handful of officers and gunners were British. Their life was inactive and demoralizing. Bencoolen lay far enough from the main currents of warfare never to be seriously threatened even during the Napoleonic era, and, because of their idleness, the soldiers who served there were even more subject than the civilians to the temptations of debauchery, with the customary effects. In a bill of mortality for the factory of Bantal in 1713 more than half the European deaths were those of ensigns and gunners. Idleness and boredom also produced quarrelsomeness, and at Bencoolen, as later elsewhere in the Far East, a condition of smouldering hostility prevailed between civilians and soldiers. The latter particularly resented the subordinate part they were forced to play, especially in view of the dramatically active role which the soldier was assuming in India proper.

By the end of the eighteenth century events in Bengal had created a sharp distinction between the Company's interests in India and its interests in the Far East, and this distinction determined the differing status of the soldier in the two regions. In India, after 1765, the Company quickly became a vast revenue gathering agency which turned the tax farm it had obtained from the Nabob of Bengal into the nucleus of a territorial empire. Tax gathering was more remunerative than trading had ever been, and the Company was able to view with equanimity the abolition in 1813 of its Indian trading monopoly, particularly as its commercial interests were still protected by a monopoly in China. The profits of tax gathering in Bengal could thus be used to purchase Indian opium, whose sale enabled the Company to buy tea in Canton, and in this form the surplus revenues of Bengal came to London and reaped a further profit in the tea auctions.

The maintenance of the Bengal end of this commercial pattern demanded the rapid development of a mass army, capable of overawing the rival native and foreign powers in the subcontinent and of policing effectively the ever growing territory over which the company wielded *de facto* sovereignty. By 1808 the company's forces in India had grown into a mass army of a size rarely seen – in Europe at least – up to this time. Its peacetime establishment consisted of 154,500 men, of whom 24,500 were European. The latter included the king's regiments, stationed in India, the Company's own European regiments, recruited mainly from Ireland, and the officers of the native regiments who, except for the Scottish surgeons, were almost invariably English. When one remembers that European civilians in India at this time numbered no more than ten thousand, and that of these no more than two thousand were actual civil servants, the leading role played by the army during the nineteenth century is not surprising.

India possessed – until the very end of British rule – a full-scale and largely autonomous military establishment. The viceregal court and the local courts of the presidencies blazed with the splendour of military uniforms, and the cantonments of the Indian Army, even more than the growing commercial centres of Bombay, Calcutta and Madras, were the centres of British society in India, since the army, rather than the civil service or trade, attracted to the subcontinent many younger members of the landed aristocracy, which, until the end of the nineteenth century, was the effective ruling class of Britain. Even in non-military fields of administration, until well into the nineteenth century, army men often held the key posts; they were particularly influential as representatives in the courts of native princes.

In the Far East a military power of this kind never developed. The predominantly commercial – rather than territorial – intentions of the British in this region, and the scattered pattern of colonies, protectorates and points of influence, prevented the creation of a massive and monolithic army. Military forces, even a tenth as strong as the Company's standing army in India, appeared in Malaya and eastward before the Second World War only on a few critical and memorable occasions: the invasion of Java in 1811; the Opium Wars of the 1840s, and the Anglo-French expedition to Peking in 1860; the fighting against the Boxers in 1900, and the Shanghai Defence Force in 1927. At other times British possessions and strong-points in the Far East were guarded by military forces so weak that they would have been of little avail in the event of serious warfare. Their presence served mainly as a token to remind local rulers and their peoples that, once offended, the British were likely to appear in force and impose disagreeable terms on their defeated enemies. The relative coolness of nationalist sentiment in the Far East until after the First World War helped to perpetuate this situation; so did the absence, between the fall of Napoleon and the rise of Japan as a naval power in the early twentieth century, of any imperial rival in the Far East strong enough to cause the British serious concern. Furthermore, the main centres of British rule and commerce throughout the Far East, with the sole exception of Kuala

Lumpur, were built beside the sea, so that in their defence naval power was even more important than land power.

Thus, while in India the man of war was almost invariably a professional soldier, in the Far East his role was varied by special circumstances and needs. It is true that we encounter the regulars of the Company's regiments, both European and native, and – with growing frequency – of the king's regiments; we encounter the professional sailors of the Navy and its poor relation, the Company's marine. But we also meet the taipans and griffins, transformed into part-time soldiers, who as volunteers played a considerable role in defending British communities on the China coast and in the Straits Settlements.

On the China coast especially, the sense of danger and of the need for defence was never allowed to disappear; whenever the internal cohesion of China showed signs of breaking down the tension in the British settlements grew proportionately greater, since the treaty ports offered rich and tempting prizes to peasant rebels and war lords alike. There was also a constant demand among the mercantile community for widening commercial opportunities, which demanded occasional military adventures. But the flow and ebb of peril and action were such that no military man could look forward – as many did in India – to making the Far East the centre of his life's career. Soldiers – sailors even more – usually came from Britain or India on short terms of duty; even compared with the men of commerce, they were transients who stayed too short a time and were too few to affect profoundly the social life of the British communities. Since there were no elite regiments stationed in Singapore or Shanghai or Hong Kong, aristocratic officers rarely found their way to Far Eastern stations, and the presence of a few naval and military officers of modest gentility hardly disturbed the middle-class homogeneity of British colonial society east of Burma.

How slight many of the military operations were which had far-reaching historical consequences in the Far East can be seen from the accounts of the annexation of Penang and Singapore, which gave Britain effective domination over the Malay peninsula and for more than a century guaranteed the safety of the trade route to China.

Francis Light, master of a country craft, who was given for the occasion the rank of captain in the Company's marine, in 1786 occupied Penang with a minute force of one hundred and fifty men; a hundred of these were newly raised sepoys of the marine, uniformed in red serge, thirty were lascar infantrymen, and only the five officers and fifteen artillerymen were British. Though Light subsequently argued that for a proper defence of Penang he needed at least a battalion of sepoys and fifty European artillerymen, no serious attention was given for almost twenty years to increasing the defences of this outpost.

In 1819 Sir Stamford Raffles founded Singapore with a force twice as large as Light's, but still minute by Indian standards. Sailing from Penang in two cruisers of the East India Company's marine, with four smaller hired craft, he landed in the island with 340 scarlet coated and shakoed sepoys of the Bengal Native Infantry and a hundred sailors. Drawing on the various ships, he was able to assemble some thirty British officers of the Company's army and marine to sweat under the Malay sun in their cocked hats and broadcloth uniforms as he signed the treaty of annexation with the Sultan of Johore.

The expeditions to Penang and Singapore took place after negotiations which led Light and Raffles to expect no opposition; their minute forces had ceremonial rather than military roles to play. But so assured did the Company subsequently feel of its position in Malaya that by 1819 a single battalion of Bengal Native Infantry was considered sufficient to garrison not only Penang and Bencoolen, but also Singapore. After Bencoolen had been ceded to the Dutch, the garrison of Singapore was further reduced. 'In 1825,' recorded John Crawfurd, one of Raffles' successors there, 'the military amounted only to about a hundred and fifty sepoys, and native artillery, without a single European, except the officers. In a period of peace, and among an industrious population, in which the elements of anarchy, discontent, or insurrection, had no existence, this small force was quite adequate for every useful purpose.'

When the Company's rule ended after the Indian Mutiny, and British interests in Malaya came directly under the India Office, there was little change in the military situation; regiments raised in India predominated and garrisons were still small. A report issued in 1865 records that 'the garrison of the three Settlements consist of two Batteries of European Artillery, a company of Native Artillery and two regiments of Sepoys of the Madras Presidency. The entire force numbers 1,811 persons, embracing the unusual number of 46 Commissioned Officers, among whom there are no fewer than seven Field Officers'. After 1867, when the Straits Settlements became a crown colony and the link with India was finally severed, units of the British army were more frequently stationed there, but their numbers remained small, and until the end of the nineteenth century the garrison at Singapore was rarely more than five hundred strong.

Even when the prevalently peaceful atmosphere of the Malay peninsula was disturbed by local warfare, the forces involved were miniature armies welded out of small units and fragments of units gathered from the scattered corners of Asia. One such motley expedition was collected from Hong

Kong and India in 1876 to deal with the disturbances which followed the assassination of James Birch, the first British resident in the native state of Perak. The combat force consisted of 300 officers and men of Her Majesty's 80th Regiment, 200 of the 1-10th Regiment, 60 of the Buffs, 450 of the 1st Gurkhas, 80 Bengal sappers, a battery and half of Royal Artillery, and a small naval brigade drawn from the crews of the five vessels which had transported the troops. All this multiplicity of units, though it was commanded by a major-general and a brigadier-general, comprised no more than fifteen hundred men.

The change from Indian to colonial status not only brought more regiments of British soldiers to Malaya than in its earlier days; it also meant a change in the type of officer commanding the local garrisons. Typical of the Company's dispensation was Major Farquhar, whom Raffles appointed first resident of Singapore. Farquhar's whole career, and twenty-eight years of his life, had been passed in the east by the time he received this appointment. Joining the Company's service as a cadet in 1791, he reached Madras in the same year; the death rate among officers was so high that he was immediately promoted to ensign. After serving against Tippu Sultan at Mysore and the French at Pondicherry, Farquhar came in 1795 as a lieutenant to Malacca. Apart from a few months in Madras, the only occasion on which he left the Malayan peninsula during the following twenty-eight years, was to take part in the Java expedition of 1811. Before going to Singapore he had served for a time as commandant at Malacca. Farquhar had his faults of vanity, and, like many men whose adult lives were passed wholly in the east he did not possess a very wide vision; unlike Raffles, he failed to foresee the greatness of Singapore's commercial future. His virtue – in which he resembled many other Old Asia Hands of his time – was his understanding of the native mentality and his tactful way of dealing with Asians. One of the Malays described him as 'a man of good parts, slow at fault-finding, treating rich and poor alike, and very patient in listening to the complaints of any person who went to him, so that all returned rejoicing'.

The fact that Farquhar reached Malaya when he was still young and impressionable was fortunate. Many other officers who served there had already been shaped by the different circumstances of India, and proved as ill-adapted to Malay conditions as the officers from the British Army who succeeded them. One of the negative results of the lack of any separate army establishment in the Far East was the absence of any effective means of providing officers with a specialist knowledge of local conditions.

Until Raffles deposed him from the residency in 1823, Farquhar combined both military and civilian control of Singapore. More often these functions were divided and this led to a rivalry between the two branches of authority which continued throughout the British presence in the Far East and helped to shape the social relationships between soldiers and civilians. The central issue was the extent to which the soldier should be subordinated to the civilian.

This emerged during the earliest days of settlement at Penang. Under Light's government, a Captain Hamilton was given command of the local company of sepoys. In a dispute between a European sailor and the crew of a local junk, he court martialled the three Malays involved and sentenced them to several hundred lashes each. The sentence had been carried out by the time Light was informed of these wholly illegal proceedings. The European merchants, led by James Scott, protested against this arbitrary treatment of civilians by the military commander. The affair finally reached the attention of the governor-general in Calcutta, who laid down the principle later to be followed throughout British colonies and settlements in the Far East; that 'the authority of the commanding officer of the troops is restricted to the men under his command', and that all cases involving civilians must be heard by a civilian magistrate.

Even when this important principle of jurisdiction had been settled there remained the question of the responsibility of army officers. How far, in the exercise of their military functions, were they subject to the local civilian authorities? This question, and the bitterness it could arouse, emerged extravagantly during the invasion of Java, the first large-scale British expedition undertaken in the Far East.

When Holland was incorporated into the Napoleonic empire, its colonies, ruled by Dutch puppets, were transformed into French strongholds, and Java became a threat to the China trade route and, potentially, to the Company's position in India. Lord Minto, the governor-general, not only ordered an expedition to capture the island; once it had been organized by Stamford Raffles, he led it in person. The expedition was planned on a scale to fit the occasion. It was the largest British army – carried by the largest British fleet – that had sailed east of India. A force of twelve thousand men, under Lieutenant-General Sir Samuel Auchmuty, foregathered at Malacca; they included five thousand European troops, as well as marines and native regiments from the Bengal and Madras armies, all – whether English, Irish or Indian – dressed in red or blue serge uniforms suited to northern battle fields, and shining shakoes or steeple hats. At Penang the European troops gorged themselves on the ripe, luscious pineapples, and this, according to the medical theoreticians of the time, was why twelve hundred of them were so sick that they had to be left behind at Malacca. By the time other sick men had been put ashore at Palambangan, Auchmuty's force had been reduced to nine thousand men who were still fit to drag their heavy accoutrements through the humid heat of an Indonesian August. A fleet of eighty-one sail finally appeared off Batavia; there were twenty-five ships of the line, frigates and sloops of the Royal Navy, and eight cruisers of the Company's marine; the remaining forty-eight ships were transports, including East Indiamen and hired country craft. To fill out the depleted forces, sailors were sent ashore to act as cavalry; they were known as the Marine Light Dragoons.

The story of the campaign, won with surprising ease against the numerically superior enemy, belongs to military rather than social history. Batavia fell without a struggle and the decisive battle was fought when the British troops, led by Colonel Gillespie, stormed through the breached walls of the fortress of Cornelis and routed the Dutch troops whose allegiance to the tricolor was, at best, lukewarm. By October Lord Minto and General Auchmuty departed, leaving Raffles as lieutenant-governor, with Colonel Gillespie and two Dutch civil servants as his council. It was only after much thought that Minto decided to make the government of Java a civil one dedicated to reform rather than a military one dedicated to repressive occupation; even in the benevolent administration which Raffles sought to establish, the shortage of officials often made it necessary to draw upon the army for men to serve as residents or in other important posts. In spite of this kind of cooperation, friction between civilians and soldiers developed owing to the extravagant behaviour of the younger – and even some of the older – officers. It was a time when little moral stigma attached to those who availed themselves freely of the spoils of conquest, and every officer took his concubine from among the half-caste or native women, while few showed any great delicacy of scruples when it came to appropriating property. Any hesitation his subordinates may have felt was removed by the example of Colonel – now General – Gillespie, who had no less than four houses, and bought himself a retinue of slave girls, an act which one of the Dutch described as 'something very unusual for an Englishman'.

Endued with the retarded juvenility which so often accompanies physical gallantry in a man of forty-five, Gillespie was not only attached to worldly display and slave girls; he was also contemptuous of civilians and chafed under his subordination to Raffles. Since he was senior member of council as well as military commander, this led to serious disagreements. Raffles proposed that, to make the economies which Minto thought desirable, the European regiments might be sent away from Java and replaced by sepoys. Fearing that this would diminish the dignity of his command, Gillespie bitterly opposed the suggestion. He also demanded that the finances of his army on Java should be independent of civilian audit or control. Minto over-ruled Gillespie on both points, and asserted the supremacy of civil rule – represented by Raffles – over military. The dispute did not end there, for after an apparent reconciliation with Raffles, Gillespie went to Calcutta and there laid false charges of financial irregularity against him, with the result that the new governor-general, Lord Moira, removed Raffles from the governorship of Java. On no later occasion did the rivalry between soldiers and civilians assume such extravagant form, but it remained a factor in the pattern of British societies in the Far East.

West of Java – except for the pointless expedition which captured Manila from the Spanish in 1762 and held it for less than two years – British military activity did not commence until the mid-nineteenth century. So long as the East India Company accepted the conditions imposed by the Chinese government for carrying on the tea trade in Canton, there was no question of armed forces being involved. It was only after the Company's monopoly came to an end in 1833, and the demands of the individual merchants for free trade precipitated a confrontation between the governments of Westminster and Peking, that British soldiers appeared on the China coast. They came in June 1840, in a fleet of twenty-seven transports, escorted by Her Majesty's men-of-war and by Company cruisers, and carrying the Cameronian Highlanders, the Royal Irish, the Hertfordshire Regiment, and Indian troops, a total of four thousand men. In July, while the fleet blockaded Canton, the military expedition sailed northward to seize the Chusan Islands. The operation was successful, and Tinghai, the principal town of the islands, was seized, followed by the occupation of Ningpo and Amoy on the mainland of China.

While these virtually unopposed actions must be counted as victories, since they were part of the series of campaigns which eventually obliged the Chinese to open the first treaty ports, Asia claimed its own victory in the deaths from sickness which decimated the British troops encamped in Chusan. The heat there was formidable and the soldiers were forced to wear their serge uniforms buttoned to the neck in temperatures which at times ranged between 90 and 100 degrees Fahrenheit. The food, much of which had been bought from dishonest Indian contractors, was putrid by the time the troops came to eat it. Malaria, dysentery, heat-stroke, all took their toll. By the end of the year, when the British forces were withdrawn from the Chusan Islands, a sixth of them were dead, and hundreds more so weak that they were unfit for service. One regiment, the Cameronian Highlanders, lost 240 men from disease, and out of its original complement of 930 officers and men, only 110 were fit for service by early 1841.

The Chinese interpreted the British withdrawal from Chusan as a sign of weakness and refused to ratify the agreement concluded after their defeat during the summer. Indeed, when Sir Hugh Gough invaded Canton to enforce the treaty in March 1841, his act was hardly a show of strength, since he could assemble only 2,400 men fit enough to totter into action; though the Westmorland Regiment arrived shortly afterwards, there were still only 2,700 men available in August 1841 to retake Tinghai and Ningpo. Ningpo was now made the headquarters, and the following winter contrasted sharply with its predecessor, since there was plenty of fresh food to be bought and the men exercized themselves playing football and snowball while the officers went on shooting parties into the surrounding countryside. Exercize and good food brought their dividends; there were not enough deaths to be statistically significant. By the next summer the troops were in excellent trim, and though they still had to sweat in heavy uniforms as they manhandled cannon through the muddy farmlands around Shanghai, they fought the Opium Wars to a successful conclusion which resulted in the Treaty of Nanking, by which the Son of Heaven finally bowed to military realities, ceded Hong Kong and established the first five treaty ports.

The later Chinese wars differ from those of the 1840s more in their military aspects, which are outside our field of consideration, than in the actual physical circumstances of the soldiers' lives. In 1860, when the joint British-French expedition marched on Peking to force ratification of the Tientsin Treaty of 1858, an army of 18,211 men – the largest British force ever to serve on the China coast – was transported to the Far East; nearly seven thousand men stayed behind to guard Hong Kong, Canton and Shanghai, but almost twelve thousand, plus six thousand French soldiers and a Cantonese transport corps more than two thousand strong, took part in the capture of the Taku forts which began the campaign and in the notorious sacking of the Summer Palace at Peking which marked its climax. Though the soldiers were still forced to fight in uniforms completely unsuited to the climate, the relative efficiency of the commissariat arrangements at least ensured that this time they did not have to eat bad food, and the losses from sickness were much less than in 1840. During the Boxer Rebellion of 1900, when the foreign legations in Peking were besieged by imperial troops who had joined forces with the rebels, the British contribution to the international relief force was considerably smaller – round about three thousand out of a total of seventeen thousand – but some ten thousand British troops were in the area to provide a reserve in case of emergency; most of them were stationed in Hong Kong.

Such times, when relatively large military forces operated, were rare enough on the China coast to be exceptional. In the twentieth century they happened only during the uneasy period of rising Chinese nationalism and Japanese imperialism between 1927 and 1941. Until the 1920s Hong Kong was in fact the only locality which maintained a considerable garrison, and even that was rarely of brigade strength. For a few years during the 1860s, when anti-foreign feeling was still strong in Japan, a British battalion was maintained at Yokohama, and in Shanghai the regular troops were usually of the same strength, or at most of two battalions, with much smaller detachments at the other treaty ports. In Malaya the establishment of the Singapore base during the 1920s created something more than mere token protection, but even there, with three British battalions in Singapore, a Burmese battalion at Taiping in the Federated Malay States, and the locally raised Malay Regiment at Port Dickson, the military forces remained minute in comparison with those maintained in India. In what seemed then the unlikely event of an invasion, the troops in Malaya were expected to sustain a limited holding action until reinforcements had time to arrive.

Whenever a census was prepared in Malaya or in the British settlements on the China coast, army personnel was always enumerated – if at all – separately from the European civilians. Doubtless there were good administrative reasons for the practice, but the presence of the two separate figures tends to emphasize in the historian's mind the extent to which the soldiers were in fact differentiated from the other British. Their roots were even slighter than those of the taipans and they lived apart.

During the early years in Hong Kong, indeed, both the generals and the admirals had aroused a good deal of animosity among the merchants by their unsuccessful efforts to pre-empt valuable real estate in the middle of Victoria for their barracks and bases. Later, however, Indian practice was followed by establishing cantonments well away from the urban areas where commercial life went on. In Hong Kong most of the soldiers were eventually stationed in Kowloon across the harbour; in Singapore at Tanglin in the hills outside the city. Here the officers were segregated from their men except at times of duty. They had comfortable bungalows, large enough to accommodate their families if they happened to be married; they ran their own clubs; they indulged fervently in all the sports the country afforded. They were accepted freely in civilian society but played a very minor part in the general activities of the communities on whose edges they lived; the names of army officers – in contrast with those of naval officers – appear surprisingly infrequently in the memoirs and anecdotal histories of Old China and Old Malaya Hands.

The other ranks were sharply divided from both the civilians and their own officers and shared with seamen the unenviable role of a white proletariat in a society especially rigid in its class distinctions. Except when he listened to the military bands which played on the Esplanade at Singapore or on the Bund at Shanghai, the average Far Eastern merchant knew as little of the life of the common soldier in his community as the London merchant in the nineteenth century might know of the life of Thomas Mayhew's outcasts. The comparison is not strained, since the life of the soldier in the Far East during most of the nineteenth century was almost as wretched as that of a London outcast and even more unhealthy. He dressed in a manner which made Edward Bowra remark of a scarlet-coated sentinel in Singapore, 'I do not like to take my eyes off him, for I expect every moment that he will burst into flames.' He ate monotonously and supplemented his coarse meals by swilling beer when he could get it, and arrack when he could not. He lived in crowded and badly built barracks; for years the European troops at Tanglin were housed in attap barracks and the Indian troops in Hong Kong's unpredictable climate in 'matsheds', whose name exactly describes their flimsy construction of bamboo and rush mats. In lieu of marriage he solaced himself with Chinese or Malay prostitutes. And even these brutal pleasures were often cut short by the sicknesses resulting from bad water, bad sanitation and marshy ground. Whenever epidemics of smallpox, cholera and typhus swept the treaty ports, it was always – among the Europeans – the soldiers and seamen who suffered most. In 1862 alone, more than two hundred of them died in Shanghai of these sicknesses. Even worse, because more regular, were the ravages of malaria, which was particularly prevalent in Hong Kong, where its presence was attributed to 'the breaking up of the soil, which is composed of decomposed granite'. In 1843, 373 soldiers died in Hong Kong of fever; in 1848 the mortality among European troops rose to 20 per cent and in 1850 reached a peak of 24 per cent, four times that among the European civilian population. Later, as the land was settled and the marshes were drained, there was less fever, but otherwise the soldier's life in the Far East did not improve greatly until after the First World War.

The private or the sergeant who survived and took his discharge in Shanghai or Hong Kong usually found himself a social pariah in the middle-class world of the China Hands. At best he might hope to earn a living as a policeman, one of the few occupations open to Europeans of the wrong class. Failing that, he might join the motley company of adventurers and mercenaries who formed a disreputable fringe to the British communities in the Far East and end his days fighting for a Malay raja, smuggling for Chinese merchants, or running guns into the Philippines, a better fate probably than going home to rot in an English workhouse.

If the merchants of Singapore, Hong Kong and Shanghai had little to do with the common soldier, they often learnt something of the professional side of his life by enrolling in the volunteer corps which appeared in the British communities of the Far East when the Crimean War aroused fears of Russian aggression, complicated, in the case of Shanghai, by the proximity of an army of rebellious peasants, who had seized the native city and in the spring of 1854 were skirmishing with the imperial forces on the outskirts of the International Settlement.

The Shanghai Volunteer Corps had been founded and had distinguished itself in a victorious action before the rival corps in Hong Kong and Singapore were even enrolled. Early in 1854, when the news reached Shanghai that the formidable Taiping rebels had captured Nanking, the British residents gathered to found their own volunteer company, and a subsequent meeting, attended by British, American and French consuls and by the captains of the naval vessels in port, set up a more international force. It was to be self-governed and self-supporting; its rifles were bought from the local gun runners, but a committee of coordination was set up to provide a link between the volunteers and the official representatives of the western powers. A flavour of professionalism was introduced when Captain Tronson of the Bengal Fusiliers was brought over from Hong Kong to act as full-time commanding officer.

On 3 April 1854 a chaotic army of imperial troops, estimated at twenty thousand strong, began to advance menacingly on the International Settlement and to plunder buildings on the periphery. The British Consul, Rutherford Alcock, thereupon sent an ultimatum to the Chinese commander, demanding that his troops withdraw immediately, and at the same time called on the volunteers to muster at the English church. On 4 April, when no answer came from the Chinese, Alcock marched out at the head of a tiny improvized army of four hundred men, consisting of sailors from British and American warships, a handful of merchant seamen, and about two hundred armed merchants and clerks. As they left the settlement the news came that the ultimatum had been rejected, but not a single volunteer dropped out of the ranks. By the end of the day, aided by a flank attack on the imperial forces by the rebels inside the city, they had defeated a force many times larger than their own, at a cost of one griffin killed and one American merchant skipper who died of his wounds.

It was later in the summer that Singapore and Hong Kong followed Shanghai's example. In Hong Kong, where sickness had left only four hundred regular soldiers fit for duty, it was the fear of attack by a Russian fleet rumoured to be roving the Pacific that led, in June 1854, to the founding of a volunteer corps in which 127 men enrolled. In Singapore, plagued since the 1840s by faction fights between rival Chinese secret societies, the idea of a European volunteer corps for internal protection had long been mooted, but here also the Russian scare was the reason why in July a small company of sixty-two local residents was raised.

The fortunes of these volunteer corps rose and fell with the political tensions in the areas where they operated. When war scares diminished they languished and sometimes were even disbanded, as happened in Hong Kong before the end of 1854 and in Shanghai during 1869. But the slightest hint of insecurity was enough to bring them back into existence and continuing crisis kept them on their mettle. The volunteers in Singapore, the least threatened of the three main British centres in the Far East, were thus the weakest in numbers and the most backward in training. The British in Shanghai, where feelings of insecurity were strongest, were the most conscious of the need for a local defence force to hold the perimeters of their settlement at times of crisis, at least until aid came from outside, and here, as in Hong Kong when Far Eastern tensions mounted during the 1930s, it became almost a social obligation for young men of the community to enrol.

By 1937 there were two thousand, five hundred active volunteers in Shanghai, including a considerable number of White Russians, and in Hong Kong there were almost two thousand. An increasing *esprit de corps* was shown in the emphasis on good discipline, in the promptness with which the call to arms was answered when the power station siren gave notice of an emergency or an exercise, and in the pride taken in the ever-changing uniforms. In 1870 in Shanghai there were blue jackets with Tyrolean hats in winter and pith helmets in summer, but later on scarlet jackets were adopted, and eventually the Corps went over to khaki, with the American volunteers insisting on wearing stetsons. By the 1920s the corps in Shanghai and Hong Kong had developed from the simple rifle companies of the 1850s into relatively sophisticated miniature armies, with batteries of artillery, machine-gun and armoured-car companies and engineers. Their equipment and maintenance were provided out of local funds, raised by taxation, and they were genuine citizen armies, operated with the kind of internal democracy which is inevitable when officers and other ranks come from the same social level.

The Shanghai Corps was the most frequently under arms. During the crisis of March 1927, when Chiang Kai-shek's forces appeared on the outskirts of Shanghai, it was mobilized and held key points until the three regular brigades of the Shanghai Defence Force arrived. In 1932 and again in 1937 it was under arms for considerable periods, while business activity languished and Shanghai took on the air of a city whose men have departed for the wars. But in the end it was the Hong Kong Corps, the Strait Settlements Volunteers (into which the Singapore Volunteers eventually developed) and the Malaya Volunteer Corps (recruited mainly from the plantations and mines of the Malay states) who were to see the real action when the Japanese invaded the British possessions of the Far East in 1941 and 1942. To these events I shall return in the final chapters.

In spite of their intermittent enthusiasm for amateur soldiering, the merchants of Malaya and the treaty ports remained on much more cordial terms with naval officers than with their military counterparts. There are several reasons for this difference. Except for the brief period at the beginning of the nineteenth century when the Royal Navy attempted to establish a base at Penang, and a time of disagreement over land in Hong Kong, there were few conflicts of jurisdiction that might embitter relationships between the admirals and the civilian authorities. The naval vessels used the harbours in the same way as merchant ships, for watering, victualling and fuelling, and they were always moving in and out of the commercial hearts of the Far Eastern ports, establishing relationships with the merchants whose interests also centred on these enclosed sheets of water. The merchants entertained the naval officers lavishly, the captains reciprocated, and in Singapore the social event of the season was often a ball given on a visiting flagship.

Behind all this mutual cordiality lay the hard fact that in a scattered empire like that which the British created in the Far East, more commercial than territorial, the navy was in the long run more important than the army. When campaigns had to be fought to extend markets, when defences had to be manned to defend them, the army was useful and hence popular, but in the long years between, the idle depleted garrisons, carrying out their undramatic functions as tokens of the remote sources of power, could not compete with the sailors who, for the whole period of British involvement in the China Seas, performed active service in protecting the trade route to Canton and beyond from enemies actual and potential.

It was during the Napoleonic era that the Royal Navy first began to play an important role in the Far Eastern seas. The presence of French ships in the Pacific, with their main base at Mauritius, not only threatened the British position in India. It imperilled the tea trade on which the East India Company depended to balance its complex financial operations. The Company was provided with vast armies but it had no adequate maritime defences. Its own marine consisted of small boats designed for defending coastal ships against piracy, and though the East Indiamen could on occasion give a good account of themselves in a fight they were no match for ships-of-the-line. It was in defending these great slow vessels and the more numerous country craft in their annual voyages to and from Canton that the navy was most regularly employed during this period, though it also took part in such important operations as the seizure of the Moluccas and of Java, to prevent their being used as supplementary bases by the French.

Life on naval ships in eastern waters at this period was certainly worse than life on the East Indiamen, but it was probably better than army service in the tropics. The discipline was more strict and brutal than on merchant ships and it was imposed on unwilling men, since, as we have seen, the crews of warships in the China Seas were made up largely of men pressed into service from the merchant ships. They were paid less than merchant seamen and they usually had to wait for their money until they returned to England, which might be in ten years – if they survived cannon balls and fever. The most they could expect to receive while in service in the eastern seas was a share in the prize money gained from the sale of captured ships and their contents. Admirals and captains, each of whom took an eighth share in every prize, could amass fortunes; Admiral Rainier, during his service at the Penang station, is said to have accumulated £300,000 in this way. But the ordinary seaman, who had to share a quarter of the prize with all his shipmates, would be lucky to find himself with four or five guineas as the price of his daring and endurance. On the other hand, by the beginning of the nineteenth century some serious attention was being paid to the health of the men in the navy, and in 1809 a hospital ship was established at Penang, which seems to have been less of a death trap than the notorious naval hospital at Bombay, no doubt because it was moored out of reach of fever-bearing mosquitoes. The seamen also enjoyed one incalculable advantage over the soldiers serving in the east at that time; they were issued with light duck clothes far better adapted for the climate than the serge uniforms which the marines, like the soldiers, were still forced to wear.

If discipline was strictly maintained in other respects, it was generally relaxed in matters of dress, and even the officers on ships in eastern waters were inclined – except at the sacred hour of dinner – to doff their uniforms for lighter and less formal dress. In general, these officers were mostly younger and less experienced than their counterparts on ships serving in European waters. Since officers as well as men died or were invalided out of the service at an alarming rate, and since they could not be recruited by impressment, promotion was sensationally rapid and there were instances of boys serving as acting lieutenants at fourteen and commanding frigates at seventeen or eighteen.

After the end of the Napoleonic Wars, the navy, like the army, entered the China Seas in force only on the dramatic occasions of wars and threats of wars and then mainly in actions, like the two China wars, which aimed at extending the commercial empire. Only once did the navy come to the defence of the territorial empire which the British eventually built up in Malaya, in 1941, when its efforts ended in total and unique disaster with the destruction of the *Prince of Wales* and the *Repulse* by Japanese planes.

To a certain extent the place of the navy was taken, at least until the 1850s, by the Company's marine, which extended its operations to Malayan waters after 1815 and concentrated on the suppression of pirates. From the early days in Singapore, piracy had been one of the main problems in ensuring the free trade which Raffles and his successors sought to establish. As in the ancient Levant, it had long been considered a legitimate occupation in both the Malayan region and on the China coast and the situation was complicated by the fact that *bona fide* traders would sometimes, when the opportunity arose, double as pirates. There were Malay pirates in the Straits of Malacca, and Chinese pirates everywhere; but probably the most formidable of all these corsairs were the tribes which operated from Sulu and Mindanao in the Philippines and in long galleys ranged far through the Indonesian archipelago. Often the petty sultans of the islands protected the pirates and shared in their spoils. The virtual elimination of piracy was undertaken between 1830 and 1860 by a formidable combination of the Royal Navy, the Company's marine – which shortly became a separate establishment under the title of the Straits Marine – and Sir James Brooke, the famous white raja of Sarawak.

It was in this service that the marine came into its own, operating small gunboats adapted for this task. The most famous of these was the *Diana*, the first steam warship to operate in these waters. Malay pirates preferred to operate in windless conditions, when their swift prahus, operated by oars or paddles, could surround and easily capture a becalmed craft. This made it difficult for sailing warships to deal effectively with them and many of the early naval expeditions against pirates failed because the prahus simply rowed out of firing range of frigates that were unable to follow them. The *Diana* could follow its prey, particularly as it was a comparatively small boat of 160 tons, operated by a crew of thirty Malays with three European officers. Following the example of the *Diana*, the steam gunboat, usually with a shallow draft which enabled it to go almost everywhere that any boat could sail, became in time the characteristic naval vessel of the Far East. Frigates and cruisers were useful to escort transports, to terrify small rulers with their big guns, to show the flag and maintain the prestige of the empire, but it was the small vessels, with their minute crews, commanded by resourceful young officers, which from this time onwards did most of the hard work of maintaining a commercial empire. The first naval steam gunboat, the *Nemesis*, which followed the *Diana* into the China Seas in 1840, showed its worth in coastal actions against both Chinese war junks and Borneo pirates. Later, after 1860, when the Yangtse was opened to merchant ships, followed by other Chinese inland waters, the gunboats carried their patrols into the heart of China and gave their protection to British shipping and British citizens until in 1949 the last of them fought its way out of a battle with Communist artillery on the Yangtse, as the curtain fell on the old British commercial empire in the Far East.

It is in this guise, as the commanders and crews of small and dogged craft, sailing into narrow waters, weaseling out pirates and on occasion terrorizing obstreperous local rulers with the threat of their long guns, that the men of the Company's marine and those of the navy who replaced them after the 1850s appear as the most immediate protectors of the British commercial empire in the Far East. But, as the instinct of merchants who lavishly entertained their captains recognized, the frigates and the cruisers were also necessary, for in the long run it was the knowledge that greater guns loomed behind the gunboats that preserved the colonies, cities and treaty ports strung along the great trade route from Penang to Yokohama from the envious grip of predators more potent than the pirates of Sulu or Mindanao. Seaborne or land-based, the man of war took his inevitable place beside the merchant and the mariner in the creation of the empire in the Far East. With the administrator, whom we now introduce, he also worked to preserve it.

4

THE ADMINISTRATORS

The shift from merchant to administrator followed inevitably on the change in the East India Company's activities from commerce to tax gathering and, ultimately, government. It affected the whole structure of the Company's service in India and its dependencies, encouraging the development and proliferation of bureaucracies, even in areas where territorial domination had not yet been established. Canton was an exception; there the Company had obtained no rights other than those of trading through a limited group of local merchants, and the men who acted on its behalf were – at least nominally – supercargoes of the East Indiamen which had docked at Whampoa.

But only in Canton did this arrangement reminiscent of the early days continue; only here were the Company's representatives, by the beginning of the nineteenth century, merely merchants. Even Bencoolen, where the Company governed no land outside its forts and posts, and gathered no taxes, supported in miniature the establishment of an Indian presidency of the late eighteenth century, with a company of secretaries, accountants, superintendents, collectors and military officers whose only function was to gather the produce of a dwindling plantation economy and each year send a few hundred tons of pepper to Calcutta. To maintain this organization at a place which was not only commercially moribund but also strategically useless (the main shipping route to the China Seas lay along the eastern and not the western shores of Sumatra) cost £100,000 a year, a colossal wastage in pre-Victorian terms.

If the establishment at Bencoolen had the dimensions, but not the functions, of a territorial administration, the first true territorial administration in the Far East, that which Francis Light established on the island of Penang in 1786, had ironically to carry out its functions with a totally inadequate establishment. Penang was different in one important respect from all the earlier establishments of the East India Company. While India remained, at least in law, a closed commercial preserve of the Company until 1813, and Canton until 1833, Penang – whose reason for existence was largely strategic – was established in the beginning as a free port and quickly became dominated commercially by the country traders or – to be more correct – by the firm of James Scott and Company, in which Light had a share. Light, as superintendent, with a salary of 1,000 rupees a month,* combined all the important civil functions; the first magistrate, John Dickens, did not take up his duties at Penang until 1801, and in the meantime Light and his successors tried to keep the peace with slight knowledge of their legal powers. For the rest, he maintained his administration with two assistants, as he told Lord Cornwallis in May 1790, at the monthly cost of '1,500 dollars [about £350] including buildings', and this he appears to have met from his salary and 'the emoluments arising from trade'. When Light died, and Major Macdonald was appointed in his place in 1796, the salary of the superintendent was raised to 2,000 rupees a month, but Macdonald was forbidden to indulge in private trading.

With the appointment of Sir George Leith as lieutenant-governor in 1786, the establishment at Penang increased in both stature and expense but it was not until 1805 that it burgeoned into its greatest splendour with the decision of the Company's court of directors to raise this small port and settlement, hitherto so penuriously managed, to a presidency on a level with Bombay and Madras. The decision had little to do with the commercial interests of the Company, nor did it portend the creation of a territorial empire like those which were rapidly taking shape in the Indian presidencies. It appears to have originated in the mind of Viscount Melville, first lord of the Admiralty, whose past experience as chairman of the Board of Control (the governmental body which supervized the activities of the East India Company), had made him sensitive to the problems of defending both the Bay of Bengal and the route to China. Penang seemed to him as ideally suited for this role as Singapore did to the strategists of the 1930s, and it was hoped to create there not only a base for the naval squadron intended to protect the eastern shores of India, but also a yard where ships of the line might be built. As early as 1797 the future Duke of Wellington had noted the potential importance of

---

* During the period of British rule in India and the Far East, the rupee varied generally between 1s 4d and 1s 6d. Today, of course, its relative value has fallen. It is not easy to assess the buying power of rupees or dollars at any time in the period covered by this book, since imported goods were considerably more expensive in England, while local produce and services were comparatively very cheap.

Penang to the Company's 'military operations to the eastward', i.e. towards China, and the advantages of its calm and easily accessible harbour. Penang failed to fulfil its strategic expectations and its shipbuilding yards proved a wasteful folly owing to the lack of local supplies of usable timber. But Melville's mistaken initiative at least introduced into the Far East the first of its great imperial administrators, Thomas Stamford Raffles.

The appearance of Raffles was almost incidental to an operation in which a passing military fad was combined with the Company's recurrent need for opportunities for its directors to exercise their privileges of patronage. To administer the presidency of Prince of Wales Island – as Penang was now called – a splendid assemblage of officials and attendants came sailing over the Bay of Bengal in the East Indiaman *Ganges* and cast anchor in the deceptively benign setting of Penang, with the pearly light brooding over the tranquil waters surrounded by jungle hills receding into blue and violet distances. It was, as it is today, one of the most hauntingly beautiful places in Asia; then it was also, as many of these men who landed on 18 September 1805 were to find, one of the most deadly.

At the head of the mission – not unexpectedly – was Melville's brother, Philip Dundas, who held the position of governor of Fort Cornwallis; his salary was £9,000 a year. Below him ranged three councillors, a secretary and his assistant, and various other officials, bringing the total membership of the establishment to twenty-seven, not counting Eurasian clerks and other supernumeraries to the number of a further sixty. When Lord Bentinck later visited Penang he complained that he 'could not see what the island looked like for the number of cocked hats which shut out the view'. It may be significant that the schoolmaster, representative of western knowledge, was the poorest paid of all the officials; he received £225 a year, a fortieth of the Governor's salary. Dundas and many of his assistants had already served in India, but they were completely ignorant of Malaya and the Malays. The exception was the assistant secretary, Thomas Stamford Raffles, whose salary was £1,500. He had come straight from a clerkship in East India House in London, and on the long voyage from England to India he had painfully taught himself the elements of the Malay language.

Raffles was the only member of Penang establishment of 1805 to be remembered. Some – like Philip Dundas himself – died early from the sicknesses which haunted the visual Eden of Penang. The rest drew their pay and departed a few years later when the presidency was abolished. Numerous though they were, they never succeeded in raising enough revenue to pay their inflated salaries, and under their rule the development

53

of the island proceeded slowly because they could never decide in their minds what was the purpose or the destiny of a British possession as far away from India as Prince of Wales Island.

Raffles, who was to die at the age of forty-four after a career as rapid in its rise and decline as that of his contemporary Napoleon, reached a position of influence in 1807 when the chief secretaryship at Penang fell vacant and he was appointed to it. Almost his first act was to bring forward a convincing humanitarian argument against the evacuation and destruction of the ancient town of Malacca, an act which the East India Company's officials contemplated in 1808 out of a desire to deprive the Dutch of a strongpoint in case the port were returned to them at the end of hostilities. Raffles' plea for Malacca attracted the attention of the governor-general, Lord Minto, a man of like humanitarian views. Minto was disturbed with the threat to British security in the Far East presented by the subordination of the Dutch empire to French military designs, and in 1810 he created for Raffles the appointment of agent for the governor-general in the Malayan region, with his headquarters at Malacca and a commission to prepare the invasion of Java. Raffles, who had used his knowledge of the Malay language to establish contacts with the local rulers, was the ideal man for the task, unburdened with the preconceptions of men trained in India, and sympathetic, because of his interest in Asian history and culture, to the feelings of native peoples subjected to the hard mercantile control sustained by the Dutch, who had been through no American rebellion to teach them imperial wisdom.

More than any other man, Raffles planned and organized the expedition to Java; he even made recommendations, which were in the main accepted, on the disposition of military forces and the sailing instructions to be issued to the navy. The invasion was successful, and Raffles was appointed lieutenant-governor of the island, with a salary of £8,000 a year, palatial establishments in Batavia and in the country, and a populous land the size of England to govern. The British stayed only briefly in Java, and Raffles himself ruled less than five years, but during that time he attempted to set up the first territorial administration in Asia based on principles of liberal reform. He sought to end the system of forced cultivation, by which the Dutch had attempted to make Java commercially profitable, and in its place to create a modified version of the system which the British had inherited from the Moghuls in India. Instead of being obliged to grow crops for export, often to the detriment of his own subsistence, and to perform various *corvées*, the Indonesian peasant was to be regarded as the lessee of the government and to pay a rent or tax for his land which he would then be allowed to use as he wished. To administer this new system, Raffles sought to lessen the powers of the regents (the native territorial magnates on whom the Dutch had relied), and to set up, parallel with their system of native rule, a civil service in which residents would assure the equitable reign of law in their localities, while the task of revenue gathering would be separated from general administration and confided to a different class of officials, the collectors. Into this system the regents, the lesser chiefs and the village headmen were introduced, with specific revenue collecting and police duties.

The system failed to work, partly because it did not take into account the complex pattern of land ownership in the Javanese countryside, but even more because Raffles could not find enough reliable British and Dutch officials. He was hampered by the policy of the East India Company, which regarded Java as an embarrassing, but fortunately temporary, addition to its already vast responsibilities in India; the directors were unwilling to incur the deficits which were inevitable in a period of radical reform, and when Raffles tried to replenish his exchequer by selling government lands, he merely gave his enemies the means to discredit him with false charges of dishonesty.

After Java, Raffles was relegated to the moribund governorship of Bencoolen, where doubtless his enemies hoped the prevalent diseases would kill him quickly, as they were to kill his three eldest children. There – in view of the decline of the pepper trade – he could do little more than preside over the dismantling of the vast establishment his predecessors had created; but he was not the man to fade into inaction, and in 1819, by founding Singapore, he provided the southernmost point in the chain of British beach-heads in Malaya, which in 1826 were formed into a single government as the Straits Settlements. Since Raffles envisaged Singapore not as a centre of territorial expansion but as the free entrepôt of the Malayan world which it eventually became, he was content with a miniature establishment. His instructions laid down that the first resident, Major Farquhar, should act as his own magistrate and police superintendent. He would have a secretary at 400 dollars a month and a master attendant to supervise the port at 300 dollars. Also provided for was a 'careful and steady European at St John's with a boat and small crew, for the purpose of boarding all square sailed vessels passing through the Straits and of communicating with you either by signals or by a small canoe as you may find most advisable'. There were Eurasian clerks and native *peons*, but the total cost of the establishment, in 1832, when Raffles handed the administration of Singapore over to John Crawfurd, was 3,500 dollars a month, or less than £1,000. This provided for a resident drawing – with salary and expenses – 1,400 dollars, an assistant resident at 300 dollars, a master attendant at 300 dollars, a newly appointed police super-intendent at 450 dollars, a chaplain at 100 dollars, a surveyor at 200 dollars, plus Eurasian clerks, and interpreters and – a characteristic Raffles touch – an allowance of 60 dollars for the Botanic Gardens.

More interesting than the details of the minute establishment which Raffles created are certain paragraphs in his instructions which show that he conceived Singapore not merely as a focus of trade but as a centre from which British political power could radiate its influence under the guise of protection. Talking of the states which have not yet fallen under Dutch authority, he tells Farquhar:

... it is justifiable and necessary that you exert your influence to preserve their existing state of independence. If this independence can be maintained without the presence of an English authority it would be preferable, as we are not desirous of extending our stations; but as from the usual march of the Dutch policy, the occupation of Tringano, and the extension of their view to Siam, may be reasonably apprehended, a very limited establishment in that quarter may become ultimately necessary.

The 'very limited establishment' envisaged by Raffles was eventually to be fulfilled when the British authorities in Malaya intervened in the native states more than half a century later and introduced that peculiar com-bination of advice and authority which was the function of the residents.

Thus in his actions in Java and at Singapore we see Raffles anticipating the two main directions which British administration was to take during the century of imperial power in Malaya and the China Seas, the creation of a territorial empire largely based on the protection of 'independent' local rulers and the parallel creation of a commercial empire based on a freedom of trade in which, thanks to their early start on the industrial revolution, the British would be in a competitively favourable position.

If, during the first quarter of the nineteenth century, the focus of adminis-trative innovation lies in Malaya, in the 1840s it shifts to China. In Hong Kong during this decade a new colony was added, the first territory in east Asia to be administered by the Colonial Office instead of the Company. And with the creation of the treaty ports the Foreign Office was faced with the problem of providing a new type of consular official, whose duties would in practice go far beyond those of a mere protector of the rights of British subjects.

It was not until the middle of the nineteenth century that the British, those hesitant imperialists, began to establish a thoroughly professional colonial service, and the first administrators at Hong Kong, like those of many another early Victorian colony, were drawn rather haphazardly from men who happened to be available locally. In 1841 Captain Charles Elliott formed the first skeleton government, with a magistrate, a harbour master, a clerk of works and a land officer to look after the immediate needs of the settlement. Hong Kong was not actually ceded by treaty until 1843, and it was only then that the secretary of state decided on the appropriate form of government and the necessary appointments.

At this time it was thought that Hong Kong would become and remain the centre of British trade in the Far East and that administration might appropriately radiate from it. The governor (with his salary of £6,000 a year) was also appointed superintendent of trade, with responsibility for all commercial arrangements in the treaty ports and also for protecting the extra-territorial rights granted to British subjects.

This combination of functions was soon revealed as impracticable. Shanghai rapidly became a much more important centre of commerce than Hong Kong and it was inconvenient to administer it from a distance. The problems of governing a colony and of keeping peace in the international colonies of merchants on the foreign soil of treaty ports were found to be essentially different. And, since in one role the governor was subordinate to the Colonial Office and in the other to the Foreign Office, he became involved in insoluble conflicts of administrative loyalty. In 1859 the governor of Hong Kong ceased to be superintendent of trade for the China coast and the affairs of the colony were completely separated from those of the treaty ports, which came under the jurisdiction of the British consul-general in Shanghai and his subordinates in the other concessions.

For some time the administrative service in Hong Kong remained amateurish in character. Sir Henry Pottinger, who as plenipotentiary had brought the Opium Wars to a successful conclusion and had negotiated the Treaty of Nanking, became the first governor, holding the position until Whitehall's nominee, Sir John Davis, could arrive in 1844. Pottinger's appointments indicate the shortage of professional administrators, which at this time was experienced everywhere in the expanding empire. He had to rely on soldiers and on civilian adventurers. The magistrate and the colonial secretary were army officers, the harbour master a naval officer, the private secretary an army surgeon, the assistant magistrate at Stanley a former ship's mate, and the legal adviser was a Bombay lawyer who had come to Hong Kong as a seeker of fortune. The high officials who came out with Sir John Davis were, if anything, even less well fitted for their posts, since, unlike the governor himself (who had served the East India Company in China), they knew little of the customs and attitudes of the Chinese people who from the beginning formed the vast majority of the population of Hong Kong. The score of assistants and junior staff who made up the early civil service continued to be recruited locally, from men who could not hope to make a better living by trade.

In the circumstances, it could hardly be other than an inefficient and chaotic administration. Discipline hardly existed. In the days of Davis, the governor, the colonial treasurer and the colonial judge spent their time mainly in bitter administrative feuds. The corrupting temptations of the east often exerted their baleful influence on the civil servants, and even the highest officials were involved. In 1858 Dr W. T. Bridges, a prominent local lawyer who had been in turn attorney-general and colonial secretary, was caught out in collusion with an opium trader, and in 1861 the registrar-general and protector of Chinese, a brilliant linguist named D. L. Caldwell, was so deeply involved with a local Chinese extortion racketeer and pirate that he had to be dismissed from the service.

By the 1850s it was clear that in the Far East, whether Malaya or the China coast, a civil service must be built up of men interested in their professional responsibilities to the exclusion of external profit making and educated in the circumstances of the region where they would serve, including, not least, the customs and characters of its peoples. Lord Canning, governor-general of India, had stated the problem in so far as it affected officials with Indian experience serving in Malaya, but his remarks applied everywhere in the east:

But whether the main system of government be altered or not [he remarked] that under which officers are provided for service in the Straits is, so far as civil administration is concerned, a positive evil, which ought in any case to be remedied. Indian officers have no opportunities of acquiring experience of the habits or the language of either Malays or Chinese, and accordingly, when officers are sent to the Straits, they have everything to learn. The government of India is unable to keep a close watch on their efficiency: the field is so narrow as to afford little or no room to the Governor of the Settlements, for exercizing a power of selection in recommending to a vacant office; and there is consequently so complete an absence of stimulus to exertion that it may well be doubted whether Indian Civil officers sent to the Straits ever become thoroughly well qualified, or heartily interested in the duties they have to discharge. The character of the Chinese, the most important and at times a very unmanageable part of the Straits Settlements, is quite different from that of any people with whom Indian officers have to deal. . . . I am satisfied that if the Straits Settlements are to remain under the control of the Indian Government, it will be absolutely necessary to devise a plan by which the persons employed in administering the Civil Government shall receive a special training; and that without this the Indian Government cannot do justice to these Settlements.

It was, however, neither in Hong Kong nor in the Straits Settlements, but in the treaty ports that the first steps were taken to establish a service adapted to the special needs of the Far East.

Until the appointment of the consuls to the treaty ports, the relations between the British and Chinese governments had been dramatic but strictly episodic. No legations were allowed in Peking; intercourse between the two countries took place only at Canton. Even this was deliberately indirect, carried on through the merchants of the Co Hong. During the whole period up to 1840 only two British envoys, both charged with securing freer conditions of trade, succeeded in entering China; both missions were fruitless. In 1793 Lord Macartney arrived with an entourage of ninety-five persons, including an escort of dragoons, artillerymen and infantry, and five German musicians. Having made his way to the emperor's summer palace at Jehol, Macartney was received politely. He refused to kowtow; his presents were unimposing. He was dismissed as a mere 'bearer of tribute', and the requests he carried from George III (classed by the Chinese as a vassal king) were refused. Lord Amherst, who headed a similar mission in 1816, was even less fortunate. He succeeded in reaching Peking, the capital, but when he arrived there at five in the morning, after travelling all night, the Chinese officials tried to force him, unwashed and without his court dress or his credentials, into the imperial presence. When he refused, he was turned away without even an audience. The final attempt to establish peaceful diplomatic relations came when the East India Company's monopoly ended in 1833. The Company had enjoyed at least quasi-governmental status; when its responsibilities ceased, the British government tried to regulate the chaos that might ensue by appointing a chief superintendent of trade. Lord Napier, a Scottish peer with a profound ignorance of Asia and its people, was chosen. The Chinese authorities refused to accept his credentials or to modify the system of negotiation through the Co Hong. Napier tried to use force, but the two ships he brought into the river at Canton were trapped, and, outmanoeuvred by the Chinese authorities, he was forced to make humiliating apologies. He died of fever on his way back to Macao.

After Napier's attempts at forceful diplomacy with inadequate firepower came the turn of the plenipotentiaries who used armies and navies effectively during the Opium Wars to force the Chinese to the conference table and to ensure that treaties were sustained. In 1860, supported by their combined armies, the envoys of Britain and France forced their way to Peking and the right of the western powers to maintain permanent embassies in the Chinese capital was won. Later, in 1900, the western envoys were obliged to defend that right with force when they were besieged in the Peking legations and an international military expedition was mounted in order to relieve them. After relief, the foreign ambassadors were granted the right to fortify the legation quarter and to establish a series of garrisons between Peking and the coast to safeguard communications.

The drama and danger which surrounded the embattled lives of British diplomats to China during the nineteenth century (minor diplomats died at Chinese hands in both 1860 and 1900) belong to the periods of crisis on the China coast which were usually attended by expansions of foreign power, including the British commercial empire. The daily administration of that domain, once it had been won, lay with the consular as distinct from the diplomatic service.

Not that the consular service was without its own dramatic occasions. In the early years, especially, consuls maintained a resolute struggle to establish and keep face in their relations with Chinese authorities. In this field the pioneer was J. Rutherford Alcock, whom we have already seen leading the Shanghai Volunteers to victory at the battle of Muddy Flats. Alcock, who had served in Spain as a volunteer during the Carlist Wars was appointed consul first at Amoy and then at Foochow; he reached Shanghai in 1846, and later served in the treaty ports of Japan. Alcock combined the vigour and decisiveness of the Victorian imperialist with an intuitive power of assessing a political situation which enabled him to fit quickly into the pattern created by the British entry into Asia. Even after the treaty ports had been established the Chinese officials sought to maintain the fictional superiority of the Celestial government; they seem to have assumed that if the red-haired foreign barbarians lost enough face they would somehow fade away. Alcock countered this tendency by asserting on every occasion the power of Britain and its representatives.

His first serious clash with the Chinese authorities came at Foochow, where his predecessor, Consul Lay, had been relegated to what a visiting *Times* correspondent described as 'a miserable house, built on piles on a mud flat, apart from the city, and above the bridge, where the tide, as it ebbs and flows, daily sweeps up to his door'. Lay's efforts to gain better accommodation had met officially inspired evasiveness and it was not until Alcock arrived, and strengthened his insistence with lightly veiled threats, that the dignity of the British consul was symbolically established in a house on a hilltop which looked from above on the city and its port. Alcock was always ready to unveil his threats; in 1847, not long after his arrival in Shanghai, three English missionaries were assaulted in a nearby village. Alcock demanded the punishment of the culprits, and when the Chinese officials were dilatory, he arranged for one warship to stop the grain ships bound from Shanghai to the north of China and another to appear off Nanking with a firm message to the local viceroy. The Chinese speedily took action. While such strong-arm methods were officially disowned by the Foreign Office, in practice they were often condoned, and the power of British consuls was largely due to the fact that gunboats could be – and often were – called in to make warlike demonstrations.

Apart from protecting British interests with firmness and occasional force, the consuls were deeply involved in the special day-to-day problems of administering territories so peculiarly constituted as the treaty ports. Shanghai was the classic example. The Chinese government, acting through its local representative, the taotai, remained sovereign of the soil, and, in the early days, only the British consul could treat with the taotai on matters concerning the concession. Later, when treaties were signed with France and the United States, the representatives of the three western powers usually acted in concert on matters of territorial negotiation. Within the concessions, however, a tangle of sovereignties existed, since the foreigners of many nations were responsible to their own consuls, while the Celestial government retained rather nebulous responsibilities towards the Chinese who went to live in what – through the fusion of the English and American concessions and the addition of new land – became the International Settlement. Under Alcock's consulship the internal affairs of the foreign community were regulated by a series of Land Regulations which created a municipal authority dominated - until the 1920s – by the British merchants. But a great deal of power remained in the hands of the consuls; they alone could negotiate with the Chinese authorities and they supervized the delicate relations between Chinese and foreign residents. Finally, each consul was responsible – under extra-territorial jurisdiction – for administering justice among subjects of his own country, and, while the smaller powers often dealt with such matters in a very haphazard manner, the British established regular courts.

Though strong willed ex-adventurers like John Rutherford Alcock might admirably meet the challenge of maintaining British dignity and power during the early days of the treaty ports, it soon became evident that the complicated duties of the consular offices demanded the kind of special-ized officials who could not easily be recruited either in England or in other branches of the consular service. A knowledge of Chinese language and customs, and of the philosophy which inspired the Celestial govern-ment, was not quickly or easily obtained, and Sir John Bowring, the last of the superintendents of trade, established a cadet system by which young men recruited in England could be brought out to China and spend a probationary period receiving an education in the ways of the east which in those days no western university could provide. Having persuaded the Foreign Office to accept his scheme, which made the consular service in the Far East a specialist enclave, Bowring went on in his other capacity as governor of Hong Kong to present the case for a similar reform to his superiors in the Colonial Office. Under his successor, Sir Hercules Robinson, the suggestion was finally put into operation. Officials recruited for the Hong Kong service would henceforward spend two years as cadets studying Chinese; they would then become interpreters and eligible for higher posts in the service. The first cadets arrived in 1862, and the superiority of the system was shown by the fact that these three pioneers quickly rose to high administrative posts. Shortly afterwards a system of examinations was introduced, and the final touch was given to the professionalization of the service by the introduction of a non-contributory pension scheme. By the 1870s most colonial administrators in Hong Kong regarded the service as a life-time career.

The Straits Settlements was slower to accept the cadet system, owing mainly to the fact that during the 1860s the administrative fate of the colony was in doubt. Was it to remain, like Burma, subordinate to Indian administration? The British residents, and particularly the merchants of Singapore, were bitterly opposed to the continuance of Calcutta's distant rule, and finally, in 1867, uncertainty was ended by the transfer of the Straits Settlements to the Colonial Office. In the year of transfer the first cadets arrived, selected by nomination; from 1869 onwards they were selected by examination. The first of them received their instruction in Malay, but soon, with the steady stream of Chinese immigration, it became evident that specialists in their language were equally necessary. In 1871 Walter Pickering, who had learnt his oriental languages as a third mate in a tea clipper, was appointed Protector of Chinese, and set about creating a department staff with Chinese speaking civil servants. Soon the cadet in the Straits Settlements service was given the alternative of learning either Malay or Chinese. Victor Purcell, in his *Memoirs of a Malayan Official*, has vividly described the life of the Chinese speaking cadets during the 1920s; after a preliminary six months in Malaya they were sent to the British concession on the island of Shameen near Canton, where they joined the cadets from Hong Kong in receiving lessons from Chinese scholars.

The experiences of a Malay speaking cadet fifty years earlier were recounted by Sir Frank Swettenham in his reminiscent essay, *Getting into*

Harness. Swettenham, who entered the service in 1871 at a salary of £240, and eventually reached the highest of all administrative posts in Malaya – governor of the Straits Settlements and high commissioner for Malaya – represented in many ways the fruition of the Raffles tradition. A flamboyant figure, with dashing cavalry moustaches, Swettenham possessed a literary eloquence which made him one of the best apologists for the British regime in Malaya. He also played a great part in the development of that regime, and in the manner of the best colonial officials of his time combined sentimental feeling for the Malays and their traditions with an enthusiasm for efficient and just administration on the western model which, by a fatal paradox, was destined to weaken the very aspects of native life he most admired.

Northcote Parkinson has stated, with his tongue only partly in his cheek, that 'The first Malayan patriots were British administrators, and it was they who decided exactly where "Malaya" should begin and end.' The welding of Malaya into a single political entity in fact began when the colonial administrators in the Straits Settlements were complemented by the residents in the native states. As long as the Straits Settlements were the responsibility of the East India Company, and afterwards of the India Office, the authorities were disinclined, despite rising demands from the merchants in Singapore, to intervene in the affairs of the native states. After the conduct of Malayan affairs passed into the hands of the Colonial Office, events began to push policy in a different direction. By the end of the 1860s, tin mining in the native sultanates had become an important factor in the Malayan economy. It had also contributed to disturbing the precarious peace of the region, since the Chinese who worked the early tin mines were divided into mutually hostile secret societies which soon became involved in the tortuous succession intrigues of the various sultanates, with the result that bloody wars involving Malays, Chinese and even Eurasian and European mercenaries were fought in the jungles and marshes of the peninsula. In addition, some of the sultans gave protection to the pirates who still occasionally raided Malay prahus and Chinese junks bound for Singapore.

By 1873 the Colonial Office, urged by merchants and by high local officials, was ready to act. The governor of the Straits Settlements was instructed to investigate conditions in the various states and, where necessary, to appoint British resident officers, only, of course, 'with the full consent of the Native Government'. In 1874 Sir Andrew Clarke intervened first in Perak, where the internal troubles were most pronounced, and then in Selangor. In both cases the native rulers accepted residents, whose advice – under the treaties – must be asked, and also acted upon, in all questions except those affecting Moslem law and religion. Shortly afterwards Negri Sembilan and Pahang accepted residents.

It was not easy in the beginning to find the right men for the difficult task of imposing western concepts of law and administration on peoples who had hitherto lived in mediaeval isolation and who remained at least nominally independent (for the Malay states, unlike the Straits Settlements, were never actually declared British territory). The first resident of Perak was murdered, in part because of his tactless handling of local princelings resentful of their loss of privilege, but his death provided the excuse for a military expedition which displayed the power and promptness of British vengeance, and there was no more resistance to the residents or their pretensions. Eventually the new generation of trained civil servants took over the residencies; Swettenham, for example, became assistant resident at Selangor in 1874 and – after a period of service in Singapore – returned there as resident in 1882.

The residents presided over the emergence of inland Malaya into the modern world. They entered a land where the tortuous jungle rivers, which they followed with their white residency boats, were the only avenues of transport; overland, through the swampy forest, an elephant was the only reliable means of conveyance. The villages and the little courts of local princes, where Moslem and Hindu traditions mingled, were scattered on the banks of the rivers, usually in the sluggish lower reaches. Beyond, where formerly there had been only the wandering, food-collecting aborigines, the Chinese tin miners were prospecting with the help of Malay diviners and scarring the earth with their pits and their mountains of spoil. But the earth they spoilt was only a fragment of the great lush jungle which climbed upward to the slopes of the central mountain spine.

Here the residents advised, and, since no one else knew how to follow their advice, they acted, creating out of nothing the skeleton outlines of westernized administrations, with law courts, police systems, land surveys, inspections of mines, and, eventually, the refinements of education and town planning. Swettenham, in Selangor, not only established an efficient administrative system and balanced the state's budget; he also rebuilt Kuala Lumpur from a Chinese jungle village into a modern city, brought in the first railway, and encouraged the introduction of European capital and initiative by the coffee planters whose appearance preceded the great rubber boom.

Slowly, the native states built up their own administrative services. 'In the first instance,' Swettenham remembered when he came to write out of his own recollections the history of British Malaya, 'the resident was quite alone; then he had a clerk or two; a native or a European non-commissioned officer at the head of his police; a Eurasian apothecary in charge of his first hospital; a Malay warder to look after the flimsy building dignified by the name of prison.' Afterwards, the resident was able to appoint local officers, who were called district magistrates, though every aspect of administration became their responsibility.

In 1895, the sultanates which had received residents were brought together in the Federated Malay States and accepted a common civil service with professional standards similar to those of the Straits Settlements. Inevitably, the two services began to coalesce, cadetships and appointments becoming interchangeable, until in 1906 the existence of a single service was recognized. As Johore, in 1882 and the states of Trengannu, Perlis, Kedah and Kelantan in 1909, came under the aegis of British protection, accepting advisers with more limited powers than residents, the British officials appointed to serve in them were integrated into the pyramidical administrative structure controlled by the governor of the Straits Settlements in his *alter ego* as high commissioner for Malaya.

Almost until the Second World War, the Malayan civil service itself remained exclusively British, largely because the Moslem sultans of the Federated States would not have accepted officials, however well educated, belonging to the large Chinese and Tamil minorities. In 1910 a separate administrative service to which Malays were recruited was set up in the states; after a quarter of a century there were twenty Malay district officers. Not until the late 1930s were Chinese or Indians given responsible public employment; then a Straits Settlements civil service was established – strictly for posts outside the states – to which Asians or Eurasians who were British subjects might be admitted. In practice, Asians, whether Malays, Indians or Chinese, filled only a tiny minority of administrative posts by the time the Japanese invaded the peninsula in 1941. About seventeen hundred British held the key posts in all departments and determined the political and economic directions Malaya would take. Since it had become by the 1920s one of the most prosperous and progressive countries of Asia, their achievement is evident.

The administrative service in Malaya was the model on which were based – with variations – the services operated in Sarawak by the Brooke dynasty and in North Borneo by the Chartered Company. These remained exclusively British and small in numbers. Even during the 1920s there were never more than sixty officers in the North Bornean service, and there were fewer during the pinched 1930s. In 1877 Charles Brooke kept Sarawak administered with nineteen European officers and a handful of Eurasian clerks; the numbers increased during the following century but it remained a small, almost patriarchal service, with the raja keeping a great deal of responsibility in his hands and the officers chosen so informally that it was not until 1934 that, under pressure from the Colonial Office, Sir Vyner Brooke introduced competitive examinations. Up to 1939, despite theoretical concessions to Asian demands for equality, it was still in practice British officials who ruled and shaped the colonies and protectorates everywhere in the Far East.

The evolution of a judicial system in the three areas has a special history. It begins in a rudimentary form in early Penang. Like most pioneer settlements, Penang was in its first years a place with neither law nor any innate respect for it. Only a year after the settlement was founded, Francis Light was complaining of 'the riots the European seamen caused by striking and abusing and plundering the inhabitants', and later he remarked on the fact that the colony had become infested 'by thieves, house-breakers and disorderly persons'. He asked permission to set up a court of enquiry in which two Company's officers, assisted by 'three or more nautical gentlemen', could send offenders to Bengal to be duly tried. When in 1793 a seaman killed a captain who had been maltreating him, and thus committed the double crime of murder and mutiny, Light decided to deal with the matter by court martial. The seaman was found guilty, but instead of executing him, Light sent him back to Calcutta. There the attorney-general ruled that the man had been wrongfully imprisoned, since the Charter of Justice granted by the king to the presidency of Bengal did not apply to its dependencies, and thus there was no means of trying a British subject for a crime committed in Penang. Even when John Dickens was appointed magistrate in 1801 he was in the strange position of being allowed to try and sentence non-British subjects, while against a British defendant the only penalty the local government could impose was banishment. Not until 1807, after the island had become a presidency, was a charter granted establishing a court of record to administer English law as it existed at that time, with powers similar to those of the King's Bench. In 1826 Singapore, which only possessed a magistrate's court established in 1823, was brought under the court in Penang, which in 1855 was finally transferred to Singapore.

Not only was British law observed in the court of Penang; so, also in the early days, was the elaborate ceremonial established under the East India Company in India. Each day the recorder would be escorted to the bench by a procession which the sheriff led with his white wand, followed by the bailiffs with black wands, the jemadar with a silver stick and the two subadars with silver dragon-head staffs. The abolition of this custom at the end of the Company's rule in the 1850s was symbolic of the new attitude in the law courts as well as the administration, based on that conception of the imperial government as a means to civilization which played so great a part in late nineteenth-century British rule in Malaya.

At the lower levels, in all the actual British possessions of the Far East, the process of law and the process of administration flowed together; the administrator – even the police officer – was often also the magistrate. At higher levels the differentiation between the barristers who became judges and the officials trained in the cadet system was more pronounced; the judges' frame of reference was often broader – as broad as the traditions of English law – but their sympathies were likely to be less involved with the Asian peoples with whom they had to deal.

But it is perilous to make sweeping distinctions. In the end, all, judges and officials, were dominated by the mores of the British communities to which they belonged and it is doubtful if either class subscribed with less conviction than the other to that belief in the innate superiority of Britain and the British which every member of a tiny ruling community maintained as a necessity of physical and mental survival. In all the memoirs of civil servants and judges who lived in the Far East one catches the unmistakable tone of men convinced of the essential *rightness* of their acts. Victor Purcell is typical in referring to the Malayan civil service as 'a body of disinterested individuals whose only aim was to do the best they could in their several offices'. One may argue whether their best was in the larger sense the best of possibilities, but in forming an image of the administrators' attitudes this is really irrelevant, since it was characteristic of them to see themselves in such terms of efficient, disinterested service. Long before the end of the nineteenth century the adventurers had vanished from among the public officials of the Far East; those who continued saw themselves as part of an elite group, a dedicated caste, and the fact that many were weak and a few even corrupt did not detract from the force which the idea of their purpose generated within the best of them.

Demanding a place in our mass portrait of the administrators, there remain those who served in the Far East for governments other than the British, yet, in their own ways, served the wider pattern of the empire. If the residents in the Federated States faded away in the unfederated states into advisers with less positive functions, in Siam the process went a further step in rarification. Under King Mongkut, whose fame has reached the west in a remote and distorted form through the popular entertainments based on the somewhat imaginative memoirs of Anna Leonowens, the barriers erected against foreigners since the end of the seventeenth century were dissolved and Siam was opened to western influences. In 1855 Sir John Bowring negotiated with Mongkut a treaty which opened Siam to British trade, and allowed extra-territorial rights and the establishment of consular courts that eventually operated as far north as Chiengmai. Mongkut's son and successor, Chulalongkorn, educated by English teachers, carried the process several steps further. Not only did he encourage English schools for the upper classes and tolerate the adoption of English manners and clothes; he also, like those seventeenth-century predecessors who had employed White and Phaulkon, decided to modernize his army and his administrative services with the aid of foreign advisers, and so established a practice that continued until the eve of the Second World War.

Theoretically, the advisers to Siam could be chosen from any nation, since their presence was not a matter of treaty. In fact, because Britain controlled most of Siam's external trade and had made large investments within the country (including ownership of almost the whole teak industry), the tendency from the beginning was for British advisers to be more numerous than those of other countries and this trend was intensified as the rulers of Thailand – as it later was called – began to feel the need for British support against French encroachments. Siam was not in name a protectorate; for a long period it was in fact not far from being one. The key post of financial adviser was always in British hands; the British also held important posts in such key departments as police, inland revenue, education and forestry. The financial adviser usually wielded a great influence over government policy; in the case of his colleagues, their task was often quite genuinely that of merely advising inexperienced Thai officials who made the ultimate decisions. As Thais gradually became more highly trained in administrative procedures, the decision-making function of the British advisers diminished, and their importance declined rapidly with the upsurge of Thai nationalism during the 1930s.

The advisers in Thailand can hardly be regarded as forming a corps of foreign administrators, but this is the only description one can appropriately give to the Imperial Maritime Customs of China. One of the demands of the merchants when British commercial power was being established on the China coast was that a customs system should be established which would replace the multifarious and often capricious exactions of the local Chinese officials by a uniform and practical way of collecting reasonable tariffs. From the beginning it was argued that the collection of dues should be placed under foreign control. The first move in this direction took place at Shanghai in 1854, when rebels captured the Chinese city and the imperial authorities could not collect the dues. The British, American

The Rulers

Lord Macartney, who in 1793 led an entourage of ninety-five on an embassy to the Chinese Emperor's summer palace at Jehol, on behalf of George III.

(*right*) A quick sketch of
the Chinese Emperor,
Tchien Lung, by
Alexander to 'describe
the features of the
Emperor' for Lord
Macartney's delegation,
and (*below*) a watercolour
portrait of the Emperor.

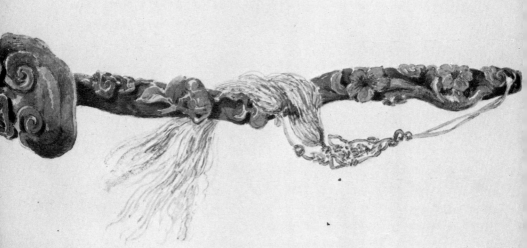

(*top*) Scientific instruments from the Planetarium, the principal gift to the Emperor, with which he was not impressed.

(*below*) An agate sceptre of peace, presented by the Chinese Emperor to Sir George Staunton, a member of the Macartney embassy, in September 1793.

An on-the-spot sketch, by
Alexander, of the son of Sir
George Staunton receiving a
purse from the Emperor. This
occurred in 1793 during Lord
Macartney's embassy.

(*left*) The scene on 2 November, 1793, as the embassy crossed the Whang-ho river, with a guard of honour drawn up on the bank.

mandarin carrying the Emperors letter before the Ambassador

(*left*) A mandarin carrying the Emperor's official letter before the ambassador.

Chinese soldiers by a fort.

The garden of the temple at Lewchew on a visit of the *Alceste* in 1817. The chronicler of the voyage noted that 'instead of permitting only a few to visit the shore at a time, they fitted up the garden of the temple as a sort of general Arsenal for us'.

Manilla, the evening parade on the Calzada by the monument to Magellan, with the harbour in the background.

The race-course in Happy Valley, Hong Kong, 1848. The English love of horse-racing led to the foundation of Jockey and Turf Clubs in most of the larger settlements in the Far East. (Watercolour by N. A. Baptista.)

A Chinese law-court photographed at work during the 1870s.

Forms of punishment used
in China: (*left*) the cangue,
a wooden collar, photo-
graphed in use in 1874, and
(*below*) three women
prisoners yoked together in
Shanghai, 1907.

A statue to Sir Stamford Raffles outside the Victoria Hotel in Singapore.

(*left*) Sir Rutherford Alcock.

(*below*) The first meeting of the British commissioner and the village headman at Weihaiwei in 1898.

Celebrations at the Royal Wellington Barracks on the occasion of Queen Victoria's Diamond Jubilee.

Celebrations in Shantung at the time of Edward VII's coronation: (*top*) Mr Johnson and the man who bore the king's picture in the procession, and (*below*) the governor and chief officials photographed at the start of the festivities.

General Mei and his watch.

Customs post between Hong Kong and China in 1890.

The British commissioner and Mr Wong, the Chinese commissioner, fixing the
first boundary mark on the shore at Starling Islet, New Territories, Hong Kong.

(*left*) British and Chinese officials outside government offices at Sham Chin, New Territories.

Scene at a Japanese court as the compensation money, for the murder by a samurai of Mr Richardson, a British diplomat, was being counted out in September 1863.

and French consuls, with the agreement of the Taotai, set up an international board of inspectors. The arrangement did not work particularly well, but the British had no intention of abandoning the hold over Chinese finances which it gave them, and various expedients were tried until, in 1863, the Imperial Maritime Customs was finally reorganized under the capable one-man control of Inspector-General Robert Hart. The British had gained an important and bloodless victory over the other foreign powers who competed for influence in Chinese affairs.

Hart, afterwards Sir Robert and a mandarin many times honoured, took seriously his responsibilities to China and was often abused by the British merchants for his thoroughness and incorruptibility. Nevertheless, he became one of the main instruments of British power on the China coast. His position proclaimed the primacy of his nation in Chinese trade, and his long tenure in office created a precedent on which the British government based successful demands that the inspector-general should always remain one of their subjects. Moreover, while the numerical majority of the customs staff was Chinese, the thousand or so European employees held, until the late 1930s, most of the senior and executive positions, and of these Europeans, more than half were always British. To pick two years at random, in 1899 they numbered 503 out of 993 foreigners, in 1911 the proportion was 738 out of 1,387. They were divided between the higher administrative staff, who underwent the same kind of training as cadets in the British consular service on the China coast, and the outdoor staff, who entered the service as raw juniors and learnt their trade in the often perilous rough and tumble of the Shanghai dockside. The higher positions were so well paid that promising young men would often leave the foreign service in Hong Kong to join the Imperial Customs. The Imperial Customs was the largest single employer of British nationals on the China coast, and its employees, with the families of those who were married, formed an important element in the British community on the China coast, particularly in the smaller treaty ports where the senior customs official would compete with the local consular representative for leadership of the miniature expatriate society.

In practice, with the consular service and the colonial service, the Imperial Customs formed the third among the services which represented British power in the Far East. However deep may have been the loyalty of some of its officials to their Chinese paymasters, the fact remains that through them the British indirectly controlled the one reliable source of income which the Chinese government possessed. And what can be a more effective form of commercial imperialism than to trade to a country and at the same time to have one's hand firmly on its customs service?

69

And so, when we consider the administrators as a class contributing to the structure of British power in the Far East, Sir Robert Hart and his successors take their inevitable place. For the Manchu rulers – that proud race of decayed imperialists – employed them only because they feared the power of British cruisers and of those seaborne armies which three times in the sixty years between 1840 and 1900 had beaten their way through the mediaeval defences of the Celestial Empire.

5
THE ADVENTURERS

In the beginning every man who went to the east from Europe was an adventurer, in the sense that he risked his life and often his wealth in a perilous venture for uncertain reward. When a successful voyage brought home a ship loaded with spices the profits were enormous; but hundreds of ships and thousands of men never returned. The title of Merchant Adventurer was not merely a badge of pride; it was a definition and a true identification, for no one who did not possess the spirit of adventure was likely to become a merchant trading to the East Indies in the reign of Elizabeth or James. Among these men one found not merely the willingness to take risks which is associated with the idea of adventure, but also an adaptability that often meant survival when they were plunged into the most unexpected of circumstances and the most alien of environments.

Among the early voyagers to the eastern seas there are many men who exemplify this true adventurer's ability to endure and even succeed in adversity. Will Adams, first Englishman in Japan, landing in 1600 as a castaway threatened with execution, becoming a favourite of the reigning Shogun, is a prime example. Adopting the customs of the country, he married a Japanese wife and died a country landowner, and today in the country he adopted three and a half centuries ago he is remembered in a street named after him – the Street of the Pilot – and Japanese children sing at his tomb in the little town where he died in 1620, having survived for twenty years the perils that beset a stranger among the intrigues of an Asian court.

More obscure, but equally talented in the arts of adventure and survival, was the English merchant Charles Lister, who arrived in 1701 at the Cambodian court in Pnom Penh and in self-preservation pretended to a knowledge of the art of medicine. With luck and shrewdness he not merely ensured his own survival but gained a trusted position in the king's entourage and founded a dynasty of Cambodian court physicians which was still flourishing when John Crawfurd went on his famous and fruitless embassy to the courts of Siam and Cochin-China in 1822.

There were many like Adams and Lister, making their way in the courts of Asia by various combinations of good sense and skill, varying from Adams's useful arts as shipbuilder and navigator to the tumblers' antics of those shipwrecked British ships' officers of the early eighteenth century described by Captain Alexander Hamilton, who bought their lives at Johore by amusing the sultan with nautical dances. If a merchant adventurer could become shipbuilder to a Japanese prince, doctor to a Cambodian king, or clown to a Malayan sultan, his adventurous resourcefulness could equally well run in other directions, such as piracy, which in the days of Drake was thought as little worthy of reproof as it would have been among the Achaeans who invaded Troy. Within a century a change in official opinion had taken place, and Samuel White, that formerly respectable mariner who became the King of Siam's harbour master at Mergui and used his opportunities to plunder Indian ships in the Bay of Bengal, found himself the object of a manhunt by the Honourable Company's warships, supported by the royal authority of King James II, and only by elaborate ruses did he contrive to escape with both his life and his gains.

A division had in fact begun to appear by 1680 between the Merchant and the Adventurer. John Company had ceased to be a combination of questing fortune hunters; it had solidified into an institution, and in another hundred years, after the downfall of Warren Hastings, it would be incorporated into the British governmental establishment through the supervision exercized by a board of control established by Parliament. Its servants were the administrators of vested rights, and though they might, and sometimes did, make dubious fortunes, it was not by venturing, but by the misuse of a position guaranteed by conquest and treaty.

In the eighteenth century it was the country traders who had become the adventurers, and the combination of ruthlessness and resourcefulness that marks the venturing type characterized equally their opium running expeditions to the Dutch East Indies and their illicit ventures to the coast of China. But after the treaty ports were won, the great firms of smugglers became the trading hongs, pillars of that Victorian and Edwardian respectability and power in whose protective shadow they carried on the legitimized exploitation of China. They too ceased to be adventurers.

In fact a shift in connotation had overtaken the word 'Adventurer'. Though it still contained the idea of the venture, this was accompanied by the suggestion of an anti-social motivation. The adventurer, as he was now seen, operated on the outskirts of the European society that had become established in the east; he sought his own satisfactions, material or otherwise, and he sought them in ways that did not always fit the hardening stereotypes of imperial authority. At his most harmless he was the kind of man who might be described by that eloquent American term, 'a loner'. One such was the French Canadian who had fled from his own country after being involved under Jean Louis Papineau in the rebellion of 1838, and after many wanderings arrived at the southern tip of Malaya, where he gained local fame as 'Carrol, the tiger hunter'. Carrol lived partly from the bounties he collected from the government for the beasts he killed, and partly from the hospitality of Chinese planters whom he protected from untimely death. He preferred the life of the forests to even so mildly urban a centre as Singapore in the 1860s, and springs to life in our minds from one sharp detail remembered long afterwards by a newspaper man: 'he always wore a gold ring half way up a long greyish beard, like a necktie ring'.

While the harmless adventurer expended his courage on tigers, others used it to gain fortune, and others knowledge, and others glory, and the most formidable used it to gain power. Sometimes they sought power insanely, like a minor official in the Imperial Maritime Customs named Mason, who served obscurely at the Yangtse port of Chinkiang. Mason became connected with a Chinese secret society, the Venerable Brothers (Kolaohwei) which about 1890 was active in the Yangtse Valley. Most of the activities of the Venerable Brothers were directed against foreigners, but there was a strain of anti-Manchu rebelliousness in the movement reminiscent of the Taipings, and Mason appears to have conceived the idea that with their aid he might make himself Emperor of China. He undertook to arm the rebels, and actually bought in Hong Kong thirty-five cases of rifles and ammunition which he shipped in piano cases on the freighter *Chi-yuan*, bound for Shanghai. Mason hoped to avoid discovery in Shanghai by the simple expedient of seizing the ship with the aid of a group of Chinese associates before it reached that port and sailing it up the Yangtse to Chinkiang. Perhaps the most insane feature of Mason's adventure was that when the mutiny had once begun he changed sides and helped to suppress it. Tried by the British court in Shanghai under the privilege of extra-territoriality, he got away with a light term in the consular prison.

Mason, whose unbalanced activities might easily have endangered European lives and disturbed trade on the Yangtse, was universally execrated by the British community in the Far East. But an adventurer in

search of power whose aims were more rational, and who actually succeeded, was likely to bring out all the ambivalence which confused the
British mind in the Far East when it dwelt upon the ends and means of
empire. The official hierarchy, intent on guarding what had been gained,
looked on every adventurer with distrust until he became so successful
that he was absorbed into the establishment. But among the merchants
there remained a feeling of sympathy for the adventurer which was not
merely an atavistic yearning back to their own past of venturing. It was also
a knowledge that those who pushed in their own ways beyond the established frontiers carried trade with them, whatever flag they bore. In
no case was this divided attitude more clearly shown than in the case of
that literal prince of adventurers, James Brooke, who grabbed himself a
kingdom and founded a dynasty of white kings in the heart of the Malay
world that ruled in practice for exactly a century, from the day in 1841
when Brooke became Raja of Sarawak to the day in 1941 when the Japanese invasion swept his realm into history.

James Brooke was the most famous and successful of the Englishmen
who dreamed of a principality in the eastern seas, but he was not the first
of them. More than a century before he arrived, the roving country trader,
Alexander Hamilton, had been tempted by the offer of a fief by the Sultan
of Johore, and had refused what later was to become the great prize of the
east.

In the year 1703 [he records] I called at Johore on my way to China, and he (the
King of Johore) treated me very kindly and made me a present of the island of
Singapore but I told him it could be of no use to a private person, though a proper
place for a company to settle a colony in, lying in the centre of trade, and accom-
modated with good rivers and a safe harbour, so conveniently situated that all
winds served shipping both to go out and come into these rivers.

Alexander Hare, the first of the white rajas, had no such hesitations as
Hamilton when the Sultan of Bandjermasin offered him a principality on
the southern shores of Borneo in 1811. Hare was a country trader living in
Malacca who in 1809 visited southern Borneo, where he found that the
Dutch had virtually abandoned their former trade on the Bandjermasin
River. Hare's trading on this occasion seems to have been rather profitless,
but he had established a link with the Sultan, and when Stamford Raffles,
the most splendid true adventurer of them all, arrived in Malacca as
agent for the governor-general, Hare was able to interest him in the
relevance of Borneo to his plans for destroying the power of the Dutch in
the archipelago. Raffles concluded a treaty with the Sultan, and once Java
was conquered, Hare set sail as his representative to establish a factory

there and to take over the monopoly rights which the Dutch had acquired in south Borneo.

Hare had an eye to his own advantage even more than to that of the Company and concluded a private agreement with the Sultan by which he acquired sovereign rights over a tract of fourteen hundred square miles of land. Thus he became resident for the East India Company and at the same time a Bornean raja. In the beginning everything seemed to work well for him. He had enough money to make a start on his plantations and he gathered around him adventurers of his own megalomaniac kind, including his brother John and, more important, a Scot named John Clunies-Ross. When he found labour hard to get in thinly populated Borneo, Raffles assisted him by recruiting coolies in Java and by declaring Hare's little kingdom a convict settlement for minor offenders. In all, some three thousand Javanese became Hare's bondsmen, and their numbers were augmented by women whom the new raja's agents kidnapped in Borneo and among the islands. Bandjermasin was also declared – with Brunei on the north coast and Pontianak on the west – one of the three ports to which trade to and from Borneo was to be restricted, and the increase of prosperity which this arrangement seemed to promise kept the Sultan, at least for the time being, favourably inclined to Hare and his pretensions.

But Hare's own weaknesses and the march of events alike conspired against his success as a ruler. He conceived oriental kingship in highly romantic terms, spent his money building a palace and his energy enjoying the girls of his numerous harem. Clunies-Ross, his principal lieutenant, strove in the face of Hare's neglect and extravagance to keep the plantations from failure and to attend to the business of the East India Company at the same time. In the event, it was immaterial whether Hare managed his kingdom well or ill, since his fortunes were bound up with those of the archipelago in general; when the East India Company decided to leave Java his position became untenable. In 1816, prior to the evacuation of Java, John Fendall – Raffles' successor as lieutenant-governor in Batavia – closed down the East India Company's establishment at Bandjermasin and withdrew the British forces, leaving the Sultan to conclude whatever agreement he might with the returning Dutch. The Company regarded itself as in no way responsible for safeguarding Hare's regal pretensions, and the Sultan, bowing to the prevalent wind, claimed that he had lost his agreement with Hare, which was tantamount to repudiating his grant of land and sovereignty. Hare protested volubly but his threats of armed resistance to the Dutch evaporated when Clunies-Ross decided to leave Borneo, and though he himself remained for some years in Batavia, clamouring for his rights, he gained nothing and was expelled by the Dutch authorities in 1820.

Meanwhile, on a group of islands too far into the Indian Ocean for even the Dutch to be interested, Hare's lieutenant had picked up the dream of kingship. Trading southward, Clunies-Ross came to the tiny archipelago of twenty-three coral islands known sometimes as the Cocos Islands, and sometimes – from Captain Keeling who discovered them far back in 1609 – as the Keeling Islands. There, out of the timbers of wrecked ships, he built a house and a small trading schooner, with which he sailed through the Indonesian Islands, buying pepper where the prices were low and storing it in the Cocos while he waited for a profitable selling time. Not long afterwards, in 1823, Hare appeared, in a ship loaded with two hundred slaves, the only possessions he had been able to salvage from his Bornean empire. At first the two old associates thought of reigning in concert, but Hare became increasingly more arrogant and overbearing, and in 1831, after a final quarrel, he departed, to die two years later in Sumatra. Clunies-Ross, now the undisputed king of the Cocos Islands, liberated Hare's slaves, who became his first subjects, and his realm slowly achieved a modest prosperity. Though Clunies-Ross had declared the Cocos Islands a British possession in the 1850s, Whitehall did not choose to recognize the fact until the end of the century when the competition for colonies became acute. Then, in 1886, the Cocos Islands were annexed to the Straits Settlements. The reigning family still remained the principal landowners, but their eventual prosperity came from a settlement they had made on Christmas Island, 550 miles away, where, even after the island's annexation in 1889, they controlled the exploitation of the rich deposits of phosphates.

Other pretenders came and went in the archipelago: men like Adam Wilson, a merchant's clerk who in the 1820s obtained from the Sultan of Siak a grant of the island of Bengcalis, off the eastern coast of Sumatra, and Joseph W. Torrey, the American merchant from Hong Kong, who in 1865 was granted land in North Borneo and the high title of maharaja by the Sultan of Brunei. Wilson fell foul of the Dutch, whose gunboats drove him out of their sphere of influence. Torrey never ruled his principality, but in devious ways the grants he received became the foundation on which the British North Borneo Company was later established.

Brooke succeeded, and on a much more impressive scale than his only real rival, Clunies-Ross, because his personality and his ideals in a peculiar way fitted the needs of the time. He was an adventurer, but though he loved power he was less concerned with material gain than most men who went to the east in his time. He was an intellectual, a lover of ideas and literature who kept his remote oriental palace filled with the latest English books and who enjoyed few things in his life so much as the long evenings of talk on philosophy and science in which he was able to indulge when the great naturalist, Alfred Russel Wallace, was his guest in Sarawak. He was also an idealist of the imperial stamp, and probably, after Raffles, the finest of his kind in the east. When we consider his record, we may begin by imagining the distrust with which Wallace, that life-long Owenite socialist, must have first approached this self-made autocrat; we shall hardly end without in some way echoing the final verdict of unwilling approval which the great evolutionist passed upon the autocrat of Sarawak.

Brooke was born into the Indian establishment. His father was judge in Benares, and his childhood to the age of twelve was spent in the valley of the Ganges. His adolescence in England was dominated by the thought that to the east he belonged and must return, and it seemed inevitable that a few days after his sixteenth birthday he should receive his ensign's commission in the Bengal army. Less than five years later, fighting in Burma, he was shot in the lungs and left for dead on the battlefield. Returning to collect his body, his colonel found that he was still alive. Brooke was sent home on furlough and given a pension of £70 a year which in many a dark period of his later years was to be his sole means of income. After a breakdown in England and a long convalescence, he returned to India in 1830, only to break impatiently with the rule-bound Company and to return home with plans of an adventurous independent career in mind.

He thought first of becoming a country trader, and bought a 290-ton brig which he sailed to Macao with a cargo of mixed merchandize. The venture was a failure and Brooke sold the boat and returned to England. His experience in the China Seas had set him thinking and reading. He developed a great admiration for Raffles, whom he regarded as something of a martyr to outdated mercantilist ideas. He published in the *Athenaeum* in 1838 an article in which he declared that the oppressiveness of the Dutch and the weakness of the English had reduced the Archipelago (this 'Eden of the Eastern Wave' he called it) to 'a state of anarchy and confusion, as repugnant to humanity as it is to commercial prosperity'. Brooke, indeed, was no enemy of commerce. But he felt that it should be linked with 'territorial possession', which, by creating an efficient administration, protects and nurtures trade. Yet he was anxious that the progress of western power should not be accompanied by the advance of western rapacity, and that whatever was good in native life should be fostered and preserved.

Having revealed the principles on which the rest of his career would be based, Brooke proclaimed his intention of going to Borneo with the purpose of making friends with the Dyaks and assessing the possibility of founding British settlements. In December 1838 he set sail in a small schooner, *The Royalist*, a vessel made for adventure rather than trade, and in May the following year he was in Singapore, where the merchants feted and encouraged him. In July he set sail for the Sarawak River at the western end of the sultanate of Brunei, which in those days extended over the whole northern shore of Borneo. He arrived at the opportune time, and made the best of the circumstances chance afforded.

Brunei was in the hands of a weak government. The Sultan, Omar Ali, was a half-wit and a physical freak (he had two thumbs on his right hand), and his uncle Hasim, as Raja Muda, was both heir and regent. The country was torn by strife between the ruling Malays and the aboriginal peoples, including the Dyaks and Ibans, whom they sought to oppress, while the immigrant Chinese, who worked as gold miners in the interior, added a powerful new element to an already complex pattern of races. The instability created by racial strife and the weakness of the dynasty was compounded by rivalries among the ruling Malays, while the coast was infested by pirates, and head-hunting was a widespread and tolerated sport among the aboriginal peoples.

When Brooke arrived in Kuching, at the mouth of the Sarawak, the Raja Muda was there, attempting in vain to suppress a powerful rebellion of local Malay chieftains supported by the Dyaks, who had been repressed beyond endurance. It was only through the intervention of Brooke, who led his crew in a surprise attack on the enemy stockade, that the uprising was brought to an end, and the rebels sued for peace. Brooke's reward, which the Raja Muda had promised him beforehand, was the government of the province of Sarawak and the title of raja; undoubtedly the ruler of Brunei calculated that if an Englishman were established in a small and remote segment of territory he would serve as a protector from predators of other nations without endangering Brunei's interests.

It was an elephantine miscalculation. On the pretexts of extending peace and civilization, of punishing pirates and eliminating head-hunting, James Brooke and his nephew and successor Charles Brooke contrived by 1905 to build the tiny river state of Sarawak into a country of fifty thousand square miles, while the parent sultanate of Brunei, squeezed between the realm of the Brookes and the spreading domain of the British North Borneo Company, which eventually acquired some thirty thousand square miles, had been reduced to a tiny fragment of a little over two thousand square miles. It was almost miraculously saved from total extinction by the discovery of oil in 1914.

Yet the record of the Brooke dynasty, though it was embellished at times by the most flagrant acts of land grabbing, was far from completely negative. All the rajas, James (1841-68), his nephew Charles (1868-1917) and his great-nephew Vyner (1917-46), ruled as benevolent despots, with a mere promise of constitutional rule appearing at the very end of Vyner's reign. They brought to the land peace and patriarchal justice (which the raja often administered in his own palace at Kuching) and, since Borneo was a fertile and uncrowded territory, this alone guaranteed a measure of internal prosperity. By suppressing piracy they performed a service to commerce in general and by ending head-hunting they conferred a special if unwanted blessing on the Dyaks. They carried out these operations and maintained their rule without great European forces; indeed, they had only a single gunboat and a few European officers to train their native levies, and in their operations against the formidable pirates of Sulu and Mindanao had to rely on the capricious assistance of the Royal Navy. Since they did not greatly approve of westernizing Asian peoples whose ways of life they tended to admire, they were slow to introduce education and social services. On the other hand, they were so simple in their personal tastes and so economical in their administration that the tax gatherer never became among their subjects the personification of a hated rule; there were in fact times during his reign when James Brooke suffered from actual poverty. Having rooted out the more murderous evils of primitive life and introduced the basic rule of law, they were inclined to leave their subjects to themselves, and one may justifiably wonder, in these days of excessive administration, whether that is not after all a good way of governing.

The record of the Brookes was the subject of continued controversy in England and in the east, and they were often approved – and condemned – for the wrong reasons. The merchants of Singapore and Hong Kong applauded their services to commerce through the suppression of piracy but became less enthusiastic when the Brookes showed themselves reluctant to open their realm to unrestricted exploitation. The British government wavered for decades between cautious encouragement and positive hostility. Palmerston would not recognize the independence of Sarawak, since he had not yet worked out the complexities involved when a British subject became the ruler of a foreign state, but he recognized Brooke's achievements by making him governor of the colony of Labuan (acquired from Brunei in 1846), and consul-general to Brunei, and by sending him on a mission to Siam. Later governments deprived Brooke of his offices under the British crown, and it was not until 1865 that Sarawak was recognized as an independent state. It became a British protectorate in 1888, and a British colony in 1946 when the last of the Brookes, Sir Vyner, abdicated a rule which had in practice become a dead letter since the Japanese invasion of Borneo in 1941.

By seizing and holding a kingdom for themselves, the Brookes were the most successful of British adventurers in the Far East. Their only real rivals were the group of latter day merchant adventurers who competed with Charles Brooke in dismembering the realm of Brunei. The British North Borneo Company which they formed was the last of the British chartered companies to hold rights of territorial government; it abandoned those rights in 1946 at the same time as the Brooke dynasty.

Though in later years respectable taipans from the China coast were involved in the operations of this Company, it was born as the result of a number of wild and dubious operations by some of the most shady adventurers in the Far East. The first of them were not British, but American. In 1865 an ex-seaman named Charles Lee Moses, who claimed to be a former naval officer and newly appointed American consul at Brunei, arrived penniless in Borneo and talked the sultan into granting him a tract of territory in the north-east, beside the Kimanis River. He immediately sold the grant to two American merchants, one of them the Maharaja Torrey whom we have already encountered. Torrey and his partners brought in two Chinese merchants and founded the American Trading Company. They even established a jungle settlement called Ellena and planted about ninety acres of cleared land, but the money ran short and Ellena was abandoned in 1866. In 1875 Torrey sold his rights to a German-born speculator, Baron von Overbeck, who was Austrian consul-general at Hong Kong. It was Overbeck, desperate for a backer, who interested the old China coast firm of Dent Brothers and thus acquired the support of the more respectable merchant interests. Eventually, after tortuous negotiations, the new combine bought out the American Trading Company, acquired further land rights from the Sultan of Brunei, and the North Borneo Company received its charter.

The terms of the Charter are illustrative of the equivocal attitude which the ruling Gladstone government showed towards extensions of empire. The government categorically declared that the Charter did not vest sovereignty of North Borneo in the British crown. Nevertheless, through the provisions of the document, Britain did assume sovereign powers if not responsibilities, since it specified that the Company must remain British, must not transfer any of its grants without Whitehall's permission, must suppress slavery and protect native customs, and must act on the advice of the British government in all questions dealing with foreign relations or the rights of natives. Once again the actions of a group of adventurers – and American adventurers at that – had been the wedge that opened the way to imperial rule.

The Company lived up to its charter. There were indeed times – particularly during the years when it was under the control of another noted adventurer, the former gun-runner W. C. Cowie – when its methods of developing the territory took on a flavour of speculation: unusable railways were laid to unprofitable destinations in uninhabited jungles. But in its dealings with the native peoples the Company on the whole was as just and equitable as its bitter enemies and rival adventurers, the Brookes of Sarawak. Native institutions were respected and there was a good deal of indirect rule based on tribal law. Perhaps the most telling tribute to the Company's rule is that the native administration it had established was taken by the Colonial Office in 1946 and continued almost unchanged by the Malayan government when it assumed control in 1963.

The adventurers who won power for themselves were few in number. Those who served the power needs of other people were many and various, and for at least two and a half centuries the mercenary was a familiar and sometimes even a respected outrider of the British Far Eastern community.

The first of them appeared in the seventeenth century, almost as soon as English ships began to thread their way through Malayan waters, and English sailors, shipwrecked or deserting, began to realize that their services had a market value among the princes of the east who were anxious to avail themselves of western skills, in war if in no other way. In the Moslem sultanates they often became renegades, changing their religion to save their lives or merely to advance themselves in the royal favour. Dampier encountered two such men at the court of Acheen on the northern tip of Sumatra. But the country that undoubtedly employed most Englishmen during the seventeenth century, whether as mariners or soldiers, was Siam. These mercenaries were attracted largely from the service of the East India Company, whose employees in Ayuthia freely indulged in trade on their own account and were often willing to change allegiances for the large rewards the Siamese offered. Even the man sent out by the Company to investigate the chaos in its affairs – a certain George Barnaby – eventually joined the service of the Siamese king, and became governor of the seaport town of Mergui on the Bay of Bengal, where Samuel White was shahbander or harbour master. Barnaby and White gathered around them many other seekers after fortune and by 1687 there was a whole colony of Englishmen at Mergui, some of them accompanied by their wives; sixty English were killed when the Siamese that year decided to massacre the foreigners. Most of the English at Mergui were mariners – captains, mates, or even seamen on the ships which nominally belonged to the King of Siam and which were often used by Barnaby and White in private ventures of trading or piracy. There were almost certainly others who were at sea when their comrades were slaughtered. One ship alone, the frigate *Revenge* under Captain English, is said to have carried a crew of seventy European sailors.

At the capital of Ayuthia, other Englishmen served the King of Siam, in this case mainly in the capacity of gunners and infantry soldiers. According to Dampier it was they who played the most important part in crushing the rebellion of the mercenaries from Macassar in 1686; in this fight a certain Captain Coates, who had just been appointed admiral to the King of Siam, died through sinking in the water under the weight of his armour. In spite of these services, the English were thrown into prison with all other foreigners (except the intriguing Dutch) by the revengeful mandarins after the downfall of Phaulkon. Later, when the French had all been slaughtered or expelled, the Siamese admitted the English mercenaries had served them faithfully and invited them to stay on in their former offices. Not unnaturally they refused and sailed away on a country trading ship, the *George*; Dampier saw them on their arrival at Acheen. Among them were some 'Families of Men, Women and Children', who admitted that, until the change in government, they had been 'maintain'd . . . very well in that employ . . .'

There can have been few sultanates in the eastern seas where European and especially British adventurers did not arrive during the eighteenth and early nineteenth centuries, either to run guns for the local rulers, or to give a semblance of western training to the native levies. During the internecine wars which led to Colonial Office interference in the Malay states during the 1870s they occasionally emerge from obscurity into a brief and clear light. There was, for instance, Sergeant Pennefather of the British army, converted to Islam and commanding a ragged company of Arab and Indian mercenaries for one of the warring factions in Selangor. Placed in command of the fort at Kuala Selangor, he proved a worse fighter than his Malay opponents and lost his life with fifty-two of his men. Even noted soldiers of fortune, like Captain T. C. Speedy, who had trained the emperor's army in Abyssinia, were drawn into this conflict, but faded from the scene or, as in Speedy's case, joined the imperial service in 1874, when the British authorities began to take a serious interest in the affairs of inland Malaya.

It was China, from the 1850s down to the 1930s, which provided the richest field for mercenaries of all kinds, from ascetic professionals like Charles Gordon to flamboyant *condottieri* like One-Arm Sutton and Two-Gun Cohen. The vast internal struggles which preluded the end of the Manchu dynasty gave the soldiers of fortune their way of entry into the Celestial Empire; the mercenaries in their turn assisted notably in the titanic travail of social disintegration and civil conflict by which China emerged from its ancient dreams into the realities of the modern world. The adventurers were of many nationalities. Some of the most notorious, like Frederick T. Ward and H. A. Burgevine at the time of the Taiping rebellion, were Americans. Others, particularly during the rise of the Kuomintang in the 1920s, were Russians, or European agents of the Comintern, looking for ideological and political rather than financial rewards. It is only with the British that we are concerned, but there were plenty of them, and the British settlements on the China coast, particularly Shanghai and Hong Kong, served as their points of contact with the outer world.

The majority of the mercenaries were neither very successful nor very romantic. They were members of the uneasy white proletariat of the treaty ports, discharged soldiers and deserting seamen, and drifters who had found their way to the treaty ports from all the beaches of the South Seas and Australia. Stiffening with a pretence of European discipline the Asians and Eurasians of various origins who always formed the majority of the mercenaries in China, they themselves were mainly the tools of more celebrated leaders who made their names or their fortunes, and sometimes both, in the service of China's clashing factions.

The mercenaries first appear in considerable numbers during the Taiping rebellion. The Taipings, who had developed a strange local perversion of Christianity (in which their own leader Hung Hsiu-ch'uan became Heavenly King and Younger Brother of Christ), were at first regarded sympathetically by Europeans on the China coast, partly because of a supposed religious affinity, but even more because their rebellion appeared to be softening up the Manchu empire for further incursions by western commercial imperialists. In this initial period, during the early 1850s, British firms in Shanghai happily sold guns to the rebels and scores of British adventurers enlisted in their forces. By 1860 enough had been seen of the ferocity of the Taipings and their ability to disrupt normal trading patterns for the attitude of the British community to veer in the opposite direction. As the rebels approached Shanghai in that year British and French troops were disembarked to reinforce the garrison, and the Volunteers more than once stood to their arms. The local Chinese merchants took advantage of the changing climate of opinion to form themselves into a Patriotic Association and hire their own mercenaries. A local American adventurer, Frederick T. Ward, undertook to raise a force and liberate the town of Sunkiang, about twenty miles from Shanghai. The army he recruited was about the size of an infantry company, but it consisted largely of British merchant seamen, strengthened with deserters from both British and American navies, the very sight of whom put the Taipings at Sunkiang to flight. Returning in triumph, Ward was immediately arrested at the insistence of Admiral Sir James Hope and accused of seducing British sailors from their duty. Availing himself of the complex pattern of jurisdictions in Shanghai, Ward maintained that he could be tried by neither the British nor the American consular courts because he was in the imperial service and had become a citizen of China. Liberated, he proceeded to expand his corps on a new basis, with European and American officers, and Chinese rank-and-file in western style uniforms. Its strength grew to a thousand and then five thousand men, and a victory over the rebels early in 1862 earned Ward the rank of brigadier-general in the Chinese army, and his mercenaries the title of 'The Ever-Victorious Army'.

Ward was killed in June 1862, and the command was given to his lieutenant Burgevine, who immediately quarrelled with the Chinese authorities, assaulted a mandarin and then joined the rival mercenary force employed by the Taipings. By now the Ever-Victorious Army had shown itself too useful a force for the Chinese authorities to abandon or for the British to leave under any but one of their own nationals. General Staveley, commander of the British forces in Shanghai, offered to find a suitable officer. Captain Holland of the Royal Marines was the first choice; under his command the Ever-Victorious Army lost any just claim to its title. His place was taken in March 1863 by a hitherto obscure officer of the Royal Engineers, Captain Charles George Gordon.

Some of the *condottiere* virtues Gordon possessed in abundance. He was superlatively courageous, marching at the head of his men with only a light cane in his hand. He was immensely resourceful as a tactician. He was able to inspire a force gleaned from the international riff-raff of Shanghai and Hong Kong with an extraordinary *esprit de corps*. He was original, dynamic, efficient. But he differed from any true soldier of fortune in his Victorian rectitude and mystical piety. Normally a generous and charitable man, he could be moved to passions of extreme rage when his principles as an English gentleman and an Evangelical Christian were in any way called in question. Perhaps, in the last resort, he fits only technically into the category of mercenary. After God, it was England he served, and he remorselessly drove the Taipings to defeat after defeat because he had been given that duty as a British officer rather than from loyalty to his temporary employers. At last, in June 1864, the Ever-Victorious Army had served its purpose and was disbanded; all that remained was the capture of the last Taiping stronghold at Nanking, and the imperial generals reserved that final victory – which would have been impossible without Gordon – for themselves alone.

Gordon was unique, in generalship as well as in character, among leaders of mercenaries who continued to flourish in China during the nineteenth century and burgeoned as never before in the age of the warlords who sprang up as China sank into civil war after the downfall of the Manchu empire in 1911.

The twentieth-century mercenaries clothed themselves in a thin garment of respectability by calling themselves advisers. There had been earlier advisers of less dubious standing in the later nineteenth century, when British naval officers were loaned to China, Japan and Siam; under the inspiration of such men the old war junk fleets of the China Seas were replaced by modern steam vessels so that by 1905 the Japanese fleet was so powerful and efficient that it could effect the almost complete destruction of the Russian navy. But the advisers of the Chinese war lords hardly fitted into this category, since they were serving factions rather than established governments and had as little care for legality as their employers.

The names of the most famous of them still revive in the minds of Old China Hands the violent and chaotic atmosphere of that dead era. Two-Gun Cohen went into the service of Sun Yat-sen at Canton, as bodyguard and military agent, arranging arms shipments through the flourishing dealers of Shanghai, and on no less than three occasions saving the first president of the Chinese Republic from assassination. But even Cohen's services did not prevent Sun from being driven from Canton in 1922 by a rival leader. An even more striking figure, One-Arm Sutton personified inimitably in many minds the spirit of the 1920s in China. Sutton had served generals in western Szechwan and northern Manchuria, had killed one general, Ma Jui, in single combat, had carried out an epic defence of the Mint at Chungking against formidable odds, and in Mukden had trained the forces of the Marshal Chang Tso-lin, the most successful of the warlords.

The growing ascendancy of the Japanese, and the subsequent rise of the Communists, progressively narrowed the field of operation for the European mercenaries from 1931 onwards. But while their heyday lasted, they were popular in the British community on the China coast.

85

Psychologically they externalized the barely-repressed aggressiveness which had been bred during two generations of looking out of tiny beach-heads at the threat of a dormant but powerful people whose sleep burst at times into violent dreams like the Boxer and Taiping rebellions, and whose final awakening was to be dreaded. At a time – after 1918 – when Britain and the other western powers were already going on the defensive in the Far East the mercenaries seemed to assert the enduring superiority of European courage, and the more flamboyant their gestures the better they were loved. However embarrassing his actions may sometimes have been to the British authorities, One-Arm Sutton was welcomed by the British merchant community whenever he came down to see his horses win the races in Shanghai, and the time he won £30,000 in the Shanghai Sweepstake was remembered as the deserved victory of a hero. For One-Arm Sutton and his kind were not only brave men to be admired; they were also good for business – the arms business. Few of the merchants of Shanghai were perspicacious enough to realize that by encouraging the warlords, the British mercenaries opened the way for forces – Japan and later Communism – which would destroy the British commercial hegemony in China.

After observing vultures, it is consoling to reflect that larks are also birds, and when one has finished with the soldiers of fortune who battened on the distresses of China and the Chinese, one remembers with relief a different group of men who lived by courage on the edge of the British community, and adventured without a thought in their mind of power or wealth. These were the wandering scientists who so often combined the functions of explorers.

During the nineteenth century, the great age of natural history, there were no wealthy foundations to subsidize research, and scientists – even of Darwin's stature – were often splendid amateurs without even a university to employ or support them. Fortunately the museums of the world were just beginning to build up their natural history collections and the greatest naturalist who came to the Far East, Alfred Russel Wallace, financed more than seven years of residence and travel in the Malay world by the sale of his duplicate specimens of insects, birds and mammals. During that time Wallace collected thousands of new species, studied the habits of such exotic creatures as the bird of paradise and the orang-outang, and experienced native life in a depth achieved by few of those who remained within the enclaves of the port cities. He was the guest of remote sultans in the Celebes and of European hermits who considered their past world well lost as they lived out their days trading in remote inlets in the heart of the archipelago. He made long and risky voyages by native prahus, and one such, from Macassar to the remote Aru Islands west of New Guinea, was, apart from its scientific interest, a remarkable feat of seamanship. He even went to New Guinea and stayed there for several months, the first European to live alone on that dangerous and virtually unknown island. As the crown of his voyage he experienced on the island of Amboyna the famous flash of intellectual light which led him to formulate, contemporaneously with Darwin, the theory of evolution by natural selection.

There were many lesser men, bird hunters, entomologists and botanists, who made modest livings during the nineteenth century collecting specimens in the Far East, but none of them achieved as much as Wallace or left such a remarkable record of the life of the region as his *Malay Archipelago* (1869). But there is one among them whose work was sufficiently different from Wallace's to be worth remembering, particularly as it brought about a revolution in the trade of the China coast.

The botanist Robert Fortune first arrived on the China coast in 1843, as a collector for the Royal Horticultural Society. He gathered a number of valuable specimens, and after almost losing them and his life in a foray with pirates, returned home successfully. He had acquired a serviceable knowledge of Chinese and had shown a peculiar talent for making friends with ordinary Chinese people, whose habits he observed very carefully. His next expedition was on behalf of the East India Company to the inland district of Bohea, whence came the best teas of China. It was a voyage of exploration as well as collection, for no European had been there before him. The journey had all the elements of romantic adventure. Fortune travelled in disguise, pretending to be a Chinese from a distant province beyond the Great Wall. He went through forbidden cities, sailed down frightening rapids and climbed the high mountains between Kiangsi and Fukien. At last, by dint of formidable patience and endurance, he reached Bohea, 'drank the fragrant herb, pure and unadulterated on its native hills', and secured seeds and plants which, with prodigious difficulties, he brought down to the coast and shipped to India in 1851. They became the foundation of the plantations of Darjeeling and Assam, whose trade in a few years rivalled and shortly far exceeded that of China.

In the pure Elizabethan sense, Wallace and Fortune may have been the greatest, and they were certainly the most attractive, of the celebrated British adventurers to the eastern seas.

6

MEN AND THE LAND

The relationship between the British and the soil of the lands they dominated in the Far East was directly related to the smallness of their numbers. There was no mass colonization of any portion of this region by men and women of British stock. The dreams of Captain Forrest and even – in his more exalted moments – of Stamford Raffles, remained unfulfilled. China and Japan were already too crowded for colonization. Malaya was still, in the early nineteenth century, an amazingly empty country, but its climate effectively repelled those who willingly toiled with their own hands to break the Canadian prairies and to build sheep farms in Australia and New Zealand. The British remained a minute minority. Even in Malaya, at their most numerous, they were never more than about one to every three hundred of the population; add their Eurasian descendants, and the combined population with British blood in its veins still remained considerably less than 1 per cent.

Inevitably, as in government, the role of this minority in exploiting the land became a directive one, and they evolved methods that were suited to such a situation. Where they mined, or exploited the forests, it was with great companies of Asian labourers hired on coolie contracts. Where they farmed, there was never a question of tending the soil with their own hands; it was usually done by gangs of indentured Tamil workers brought from the overpopulated regions of southern India. The plantation system they created had profound effects on the societies of Malaya and Borneo. By the mass importation of Indians and Chinese who stayed to create families, it shifted the balance of population until the Malays became a minority in their own land. And by evolving a system of cultivation directed towards cash profit rather than subsistence, and towards export rather than home consumption, the planters and the tin miners created in Malaya an economy mainly dependent on the fate of two commodities in the world market. Still, a decade after liberation, these consequences of the plantation and mining systems have profound social and economic effects on Malayan life.

Like so much else that was British in the Far East, the plantation system began in the East India Company's unprofitable settlement of Bencoolen. Fairly early at Bencoolen, the Company had begun to supplement its collection of pepper from native growers by establishing its own pepper gardens, but in the latter half of the eighteenth century independent European planters appeared, particularly in the locality of Fort Marlborough, and by the early nineteenth century they controlled a considerable proportion of the plantations. Some of these planters were men who had found their way to Bencoolen as country merchants, but many were former company's servants who had retired on the profits of private trade or had been dismissed in one of the reductions of staff which took place periodically at Bencoolen in the interests of economy.

Labour is always one of the prime problems in a plantation economy, and the pioneers at Bencoolen were no exception. At first they used slaves, largely imported from primitive areas like Nias Island off the west coast of Sumatra, but Raffles ended chattel slavery and in its place the planters resorted to the local custom of debt slavery by the simple expedient of offering monetary loans to the local Sumatrans, who rarely succeeded in more than paying the interest. By 1819 it was estimated that half the native population of the region around Fort Marlborough were debt slaves. The remaining needs of the planters were met by convicts whom Raffles obligingly imported.

All these efforts came to an end when the Dutch regained Bencoolen. Meanwhile, the establishment of plantations in Penang, the first British settlement on the Malay peninsula, was at first hindered by the company policy regarding land grants. In the beginning Light had been given authority by Lord Cornwallis, the governor-general, to 'receive such colonists as you may think it safe and advisable to admit and to give each family such portion of the land as circumstances will allow and you may judge expedient'. The land was covered with dense jungle; Light was inclined to regard it as of little value and to grant it rather freely to all askers, with the promise of a future title of ownership. The result was that the best lands, particularly in the neighbourhood of Georgetown, passed into the hands of country traders, and in 1794 the Bengal government decided to remedy the situation by a drastic measure which had the effect of stifling for half a century the progress of planting in Penang. They decreed that no European should be granted more than three hundred orlongs (four hundred acres), and that grants in perpetuity should cease;

henceforward planters would receive leases limited to five years in extent.

The British were not interested in small plantations; neither they nor the Chinese were interested in short leases; clearing and cultivation alike languished. Only one man, James Scott's partner and successor, David Brown, remained confident of the possibilities of planting on Penang, and he steadily bought out or acquired through lapsed mortgages the few estates covered by perpetual titles, planting nutmeg and clove, which by the 1830s commanded more attention than pepper in world markets, but which could not be planted on short-lease land since the trees took several years to reach maturity and bear. At last, in the early 1840s, the Company changed its policy, perpetual grants were made, and many plantations were laid out, until by 1847 half the island was covered with groves of nutmeg and clove. In 1860 the spice plantations of Penang were destroyed by blight; by the time they were replanted and bearing again, the focus of plantation activity in Malaya had begun to shift to the native states.

In Penang many of the plantations remained in the hands of British settlers; in the other Straits Settlements Europeans played a relatively minor role. In Malacca the land situation left by the Dutch was so complicated that in the early days of British occupation no plantations were established there. At Singapore most of the Europeans who tried to establish plantations gave up when they found the island unsuitable for the cultivation of spice trees or sugar cane. It was left to the energetic Chinese to turn the land to quick profit by planting gambier, a shrub much used in the Far East for dying, tanning and medicine. Their methods of cultivation were extremely wasteful, since they never fertilized the soil and when they had exhausted one area of land moved on to clear more jungle for the next planting. In this way, by 1860, most of the arable land of Singapore was abandoned waste. The Chinese carried their primitive methods across the Straits to Johore, and so they became the pioneers of the great movement of plantation that changed the whole face of the Malayan peninsula during the last decades of the nineteenth century.

Early British planters in Penang and Singapore had been mainly country traders and former servants of the East India Company, with comparatively little training in the arts and sciences of cultivation. The new wave of planters who began to appear in the native states within a decade of the establishment of British protection were mostly men who had already learnt their profession in the long established plantations of Ceylon. The first of them, who arrived about 1881 in Selangor and Perak and settled particularly in the region of Klang and along the new railway line to Kuala Lumpur, were attracted by the possibilities of growing coffee, and at first they were successful; the plants grew well on the cleared soil of the jungle and the berries were of excellent quality. Less experienced men, who had failed at tin mining, joined the original planters, and a considerable industry had already developed when world over-production brought the coffee prices down; only the most experienced planters, able to economize ruthlessly, could survive.

It was these men, the pick of the Ceylon veterans, who were to play their part in the transformation of the Malayan plantations which took place after the introduction of Hevea Brasiliensis, the Brazilian rubber tree. In the 1870s the wild trees of the Amazons provided most of the world's supply of rubber, and the Brazilians endeavoured to perpetuate the monopoly of the trade by forbidding the export of rubber plants. In 1876, however, Henry Wickham succeeded in smuggling a large quantity of seeds out of the country to England. The seeds were immediately planted in Kew Gardens and before the year was out nearly two thousand rubber seedlings had been sent to Ceylon (at this time the area of most intensive plantation). Twenty-two were sent to Malaya, and out of these the world's greatest rubber industry was bred. Thirteen were planted in the Economic Gardens at Singapore and the rest at various places in the state of Perak.

There, for more than a decade, they grew almost unnoticed into mature trees, until in 1888 the botanist H. N. Ridley arrived at Singapore. He realized that the trees were ripe for production, experimented with methods of tapping, and with the support of local officials (particularly Sir Hugh Low, the resident of Perak), went around the Malay states trying to persuade the barely solvent coffee planters to experiment with rubber. Ridley's sense of mission gave his efforts the flavour of monomania, and as he wandered up and down the peninsula with his pockets crammed with seeds gathered from the trees in Singapore, he acquired the name of Rubber Ridley.

Finally, in the early 1890s, Ridley found two men with enough capital and patience to lay down a small plantation of rubber and wait until the trees produced. These were the brothers R.C.M. and D.C.F.Kinderley of Kajang; shortly afterwards a Chinese landowner in Malacca, Tan Chay Yang, followed their example. Tan Chay Yang tapped rubber in 1898 and showed it at the Malacca Exhibition of that year. In 1901 the production of plantation rubber from Malaya had reached 134 tons, about one four-hundredth of the Brazilian production of wild rubber. Both the government and the planters realized the importance of these developments. Intensive, officially-sponsored research probed the problems of rubber growing in Malaya; long leases were granted to encourage planters to sink capital in trees that took six to seven years to mature. By 1913 the production of the Malayan plantations already equalled the production of wild rubber in Brazil. The first world war gave a further stimulus to rubber production. By 1922 some 1,400,000 acres had been planted. By 1928 95 per cent of the world's rubber was produced in Malaya; by 1940, in spite of the temporary slump in rubber during the Depression and the competition of new regions of production like Malabar and the Dutch East Indies, the area under plantation had risen to 2,100,000 acres. The great regimented groves of rubber trees that net so many miles of Malaya in their regular patterns were laid out and planted at this time.

With the rise of the Malayan rubber industry came a transformation of the plantation system, based on large-scale capital investment. The jungle had to be cleared by gangs of Chinese labourers hired on contract. Then the Indians (almost always Tamils), who would be the regular workmen, had to be recruited to plant the trees and keep the ground cultivated. Long years and many pay days afterwards, they would tap them and gather and process the rubber. The individual planters who had survived from the days of coffee cultivation were largely bought up or replaced by absentee owners – companies operating from headquarters in London, though often partly financed by the savings of British men and women who had spent their lives in Malaya. When, later on, the oil palm from Africa was found to be a profitable plantation tree (yielding up to 20 per cent on capital), its cultivation was organized in the same way. By 1950 the Chinese and Indian owned plantations were more numerous than the British owned; there were about one thousand of them in comparison with eight hundred owned by Europeans. But, while the average Asian-owned plantation (not counting the smallholdings of a few acres each) was 340 acres in extent, the average British plantation was 1,800 acres, and very few were less than one thousand acres. About 98 per cent of the Asian plantations were owned by private individuals whose families often carried out much of the work. But nearly 75 per cent of the British estates had passed out of the hands of private owners into those of public liability companies.

The effect of this change was that even before the First World War the average planter had become an employee rather than an owner. While the owning companies were situated in London, the Malayan operation of their estates was usually in the hands of managing agency houses, of which Guthrie and Company, Harrison and Crosfield and Sime Darby were the best known. These companies hired the managers and staffs and were generally responsible for running the plantations and selling their products. Thus the link between the real owners and the plantations was

Adventurers, Miners and Planters

Sir James Brooke, Raja of Sarawak, 1803–68.

A Javan chief in ordinary dress, an illustration from Sir Stamford Raffles' *History of Java*.

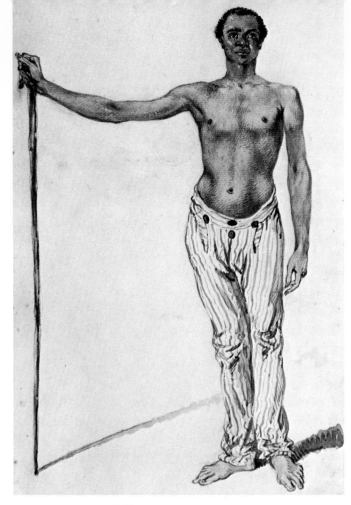

(*left*) Benjamin, a slave purchased at Batavia by Sir George Staunton and painted by Alexander.

J. Clunies Ross, the uncrowned king of the Cocos-Keeling Islands.

Alfred Russel Wallace, explorer and naturalist, author of *The Malay Archipelago* and a firm friend of Raja James Brooke.

(*above*) The tomb of Caroli Cathcart buried at a Dutch port, having died at sea in 1788, during a voyage of exploration to the Far East.

(*below*) Malayan slaves at Bencoolen, painted by Alexander in 1794.

(*above*) Englishmen embarking on the lake of Taal, for the Volcan Isle, an illustration from H. T. Ellis's *Hong Kong to Manilla*, 1859.

(*below*) A Chinese pig-farm in the mid-nineteenth century.

Junk farming: duck and other waterfowl being released onto a river.

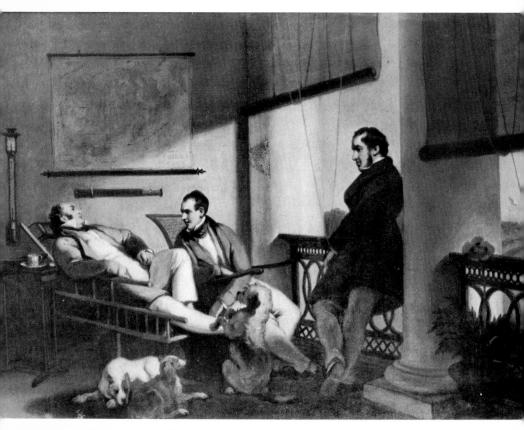

The verandah of Dent and Co.'s residence at Macao, with Mr Durand, Mr Hunter and Captain Hall.

A neglected rubber plantation: the trees have not been pollarded and the ground is unweeded.

Open-cast tin mining near Kuala Lumpur, Malaya.

A well-tended rubber estate at Penang.

1935; rest while overseeing clearing and planting.

very indirect and resulted in a highly impersonal profit-and-loss attitude towards their operation.

Most plantations were run by a British manager and one or more assistants. The number of European staff varied in accordance with the price of rubber, and during the depression years of the 1930s there were wholesale dismissals of junior assistants, so that by 1933 the average planter was supervising 1,400 acres as opposed to 700 acres in 1929. This, admittedly, was a short-lived situation, and as soon as the price of rubber began to rise with the threat of war in the late 1930s, the plantations went back to full production on extended acres of land and the staffs were increased.

The planter fitted in to the middle-class world of the British Far East, but he tended to belong to its lower stratum, since he needed neither the education required of the administrators nor the family connections which usually provided an entry into the large merchant houses of Malaya and the China coast. Economically he was generally rather worse off than either the administrator or the commercial employee. It is true that the comparatively low plantation salaries were supplemented in boom years by bonus payments, and planters were given free accommodation, but pay was cut drastically in hard times. Even in the early days, a few managers of very large plantations lived well, and in the 1950s and 1960s there has been a general improvement in conditions of employment, but generally speaking during the British period the planters lived a harder life for less money than most Europeans in the Far East.

Malaria was rife everywhere in Malaya during the early years and was not brought effectively under control until after the Second World War, so that many planters – even if they did not die on their estates – returned to England in broken health, subject to recurrent attacks of ague. Those who were married could rarely afford to send home their ailing wives, and it was almost axiomatic that the young assistant could not even afford to marry. Loneliness and boredom characterized the plantation life. Unless they lived near one of the towns in the rubber belt like Kuala Lumpur or Klang, the planters formed small, scattered communities, centred socially on dreary little clubs with minute memberships; the few white women, spending most of their time in isolated plantation bungalows, were probably the worst off, particularly when the unaccustomed pleasure of being attended by many servants had slowly worn away.

As for the planters themselves, they were dominated by a routine of singular monotony. Every morning they must be out at five to attend the muster of coolies and see them off on their respective tasks. The days were spent – often long into the sickening afternoon heat – inspecting the

93

endless military lines of trees for plant disease and poor tapping, keeping a record of yield, inspecting the cups and the pails to ensure complete sterility, supervising the coolie quarters, and ensuring the efficient operation of the factory where the rubber was processed. Long after the evening drum had called the coolies back to their quarters there would often be books to keep, the everlasting chits to sort and file. And all this took place, not in a setting of magnificent natural splendour, but of man-made regularity, as soulless to many observers as a modern prison or factory. The periodical visit of the government labour officer to inspect the coolies, the monthly trip to the nearest town with a bank to collect money for the coolies' pay, and in good years the felling of jungle and the planting of new trees, were the main occasions when the routine was varied.

Inevitably, there were many planters who became what Canadians would tersely describe as 'bushed', driven out of mental balance by isolation. Suicides were not infrequent, alcoholism was common, and incompetence familiar; a fair number of the assistants were either remittance men who had already ruined their lives at home, or war-service captains who, unable to find a job in England that would fit their acquired pretensions as 'officers and gentlemen', had come to Malaya with the thought of perpetuating their old status by commanding companies of coolies instead of platoons of soldiers, but without any real feeling either for the country or for their acquired profession. On the other hand there were some planters who either liked the role of autocrat their work gave them or were genuinely interested in the more scientific aspects of rubber cultivation; there were others who found the geometrical solitudes of their plantation a proper setting for misanthropy and yet others who preferred the society of Indian coolies, or their Malay or Chinese servants, to that of their fellow Europeans; Henri Fauconnier drew an admirable portrait of one such man in the character of Rolain, the hero of his novel, *Malaisie*. In the tropics, as in all extreme situations, temperamental differences are polarized and one man's prison becomes another man's freedom.

If the rubber planter imposed upon nature a strict and rigid pattern of his own, the men who exploited the forests lived almost entirely in the shadow of the wilderness. Here Thailand was the centre of British enterprise in south-east Asia. The valuable teak tree is comparatively rare in Malayan forests, but in the jungles of northern Siam it is abundant, and after British timber men had become established in Burma, it was not long before they extended their operations across the border into the Siamese jungles. By the beginning of the twentieth century they had acquired almost complete control of the country's timber trade, and were importing

British staff to direct the logging operations. So important did this foreign controlled industry become to northern Thailand that, apart from the officially recognized jurisdiction of the British consul in Chiengmai over all British subjects in the region, an unofficial monetary control came into being and the Indian rupee was tacitly recognized as legal tender, almost to the exclusion of the native tical.

The logging operations which the British staff supervised in Thailand were – with local variations – rather similar to those in the New Brunswick woods a century ago. The trees were first stripped of a girdle of bark so that they would die and dry out until they became light enough to float down the rivers. This would take two years, after which the trees were felled, cut into logs five or ten yards long, stamped with identification marks and dragged by elephants to the river banks where they would await the floods of the wet season. When these came – lasting from June to October – the logs would be floated singly down the rapids, and, in the slow currents of the plains, be bound into rafts and poled down to the mills in Bangkok.

Some of the forest managers and forest assistants who operated the teak trade in Thailand, particularly in the early days, were men who had learnt their trade in Burma, but in later years they tended to come without prior experience from the same lower-middle-class background as the apprentice planters, and after the First World War teak also attracted many former officers who could not settle down to the humdrum rhythm of English suburban life. Their task was even more solitary than that of the planter, but in a less deadening way, and it was certainly far from monotonous. They would be quartered in bungalows in remote jungle villages, but many weeks of the year they would be on tour, travelling through the jungle on horseback with their baggage elephants, marking trees for felling. At other times they would remain in camp where the actual felling was taking place. When the floods came they would often have to move down the rivers to make sure that as many logs as possible reached the plains. Perhaps the most arduous of their occupations was to tramp up the muddy river and stream beds after the floods had subsided, making a check of the logs which had failed to float all the way down to the plains; some logs took several years to reach Bangkok.

They were subject to jungle sicknesses, to the perils of bad water and the tediousness of unvarying menus; the air in the upland jungles of Thailand was crisp and clear, particularly at night, but the plains were always muggy and enervating, especially in high summer when it was necessary to go down to the flat lands and supervise the rafting of the logs. There were times of agonizing exhaustion and ennui, but also times of

95

delight, of splendid riding or hunting, of dawns and twilights drenched in the irresistible atmospheric beauty of the Siamese jungle which no traveller who has experienced them ever forgets. A forgotten book of the 1930s, Reginald Campbell's *Teak Wallah*, catches admirably the varying aspects of the forest man's life in the Thailand of the time of high British influence, before the current Americanization of the land began.

The planter stamped his image indelibly on Malaya, changing the look of the land, its ecology, its economy, its balance of population. The forester robbed the Siamese jungle of its teak trees, broke down the river banks with his log runs, and contributed towards the temporary British control over the trade of Siam, but in the long run he had little effect on the social life of the country where he operated and even his physical mark on the landscape has been minimized in recent years by the controls on the felling of teak trees which have been imposed by the Thai government, originally with the aid of British forestry officers loaned by the government of India.

But neither planter nor teak logger has laid such ugly and abiding scars on the landscape of Asia as the tin miners in Malaya. The British did not introduce tin mining. It is an ancient industry which in the Malay peninsula goes back long before the arrival of the white men. The first tin miners were the Chinese, who pushed into the uninhabited regions of the peninsula. They would fell the jungle and strip away the top soil down to the bed rock of the ancient streams where the particles of tin lay buried. Wherever they went, they left the bones of the land stripped bare, and ugly piles of tailings, out of which they had washed the metal.

After the British had established control in the Malay states in the 1870s, European fortune seekers were impressed by the success of the Chinese tin miners, and started operations on their own account in Selangor and Perak. They hoped to rationalize the industry and squeeze out the Chinese operators, with their primitive placer mining methods, by introducing modern machinery. They might have succeeded if tin prices had not fallen drastically in 1884. The resilient Chinese, still using primitive but cheap methods, survived; the first wave of British miners were bankrupt, and it was not until the next century that British capital and British mechanical methods, usually in the form of immense and expensive dredges, became an important element in the industry. In 1940, however, only 60 per cent of the tin production was in British control; the rest remained in the hands of Chinese, using gravel pumping methods which involve cheaper machinery.

In some ways, the social position of British miners is similar to that of the planters; they form a tiny directive group supervising the labour of large numbers of Asian coolies. But, while the planters have always been recruited untrained and have learnt by experience after arrival in Malaya, the miners in their own way form a small specialized elite. It is, however, an elite divided by class and origin, since, besides academically trained mining engineers, it has included Scottish mechanical engineers with a mere factory training and Cornish foremen from the tin mines of England; indeed, this is one of the few fields in which members of the working class have found a genuine niche for themselves within the British community in the Far East.

7

SPOKESMEN OF THE
IMPERIAL DEITY

Every Sunday, in the Victorian age, in all their communities around the
China Seas, the British would make their way to churches built, in painted
wood or hand-hewn stone, to imitate the towered Norman and the pin-
nacled Gothic of distant English counties. They went dressed as they
would have gone at home, the men in silk hats and black frock coats, the
women with veils and gloves, and long skirts trailing on the ground. As
the punkahs flapped and creaked (propelled by half-naked heathens pulling ropes from outside the building) they would doze through the sermon
of the colonial chaplain, shout the militantly optimistic hymns of the
Victorian Evangelicals, and go home – most of them – with the comfortable conviction that by a process of benign inevitability the sea of Christian faith would indeed spread some day from 'Greenland's icy mountains' to 'India's coral strand'. When the great conversion was achieved
they had little doubt that the God who had offered them so much during
the reign of the Great Good Queen would grant them credit for this as well.

Most of these people regarded themselves as religious, and some were
so, with a genuine and burning conviction; none more emphatically than
those who, in a nineteenth-century variant of the crusader complex, combined their Bible study with the efficient ferocity of the professional soldier. Charles Gordon, slaughtering the Taipings, was one of these, as
Henry Havelock, with his ever-bearing gallows, was at the same period in
India. They saw themselves as the righteous agents of heavenly wrath
against those who defied the ordained march of humanity towards Christian brotherhood. 'I . . . look to Him who is Almighty', Gordon would
say, 'and I leave the issue without inordinate care to Him'. He had little
doubt that the cause his profession as a soldier had brought him to serve

was embraced within the compass of God's will, and the other professing Christians who served the empire in Asia, or profited from it, would have agreed with him. Most people who ride a wave of history, as the British did from 1815 to 1914, believe, without necessary hypocrisy, that God is on their side. It would, after all, be foolish to deny the evidence, which showed that even when the rulers of Britain had been unwilling to 'take up the white man's burden', destiny had thrust empire upon them.

The average Victorian Christian who found his way to the China Seas believed firmly in the divine approval of his presence there, and within the Church, at least as it became constituted abroad, hardly a voice was raised in criticism of the aims of either commercial or territorial imperialism. Whether or not they developed independently, it would be hard to find systems more suited to each other than Evangelical Christianity with its missionary impulses and Victorian expansionism with its territorial and commercial aims.

Yet the harmony between them was not so complete as Sunday appearances suggested. An ostentatious observance of the Church's ceremonials did not necessarily imply a practical acceptance of its moral teachings. There were many ways in which the British in the Far East, as in India, adapted their lives to the standards of a pagan world, and when this occurred the interference of the clergy, on the rare occasions when it happened, was by no means welcome. 'Personally, I think bishops are a bit of a nuisance out here', said Raja James Brooke in one frank moment, and most British administrators would on occasion have liked the freedom to echo him. As for the missionaries, they were never fully accepted into the British community. They roved on the geographical edges, like the mercenaries; they sometimes came from the wrong social backgrounds; above all, they were often inspired by the kind of enthusiasm which the practical administrator or man of business finds extremely inconvenient when it is put into practice. A belief in the equality of all men before God, too literally acted upon, can produce patterns of behaviour which no imperial society can accept with equanimity. Yet even the zealots, dead if not alive, had their uses to the cause of empire, and without them the life of the British East would have lost much of its special character.

Anglican observances entered the Far East with the first Englishmen. By the time the pioneer ships of the East India Company set sail for the Spice Islands, the puritan revolution was already establishing itself in the City of London, and the generals of each expedition in the early seventeenth century were enjoined not only to suppress blasphemy, idleness and gambling on their ships, but to reinforce these moral prohibitions by daily prayers and Bible readings. Occasionally, a preacher was engaged, like Arthur Hatch, who in 1620 sailed to Japan on the *Palsgrave*, but for the most part religious observances were conducted by the masters of the vessels, and this practice continued on the East Indiamen into the nineteenth century. A contemporary description quoted by Northcote Parkinson (who does not identify his source), tells us:

On every recurrence of the Sunday (weather permitting) the ship's company were expected to be dressed in the neatest manner, and to be perfectly clean. The main-deck was converted into a commodious chapel. On each side of the main-mast, seats were placed for the sailors and soldiers; a table stood in the centre; the officers, passengers, and cadets, had appropriate places; and Bibles and Prayer-books were distributed. An Awning was thrown over the deck, and the sides were hung round with the ship's colours. A bell tolled in the forecastle for a few minutes; silence was ordered; and the Service was read by the Captain (his purser, or first officer, assisting) in a manner equally serious and impressive while the utmost decorum was observed by every person on board.

Even in the smallest of the Company's posts established in the East Indies, the Sabbath was similarly observed, with the chief factor or governor conducting the service. This practice continued at Bencoolen into the eighteenth century. 'If I live to come home . . . I think to turn parson,' wrote Joseph Collet from Fort Marlborough in 1714; 'I preach every Sunday and all the Natives really take me for a divine.' By the 1780s, however, there was a resident chaplain at Fort Marlborough, and in the British factory at Canton a church was built, though there was no resident officiant until 1808, when Dr Robert Morrison arrived under the aegis of the London Missionary Society. In the same year, 1808, the first British church in Malaya – for use by the presidency chaplain – was built in Penang by Hindu convict labour, and, as K.C.Tregonning has drily remarked, 'on government funds derived largely from the opium and gambling farms'.

From this time a distinction begins to appear between official clergy employed by the East India Company or the Colonial Office and the unofficial preachers sent out after 1800 by bodies like the Church Missionary Society, the London Missionary Society, the British and Foreign Bible Society, and the Baptist Missionary Society, all of which became active in the field during the early days of the nineteenth century.

The first British traders, like their Dutch counterparts, were little inspired by the urge to spread Christianity among the heathen. Indeed, one has at times the feeling that the Company's insistence on Christian ceremonials was intended mainly as a means of sustaining *esprit de corps*. The weekly service, like the elaborate protocol observed at the communal dinner table, helped to solidify the tiny community; it was a light of brotherhood – even more than of faith – in the surrounding heathen darkness. Towards other Christians, who set out to make converts (which in practice meant the Catholics of Portugal and Spain), the East India men showed a positive hostility. With their knowledge of Jesuit activities in Britain it is not surprising that they accepted the view of oriental rulers that missionary activities were a form of political infiltration. In the context of the times it is understandable, even if deplorable, that the English merchants at Hirado abetted the Japanese in their persecution of Christians to the extent of informing the local authorities of the hiding places of Franciscan missionaries.

Accidentally or not, the conversion of the heathen only became a dominant preoccupation of British Protestants during the formative years of the second British empire. The historic Anglican missionary organizations, like the Society for the Propagation of the Gospel and the Society for the Propagation of Christian Knowledge, founded a hundred years before, took little interest in the Far East, where it was the new societies founded on the impulse of the Evangelical movement that became the pioneers in British missionary activity. The Baptist Missionary Society, founded in 1792, sent its preachers to Bencoolen during the regime of Sir Stamford Raffles, who also encouraged the activities there of the British and Foreign Bible Society, founded in 1804. The London Missionary Society, founded in 1795, sent its earliest representative to the east in 1807, when Dr Robert Morrison set out for Canton, to become the first Protestant missionary operating on Chinese soil. Morrison's colleague, William Milne, reached Malacca in 1813, and John Nice opened the Society's mission at Penang in 1818, while both the London Missionary Society and the British and Foreign Bible Society had their men at work in Singapore a few months after its foundation in 1819.

The conversions in these early days were not numerous. In the Far East, relatively speaking, they never were, since the Moslems found little in Christianity that Islam did not already give them, while the Japanese and Chinese, accustomed to the essentially political religions of Confucianism and Shinto, suspected that the missionaries were really the agents of western intervention. It was for this reason, more than because of religious bigotry, that the profession of Christianity in these countries was often a perilous matter for both preachers and proselytes. The former could be represented as spies, and often there was something in the accusation, since British diplomats on the China coast during the later nineteenth century relied largely on missionaries for reports of what was going on in the interior of the country. The proselytes were often regarded, with much less justice, as traitors.

But Robert Morrison, the pioneer missionary, who stayed in Canton until his death in 1834, does not appear to have made a single convert. Chinese laws forbade him to proselytize, and the East India Company, who gave him shelter in their factory and also employment as Chinese secretary, made certain that he had no chance to disobey. Instead, he occupied himself with tasks which may well in the long run have been more useful. He was the pioneer British Sinologist. He compiled a Chinese grammar, and the first English-Chinese dictionary, which the East India Company bore the cost of printing in five volumes. He translated much of the Bible into Chinese, an accomplishment which the great Nationalist leader Sun Yat Tsen was later to regard as the starting-point for 'the awakening of China'.

Morrison's career in rather dramatic ways exemplified the ambivalances which were never completely absent from the activities of British missionaries. Always, until the end of the British presence in China, the missionary was beset by a conflict of loyalties. He owed one duty to his religion and the people he was trying to convert; another duty to his country. And there were times when, even against his will, his very presence became an excuse for his country's power to be tightened over the land in which he worked. There is no sign, however, that Morrison was unwilling to serve either his country or his countrymen. From the East India Company he received, for his invaluable services as a Chinese scholar, a salary of £1,000 and later £1,300 a year, a very considerable sum in the early years of the nineteenth century. When the East India Company's monopoly ended in 1833 and the work of the select committee terminated, Morrison willingly transferred his allegiance to the British crown and became the interpreter of Lord Napier during the clumsily handled negotiations of 1834 when the British attempted to force freedom of trade – including the opium trade – on the Chinese authorities.

From 1832 to 1834 Morrison edited the first English periodical on the China coast, the *Chinese Repository*, whose editorial tone reflected that of the more militant merchants; at times its voice, as Maurice Collis has suggested, sounded very much like the voice of William Jardine. Morrison was certainly on good terms with Jardine and the other country traders who frequented Canton during the 1830s. There is no account of his having actually taken part in the opium trade, but the same cannot be said for his rival scholar and fellow missionary, the Reverend Carl Gutzlaff, a Prussian operating in Macao who could speak Cantonese even more fluently than Morrison. In 1833 Jardine was sending an armed vessel filled with opium on a six-months' smuggling voyage up the coast from Lintin, and he needed a good interpreter. Shrewdly, he realized that Morrison was not the kind of man to approach for this task, and, putting on a frank show of admitting the regretful necessity of trading opium in order to pay the expenses of the voyage, he approached Gutzlaff with the offer of an appreciable gift for the maintenance of his mission if he would go on the voyage. Gutzlaff agreed, and while Jardine's men were selling their opium he was as busily distributing his Bibles among the local Chinese. Curiously enough, it did not even need Gutzlaff's presence for such apparently incongruous activities to go on at the same time and sometimes in the same hands; James Innes, one of the most ruthless of Jardine's supercargoes in pushing the coastal drug trade, regularly distributed Morrison's Christian tracts among his customers. The inevitable link on the China coast between the missionary and whatever kind of merchant might be operating at the time is shown with a peculiarly revealing naiveté in a paragraph from Gutzlaff's description of the voyage which Maurice Collis pointedly quotes in *Foreign Mud*, his book on the origins of the Opium Wars:

Our commercial relations are at the present moment on such a basis as to warrant a continuation of the trade along the coast. We hope that this may tend ultimately to the introduction of the gospel, for which many doors are opened. Millions of Bibles and tracts will be needed to supply the wants of the people. God, who in his mercy has thrown down the wall of national separation, will carry on the work. We look up to the ever blessed redeemer, to whom China with all its millions is given; in the faithfulness of His promise we anticipate the glorious day of a general conversion, and are willing to do our utmost in order to promote the great work.

It must be remembered, in judging this pious simpleton, that at this time opium was freely sold in England, without, as yet, any organized attempt to control its use. Missionaries, as much as other men, are children of their ages, and it is perhaps not over cynical to note that by the time the Evangelicals raised their great campaign against the opium trade, culminating in Lord Shaftesbury's memorial to the British government in 1855, the leading merchants on the China coast had already abandoned the sale of the drug in favour of other forms of commerce which were not merely more respectable but also more profitable and less troublesome.

While in Canton the Protestant missionaries were in various ways serving the aims of the East India Company and the country traders, in Malaya they were already introducing the first rudiments of western education among the Asian peoples of the peninsula, where William Milne in 1818 founded his Anglo-Chinese College in Malacca, and G.H. Thompson, another L.M.S. missionary, started a class for Chinese and Eurasian boys in Singapore, while his wife taught in the same house a class of six girls. Other British missionaries pioneered in medical work, like the formidable Dr William Lockhart, who in 1838 set up a dispensary in Canton, who in 1843 was the first Protestant missionary to reach Hong Kong, where he set up a hospital for the Chinese in the native city, and who in 1861 was the first Protestant missionary in Peking, where, forbidden to proselytize, he worked as doctor in the British legation and started yet another hospital.

But Lockhart, while he headed the rush of missionaries to Shanghai after the Opium Wars and to Peking after the Chinese war of 1860, was not actually the first medical missionary in the Far East. Dr Morrison's funeral service in 1834 had been read by Elijah Bridgman, an American missionary sent out to Macao in 1829 by the board of commissioners for Foreign Missions. In 1834 Bridgman was joined by a medical missionary, Peter Parker, who set up the first missionary dispensary in Canton, four years before Lockhart. These men were the forerunners of a great American movement which was eventually to dominate the missionary field in most Far Eastern countries. The British had taken the first lead not only in China and Malaya, but also in Siam, where Jacob Tomlin – accompanied by the already familiar Gutzlaff – set up the first Protestant mission in 1828. But – perhaps because there were so many nearer fields to harvest – the British were slow to follow up their original leads, while the Americans, once their westward drive had brought them to the Oregon territory, looked farther, into the orient that was their occident, and during the 1840s the flood of their missionaries built up until by the 1850s they outnumbered the British two to one. The same thing happened in Siam and in Japan, and it was only in Malaya and Borneo that Protestant missionary activity, such as it was, remained securely in British hands. And if, between 1840 and 1949, the Christian missionaries played a major role in the spread of western education and of western medicine in China it was due in the greater part to American effort. While until 1940 the British remained the most important western power in China politically and commercially, in the field of religion, and particularly of practical Christianity, they lost the lead almost in the beginning and never regained it.

There was, however, one British initiative which had a profound effect on missionary activity in China. That was the establishment in 1865 of the China Inland Mission, which revolutionized evangelical methods in the Far East. Hudson Taylor, the founder of the Mission, had gone to China originally in 1853 as a teacher on behalf of the China Evangelization Society, one of the many small British and American groups who between them were maintaining about seventy missionaries in China. An imperial rescript in 1844 had allowed missionary activity on Chinese soil, but in practice it was confined to areas near the treaty ports, and, except for Hankow, one could talk only of China coast missions. In Shanghai the London Missionary Society had maintained its ascendancy. Elsewhere the Americans had already established their numerical dominance.

Taylor was a fundamentalist of the purest and most intense kind, believing in latter-day miracles, and contending that faith alone was sufficient for propagating the word of God; he carried this belief so far that he never in his long and spectacular career made a direct appeal for funds. Yet the money came to him. How much it came entirely as a result of faith is another question, for Taylor was a notable publicist, and it might be argued that the highly emotional meetings which were a regular feature of the Mission's work in England and America were a very effective way of asking without words.

Fundamentalists are not, as is often supposed, completely illogical people; once one takes a leap beyond reason to accept their basic premises, everything follows after with a rather relentless rationality, and the curious combination of faith and reasonableness in Hudson Taylor led him immediately to see that was wrong with the missions of the China coast. His missionary colleagues dressed and behaved like European clergymen. They belonged, visibly, to the same world as the merchants and the administrators and the soldiers whom the Chinese collectively classed 'red-haired foreign devils'. The first step was obviously to get out of devildom by looking and behaving as much like a Chinese as possible and thus approaching one's potential converts on their own terms. The methods which Robert Fortune had used to make his spectacular journey through forbidden territories to bring the tea plants from Bohea, Taylor decided to adapt to the task of bringing souls to God. He devoted himself to learning as much colloquial Chinese as he could master. Then he shaved his head, attached a false pigtail ingeniously to the back of a Chinese cap, and, in full native garb, walked out on the Bund in Shanghai. The effect was striking. To the taipans and to all the other people who believed that the white man's dignity rested in strict adherence to British dress and British habits, his action was deeply shocking. He had gone native. He had lost face. He had broken the magic ring of white solidarity. The word *traitor* was not too harsh to describe him. But Taylor persisted in his folly, and, like Blake's fool, achieved what for his own purposes was wisdom. He could travel into the country districts without being conspicuous. He could approach the peasants and the inhabitants of inland towns without their distrust having been aroused beforehand by an outlandish European garb.

Taylor soon became convinced that to achieve mass conversions among the Chinese people a movement of dedicated men and women who would seek 'absolute simplicity in everything' was needed. Sectarian disputes should be abandoned as unnecessary luxuries. An interdenominational movement, linked to no one Church, should be established, aimed at teaching uncontroversial Protestant Christianity. And, to take it to the Chinese, a new type of missionary must be produced who would be willing to live and to travel as an ordinary Chinese might do and to look and speak like him, except that his speech would be of Christ.

Taylor succeeded in creating his mission and in gathering a company of men and later of women who would act as he had done. In their Chinese dress they penetrated into the far corners of the land where white men had never been before. They travelled by litter and by wheelbarrow and on foot; they evangelized from gospel boats on the long waterways of China. They settled in distant towns and villages, and braved the hostility of men and the malignancy of unfamiliar sicknesses. Undoubtedly they made converts, but more in proportion among the pagan peoples of the marginal regions of China than among the pure-bred Hans, and more among the educated men stirred by western ferments than among the traditionalist merchant and peasant classes. From their initiative sprang a deeper involvement, among missionaries in general, in the massive social problems of China. In this respect the relief work undertaken by British mission workers during the great famines of 1876 to 1878 was a turning point, and the missionaries turned from feeding the bodies of the starving to feeding the minds of those hungry for a liberating education. It is significant that Timothy Richard, the English Baptist who led the famine relief of 1876, should more than twenty years later have founded the Shansi Provincial University, one of the pioneer institutions of its kind in China.

The China Inland Mission not only sought to eliminate the fences of sectarianism. It also sought to intensify the appeal of its simple and united Christian approach to the Chinese by becoming international, by bringing women actively into mission work, and by recruiting its preachers from all classes. By the peak of its activity, when, in 1927, it put almost twelve hundred missionaries into the field; many of these were Americans and much of the Society's financial support came from the United States, although the headquarters of the mission remained in England. As early as 1878, a mere thirteen years after its work began, the China Inland Mission sent the first women missionaries into the interior of the country. By the 1880s the proportion of trained doctors among them had materially increased, and in 1882 recruitment among the upper classes began sensationally with the appearance of the so-called Cambridge Band. The Band combined sporting hearties with theological students and officers of elite British regiments. C. T. Studd was the Cambridge cricket captain, and Stanley Smith was stroke of the Cambridge boat; Montague Beauchamp was heir to a baronetcy, and Cecil Turner an officer in the 2nd Dragoon Guards. Its members formed the beginnings of a patriciate within the mission world. It is perhaps not surprising, given Victorian social attitudes, that after their first period of dedicated toil in inland China they levitated into positions of prestige: one became a bishop, a second general director of the China Inland Mission, and two others went off to the fruitful fields of Africa to found mission societies of their own.

Inevitably, whether they willed it or not, the missionaries were regarded on all sides as the outposts of western penetration into the Far East. Not only did their own consuls look on them as an unpaid information service, but the Chinese vented on them all the xenophobia that western encroachments aroused. Three years after the foundation of the China Inland Mission, its buildings in Yangchow were sacked and burnt by a local mob. The incident became an excuse for an exhibition of strong-arm diplomacy by W. D. Medhurst, the British consul in Shanghai, who went to Yangchow in a gunboat to rescue the missionaries and then, when the Chinese authorities refused an indemnity, appeared with two warships off Nanking and forced payment. In 1870, when French missionaries were killed and their British confrères threatened in Tientsin, British gunboats appeared again. It is true that later on the missionary societies, realizing the effect of such punitive actions on Chinese opinion, specifically renounced extraterritorial rights and the protection of the British government. But the link between the patient infiltration of the proselytizers and the encroachments of foreign power during the later nineteenth century still seemed obvious to many Chinese, particularly among the literati and the official class, with their training in Confucian doctrine that identified politics with religion. And this opinion helped to cause the worst persecutions endured by British missionaries, during the Boxer Rebellion of 1900. Eighty members of the China Inland Mission alone (including twenty-two children) were slaughtered; most of them were killed not by the fanatical Boxers, but – sixty-four in all – in Shansi at the orders of a governor, Yu Hsien, whose actions were approved by the Dowager Empress; the largest slaughter took place publicly in the capital city of Tsiyanfu, in the presence of the governor himself.

The slaughters of missionaries aroused ire in Shanghai and Hong Kong. They were used as pretexts by the local merchants and the influential China Association in London to demand a sterner attitude towards China and more direct interference in its affairs. But, though the missionary might be hailed as a martyr once he had been killed, in life he remained a marginal and distrusted member of the British community. It was not merely that he sometimes broke the solidarity of the white ruling race by associating too much on their own level with the Chinese or the Dyaks. There was a haunting suspicion that his very work of conversion and education was in some way subversive. As in India, it was said that converts were spoilt and dishonest men. The Brookes usually allowed themselves the luxury of speaking openly what less despotic administrators only dared to think, and Raja Charles gave expression to the views of many people in the Far East when he said: 'I allow no one to meddle with my Mohammedan subjects, and I will turn out any missionary neck and crop who interferes with them.' In China the educational work of the missionaries was suspect and – from the point of view of the British who wished to sustain the commercial domination there – with good reason, for the western education which the Chinese received in Christian colleges and schools helped materially to produce the nationalist and even Communist intellectuals who played a decisive part in ending the British commercial empire in the Far East and also, ironically, in ending the missions.

While the missionary played his dramatic and ambivalent role on the margins of British life in the Far East, his more domesticated fellow clergy built up in the British communities a fairly convincing simulacrum of the Victorian religious establishment at home. In the actual colonies, the Anglican Church gained its footing as the State Church, under the aegis of the East India Company and later of the Colonial Office, and its first ministrant was the residency or later the colonial chaplain, for whom an initial chapel or church would sometimes be built at government expense, though this was not always the case; in Singapore the chaplain had to officiate in a missionary chapel of the London Missionary Society until the first St Andrew's Church was completed in 1838, and in Hong Kong, when the chaplain arrived in 1842, he had to conduct services in a temporary chapel constructed of bamboo and mats; it was only in 1847 that the Anglican church was consecrated there. In Shanghai the first Church of England services were held in the British consulate, and not until 1848 was Trinity Church ready for services.

Other Churches were often ahead of the official Church of England in building their places of worship. The first Armenian church, which gave an exotic touch to early Victorian Singapore, was opened in 1831, and the first Roman Catholic church in 1833. In Hong Kong the Baptists were the pioneers, opening their chapel in 1842, while the London Missionary Society built its own non-denominational church in 1845, two years before the Anglicans.

Spokesmen of the Imperial Deity

Trinity Church, Shanghai, 1853.

China's Millions

Vol. XXXI.
No. 6.

JUNE, 1905.

Price
One Penny.

LADY MISSIONARY STARTING ON AN ITINERARY IN SÏ-CHUEN.

JEHOVAH-JIREH.

EBENEZER.

ANNIVERSARY NUMBER.

Reports of Afternoon Addresses

GIVEN AT THE 39th ANNIVERSARY OF THE

China Inland Mission.

MORGAN AND SCOTT, 12, PATERNOSTER BUILDINGS, LONDON, E.C.

China Inland Mission, Newington Green, London, N.

Title-page, from the magazine *China's Millions* issued by the China Inland Mission: the illustration shows a British lady missionary about to set off, in a litter, on her itinerary.

(*right*) That the British took with them to the East the type of architecture to which they were accustomed, is well shown in St George's Church, Penang.

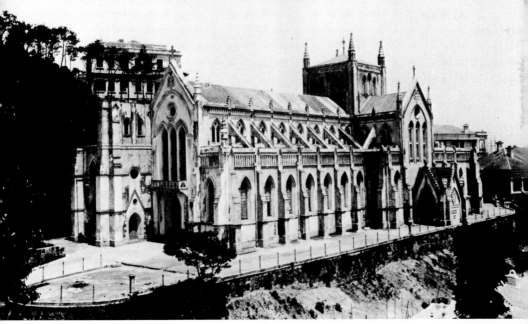

The Roman Catholic Cathedral of the Immaculate Conception at Hong Kong.

The parade at Hong Kong, August 1857, with the Cathedral in the background.

Three veteran Protestant missionaries, presenting 156 years of service for Chinese. On the left sits the Rever[J. Hudson Taylor, the founder of the Ch[Inland Mission, who first arrived in Ch[in 1854. This photograph was taken 1905, a week before Hudson Taylor's de[

Father Nani, one of many Roman Catholic priests who served as missionaries in China

A member of the China Inland Mission with a Chinese Evangelist, in 1904.

The new science room at the China Inland Mission hospital of Sui-Ting Fu in 1905.

Calisthenic display by the girls of the China Inland Mission School at Chefoo, in 1905. The school buildings are to be seen in the background.

(*above*) Boiling and testing opium, China, 1881. Early missionaries tacitly condoned the opium trade, but by the mid-Victorian period they opposed it.

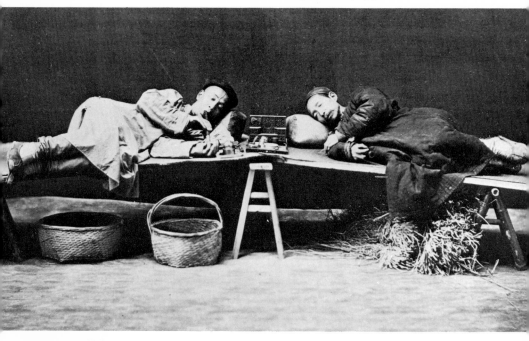

(*below*) Opium smokers photographed in 1874. Opium smoking was allowed to Chinese in British possessions in the Far East, and the trade continued openly until well into the twentieth century.

The early churches were often makeshift wooden buildings, put up in a hurry like Holy Trinity Church in Shanghai, whose roof collapsed two years after it was opened in 1848. But the desire to echo the splendours of Victorian Britain was soon felt in these distant communities, and when Holy Trinity was replaced in 1869, Sir Giles Gilbert Scott was hired to design the new building. By this time the Church of England (which remained established and partly state subsidized in Hong Kong until 1891) had begun to extend into the east its episcopal form of church government. The first bishop appeared in Hong Kong in 1849. The next, in deference to the white rajas, was appointed in 1851 to the diocese of Labuan and Sarawak, and somewhat anomalously was given control over the whole Malayan area, a cause of grievance to the citizens of the Straits Settlements, which was not removed until 1908 when a separate diocese of Singapore was established. In Shanghai, which had originally been dependent on Hong Kong, a bishop of north China was installed in 1875, and somewhat later a bishop of Tokyo ministered to the Anglicans in the treaty ports of Japan.

The establishment of these dioceses gave the hierarchy of the Church of England some control over Anglican missionaries operating in the area, but in practical terms this did not mean a great deal since most missionary work was done either by the dissenting churches or by the large non-denominational movements like the China Inland Mission. The relationships between the regular clergy, who had to live with their merchant neighbours, and the proselytizers in the field was in reality tenuous and not always harmonious. But even the non-missionary clergy were not popular in Far Eastern communities, where the bishops often aroused anger by trying to interfere in the private lives of unmarried Englishmen.

The difficulties of the Anglican clergy were increased by the shifting patterns of jurisdiction, as a result of which the bishop of Tokyo became the centre of a notable scandal. Marriages made in the churches of the treaty ports, where extra-territoriality existed, were regarded as valid under English law. Extra-territorial rights ended in Japan in 1899, and from this period British courts could only accept marriages performed in the embassy or one of the consulates. But the bishop of Tokyo, unaware of this situation, went on marrying English people in his cathedral, which was now outside extra-territorial jurisdiction. A divorce case in 1908 brought out that no less than thirty marriages of respectable English people were invalid, and the children of these marriages were illegitimate. An Act of Parliament had in the end to be passed to legitimize both marriages and offspring. Such incidents hardly enhanced the dignity of this outflung extension of the British episcopate.

Thus, while bishops and missionaries – given the nature of Victorian England – were a necessary element in the empire as it developed in the Far East, their position was more indefinite than that of any of the other classes I have introduced in presenting the composite picture of the Englishman in the Far East. One can contrast their marginal role to the central role played by priests in the Portuguese empire of the East Indies. The conquest of trade and the establishment of God's kingdom were aims of equal urgency to the Portuguese, accepted by every man who went under their flag to the east. For the British, as for the Dutch, militant religion made a late appearance, after the main structure of British dominion in the Far East had been established, and even then it was not universally welcome. One can talk of a Catholic empire of the Portuguese in a way one cannot talk of a Protestant empire of the British. Among Europeans on the China coast in the nineteenth or twentieth century no man of God occupied the position that St Francis Xavier had held in the sixteenth century.

PART II

The British Communities

8

THE WAY TO
THE EAST

Until the great jet planes of the 1950s began to wing into the airports of
Hong Kong and Singapore, the way to Malaya and the China coast was
long in time as well as distance. In the days of sail and the passage round
the Cape of Good Hope it might last more than six months; even after the
Suez Canal was opened to the steamships of the Peninsular and Oriental
Line in 1869, it still took six weeks. The journey through those thousands
of miles of empty water to Penang, and then for thousands more to the
end of the journey at Shanghai or Yokohama, formed a prelude to the life
of the merchant or the administrator, the planter or the missionary, which
he never forgot. And if he looked back with distaste on the discomforts
and the tedium of the voyage, he still looked forward, some year, to
repeating it in the other direction. For the very magnitude of the journey
affected men's lives even after they reached the east; a voyage so long and
expensive could only be taken rarely, once in a decade, once in a life, and
many who detested the east at first sight, and never changed their minds,
stayed on because they could not afford to return.

This was especially the case in the early days when nothing resembling
a regular service of ships to the east existed. The first British traders
arrived in Jacobean ships which departed from London whenever there
was capital available to outfit them and which returned when their venture
was completed, after a year's voyaging or more. When the traders themselves were ready to return, they waited without certainty for the next
unscheduled ship on its way back to England. At this time passenger
traffic to India and beyond was almost entirely confined to the servants of
the East India Company. In law, at least, only the Company's ships could
sail from Britain to the seas beyond the Cape of Good Hope, and most of

the men who by the late seventeenth century became interloper traders or mercenaries to Asian kings had gone there with at least the avowed intention of serving the Company. The few exceptions were those who in the early days of the sixteenth century enrolled – like Will Adams – in the crews of Dutch trading ships, or later sailed furtively in the English ships which plied under the flag of Ostend. By such haphazard means a considerable number of men, and even some women, found their way to the east and – if they were fortunate – returned home. But nothing resembling a real passenger service was established until, in the eighteenth century, the East Indiamen began their regular runs to and from Canton, which, if not scheduled like those of a modern liner, were at least predictable because of the Chinese limitations on the season for tea buying; they left England in the spring so as to reach Canton in October and left Canton in January or February to reach England in July or August.

The experience of travelling on an East Indiaman resembled only in a very superficial way that of sailing on a modern liner, or even a modern freighter. The East Indiamen were built to carry cargo primarily, and secondly to defend themselves against attack by anything less than a ship of the line. To carry passengers was merely the captain's privilege, and he had to find accommodation for them which would interfere with neither of his boat's main functions. Cabins as we know them hardly existed. The various rooms and galleries of the poop and gun-deck were divided, according to the number of passengers, into temporary cubicles, sometimes enclosed by wooden partitions with fitted doors and at other times merely by canvas.

Comfort depended greatly on the number of passengers. Sometimes more than forty were carried, including Company's servants, officers in the armed forces, cadets, wives, children, and, in later years, independent merchants and professional men whom the Company allowed to live within its preserves. At such times the accommodation became insufferably cramped. If a mere dozen passengers sailed, there was likely to be room for them all in the poop. But, poop or gun-deck, crowded or uncrowded, the passengers could look forward to months of discomfort; those who sailed East Indiamen in the early nineteenth century included a surprisingly large number of compulsive writers, and their memoirs and diaries are loud with complaints.

The objections to the round-house (William Hickey tells us) are the frequent noises that must occur upon the poop from the seamen performing the necessary manoeuvres with the sails attached to the mizen-mast, especially that of working the spanker-boom, and the feeding of the poultry kept in coops there, with the consequent pecking twice a day, and both points undoubtedly are extremely unpleasant and great annoyances. But on the gun deck, if you avoid the noises above specified, they are more than counter-balanced by a variety of inconveniences, the grand one that of being completely debarred of all daylight in tempestuous weather by what is very expressively termed 'the dead lights' being then fixed in all the windows in order to prevent the sea breaking in, which nevertheless it does not effectually do, for I was often set afloat in my cabin by heavy seas breaking against these dead lights, and entering at the seams, especially so at the quarter galley door and window, where it poured in in torrents, beating even over my bed.

Mrs Sherwood, with her officer husband, travelled on the East Indiaman *Devonshire* in 1805; they booked late and all they could get was the carpenter's cabin. Her description is tinged with the vividness of experience hardly won.

No woman who has not made such a voyage in such a cabin as this can possibly know what real inconveniences are. The cabin was in the centre of the ship, which is so far good, as there is less motion there than at either end. In our cabin was a porthole, but it was hardly ever open; a great gun ran through it, the mouth of which faced the porthole. Our hammock was slung over this gun, and was so near the top of the cabin that one could hardly sit up in bed. When the pumps were at work, the bilge water ran through this miserable place, this worse than dog-kennel, and, to finish the horrors of it, it was only separated by a canvas partition from the place where the soldiers sat and, I believe, slept and dressed, so it was absolutely necessary for me, in all weathers, to go down to this shocking place before any of the men were turned down for the night.

Thomas Twining, who embarked in 1792 at the age of seventeen, presents yet another aspect of the trials of passengers on the East Indiamen. He had to share a cabin, six feet wide, with six other young men.

Having made a bow to the Captain and officers . . . I inquired where my cabin was, when I was conducted down a ladder to it, on the lower or gun-deck, not far from the stern, on the larboard side. Here, the port being shut, there was scarcely light enough for me to survey my new apartment . . . I also became exceeding oppressed by a close suffocating air, and by a sickening offensive smell, to which I know nothing comparable, and can only designate by its usual appellation on board *the smell of the ship*.

For his cramped and odorous accommodation, Twining paid £100. He was fortunate; this was the rate set by the Company for cadets. Majors paid £150, colonels £200 and generals £250, but there were no rates set for those not in the Company's employment and ladies going out to join their husbands or their families were frequently charged £500. William Hickey claimed that he paid £1,000 for his return journey to England, and there is on record the case of one family, with children and servants, which paid

£2,500 to get home. The fare included food at the table of the captain or one of the other officers, and the cabin, very occasionally fitted with lockers or bare bunks. The rest of the furniture the passenger must himself provide, and dealers specializing in such items sold sofas with drawers, washstands which folded into tables, coffin-shaped cots that could be suspended from the beams during rough weather, and perforated shelves to hold cups and glasses. Most passengers also acquired some kind of apparatus for making coffee, together with a water filter (absolutely necessary since the water was always impure), and their trunks usually contained a private supply of beef tea, coffee, soap, and sweetmeats. These items added considerably to the cost of the voyage but the furniture could usually be sold at a moderate loss to people returning from England or to another set of dealers.

Reports of the food on the East Indiamen vary considerably, as the food itself must have varied on the different ships. Twining, with his boy's appetite, found the mess on the first day an ample compensation for the wretchedness of his cabin. Rushing to table at the beat of the dinner-time drum, he beheld on the table 'an abundance and variety which surprised me, consisting of many joints of mutton and pork variously dressed, curries and pillaus, chickens, ducks. . .'. From other passengers we learn that such abundance characterized only the earlier weeks of the voyage; as the live sheep, pigs and chickens carried from England were killed off, fare became notably more monotonous, and when rough weather set in and the heavy seas swamped the galley, it descended to the primitive, as 'a lady' recounted in the *Asiatic Journal* during 1835.

The dinner presented rather a melancholy spectacle, for . . . the fire had been quenched several times during the attempt to prepare for the repast. A sea-pie, a boiled leg of mutton, and two dishes of potatoes alone graced a board which had been hitherto distinguished for its ostentatious display, and even those, at least the mutton and potatoes, could not be kept in their place, but danced about, to the great diversion of some of the passengers, and the annoyance of others.

Butter was rancid; milk gave out when the ship's cow died in mid-voyage; the bread baked on board was detestable and the ship's biscuit worse; breakfast, Mrs Sherwood recorded, was 'miserable foraging'. By the time the ship drew near to Madeira the passengers were ready for a change, and a wise captain, who wanted peace on board ship, would put in there to load up with fresh vegetables and wine.

To go ashore at the ports of call was a pleasure to which the passengers looked forward with almost desperate impatience. During the six months from London to Canton, a ship would make three such calls, at Madeira, the Cape, and either Bombay or Madras. Returning, it might call at St Helena, and there the curious might – like Raffles – be fortunate enough to exchange a few stilted words with exiled Napoleon. During the long weeks between ports, boredom built up in inverse relation to the passengers' intellectual interests. Raffles, learning Malay, was not alone; other ambitious future administrators gained their first knowledge of Persian or Hindustani, their earliest smattering of Chinese, in the cramped cabins of the East Indiamen. Many went aboard with small libraries; Lord Minto read Latin verse and *Ossian*, and Scott was a steady favourite among the less studious. Other passengers formed companies to perform plays by Shakespeare and Moliére, and there were amateur concerts, and concerts by the ship's band, and sometimes dancing, though this did not happen on every ship, since it was offensive to forecastle superstitions. For those who did not read or act or play an instrument, and this appears to have applied to most of the officers and cadets – life narrowed down to gymnastics and cards, to squabbles and intrigues and flirtations. Though the average captain tried to maintain among his passengers a decorum as strict as the discipline among his crew, to such an extent that lights on most ships were put out by ten o'clock and disobedient passengers were excluded from the dining room, the ingenious often found means to carry on adulteries and even duels, and the vain and frivolous got their empty heads romantically turned.

Most of the passengers who travelled on the East Indiamen were bound for India only. Those who had to travel beyond, to Penang or Bencoolen, to Singapore or Canton, had further long weeks ahead, and it is not surprising that the fast tea clippers, when they began to ply in the 1850s, enjoyed two brisk decades of favour among travellers to the east. The clippers halved the time of the voyage and those who travelled on them entered into the spirit of the great races from the China coast to the Channel; in such sailing there was the thrill that in every age attends the invention of a faster kind of transport than those already existing. In any case the clippers were more comfortable than the East Indiamen, with proper cabins, saloons resplendent with gilding, medallion views and crimson velvet seats, and even shower baths and ice houses. With these elegant ships, in fact, the predecessors of the modern passenger carrying freighters had arrived.

But even the clippers ceased to attract any but the nostalgically adventurous lovers of sail as soon as the opening of the Suez Canal allowed direct steam communication with Europe. Even before that they had faced the competition of the Overland Route, by which passengers who had come by sea to Alexandria crossed the Isthmus of Suez and took ship

117

again in the Red Sea for the last lap of their journey to the Far East. The Overland Route had already become an issue in the 1830s, when the private merchants of India and the Straits Settlements saw in the invention of the steamship a means for a more efficient form of transport than the leisurely East Indiamen; the urge to steam was in fact part of the same movement towards speed in transport and competition in trade which had produced the clipper. In 1833 the merchants of Bombay had set up a Steam committee and solicited support in Singapore, while enthusiastic British entrepreneurs were already at work in Egypt establishing a feasible route. This utilized the Mahmoudiah Canal, which Mehemet Ali had recently completed from Alexandria to the Nile; horse drawn boats first operated on the canal but were later replaced by the first service of screw steamers anywhere in the world. At the Nile the travellers were transferred to other boats, which took them to Cairo. From Cairo it was necessary to cross the desert to Suez. For years there was furious competition between a 'travel agent' named Thomas Waghorn, who had secured a contract for the Government to transport Indian mail across the Isthmus, and two other Englishmen, Hill and Raven. Two rival transit hotels were built in Cairo and the two groups bid against each other to secure the camels on which the first passengers crossed the desert. Eventually both Waghorn and his rivals were swallowed up by the Egyptian Transit Company, which imported carriages and baggage wagons, built rest-houses along the route, and, using relays of horses, reduced the time of travel from Cairo to Suez to twenty-four hours. By now the P. & O. was running its ships from London to Alexandria, and connecting with the Overland Route at Suez. A Singapore merchant who made the journey in 1844 wrote an unflattering account.

I paid at Alexandria, for myself and servant, £25 to Suez besides £2 for extra baggage; you cannot imagine how bad was our scanty and miserable food. The transit was equally bad, we were driven by Arabs, of which they know nothing, and the consequence was, that some of the vans were capsized, some of the ladies had black eyes, and not a little burning, and I was once obliged to walk four miles, as the horses would not start. For economy's sake, the stations are now managed by Arabs, and these people have such a tendency to dirtiness, that the rooms and everything else were swimming in their element.

At this time the Singapore passengers had still to find their own way from India – where the first P. & O. services terminated – to Malaya. There were no regular ships and travellers in a hurry were sometimes forced to follow the example of Stamford Raffles, who in 1810 had to hire a local prahu to get him to Calcutta in time for an important meeting with the governor-general. In 1845, however, the monthly P. & O. mail service to Singapore was initiated. It soon extended to Hong Kong and Shanghai, and in the 1860s to the treaty ports of Japan. For a long period the line held a virtual monopoly of passenger traffic from the east to England and fares were considerably less than those on the East Indiamen. From London to Singapore cost between £130 and £140, including the journey through Egypt, and to Hong Kong between £150 and £170; in both cases beer and wine were included.

Yet, despite the reduced fares, the P. & O. boats aroused their share of complaints. In 1848 the *Singapore Free Press* publicized the grievances of the Far Eastern passengers and interpreted them as showing 'the usual effect of monopoly, an exclusive concern for their own interests, and a complete disregard for that of others'.

The passengers from China and the Straits especially [goes on the editor] suffer from the conduct of the Company, which having secured their money, gives itself no further trouble about them. There is no accommodation reserved for passengers from the East in the Red Sea steamers, so that if the steamer from Calcutta and Madras is full, the unlucky Far Easterns must wait in Ceylon for a month before they can have the chance of going on; and for this heavy expense the Company, as far as we are aware, make no allowance.

The Overland Route continued to be a subject of grievance. Improvements in speed were effected as the railway was built from Alexandria to the Nile in 1853, and then on to Cairo and finally Suez, which it reached in 1858. Passengers remarked on the European amenities of Alexandria, took time to see the Pyramids and the Sphinx, suffered the invasions of bedbugs in the hotels of Cairo and complained loudly of the railway carriages. 'They look like cattle vans,' one lady wrote home, 'no cushions, no windows, only holes to peep out of – my bones still ache with lying on the benches.'

The cost of travel to the east before the opening of the Canal could of course be reduced by chartering a ship to go round the Cape, which immigrant groups frequently did to reach Australia and New Zealand. But it was rarely that such large groups of people had reason to travel to the Far East, where ordinary colonization was impossible, and those who did often ran into trouble. In 1866, for example, the first members of the China Inland Mission chartered a sailing ship, the *Lammermuir*, to take them to Shanghai. The *Lammermuir* ran into two successive typhoons, and its situation became so critical that even the women had to work at the pumps; the missionaries later regarded their certainly astonishing survival as one of the latter-day miracles of which their leader, Hudson Taylor, talked so often.

The opening of the Canal removed the horrors of the Overland Route, and reduced to forty-two days the time of travel from London to Singapore. Moreover, the comfort and convenience of liner travel were notably improved, for the opening of the Canal encouraged new shipping lines and broke the monopoly of the P. & O., which had to compete with such formidable enterprizes as the Messageries Maritimes and, later, German and even Japanese mailboats. From this time the accounts of travellers become less discontented, dwelling rather on the social pleasures, the flirtations, the mirrored staterooms, the everlasting conversation which one Chinese mandarin likened to 'the twittering of swallows in the eaves, or of a flock of water-fowl aligned for repose', and the importance of eating, an occupation which dominated each day with its homeric lavishness as the passengers made their way through a breakfast of Victorian dimensions (9 to 10), 'luncheon with beers and wines' (1 to 2), dinner (4 to 6), tea (7 to 8), and 'supper and grog' (9 to 10). Reading some of the more enthusiastic accounts, one tends to forget that these people travelled through the damp, suffocating heat of the Red Sea and the Straits of Malacca without air conditioning or electric fans, in ships which by our standards were still small, which lacked stabilizing devices, so that in mildly blowy weather a large proportion of the passengers were prostrated with seasickness, and which were navigated so primitively that during the twenty years between 1850 and 1870, sixteen P. & O. ships were wrecked or disabled, most of them in Malayan or Chinese waters. The *Pacha*, first of the Company's iron ships, collided with another P. & O. boat in the Straits of Malacca and sank immediately; the *Corea*, with a hundred and three people on board, vanished into a typhoon and was never heard of again.

The *Corea*, running from Yokohama to Hong Kong, was one of the ships serving the long route from London to the farthest British settlements in Asia. But others among the wrecked ships of the 1850s and 1860s were engaged on feeder services between the smaller and the larger ports of the China coast and their very presence demonstrated the changing condition of local travel on both land and water in the Far East. In the early days the traveller might reach without difficulty only the ports regularly served by European ships. In the late seventeenth century it was not difficult to get to Bencoolen, or Batavia, or Ayuthia in Siam, and in the eighteenth century – provided one had the money – it was easy to reach Macao and almost as easy to enter at least the factory area of Canton. But to go beyond such centres remained – until the 1850s and in some regions for another fifty years – a matter of hardship and toil.

Inland travel was especially difficult. From Merqui on the Bay of Bengal to Ayuthia, the capital of Siam, about 150 miles as the crow flies, along a route regularly used by royal officials, took ten days in the 1680s, jolting over jungle paths in sedan chairs and riding rapids in clumsy country craft. Robert Fortune travelled similarly in China during the 1840s, and three decades later, in the 1870s, the C.I.M. missionary James Cameron, who spent six years exploring every Chinese province but one (as well as Mongolia, Manchuria and Sinkiang) had to travel most of the way on foot, crossing passes as much as seventeen thousand feet high. Even on the main routes from the coast to Peking the road system was broken by long stretches of waterway on which the British ambassadors, Macartney and Amherst, had to travel by barge.

As for Malaya, all one can desire to know of inland transport there in the beginning of the British era is contained in a vividly descriptive passage from a diary which Sir Frank Swettenham kept in 1874 when he was helping to establish the residential system in Perak. Going up the Larut River from the coast, he and the other British commissioners turned into the Limau River, and found it too shallow for their launch, so they got into 'the big boat' to continue their cross country journey to Kuala Kangsar.

She was so intensely slow that, after half a mile's progress, we were obliged to change into the small boat, and here our real troubles began. This boat would only just carry us and our baggage, so we had to leave the servants and some of the things behind for a second trip. After going perhaps three miles in the boat, there were only a few inches of water, so we had to get out and walk in the river. The boatman and I dragged the boat, thus lightened, a few hundred yards farther, and then I left him in charge and pushed on after the others, whom I found higher up the river, in an old stockade on the bank of the stream. Here, with some difficulty, we found a few Chinese, and persuaded them to come and fetch our luggage and send the boat back for the servants. The things came in a short time, but the servants did not arrive for an hour and a half.

Meanwhile we had ascertained that, the day before, there had been five elephants for us; now there was only one, and that one had come by accident. We were therefore obliged to compel the Chinese to carry our things through the jungle to Bukit Gangang, and we sent them off at once. At 5:50 p.m., daylight closing, we four – Dunlop, Pickering, Ah Yam and I – mounted the solitary elephant, the interpreter and three servants following on foot.

The elephant was the slowest, and the path the worst, that it has ever been my misfortune to meet. In fact, the path was no path; it was a 'slough of despond', as indeed we found to our cost. It had been raining at intervals all the day, and the track, where it was not an unbroken stretch of water, was a succession of holes, at least two feet deep, and full of water. These holes had been made by the feet of elephants walking over the track. After an hour's progress it became darker than I have ever known it before and darkness in dense jungle feels at least doubly dark. We could no more see our own hands than if they had been in the next State, so we were obliged to abandon ourselves entirely to the sagacity of the elephant, and never knew whether he was off the track or on it, or whether there was a track at all. We were sitting back to back on some wet grass, in an open pannier, with no covering of any kind, and, to make us thoroughly miserable, it began to pour with rain – buckets of tropical rain – and never ceased till late the next morning. We had no waterproofs, and umbrellas were impossible; they would have been torn to pieces by the branches we could not even see.

If we were miserable, our servants were in a far worse case. Floundering through mud and water, tumbling over fallen trees, and tearing through briars and thorns, all in pitch darkness, I believe they wished for a speedy end to save them from their intolerable woes. Indeed, they were in constant fear of being carried off by tigers, and as they could neither see the elephant nor each other, we tried to keep them together by constantly shouting to them, and by the two men who sat behind on the elephant smoking without ceasing. Those on foot followed our voices and the lights of our cigars for many miles. Occasionally the elephant, either frightened or doubtful of the road, would turn right round, and the servants were then obliged to scatter into the jungle, and wait there until he made up his mind to go on again; when he did so, there was no little difficulty in getting them back on his track. . . . We crossed three considerable rivers in flood. We saw nothing, but we felt the elephant make preparations as though to stand on his head; then he evidently slid down a steep bank; we heard him ploughing through the water, and held on for our lives as he crawled up the opposite bank.

(*British Malaya*, 1906)

After nearly six hours, the party reached a jungle road, and, leaving the elephant, tramped on through mud and water for three miles until they reached a post commanded by the mercenary Captain Speedy. In this way they travelled on for weeks in a similar manner, seeking women and children captured during the recent civil war, until they reached the Perak River at Kuala Kangsar; there they got a country craft and paddled it a hundred miles down river to the coast. The journey was typical of many by administrators in Malaya and Borneo at this period.

Japan, in fact, was the only Asian country where travel was at all easy on the first arrival of the Europeans, and that only in the southern part of the main island of Honshu, where the military government of the shoguns kept a network of roads open between the chief towns; the principal highway was the great tokkaido linking the shogun's capital of Edo with the emperor's capital of Kyoto. Along this John Saris, commander of the East India Company's first expedition to Japan, travelled in 1613 when he went to visit the shogun Ieyasu.

Thus we travelled ... each day fifteen or sixteen leagues of three miles to a league, as we guessed it. The way for the most part is wonderful even, and where it meeteth with mountains, passage is cut through. This way is the main road of all this country, and is for the most part sandy and gravel: it is divided into leagues, and at every league's end are two small hills, viz. on either side of the way one, and upon every one of them a fair pine-tree trimmed round in fashion of an arbour. These marks are placed upon the way to the end that the Hackney men, and those which let our horses to hire, should not make men pay more than their due, which is about three pence a league. The road is exceedingly travelled, full of people. Ever and anon you meet with farms and country houses, with villages, and often with great towns, with ferries over fresh rivers.

When the British returned, more than two hundred years later, after the opening of Japan to foreign commerce in the 1850s, the great tokkaido was still open and still crowded with horsemen, chairman, bullock carts and foot travellers. It was a well metalled road, adequate for European carriage traffic, and very soon an Australian named Cobb was operating a service of four-horse coaches, the Yedo Mail, which travelled in four hours from Yokohama to the European merchants' settlement in Tokyo. But the tokkaido had its dangers, owing to the number of armed samurai who used it and the elaborate customs which governed the behaviour of travellers. One day in the autumn of 1862 an Englishman from Yokohama named Richardson was riding on the tokkaido with two other men and an Englishwoman. They met one of the great daimyos or feudal chieftains of Japan, a notorious xenophobe named Shimadzu, coming along the highway with his company of retainers. Etiquette demanded that those who travelled on horseback should dismount and bow to the nobleman as he passed. This the English – whether out of ignorance or pride – neglected, and Shimadzu ordered one of his warriors to attack them. When the samurai's sword had ceased to flash, Richardson lay mortally wounded, and the other two men were seriously hurt; the samurai's own pride prevented him from attacking the woman.

As trade spread, during the nineteenth century, the pattern of transport also changed. First came steamship services uniting the scattered ports of the Straits Settlements. Experimental trips were made in the 1840s, with the *Victoria* and the *Royal Sovereign,* but a successful service was not established until 1864, when two small ships of less than 60 tons each, the *Enterprise* and the *Fair Malacca,* began to travel between Singapore and

Malacca, providing cabins for Europeans and deck passage for Asians. Shortly afterwards the service was extended to Penang, and at about the same time a link was made to India by the British India Steam Navigation Company, whose boats ran from Rangoon down to the Straits Settlements and established a regular connection through Rangoon with Calcutta. Similar services spread up the China coast and up the Yangtse. Eventually they linked Borneo with Singapore.

Such transport was sufficient while British settlements remained points on the map, ports without hinterlands, concerned mainly with gathering goods for export. When planters and miners began to open up the back country and trade began to reach inland from the coasts, land transport was needed to supplement the seaways and the rivers. The first railways appeared in Japan, linking Yokohama and Tokyo in 1872 and extending to other towns, until, by the end of the treaty port system there in 1899, a nucleus of a modern transport system existed, due largely to the work of British engineers and even British engine drivers, who manned the first trains. An attempt was also made in the 1870s to build railways in China, but it was frustrated by the opposition of the traditionalists in power. Extensive construction did not begin until after the Boxer rising, and even when railways were built they formed such a thin network that vast areas of the country were still accessible only by water or by primitive roads, a condition which persisted until the advent of the present regime in China, growing worse during the troubled years of the 1920s and 1930s, when bandits and warlords made travel in some regions virtually impossible and even the railways were unsafe; on one occasion in 1923, an express travelling to Tientsin was attacked by bandits who kidnapped thirty-five European passengers and held them for ransom.

Western Malaya was the area of British concern where a modern transport system was most effectively developed. The first railways appeared for the convenience of tin miners and planters in the native states of Perak and Selangor; the first train ran into Kuala Lumpur in 1886, long before the railway reached any of the Straits Settlements. (It still has not reached Malacca.) Gradually these various utilitarian lines, which carried the planters into the country and took their produce out, were extended and linked together until it became possible to travel by rail from the Siamese border to Singapore. During the twentieth century roads were built into the regions of Malaya untouched by the railways. The first motor car reached Singapore as early as 1898. Ten years later there were 214 people in that city alone licensed to drive motor cars, and by the 1920s a road system of four thousand miles had made the automobile a more familiar means of transport than anywhere else in the Far East. Only on the

Days of Peril—
The Boxer Rebellion

The Empress dowager of China, 1900.

"THE OLD FIRM."

Dowager Empress of China (*to* Old Li Hung Chang). "THEY SAID WE WERE WRONG 'UNS, DID THEY ? TRIED TO SHIFT US ! BUT WE 'RE BACK IN THE OLD PLACE IN SPITE OF 'EM."

A cartoon that appeared in an English journal at the time of the Boxer Rebellion.

西人避亂圖

同文滬報隨報附送不准及售畫報第卅頁六月初二日

(*above*) Print from a
Chinese newspaper
showing Europeans
retreating before the
Chinese at the time of
the Boxer rebellion,
August 1900. It was the
first illustration of the
fighting in Peking and
Tientsin to reach
Britain.

(*left*) Li Hung-Chang
photographed in 1912.

The scene within the walls of the British legation when it was under siege during the Boxer Rebellion.

(*right*) Lady Macdonald, wife of Sir Claude
Macdonald, the British minister to China:
with her husband she was besieged in the
British legation and was among the survivors.

(*below*) The approach to the British legation in
Peking. The large building is the residence
of the chief secretary.

Royal Marine artillery detachment embarking on the *Jelunga* at Portsmouth *en
route* for Peking.

Peking in flames, Chinese houses burning near the American legation.

Peking was fortified with walls about 50 feet thick at the base, narrowing to 40 feet at the top. In height they were approximately 50 feet.

Foreign troops parading through the Forbidden City, two months after the defeat of the Boxer revolutionaries.

conservative eastern coast of the Malay peninsula, as in Borneo, did the rivers remain the principal means of communication.

By the eve of the Second World War, the major problems of inaccessibility in regions under British control and influence around the China Seas had been eliminated. The age of air transport had already begun. By 1936 Imperial Airways planes were already flying from London to Malaya and Hong Kong, and the possibility of reaching the China coast in a few days instead of a few weeks began to change the attitude of eastern merchants and the pattern of their lives. For it is probably from these first aeroplane passenger flights that we can date the evolution that has finally made the business life of Singapore and Hong Kong in the 1960s so similar to that in other world centres. Yet, until the 1950s, few people actually travelled to or in the east by air. Most of the men and women who went there were still content with the improvements in surface transport: with the roads and railways, with the power boats that opened the rivers of the jungle, with liners which each year became larger and faster and more endurable, through inventions like the electric fan. The man who went to find his place in the east during the 1930s did so without hardship, unless he sought it deliberately, and yet he travelled at a pace leisurely enough to absorb and to begin to understand the uniqueness of the world he entered. Above all, he saw the centres of British territorial and commercial power in the Far East at the zenith of their pride, on the eve of imperial decline, as we shall portray them in the chapters that follow.

9

THE WAYS OF
GOVERNMENT

Once the apprentice China or Malay Hand had found his way to the corner of the east that would be his dwelling for the next four or five years, and probably the next decade, he would find himself in a society which was in most respects extraordinarily rigid and stratified. Its first impression might well be deceptive. There was often a look of rawness, of transition, about a Far Eastern settlement that might remind him at first sight, if he had been to the Canadian prairie or the Australian outback, of a frontier town. And the numbers of brown and yellow and black skinned people might give him, for an uneasy hour at least, an emperor-without-his-clothes vision of the weakness of the British hold over the territory he had just entered.

The rawness was there indeed: it was inevitable in towns that emerged, for the most part, in the middle of the nineteenth century and which did not begin to take on the solid stony look of established places until the Edwardian or Georgian decades. But the superficial resemblance to the pioneer towns of the white dominions was as deceptive as, at that time, the impression of the weakness of the British hold would have been. The commercial ruthlessness of the classic frontier was there; so was some of its lawlessness, though this dwindled quickly as respectable means of extracting wealth from the east were evolved. What did not exist was the rough, egalitarian democracy of the frontier. Britain did not export its rebels to the east. Among its proconsuls there were none like Lord Durham, whose radical reputation made him so appropriate for assessing the situation of a Canada beset by the rebellions of the 1830s. Indeed, there were no rebellions and few radicals in the British communities of the Far East for two simple and interdependent reasons; the British population was almost homogenous in class and in its adherence to the mercantile interest, and any divisions which may have appeared within it were controlled and restrained in order to present to those below – the great Asian masses – a solid appearance like the bottom of the airborne island of Laputa which, in *Gulliver's Travels*, hovered over its subject realm, ready to crush all rebellion by the weight of its cohesion. Swift invented the island of Laputa as a figure to represent English rule over Ireland, but it would do just as well to represent English rule over the east, which in social and political terms was characterized by its close-knit pyramidical structure.

Enough has already been said in previous chapters to give an idea of the varying political forms which British occupation and influence took in the Far East – the crown colony, the protectorate, the treaty port settlement with extra-territorial rights. In each case the form of government chosen was intended to be political in character rather than purely mercantile as in the earliest East Indian trading factories or even in Bencoolen. It was an attempt to regulate a free trade society whose prototype, without any form of colonial government, appears in the eighteenth-century settlement on Junk Ceylon (now known as Ko Phuket), an island off the west coast of the Kra Isthmus which connects Malaya with Thailand.

Junk Ceylon, a dependency of Siam, had good tin mines, an excellent situation for trading with Burma and the Malay sultanates, and was sufficiently removed from the normal spheres of the Dutch merchants and the East India Company to become a favourite haunt of British country traders, who built their houses in the little settlement of Chaulang and settled down with mistresses from among the local Eurasians of Portuguese extraction. Here a kind of rudimentary hierarchy established itself. The leaders of the settlement during the 1770s and 1780s were the British country traders, headed by Francis Light and James Scott, the founders of Penang. Beneath the British came the Eurasians who, apart from providing wives according to the native fashion, served the traders in many other ways. Below them, in terms of wealth, came the wretched Malay inhabitants who, in the constant local wars that were fought up and down this coast, fell by turns under the rule of Burmese, Siamese and local Malay sultans. It was this political insecurity, reflecting on the success of trade, that induced Light to call on the East India Company to take over the government of Junk Ceylon, and, when this did not happen, to create the settlement of Penang as a dependency of the Presidency of Bengal.

The combination of free trade and a government strong enough to repel any possibility of native uprising or invasion by local rulers became from this time the pattern of British communities in the Far East. Political and social rigidity were paradoxically the only conditions that would give commerce enough protection to grow and flourish without interference. Stability could only be secured – it was believed in Whitehall and generally accepted among the Far Eastern British communities – by vesting power in the colonial executives. For this reason neither responsible, or constitutional government in any true sense began to emerge under the British in the Far East until the empire was already disintegrating.

Population figures provide the key to this political rigidity. From the beginning, in all the settlements in the Far East, the British were in a tiny minority. Either, as in the smaller treaty ports, they formed minute enclaves on the edges of existing native cities. Or, as in Singapore, Penang, Hong Kong, Kobe, Yokohama, the International Settlement of Shanghai – all of them cities created wholly or largely through British initiative where no cities had stood before – they were immediately outnumbered by the tens of thousands of Asians who hurried to avail themselves of the profit and protection they might enjoy under the British crown. A few figures will suffice. In 1824 the first census was taken in Singapore. The population was 10,683, and of these a mere 74, less than 1 per cent, were Europeans; the rest were Asians of various kinds, including 4,580 Malays, 3,317 Chinese and 756 Indians. By 1901 there were forty times as many European civilians in Singapore, but they were still only 2,861 in a total population of 228,555. In Hong Kong, by 1845, four years after the colony's foundation, there were 595 Europeans, but there were more than 23,000 Asians, mainly Chinese. Shanghai, by 1863, contained 1,657 Europeans, as against 195,000 Chinese; by 1935 there were about 11,000 British subjects (including some Indians) in a foreign dominated city of a million and a half Chinese. In the whole of Malaya, at the high point of imperial power in 1931, when the total Asian population was nearly five million, there were 16,332 British civilians dominating administration and exerting a controlling influence over business, plantations and mines. In all it is doubtful if at any time during the high period of British influence in the Far East there were as many as 60,000 British civilians in the whole region, with military and naval personnel varying between 10,000 and 20,000 according to the political climate. In other words, an average of about 75,000 members of the alien ruling race – including a fair proportion of women and children – ruled fairly directly over about ten million Asians in Malaya, Borneo, Hong Kong and Shanghai, and wielded a deep influence over the lives of many millions more through commercial, missionary and mercenary activity in the hinterlands of China, Siam and, to a dwindling extent after 1899, of Japan.

In Malaya, and also in Borneo, where Malays, Dyaks, Ibans and other aboriginal people mingled together, the British rulers had to deal with multi-racial Asian societies whose explosive potentialities were mitigated mainly by the disinclination of Malays to live in cities or to mingle with non-Moslem peoples. On the China coast the situation was different but even more explosive in its potentialities, for the people over whom the British exercized their domination in Hong Kong and Shanghai, and to a lesser extent in the other treaty port, concessions were of the same race, traditions and loyalties as the people of China, just across the narrow border and were bound to be affected by the waves of xenophobia, and particularly of Anglophobia, which periodically swept that great country. Emergent Asian nationalism did not create a problem for the imperialists in Malaya and Borneo until after the Second World War, but by the 1930s the British faced it on a double front on the China coast, as a movement towards national self-determination among the Chinese and as a movement towards an Asian imperialism on the part of the Japanese.

Such situations inevitably affected the functioning of British rule in the Far East and, indirectly, its social hierarchy. The social exclusivism of the European community, which tended to increase as more English women arrived towards the end of the nineteenth century, never became a great issue as it was in India, largely, no doubt, because both the Chinese and the Malays were themselves proud and exclusive peoples, without the neurotic itch which made the educated Indian wish to become an imitation Englishman. But political power was a different matter, and here an authoritarian paternalism was the pattern followed by the British until after their return to the Far East as victors in 1946.

They were assisted by the fact that there were no large areas subjected to direct colonial rule. In the Malay states the traditional ruling classes of Malays were left intact and allowed the shadow of power; the British residents, who really represented the imperial power and protected British plantation and mining interests, were by a convenient fiction regarded as administrators on behalf of the native princes who accepted their advice. The fact that there was no alternative but to accept could be easily forgotten by rulers whose revenues had never been so capably collected, while nobody in the Malay world was interested until long afterwards in political democracy of the western kind. The preservation of the traditional structure of Moslem society was sufficient for most Malays, and British officials took care that in this respect their wishes were fulfilled.

The nearest approach to constitutional government in the protected settlements was the creation, in 1909, after the establishment of the Federated Malay States, of a federal council consisting of the four rulers, the four residents, and four unofficial members, three of whom were

Europeans and one Chinese, with the governor of the Straits Settlements, in his capacity as high commissioner for Malaya, acting as chairman. In this arrangement there was no semblance of democracy. The four unofficial members of the council were all appointed by the high commissioner, and the majority of the council – seven out of twelve – consisted of Europeans. But, offensive as such an arrangement would have been in England, or in a white dominion like Canada, where responsible government had been in operation for more than half a century, it was in practice a paternalistic rather than a tyrannical form of administration. The Malays, with their respect for traditional hierarchies, were content to be represented by their rulers. The presence of a single Chinese recalled an arrangement traditional in Malaya, where the Chinese, living in their own kampongs or quarters of towns like Malacca and – later – Kuala Lumpur, were allowed by Portuguese, Dutch and Malay rulers to carry on the internal affairs of their communities under the leadership of a respected merchant, who acted as their representative in dealings with the sovereign authority and was generally known as the Capitan China. Such a Chinese representative was the spokesman of his people and at the same time the protector of their autonomy; so long as their business interests were unharmed, few Chinese at this period had any concern with general policies in the states they inhabited. In the unfederated Malay states, where neither rubber planting nor tin mining became very important, and where European and Chinese residents were few, there was not even a pretence of communal representation in the government. The sultan and his British adviser governed without any officially recognized council. Later, in 1927, the council of Federated Malay States was reconstructed on a more popular if not a more democratic basis. The princes withdrew from it. Their place was taken by four other Malays – usually of noble ancestry – who formed part of an enlarged group of eleven appointed unofficial representatives. The other seven included the Chinese representative and an increased group of British planters, miners and merchants. But the official membership of the council, consisting of British administrators, was increased at the same time to thirteen, so that there was always a marginal majority of bureaucrats, and, counting the plantation contingent, a large majority of the British who formed numerically such a minute proportion of the population of the Malay states.

If, in a group of protectorates ruled nominally by native princes, the British – through official and nominated representatives – had acquired virtual control of government, it is not surprising that in the urban communities of the Straits Settlements and Hong Kong, where their commercial interests were focused and the subject peoples were concentrated in greater masses, they should perpetuate the very kind of authoritarian colonial government which had provoked rebellion among American colonists in the 1770s and Canadians in the 1830s. In Malaya and China, because of the Asian traditional acceptance of a stratified form of society and also because of the willingness of various racial communities to accept political tutelage so long as they were allowed to pursue in peace their traditional customs, such a system worked so well that until the late 1940s the only serious initiatives for reform came from within the British community.

Under the crown colony system, as it operated in Hong Kong and the Straits Settlements, the governor ruled with the assistance and advice of a legislative council. Since the Settlements remained until 1858 under the Company's more authoritarian rule of governor and resident councillors (all bureaucrats appointed from Bengal), it was Hong Kong, which came directly under the Colonial Office in 1843, which acquired the earliest legislative council. At first this also consisted merely of the senior officials, but in 1850 the governor was empowered to appoint two unofficial members. Though his instructions did not provide for any kind of popular choice, Sir George Bonham asked the unofficial justices of the peace (who were chosen from among the more influential merchants) to nominate their representatives. The two men chosen belonged to the richest commercial houses in the colony. One of them was William Jardine. During the 1880s a progressive broadening of the Hong Kong Legislative Council took place. In 1880 a Chinese barrister was appointed to represent his people and in 1881 an Indian banker. In 1884 the principle of nomination by public bodies was formally recognized; one of the unofficial members was henceforward appointed by the justices of the peace and one by the powerful Hong Kong chamber of commerce. But the majority of the unofficial members were still nominated by the governor until after the Second World War.

In the Straits the principle of Chinese representation was recognized immediately the Settlements became a crown colony; in 1867 the Chinese merchant, H. A. K. Whampoa, was appointed to the new legislative council. Whampoa was a safe man; he made a great deal of money from supply contracts to the Royal Navy and the hospitality he dispensed at his mansion on the outskirts of Singapore was legendary among the captains and admirals of the China Seas, who would go out regularly when they were in port to share his lavish dinners and to admire his magnificent Victoria Regina water lilies. Whampoa's presence, in fact, reflected the real identity of interest between the Chinese and the European merchants, and, since the British working class was virtually absent from the settlements except as transient seamen and soldiers, and the poor Chinese had not yet wakened to ideas of democracy, this harmony among men of wealth, influence and varying races was enough to ensure the smooth working of the governmental machinery. Cautiously the scope of representation was widened, until in the 1920s the legislative council for the Settlements included thirteen unofficial members, seven of them representing the few thousands of Europeans, one representing the Eurasians (more loyal than the British themselves), and five (three Chinese, one Malay and one Indian) representing the hundreds of thousands of Asians. Only among the Europeans was the elective principle allowed a modest toehold. Two members were voted in by the chambers of commerce in Singapore and Penang, which meant that only those British who belonged to the merchant community were enfranchised. Both Hong Kong and the Straits Settlements were, essentially, trading communities, and it was natural that in their governments the merchants should, next to the administrators, be most strongly represented.

In the treaty ports, even the measure of diffused authority represented by a legislative council did not exist. Under Foreign Office domination, all matters affecting sovereignty were handled by the consular officials in consultation with the corresponding Chinese officials, and on this higher governmental level the merchants were not, at least openly, consulted. They wielded their influence, nevertheless, through their chambers of commerce on the China coast, through the chambers of commerce of manufacturing towns and port cities in Britain, through the prestigious China Association, and, on a less formal level, through the Thatched House Club in London, to which most of the retired taipans and China coast administrators belonged. The nineteenth-century English equivalent of the China lobby was powerful in Westminster circles, particularly as many of the wealthier merchants, on retirement, found their way into the House of Commons, William Jardine among them.

It will by now be clear that in the imperial territories and the concessions of the Far East the British rule, far from being entirely administrative, was based on a shifting pattern of arrangements amongst three parties, the appointed civil servants, the European merchants, planters and miners, and a small group of wealthy and influential Asians, principally Malay princes, Chinese merchants and, at least in Hong Kong and Shanghai, Indian bankers like E. R. Belilios and Frederick Sassoon, a Bombay Jew who founded a family that in the early twentieth century played as extraordinary a role on the China coast as it did in England. Conflicts amongst these interests did appear, but they were never so intense as to cause any rift in the underside of the governmental Laputa. In the early days, particularly in Hong Kong, there were some high-handed and opinionated governors, and there were also ruthless and self-interested merchants, who objected to the minimum of law that became necessary as the colony developed. But as soon as procedures were established, frictions diminished, and by the Edwardian age the legislative councils had become so expert in achieving consensus that it was rarely necessary for the governor to save the face of his officials by throwing the casting vote. 'Tact oiled the wheels', as one historian of that time has remarked. But tact succeeds only when a community of interests exists, and this necessary condition of tranquil colonial government only lasted until the end of the 1930s. What happened then, after the summer of empire had ended in the storms and landslides of Japanese invasion, belongs to my closing chapters.

The colonial administrations, with their legislative councils, and the consular authorities without them, represented only the higher level of government in the larger British communities of the Far East. In each region the Europeans – except for a minority of officials, planters, miners and missionaries – tended to live in urban centres, and in the internal government of these centres their activity was much more direct and autonomous than on the colonial level. They did eventually create municipal organizations of considerable complexity, and, in Shanghai especially, but to a lesser extent in some of the other cities, established political organisms which in many ways resembled the patrician commonwealths of merchant cities in mediaeval Europe. The ability to build up and operate such oligarchic urban governments undoubtedly contributed greatly to the willingness with which the China Hands accepted the rigidities of colonial government. But to understand this situation we must trace the growth of the various cities which the British founded in the Far East. The next two chapters will be devoted to them, dealing first with the purely British foundations in Malaya and Hong Kong, and afterwards with the somewhat different evolution of the cosmopolitan but largely British dominated settlements on the China coast.

10

THE CITIES

The cities of the territorial empire in the Far East were, with one exception, British creations. The exception was Malacca, founded by Malay princes and given the solidity of stone by Portuguese and Dutch rulers. But Malacca was, also significantly, the only one among these cities which did not take on a British character, owing mainly to the fact that its harbour had silted up by the eighteenth century and the newer settlements of Penang and Singapore drew away the Malayan trade which in former times it had dominated. Malacca had ceased to grow and it changed slowly; few British merchants or officials settled there and the Dutch and Portuguese strains have remained evident to this day in its culture and its population. Like Macao, it retained the flavour of an earlier phase of European domination and in the nineteenth century it was – as it remains – the only town in Malaya that gave, even at first sight, the impression of age. In 1865, the Singapore editor, J. N. Cameron, saw it in this way:

The appearance of the town from the roadstead is to say the least pretty. The anchorage for vessels of any great draught of water is about two miles out from the landing; and from this, the eye embraces a view of nearly twelve miles along the coast, extending from Tanjong Kling on the westward to Water Islands on the eastward. Close to the Stadt House runs the Malacca River, and this divides the native part of the town on the westward from the European to the eastward. The former is not attractive, though from a distance, the tiled and closely packed roofs, which gradually lose themselves among the cocoanut and other foliage, have no bad effect. The European part of the town is, on the other hand, very picturesque; for the houses, which line the sea wall, are tastefully built and in most cases surrounded by trees and flowers; and these also become gradually shut in by the foliage on the islands to the eastward.

... Unlike our own modern buildings in the East, which are too often but the pasteboard representations of their original types, all is solid and substantial. Indeed with respect to every one of the old buildings at Malacca there is nothing that will strike the thoughtful observer more powerfully than the substantial character of their construction. It would almost seem, and this conjecture will be borne out by subsequent observation, that the emigrants of the old days were colonists, and not birds of passage merely. They must not have come, as the people of England now flock to the east, to gather together as much of the wealth of the land as they could grasp and then to hurry back and spend it at home heedless of the after fate of the country from which it had been derived. Both the Portuguese and the Dutch appear to have determined to deal more fairly by their Indian possessions, and to content themselves with a luxurious life in the east as the reward of their enterprise and industry.

(*Our Tropical Possessions in Malayan India*).

The comparison Cameron makes between Malacca (he might have added Macao) and the newer British cities reflects a true insight into the differences between the British form of commercial imperialism and those practised by the Dutch and Portuguese, who were much more inclined than the British to assume that when they came to the east it was for life, and that they must build and plan with that in mind. Like the Moslems before them they often became settlers rather than transient exploiters, but the change that took place during the nineteenth century was determined as much by the improved means of transportation between Europe and Asia as it was by the national character of the British. Undoubtedly, the easier links with Europe affected the attitudes and the way of life of all those who came to the cities of the east in the Victorian age and afterwards, but it is probable that the difference between solidity and impermanence which Cameron perceived was due even more to the fact that in the 1860s British-founded Singapore was still in a process of active growth which had not halted since the first buildings of attap or palmleaf were run up after the annexation of the island in 1819.

In fact, despite the differences of appearance and atmosphere which to this day remain evident to the traveller, Malacca set one pattern which was to be followed by the British in establishing their settlements; the division of the town into quarters where the members of various races lived their separate existences. This was no matter of European colour prejudice, of which in any case the Portuguese had hardly any and the Dutch much less than the British. It was an inheritance from the Asian past. Under the Malay kings of the fifteenth century, Malacca had been divided into kampongs or quarters, some for the natives of the region, but others for merchants from foreign lands, so that the Gujeratis and the Bengalis, the Bugis, the Burmese, and the Chinese, all lived in their separate enclaves. The practice was accepted as a convenience to the Malay rulers and to the foreign merchants themselves, who enjoyed both protection and company by living among their own people and who dealt as a group with the ruler through representative officials, of whom the Capitan China of later years was a survival.

Thus, when Francis Light and Stamford Raffles laid out their new cities of Georgetown and Singapore, it was according to accepted Asian practice that they set aside one area for the conducting of official business and separated others for the homes and businesses of European and Asian merchants. It was only in the mid-nineteenth century, when racial prejudices hardened among the British, that segregation for its own sake became a dominant element in this arrangement; before then everyone had seen it merely as a means to preserve the unity of groups. As in all ghettoes, the protective refuge was eventually to take on the aspect of a prison.

Much of the character of the British cities of Malaya, and much also of Hong Kong, is due to the fact that they were planned, in varying degrees, by the men who founded them, rather than having grown up from the haphazard initiations of private enterprise. Most of them began as almost unoccupied sites. On Penang Island, Light landed in 1786 to find a village of fifty-eight Malays living in primitive huts on the little they earned from selling wild forest products to itinerant traders. Here he began to fell the jungle for the tents and huts which were the nucleus of Georgetown. Singapore had once been the site of a walled city belonging to the ancient Indonesian empire of Srivijaya, but it had been deserted since the fourteenth century and all that remained when Raffles landed was a little village on the beach, inhabited by fishermen, pearlers and pirates, and ruled by a local chief called the Temenggong. Where Victoria was built on Hong Kong Island stood small villages, whose people also supplemented the crops they grew from a rocky soil by occasional piracy on the craft that passed along the China coast or up the Pearl River towards Canton. In all these places the builders had a free hand at planning the city they wished to create.

Kuala Lumpur, the only inland city built by the British in the Far East, is also unique in that its plan was determined by the outlines of a Chinese town which had grown up on the chosen site, under the rule of Yap Ah Loy, the Capitan China in the state of Selangor during the 1870s. Frank Swettenham, as resident of Selangor, began his reconstruction of the town in 1884 by widening the existing streets and rebuilding the old attap houses in brick, with tile roofs, to obviate the risk of fire. Thus, even today, the centre of Kuala Lumpur reproduces the pattern of an overseas Chinese settlement among the tin mines of Malaya. It was only when Swettenham began to construct the government buildings outside the centre of Kuala Lumpur that he could adopt the spacious planning that was characteristic of Penang and Singapore, and even here the age dictated the style. Kuala Lumpur, as the traveller today sees it, is the product of a public works department conception of the style appropriate to the capital city of a federation of Moslem sultanates, administered by British gentlemen. Since Malays had long lost whatever tradition of building in stone they may have had during the mediaeval Indonesian empires, a curious hybrid of Saracenic and Moghul was chosen, and reached its apogee in the many-cupolaed structure of the Kuala Lumpur railway station, an unacknowledged masterpiece of the architecturally bizarre.

Kuala Lumpur was in fact the only city built by the British which strove after an 'oriental' effect, and this striving was related to the administrative compromises of officials like Swettenham and his successors who tried to preserve an illusion of Moslem tradition in the native states, while imposing European administrative methods. Penang and Singapore, on the other hand, were Georgian foundations, and Hong Kong a city of the early Victorian age, showing Mediterranean influences and partly shaped by its proximity to Portuguese Macao. These places were built by men who believed, like the great Indian administrators of the age before the Mutiny, that Europe should bring its light into Asia – and the light they tried to bring was still unobscured by the religious obscurantism and the moral perturbations of the Victorian age.

Perhaps more than any other city of the Far East, the appropriately-named Georgetown reminds one of the age of John Nash, the great Regency architect, to which, in time, it belongs. Francis Light, that many-faceted country trader, supervised its planning, and he planned it in classical form, like the Hellenistic cities of the east and the conquistador towns of the Spanish Americas, with broad streets intersecting each other at right angles, varied by the curving roads which clung along the seashore. Most of the buildings which originally lined these streets were of wood and palm-thatch, but two great fires, in 1808 and 1814, helped Light's successors to create a handsome city. Palm-leaf construction was prohibited, and by the 1820s the muddy surfaces of the broad streets were paved and brick and stone buildings had arisen beside them, while a brick aqueduct had been built to bring water for the citizens and the ships that called in the harbour. The plan of Georgetown today is still essentially that which Light laid down two hundred years ago; the comparatively slow growth of Penang compared with Singapore and Hong Kong has helped to preserve it as a fair example of a late eighteenth-century colonial planner's vision brought to fruition.

In founding Singapore Raffles did not neglect to draw up a careful plan which he thought might be regulated by an elaborate system of registration and building permits. Conceiving the town as a long rectangle of parallel streets between the hills and the seashore, he envisaged a central area devoted to public use with – in the Raffles manner – a botanical garden established on the hillside behind. To the west on the plan lay the Chinese kampong; to the east the European town, with, beyond it, the Arab kampong, the old Malay quarter with the mosque and the sultan's palace, and, farthest away, the Indian kampong. The instructions he gave to Major Farquhar, the newly appointed resident of Singapore, on 25 June 1819, show the manysidedness not only of Raffles' preoccupations but also how, even on the eve of an era of free enterprise, men reared in the service of the Company still saw a new town as an intimately functioning unit, controlled and planned from above, like an Indian factory. (Raffles actually refers, at one point in his instructions, to 'the Factory of Singapore'.)

After dealing with the provision of watering and ballasting facilities for ships and the placing of the bazaar and the warehouses, and after discussing the problems of adequate policing, Raffles continues:

6. The whole space included within the Old Lines and the Singapore river is to be considered as Cantonments and of course no ground within this space can be permanently appropriated to individuals. Whenever you may have planned the lines, parades, &c. for the troops and set apart sufficient accommodation for magazine, &c., it will be necessary to allot sufficient space in a convenient and proper situation for officers' bungalows. . . . The whole of the hill extending to the fort within the two rivers and the fresh water cut is to be reserved for the exclusive accommodation of the Chief Authority and is not to be otherwise appropriated except for defences.

7. Beyond these limits, the opposite point of the river, including the whole of the lately cleared high ground, and a space of 200 yards from the old lines, should also be reserved entirely for public purposes, and no private building whatever for the present allowed within the same. In the native towns, as they have been and will be marked out, proper measures should be taken for securing to each individual the indisputive possession of the spot he may be permitted to occupy, which should be regularly registered in your office, certificates of which may be granted.

8. The European town should be marked without loss of time; this should extend along the beach from the distance of 200 yards from the lines as far eastward as practicable, including as much of the ground already cleared by the Bugguese as can possibly be required in that direction, re-imbursing the parties the expense they have been at in clearing and appropriating to them other ground in lieu. For the present the space lying between the new road and the beach is to be reserved by government, but on the opposite side of the road, the ground may

be immediately marked out in twelve separate allotments of equal front, to be appropriated to the first respectable European applicants . . .

9. Whenever these allotments may be appropriated, others of convenient dimensions may in like manner be marked out in line and streets or roads formed according to regular plan.

10. It would be advisable that a circular carriage road should be cut in each direction from the cantonments during the present dry season.

11. A bridge across the river so as to connect the cantonments with the intended Chinese and Malay towns on the opposite side of the river should be constructed without delay and as soon as other more immediate works are complete a good bungalow for the residence of the chief authority may be constructed on the hill.

Singapore did not in fact develop in quite the way Raffles had originally planned. The interests of merchants and the differing views of his successor John Crawfurd brought about quite radical changes, particularly in the setting of the European town, which was eventually established around the present Commercial Square, to the west of the grounds reserved for public buildings, while before very long the merchants were moving their residences out to the hillsides around Tanglin, from which they would drive or ride each morning to their offices in the city. Soon Singapore had grown beyond the dreams even of Raffles. In the early 1870s its population had reached 100,000; by 1911 it had passed 300,000, growing at a much faster rate than either Penang or Malacca. This increase in numbers, combined with the greater flexibility of organization that came with the development of a competitive free-trade community, led to the submergence of the old city of the early nineteenth century in the island metropolis which Singapore has become in the twentieth century.

Yet, large as Singapore became, the conception of its original planners was not entirely lost. It is still a city of broad thoroughfares, and the central areas around Raffles Place and the Esplanade, with the incongruous Gothic of St Andrew's Cathedral in the middle of its green lawns, remain much in the spirit of mid-nineteenth-century Singapore. Also – and this is perhaps as much due to the clannishness of the city's inhabitants as to the foresight of its planners – there remains a kind of order in Singapore which, as a hostile American traveller observed as long ago as 1885, sets it off as the most compact and convenient city of Asia.

Singapore is certainly the handiest city I ever saw, as well planned and carefully executed as though built entirely by one man. It is like a big desk, full of drawers and pigeon-holes, where everything has its place, and can always be found in it. For instance, around the esplanade you find the European Hotels – and bad enough they are, too; around Commercial Square, packed closely together, are all the shipping offices, warehouses and shops of the European merchants; and along Boat Quay are all the ships chandlers. Nearby, you will find a dozen large Chinese medicine shops, a dozen cloth shops, a dozen tin shops, and similar clusters of shops kept by blacksmiths, tailors and carpenters, others for the sale of fruit, vegetables, grain, 'notions' and so on to the end of the chapter. All the washermen congregate on a five-acre lawn called Dhobi Green, on one side of which runs a stream of water, and there you will see the white shirts, trowsers and pajamas of His Excellency, perhaps, hanging in ignominious proximity to and on a level with yours. By some means or other, even the Joss houses, like birds of a feather, have flocked together at one side of the town. Owing to this peculiar grouping of the different trades, one can do more business in less time in Singapore than in any other town in the world.

The order and vestigial elegance Singapore has retained are due in great part to George Drumgold Coleman, a fine neo-classical architect who arrived in 1826 and in 1833 became the first government superintendent of public works. Employed privately, Coleman designed a series of fine Regency mansions, including the house on No. 3 Coleman Street, with its magificently lofty dining room, which he built in 1829 as his own residence. An even more splendid collonaded house which he built for the merchant James Argyle Maxwell is now used by the Singapore Legislative Assembly. But the best of his works survives in that neo-classical gem, the tiny Armenian church, which was completed in 1836 and dedicated to St Gregory the Illuminator.

As Northcote Parkinson has pointed out, if Singapore has – and it has undoubtedly – 'a style of its own', it is due above all to Coleman, not only for the buildings he designed as the most accomplished of all British architects to work in the Far East, but also for his work as government superintendent of public works, in building most of the main streets of Victorian Singapore, as well as the roads into the country, and reclaiming from sea and morass much of the land over which the city was later to spread.

Yet it is doubtful whether Light or Raffles, or Coleman and the engineers who succeeded him, would have been able to save their cities from the chaos of piecemeal private development, if they had not been in control of an inexpensive labour force which was available throughout the formative period in the Straits Settlements, from the late eighteenth century down to the 1860s. Penang may have been mischosen as a naval base, but it was a fine and distant place to send convicts from Bengal, and by 1790 the first contingent had arrived. In those relatively untroubled days before the Indian Mutiny, very few of these transportees were kept in confinement. Instead, they were employed on public works and even in households, and allowed a great deal of freedom of movement. Convicts in

Penang built the church, most of the public buildings and the aqueduct, as well as widening and consolidating the streets in the years after Light's death. In Singapore they worked under Coleman and his successors, constructing the roads and many of the public buildings. Ironically, even the Gothic cathedral, which Joseph Conrad talks of as 'standing in solemn isolation amongst the converging avenues of enormous trees, as if to put grave thoughts of heaven into the hours of ease', was built by criminal Hindus, of whom, by 1864, there were no less than 3,500 in the Straits Settlements. They were accepted by most of the British as part of the background to Malayan life and it was only in 1855, when proposals were made to turn the Settlements into a second Botany Bay and introduce English convicts, that protests were emphatically raised by the inhabitants of Singapore. When the Straits Settlements were finally detached from the control of the India Office in 1867, it finally lost its convicts, who in 1873 were sent to the more rigorous conditions of the Andaman Islands, where the penal settlement was established in 1858.

Hong Kong gives the impression today of being less deliberately designed and a less unified city than either Georgetown or Singapore, and its present urban disorder in fact reflects the difficulties of its past. Light and Raffles had controlled their settlements from the beginning, imposing plans which though later modified influenced permanently the shape of the cities they founded. They had the time to do this before their settlements were overrun by immigrants. The early days of Hong Kong were clouded with uncertainty. The government in Whitehall was at first by no means pleased to have acquired a new colony on the China coast; Lord Palmerston dismissed Hong Kong as 'a barren island with hardly a house on it'. Captain Charles Elliott, who was responsible for its annexation, was repudiated and dismissed, and it was only in 1843 that the island was finally accepted by rulers who – despite the strictures of modern Chinese nationalists – were probably the most reluctant territorial imperialists the world has ever known.

In the prevailing atmosphere of uncertainty – for the Chinese imperial government also repudiated the terms negotiated by its own representatives and did not accept the loss of the 'barren island' until after renewed hostilities in 1841-2 – it is not surprising that urban planning should have appeared at a relatively late stage. Hong Kong was occupied by a British naval force on 26 January 1841. Elliott issued a proclamation guaranteeing to all comers freedom to exercize their social and religious customs and protection for their ships and persons; all Chinese trade, he further promised, would be exempt from any kind of charge or duty on the part of the British government. In response, thousands of Chinese of the merchant and coolie classes, with a fair proportion of vagabonds, criminals and amateur pirates among them, began to flock to the new settlement; by December 1841, twelve thousand had arrived. The British trading houses also began to set up establishments there, though in view of the political uncertainty, they were unwilling to commit themselves without reserve to the new colony and still regarded Macao or Canton as their headquarters. Temporary wooden structures and matsheds began to crowd haphazardly on the site of the new settlement. It was not until several months after the original occupation of the island that Elliot was able to begin surveys and to arrange for the proper sale and registration of land; the process was further interrupted when in August 1841 Elliot was recalled and replaced as governor of the colony by Sir Henry Pottinger. No overall plan existed before the plague of building began. The main road of the settlement – which later became Queen's Road – was built rather casually on the site of an existing track along the shore facing the harbour; it was finished within the first year. Other roads made along the coast and across the island were often mere bridle paths which soon fell into disrepair. The crowding of the Chinese quarters demanded some immediate attention, and here a regular pattern of streets was created, but it was an improvization rather than the fulfilment of any intelligent overall plan, and the bad building and crowding in the geometrically laid out streets has continued to the present as an administrative and a sanitary problem.

The absence of an early master plan for the new city was probably also to blame for the difficulties with the naval and military authorities, who combined with the vested interests of the wealthier merchants to frustrate the plans of some of the later governors to improve the city's look and layout. When Queen's Road was first built the lots were plotted to face it, and those on the side of the seashore ran down to the front, where the owners built whatever piers they wished and even reclaimed land illegally to increase their holdings. This meant that public access to the harbour was extremely limited, while the coastscape of the city was squalidly untidy. In 1855 Sir George Bowring evolved a scheme for a seafront road which, following the custom of neighbouring Macao, he called a Praya. The Chinese who held land extending to the seafront, and some of the lesser European owners, agreed, and Bowring was able to start work on portions of the Praya abutting on to their properties and on to government owned land. The wealthier taipans, however, were strongly opposed to any scheme which would interfere with their control of the waterfront, and headed by Dents they refused to give way. Bowring introduced an ordinance that would allow him to apply compulsory powers, but the merchants who were unofficial members of the legislative council won over some of the official members and Bowring was humiliatingly defeated by a combination of private interests and his own civil servants. The result was a delay in the construction of the Praya and in the creation of unity in the seaward view of Hong Kong.

After the central Praya was finally built, it was decided in the 1870s to extend it so as to unite Victoria with the growing eastern suburb of Wanchai. Between the city and the suburb lay the military cantonment and the naval yard. These cut off access to Wanchai except by the single inland thoroughfare of Queen's Road, which was becoming steadily more congested. The local naval authorities, to whom the presence of a sea wall adjoining deep water seemed an advantage, agreed to the scheme, but the military opposed it on the grounds of expense, and they were, surprisingly, supported by the Admiralty in Westminster. By this time the merchants on the legislative council had realized the benefit that accrued to them from a waterside thoroughfare and supported the incumbent governor, Sir Arthur Kennedy, but in the end both of the services refused to contribute to the cost of the new Praya and the scheme was abandoned, once again for many years.

Such obstructions did not slow down the physical growth of Hong Kong, which by 1911 had accumulated a population of over 450,000 (50 per cent more than that of Singapore), but it did prevent an effective planning of Victoria's development, so that even today a chaotic skyline of office blocks in the city and of apartments rising up the mountainside behind it spoils the great natural beauty of Hong Kong's setting, which in the Far East, only Penang excels.

In Hong Kong the attraction of free trade brought a considerable immigration of prosperous Chinese merchants, who assumed such an importance in the trade of the colony and acquired such interests in Victoria's real estate that by 1885 there were seventeen Chinese paying 1,000 dollars in rates per quarter, as against only one European concern (Jardine Matheson, of course). Some time before this, Chinese were already beginning to buy up urban sites originally purchased by Europeans, and this development was eventually to have a considerable effect on the racial geography of Hong Kong. During the first thirty years of the colony it had generally been accepted that the central part of the city was the European quarter, and the Chinese were content to live east and west of it; this pattern was followed by the surveyor-general in approving land sales. By 1877, however, a centripetal movement of Chinese interests had become evident and it was equally evident that some of the European merchants were anxious to sell up and leave Hong Kong for Shanghai, where it was easier for them to make money since the profit margins were broader. Sir John Pope Hennessy allowed the sale of certain properties in the central part of Queen's Road, which had formerly been reserved for Europeans, and, while he agreed to a new restrictive line which his surveyor placed on the map of the city, he remarked in his despatch to the colonial secretary:

I am disposed to think that the line Mr Price has now drawn cannot be maintained very long in justice either to the Chinese who want to buy property or to the Europeans who want to sell it.

The shift was commercial rather than residential, for the Chinese merchants of Hong Kong were still, as Hennessy remarked in the same despatch, inclined to locate their family homes in Macao or Canton, which he felt was 'a serious political evil'; the poorer Chinese, of course, remained in the warrens of the native town and did not attempt to overrun the European quarter. The result of Hennessy's decision to relax the regulations on land sales was a vast surge of speculation among the Chinese, who in a little over a year bought from European vendors land to the total value of 1,700,000 dollars and materially advanced their numerical position among the ratepayers, outnumbering all other races combined by 3 to 1.

Later, in the 1880s, when the wealthy Chinese finally began to make their homes in Hong Kong, there were agitations among the British merchants to restrict the slopes of the Peak, where building was now beginning, to Europeans. A European Reservation Ordinance was indeed passed in 1888, but the authorities, by now extremely alert to any suspicion of racial discrimination, were careful not to exclude Chinese as such; instead they imposed rigorous building regulations with which few Chinese at that time were willing to comply. However, it was not long before western standards and western education began to spread among the Chinese, encouraged by the schools which the British established in Hong Kong, and the attempts to maintain segregated areas were doomed to failure as Chinese residents slowly infiltrated district after district, until the present Hong Kong situation was reached, in which riches rather than race determine where any resident shall live.

The rapid acquisition of property by the Chinese in Hong Kong was undoubtedly partly responsible for the slow development of municipal government in that colony as compared with either Shanghai or the Straits Settlements. Shanghai was a settlement conceded to a group of foreign communities, who managed their own common affairs and, technically at least, merely allowed the Chinese – who remained subjects of the Celestial Empire – to live among them. This allowed the emergence of a degree of British dominated self-government among the foreign residents which was the envy of mercantile communities everywhere else in the Far East. Shanghai belongs to the next chapter, but it is significant now to observe the differences between the Straits and Hong Kong, which were both crown colonies but which differed considerably in the degree of participation in local government allowed to European residents.

Technically, until 1858, the Straits Settlements were part of the possessions of the East India Company, which had the right arbitrarily to expel any British subjects residing without its permission in settlements under its control. In practice, as Penang and Singapore developed into centres of free trading, the right was never invoked and from the beginning the merchants, who always constituted the core of the British community in the Straits, began to exercize certain rights of their own. Particularly there was the right to petition and to meet publicly with that end in view. Significant in this respect was the petition which James Scott, as spokesman for the European residents of Penang, presented to his friend Francis Light, in the role of Company's superintendent, as early as 1794. The petition asked Light to represent to the government of Bengal the merchants' feeling of the need for a regular government in the colony of Prince of Wales Island so that 'the confidence they have placed in the faith of government may be increased and they be enabled to follow their several occupations without fear of molestation'.

Right from the beginning, the public meeting was an important unofficial mechanism in the government of the Straits Settlements, and, to a less extent, even of Hong Kong. The British permanent residents in places like Georgetown and Singapore and Hong Kong were always few enough to be able to meet, like the citizens of Uri or Appenzell, in one place at one time, so that a resolution at a public meeting, followed by a petition, became a reliable and frequently used means of transmitting the opinions and grievances of Europeans to the local authorities and the British Parliament. Some important developments can be traced to agitations carried on by public meetings – such as the various campaigns in Singapore between 1820 and 1840 which resulted in an effective police force, and – much more important in its eventual results – the series of public meetings, beginning in 1855 and continuing regularly into the 1860s, at which the merchants of Singapore expressed their discontent with the government of the East India Company and with subsequent administration by the India

Office, on the grounds that the special interests of their Far Eastern entrepôt were ignored by governments based in Bengal. The fact that the Straits Settlements, unlike Burma, were eventually transferred to the Colonial Office, was undoubtedly a triumph for the public meeting as a form of political action effective in a restricted and relatively homogeneous community. As in the classic direct democracies, smallness of numbers was here an advantage.

Participation in actual local government began early in the Straits Settlements. Both Light and Raffles were aware that the success of their settlements depended on obtaining the cooperation of the local merchant community. The principle that payment of rates and local taxes must be linked with representation was recognized as early as 1796 when Philip Mannington, Light's immediate successor at Penang, formed a committee of ten British merchants to consider the question of taxation, and found them following the classic tendency of tax-granting bodies to criticize aspects of government outside their constitutional competence. A few years later, after the arrival of Sir George Leith as lieutenant-governor of Prince of Wales Island in 1800, the situation was regularized by the appointment of a committee of assessors as a primitive municipal government for Georgetown. Not only British, but also Chinese merchants, were among the assessors; they were responsible for collecting rates, for supervising the bazaars and for maintaining and cleaning the streets.

Raffles was convinced of the importance of bringing the merchants into the local administration of early Singapore. Not only did he approve the action of the merchants themselves in electing a committee to establish a night watch in 1820, but he himself appointed committees of local residents for various purposes and in 1823 wrote to the authorities in Calcutta expressing his view that 'nothing has tended more to the discomfort and constant jarrings which have hitherto occurred in our remote settlements, than the policy which has dictated the exclusion of the British merchants from all share, much less credit, in the domestic regulations of the settlement, of which they are frequently its most important members.' In 1827 the committees of assessors were finally established on a regular basis in Penang, Malacca and Singapore, with the official consent of the court of directors and the board of control, the highest governing bodies of the East India Company, and from this time there was a steady evolution, goaded periodically by petitions and public meetings, towards municipal autonomy. The committees of assessors, which later became municipal committees, consisted at first of equal numbers of officials and of nominated representatives of the local merchants. By the 1850s the unofficial representatives were in the majority. Eventually, in 1856, the principle of an elective majority was conceded, and the local commissions of Penang, Malacca and Singapore could be regarded as regular municipal governments which appointed their own officials, enjoyed a growing degree of power, and were slowly broadened to embrace Asian representatives until by the 1930s these were, at least in Penang, in the majority.

It is perhaps ironical that the East India Company, from whose rule the merchants of the Straits Settlements were so anxious to escape, in practice gave them a greater share in local administration than the Colonial Office was willing to grant to the merchants of Hong Kong. The earliest instructions for the government of that colony indeed contained what seemed the promise of municipal self-government, since Pottinger, the first governor, was told that in levying rates for municipal purposes he should confide 'to the householders the power and the obligation to assess themselves and each other'. In practice, the ordinance of 1845 which established a police rate placed the task of assessment in official hands. In protest the merchants petitioned for a municipal council 'with power to decide on the appropriation of monies raised', and this was to become the *leit motif* for agitations lasting almost a century. In 1847 a select committee of the British Parliament, well briefed by the merchants' allies in London, recommended that a share in the administration of local affairs 'should be given, by some system of municipal government, to the British residents'. But successive governors, mainly supported by colonial secretaries in Whitehall, opposed the formation of a municipal council of any kind. Their reasons, if not necessarily right, were weighty, and stemmed mainly from the fact that the Chinese were such an overwhelming majority among the ratepayers. British policy in Hong Kong, placed so precariously near the mainland of China, discouraged any legislation that appeared to discriminate against Chinese. But if all ratepayers were allowed to vote, the Chinese would dominate any conceivable elective council. In the 1880s Governor Bowen expressed the view that Chinese conceptions of sanitation, so different from the European, might in such circumstances create great difficulties and that in any case a garrison town, with a considerable British trading interest, should not be placed under the municipal control of Asians. What he did not say openly – though he doubtless thought it – was that the loyalty of the Chinese was suspect, since most of them either maintained residences on the mainland or were attached to it by strong family links.

It was this dilemma that prevented Hong Kong from getting even an urban council (with two elected members out of thirteen and advisory powers only) before 1935; the number of elected members was increased to four in 1953 and eight in 1954, and a real, fully elected municipal council is still in the future. Agitations by dissenting groups, like the Reform Association of 1867, favoured an elective council of British subjects, but what they meant by this was rarely defined, and when it was defined usually amounted to men of British race, which – as Lord Ripon pointed out in 1893 – would have meant the disenfranchizement of nine-tenths of the ratepayers.

One argument of various governors which had a certain validity was that in a restricted territory like Hong Kong it was difficult to divide the functions of the colonial government from those of a possible municipal government, and that the British merchants had in fact gained a fair degree of control over local affairs through the unofficial members of the legislative council, who gained in importance after Sir George Bowen laid down in 1885 a constitutional principle for Hong Kong that the official majority should not overbear a completely united unofficial minority on financial matters. The franchize for the elected unofficial members of the legislative council was admittedly restricted to two bodies – the unofficial justices of the peace, and the chamber of commerce. But figures suggest that no important merchant was left without a vote; the chamber of commerce included twenty English merchants, seven other Europeans and seven Asians; the justices included sixty-two Englishmen and seventeen Asians, all British subjects. The total number of English ratepayers at the time was eighty-two. In other words, an oligarchy of the wealthier merchants existed and was fully represented in the legislative council which dealt also with municipal affairs, while the less prosperous majority, even of the British, had no representation, or voice at all. It amounted to patrician rule and only on one occasion was this rule officially broken by testing the vote of the general British community. This was when Sir William Robinson in 1896 took a plebiscate on whether the sanitary board should have an official or an unofficial majority. The vote was 331 to 31 in favour of an unofficial majority. Joseph Chamberlain, the colonial secretary, immediately repudiated Robinson's action and declared that the governor of a crown colony could not 'seek the guidance of a plebiscite'. But the mechanism of the plebiscite was kept alive by the chamber of commerce which – though mostly concerned with trade matters – would occasionally interfere in matters of municipal interest, and in 1901 it finally succeeded by this means in getting the sanitary board – which concerned only matters of public health – reconstituted with an

The Cities

Batavia, a view from the inn sketched by Alexander in 1793. The very European-style carriage may have been part of the equipage of Lord Macartney's embassy.

A general view of Whampoa harbour at Canton in 1793, painted by Thomas Daniel. The numerous European ships indicate its importance as a port.

A view from Whampoa up the Canton river. The pagoda on the right is at Canton.

Factories at Canton, 1830.

Macao, junks in the harbour and the dock area of the city.

(*above*) The square in Macao, painted by Chinnery in 1831.
(*below*) A view of the Bund at Ningpo, Chekiang province. This was one of the
smaller treaty ports.

The Administrative buildings at Penang.

The head offices of the Federal Rubber Stamp Co., Penang.

View of the roadstead at Singapore, from a mid-nineteenth-century engraving.

Flints Buildings, Singapore, built in the nineteenth century in neo-classic style with an open arcade.

Japanese woodblock print of a European merchant's house in Yokohama, 1870.

The port, Yokohama.

The Bund at Yokohama in 1900, with the Grand Hotel in the centre.

Another view of the Bund at Yokohama.

(*above*) Shanghai: a mid-Victorian hong or merchant's warehouse.
(*below*) Modern hongs in Shanghai, 1920.

A refuse cart in Kuala Lumpur.

One of the many open-fronted shops in Kuala Lumpur.

A general view of Hong Kong, with the Cathedral clearly visible in the foreground.

Boats at Chikwan, Deep Bay, Hong Kong, in 1900.

(*right*) Rickshaws and motor cars in West Praya Street, Hong Kong.

The War Memorial and Queen's Square, Hong Kong.

The Kowloon Railway Station in Hong Kong, with the Kowloon Wharf on the far right. This railway was a direct link with Canton.

Holt's Wharf, Kowloon, with junks and a ship of the Blue Funnel Line loading and unloading alongside.

The Hong Kong branch of the Hong Kong-Shanghai Bank.

(*above*) A typical home of a wealthy Chinese merchant in Hong Kong.

(*below*) The house of Aw Boon Haw, Singapore. This merchant made a fortune from his 'Tiger Balm' ointment – a panacea for all ills, still sold in the Far East.

unofficial majority of six to four officials. The unofficials, however, were all nominated and the ratepayers of Hong Kong had to wait until 1935 before they could elect a single representative on a municipal level. It was little wonder that their petitions so often mentioned with envy the freedoms and responsibilities assumed by the merchants of that strange, British-dominated commonwealth, the International Settlement of Shanghai.

I I

SHANGHAI AND
OTHER PLACES

When the tide of European penetration into China reached its height in the early years of the twentieth century, no less than forty-six places in that country had become treaty ports where foreigners were allowed to trade freely, to enjoy extra-territorial privileges, and often to reside in special settlements where they were virtually self-governing. The treaty ports were not always on the sea; some of them were inland on the Yangtse and others were not on any navigable water but on commercially important land frontiers. Among them are not included the areas ceded to foreign powers (particularly to Russia) or the places which the Chinese had leased under pressure, such as the New Territories at Hong Kong, or Weihaiwei which the British obtained in 1898 and administered until 1930 as if it were their own territory. In the treaty ports, by the universal application of the 'most favoured nation' clause, all foreign merchants had equal rights of trading, provided they paid the customs duties imposed by the British directed Imperial Maritime Customs; but the concessions of land were usually made to the power or powers who had negotiated the treaty. A measure of the strength of Britain in the Far East, particularly during the early period of European penetration, is given by the fact that Queen Victoria's plenipotentiaries established no less than twenty-six of the forty-six treaty ports, including almost all the places of real commercial value, and many more which played little part in either history or trade, such as Kongmoon, Wuhu and Kiungchow.

The British treaty ports where settlement took place on a noticeable scale varied from the silt-choked and fever-ridden little Yangtse port of Chinkiang, where there were rarely more than thirty foreign residents, to Shanghai, which British and other foreign capital and initiative built up into the greatest port of China. Some settlements, like Foochow, Ningpo and Amoy, had aroused great expectations, partly because of their connections with the East India Company during the seventeenth century, and even more because of their convenience for the tea trade in the days of the clippers. But the development of the Darjeeling plantations radically diminished the demand for China tea, and in terms of general trade these ports were not well situated to compete with either Hong Kong or Shanghai. Yet they sustained enough trade to retain small foreign communities of merchants, consuls and European customs officials, who led a leisurely and uneventful existence which suited best those inclined to seclusion and intellectual pursuits.

Apart from Shanghai, however, the only treaty ports which remained commercially busy and attracted substantial numbers of foreigners were Canton, which retained much of its old importance as a commercial centre for south China, Hankow, the principal inland port on the Yangtse, where some seven hundred foreigners lived in the British concession, and Tientsin, the nearest port to Peking, whose British settlement was occupied by two thousand foreigners and more than thirty thousand Chinese.

Where territorial concessions existed at treaty ports, either in China or Japan, they were always placed outside the existing native city, on the waterside. At Canton, where xenophobic feelings remained strong after the Opium Wars, and the old factory area was sacked by mobs in 1846, the British and the French eventually obtained in 1860 the island of Shameen. This was originally little more than a large sandbank, eighty acres in extent, but when retaining walls had been built around it and the ground raised, a miniature eastern colonial city, curiously mingling English and French styles of Asian living, arose to confront the ever hostile face of native Canton. The other settlements were usually built on wasteland stretches of river bank or creek side which the Chinese conceded in mingled contempt and fear of the foreign devils whom they would not allow within their own city walls. This arrangement had definite advantages, for the British who settled in such places were removed from the irremediably unhealthy conditions of traditional Chinese urban life and were able to plan their own towns with some kind of order, a due regard for sanitation, and even at times a certain aesthetic competence, for, seen for the first time from the water, the larger settlements were often handsome in prospect. Hankow, Tientsin and Shanghai all made such an appeal to the eye of the arriving traveller. The concessions varied in size, from the tiny twenty acre strip at Kiukiang, through the hundred and fifteen acres of Hankow and the thousand acres of the British concession of Tientsin, to the 5,584 acres (little short of nine square miles) which the International Settlement at Shanghai attained as it grew to its greatest size in 1899.

Shanghai was not only the largest of the European settlements of the China coast; it was also the most populous, the most prosperous, the most cosmopolitan, the most colourful and the most dynamic. It was the principal centre of British trade in the Far East and a focus of British political influence so important that to Shanghai, rather than even to Hong Kong, the strongest military contingents were always rushed from Britain and India at times of crisis. Many aspects of Shanghai and its extraordinary society find their places in other chapters of this book. Here I am concerned with the character of the treaty ports as expatriate commonwealths. They had – like pioneer communities anywhere – to create shape out of the chaos of new beginning, to turn their raw settlements into trading towns, and then to administer them, since the peculiar circumstances of sovereignty in the concessions left a power vacuum which the inhabitants themselves had to fill. Partly because of its greater resources in wealth and talent and partly because its problems also were greater, Shanghai was the pioneer in local planning and administration; it set an example to the other treaty ports of China and Japan, and became, as we have seen, the envy of British merchants of Hong Kong.

It was some years before merchants began to realize the particular commercial advantages of Shanghai's situation near the mouth of the Yangtse. It had not been one of the ports favoured by seventeenth- or eighteenth-century traders (though one ship's master employed by the East India Company reported in 1756 that it seemed a desirable trading centre) and as late as 1832, when the Company did at last send a ship there with a commercial mission, it was somewhat contemptuously rebuffed by the local mandarins. These officials, however, did not represent the feeling of the local merchant community, and one of the advantages of Shanghai, once it was selected as a treaty port, turned out to be that the people of the city and its region were little afflicted with that peculiarly passionate hatred of pale-eyed and fair-haired beings which was so widespread among the Cantonese.

Nevertheless, it was a wretched stretch of muddy foreshore that the taotai (or intendant) of Shanghai offered to the first British consul, Captain George Balfour, when he arrived in November 1843 to establish the foreign settlement. The anchorage was a thousand yards long and stretched a thousand feet out into the Whangpoo River; the land accompanying it was a low lying semi-marsh of twenty-three acres bounded by stinking ditches. Three years later the boundary was pushed back to enlarge the settlement to 180 acres, and in 1848 it was further extended to 480 acres its western boundary being the Defence Creek, which in later years formed the fortification line when Consul Rutherford Alcock led out his little army to the victorious field of Muddy Flats.

Consul Balfour, and the few English merchants from Canton who moved up to Shanghai in the early days, occupied at first houses or huts which the Chinese reluctantly rented to them outside the walls of the city, but also outside the concession. Within the concession itself the sole improvement on nature, apart from the ditches, was an earth embankment beside the river, along which ran the tow path used by coolies dragging the grain boats. The foreign population rose steadily, from twenty-three in 1843 to ninety in 1845, and as a crop of roughly-built, sprawling bungalows began to appear haphazardly along the waterfront, it became evident to the British consul, and even to the taotai, that some kind of authority was desirable to provide the elementary urban amenities. Fortunately the consul was not provided, like the governor of Hong Kong, with a staff of senior officials, and he was forced to rely on the initiative of the foreign residents themselves. Accordingly, he and the taotai drew up in 1845 an *ad hoc* agreement which provided for a committee of roads and jetties consisting of three land-renters chosen by election from among their fellows.

At first the committee concentrated on what in merchant minds seemed the urgent necessity, the construction of jetties to obviate the costly double handling involved in loading ships from sampans. Fortunately for the future appearance of Shanghai, the Chinese authorities insisted that, to preserve the rights of the coolies over the towing path, all buildings must be set thirty feet back from the riverside. A line of piles was driven along the water's edge, and the ground filled in to make a road, which became the settlement's first thoroughfare and the ancestor of the famous esplanade known as the Bund, along which in later years the finest buildings of Shanghai would be constructed. At this early stage little attempt was made to lay out the areas behind the Bund according to any regulated plan; the main interests of the merchants were concentrated on the waterfront. A regulation minimum width of twenty-five feet was established for roads, which tended to follow the most immediately convenient direction, usually the winding banks of the creeks, where the coolies habitually carried their burdens. There was at first no effort to regulate the appearance of the buildings; drainage was left to the renters of waterlogged land to provide for themselves, and refuse was usually dumped on the shore below the Bund for the tide to wash away.

By 1847 the Americans for commercial, and the French for political reasons had established their consulates at Shanghai, where their separate treaties with the Chinese had given them equal rights with the British, and in 1847 a new stage was reached in developing the organization of the community by incorporating the *ad hoc* agreements between the British consul and the taotai into the first Land Regulations, which confirmed the existence and powers of the committee for roads and jetties. In 1849 the French obtained their own concession and, unlike the Americans who were willing to accept an international form of control even if it meant British preponderance, the subjects of the revived Napoleonic empire were so taken with their own glory that they refused any suggestion of unity, so that to the end of Shanghai's existence as a treaty port, the French concession remained separate from the International Settlement. In other respects the French pursued their own China policy which at times – as in the Taiping war – ran contrary to that prevailing in the International Settlement, but their consuls still insisted on being consulted in any agreement regarding the status of the International Settlement, and so they appear as signatories to the amendments to the Land Regulations which were carried out from time to time until, in 1869, this essential constitutional instrument of the International Settlement (including the former British and American concessions – united in 1863 – plus later additions) reached its final shape.

The Land Regulations gave substantial but definitely limited rights to the European community in Shanghai. There was no question of a transfer of sovereignty. When the British taipans in 1861 submitted to Whitehall a proposal that Shanghai should be turned into a Free City, run by its merchants under the protection of Britain, France, Russia and the United States, the Foreign Office rejected the suggestion as out of keeping with the treaties of Peking and Nanking, which guaranteed Chinese sovereignty over all territory that had not, like Hong Kong and Macao, been actually ceded to a foreign power. (One is of course tempted to speculate on the worth of a sovereignty which allowed the European powers to establish large armies in Shanghai when it suited their convenience or which allowed British subjects inhabiting China to be tried only in British courts.) Even if the merchants did not gain their Free City, they had in practice the protection of British arms, involving major defence operations in 1900, in 1927 and again in 1937. They also contrived for almost a century to manage the affairs of international Shanghai in such a way that they counted as its citizens, with the full traditional rights of tax paying burgesses, while the Chinese, no matter how numerous they might be, were treated as foreigners in their own land.

The rights of the foreign residents in Shanghai were defined in the set of Land Regulations which were drawn up in 1854 after the influx of a large number of wealthy Chinese who came into the settlement as refugees from the Taiping rebellion. The taotai and the consuls agreed under these regulations that the Chinese should be allowed to rent buildings in the settlement, but the municipal authority, which the regulations also specifically authorized, was to be appointed only by the foreign residents, who were thus given the power of taxing and policing not only those who elected them, but the disenfranchised Chinese as well. This situation seemed anomalous even to the merchants themselves and when the foreign community drew up suggestions for new regulations in 1866, provision was made for Chinese representation on the Shanghai Municipal Council. It was disallowed by the foreign diplomats in Peking, who were disturbed – like the colonial authorities in Hong Kong – by the implications of allowing any Chinese rights – except a shadowy sovereignty – in the treaty port concessions.

The Municipal Council in 1854 was something more than a continuation of the old committee of roads and jetties. It was actually a *fait accompli* by the time the Land regulations gave it authority. The need for defence as much as the need for sanitation and policing had called it into being. In the early months of 1854 the Shanghai Volunteers were formed to give protection against the Taiping rebels and against unruly imperial troops. A self-supporting and autonomous military force, its very existence betokened the resolution of Europeans in Shanghai to protect their property and their commercial interests, even at the risk of their lives. Such militancy, culminating as it did in the victory of Muddy Flats, contributed to the willingness of the taotai (who had actually been rescued from the hands of the rebels by two English residents) to accept the merchant community as a power in its own right when he approved the Land Regulations in July 1854. The Volunteers had established a committee of cooperation to provide necessary liaison between themselves, as the armed residents, and the consular officials, and the discussions which followed reached their culmination, as did so many movements among the British of the Far East, in a public meeting, presided over by Consul Rutherford Alcock, and attended, in true direct democratic style, by the entire foreign community. A municipal council of five members was elected, and a resolution was also passed providing for the whole company of rentpayers to meet each March in order to approve the rates and wharfage dues which the council would be authorized to enforce. It was only a few days later that the Land Regulations, incorporating these decisions, were formally approved by the consuls as representatives of the three treaty powers, and the unfortunate taotai as representative of the powerless Son of Heaven.

The mixture of direct and delegated democracy represented by the assembled ratepayers as a one-day-a-year legislature, functioning parallel with the elected council as the community's executive body, characterized to the end the commonwealth of Shanghai, which legally was not a Free City but in practice often looked very much like one, with its own armed force and its own folk moot and parliament.

The powers of the Shanghai Municipal Council were in fact bounded not by the sovereign powers of the Chinese government but by those of the foreign powers, acting through their consuls. The consuls alone were empowered to conduct negotiations with the Chinese authorities, and, as a practical manifestation of this fact in everyday life, all land leases had to be arranged through the appropriate consul – those foreigners whose nations maintained no representatives in Shanghai being free to act through the representatives of any friendly power. But it was the administration of law, in a settlement where foreigners came under as many codes as there were nations among them, and where the Chinese were theoretically subject to their own law, that raised the most complex problems – problems too heavily loaded with possible international complications to be left in the hands of laymen. Thus, though legislation and execution were virtually handed over to the Municipal Council and the annual general assembly, judicial matters remained the restricted province of consular officials.

Here an irremediable and perpetual chaos prevailed, because of the different methods of the countries involved. By no means all consuls were, like those who served Britain, members of a service especially trained for work on the China coast. Some were ordinary merchants who accepted the task for the prestige and profit it brought them, and these often operated with almost complete ignorance of the legal codes they pretended to administer. The British, on the other hand, endeavoured to set up a system which would make extra-territoriality workable. To deal with British subjects, they created at Shanghai in 1865 a supreme court for China and Japan, staffed by trained lawyers. Not only did this court deal with civil and criminal law, as it affected British subjects in Shanghai, it also served as a court of appeal and a school of guidance for the consuls who operated their minor courts in the other treaty ports. Later a British police magistrate was appointed to deal with the kind of petty cases that were always cropping up among the floating population of foreign seamen. To complete the pattern of British justice transplanted to the China coast, the consular service ran its own prison. This began with a few cells within the consulate; later, a small prison was built in the consulate grounds, and in 1871 a grim solid structure of one hundred and forty cells was opened in Amoy Road. The British were not so criminally inclined as the size of their gaol suggested. It was also open as a matter of courtesy to prisoners of other races whose consuls had not built a prison of their own, and it had a considerable American population until a minor international incident arose over the refusal of the American consul to pay for the maintenance of his prisoners.

The Chinese who had come to live in Shanghai presented their own kind of problem, since they could clearly not be tried by the consular courts according to foreign codes of law. At the same time, the treaty powers were jealous of any overt exercize of Chinese sovereignty in the settlement, and in the end a special tribunal was established, under the aegis of the consuls and called the mixed court. It had a Chinese judge, but in any case where a foreigner was involved his consul sat in as assessor and influenced the eventual decision. Since Chinese were also subject to arrest by the police employed by the municipal council, and when convicted were often used to repair its roads, it will be seen that even in this field the foreigners made sure that their interests were paramount.

There remained, in a settlement so cosmopolitan, the problem of solving civil disputes between foreigners of various nationalities, and a court of consuls was eventually established to deal with such questions at sittings where the various nations were represented. Since the municipal council was an international body, it was before the court of consuls alone that individuals were allowed to bring suit against it, and the court mediated on behalf of the council with the foreign ministers in Peking, who remained the final court of appeal for any matters relating to the treaty ports.

There were times in Shanghai when a dozen different courts were applying as many different codes of law in as many different languages. In comparison with this tangle of consular and Chinese jurisdictions, the role of the municipal council as the executive body of the Settlement was simplicity itself, though as Shanghai grew from a small port to a maritime metropolis, its tasks became increasingly onerous and varied. At its very first meeting in the summer of 1854, it had to extend its responsibilities beyond the mere roads and jetties of its predecessor and take on the task of creating an effective police force. Thirty-two armed British policemen were imported, and the council – with doubtful legality – turned itself into a court of first instance, since in the event of an arrest the prisoner must be brought before a council member who could dismiss the case or order the accused before a consular or a Chinese court. The growing needs of the community constantly imposed new burdens on the council. The system of mails operated through Hong Kong proved inadequate for a merchant community which depended on fast communications, and the council established its own post office. Epidemics of cholera, typhoid and small-pox eventually made it necessary to create a municipal health department. The problem of opium was dealt with by a council-operated licensing system for the shops where it was sold and smoked. A voluntary fire brigade was created. In 1870, when there were anti-foreign outbreaks in China, it was the council which revived and equipped the moribund Shanghai Volunteers; this cosmopolitan army henceforward remained the responsibility of the council which, if it did not technically have the power to declare war, could and did on occasion declare states of emergency which automatically brought about the mobilization of the Volunteer Corps. Education came within its scope in 1886 when it established the first public school in the settlement. In 1893 it took over the electric light company, and in 1894 it began providing public sports grounds. It even established a municipal band, to play of an evening in the gardens which now decorated the Bund.

The franchise for the council, like that for the British Parliament, broadened steadily as the century went on. First, only those who actually rented land could take part in the elections. Later all those who paid rates above five hundred taels were included in the voters' list. This left many Europeans without a voice in the election of the governing authority; these were all swept into the voter's list during the very last months of cosmopolitan Shanghai, when the British and American merchants frustrated a Japanese attempt to control the municipal council by creating new voters through the expedient of dividing their rate-paying properties among their employees, so that in 1940 an unprecedented eight thousand white voters went to the polls. Japanese had always been entitled to vote in the council elections provided they met the qualifications in terms of rate paying, since they were the subjects of one of the treaty powers. The Chinese, on the other hand, were voteless until the 1920s, despite the fact that under the Land Regulations approved in 1869 the government of China abandoned all claims to tax them. For two generations they paid the taxes imposed by the European-dominated municipal council without representation and usually without complaint. They found the predictable demands of the red-haired foreign devils easier to meet than the unpredictable impositions of the corrupt and tyrannical mandarins.

The size of the municipal council was not established by regulation until 1898, when the taotai and the foreign consuls agreed that it should consist of no less than five and no more than nine members; these were the limits within which it had already in practice operated, and until the First World War the council consisted of nine members whose national origins left no doubt as to which was the dominant power in Shanghai. Seven of them were customarily British, one American and one German. The first break in this arrangement came in 1915, when the British refused to observe the gentleman's agreement and a Russian was elected in place of the German. The next change in the council's composition came when the Japanese, who had become the largest foreign community in terms of numbers, demanded a share in the government of the International Settlement. One Japanese was added in 1916.

This was the first important crack in the British preponderance and it soon led to others. The resident Chinese had accepted rule by European foreigners, but to have a member of a hated Asian nation among the council which controlled their material interests was too much to be borne, and in 1919, inspired by the rising tide of nationalism, they demanded representation. A temporary compromise was reached in 1921 when the municipal council agreed to allow a committee of Chinese residents to advise them on native affairs and interests. Finally, in 1929, yielding to the pressure of the ascendant Kuomintang government, the council agreed to accept three Chinese members, to be chosen by their various native organizations. In 1930, by a further change forced by American, Japanese and Chinese demands, the council assumed its final shape, and the British at last became a minority when, in a new council of fourteen members, five were British, five Chinese, two Americans and two Japanese. The British probably considered the risk was worth taking, since they could count on the Chinese and the Japanese never working in harmony enough to form an Asian bloc. One important element in the population of Shanghai was overlooked in this arrangement: the large refugee community of White Russians which had arrived after the Revolution and, with its twelve thousand members, formed the largest of all the European groups in Shanghai. These Russians were rarely prosperous enough to pay the rates necessary to become a voter; in fact the majority of them were so badly off that they provided a resident poor white population for Shanghai, many living parasitically on the night life which grew up lushly in Shanghai during the 1920s, and others serving as policemen or forming the permanent Russian company of Volunteers which during these stormy years served the municipal council as a miniature standing army.

The change in composition of the municipal council still left the British as the dominant community in Shanghai for a whole decade after 1930. Not only had past councils packed the municipal service and the police with British personnel; most of the money which kept the council going was provided in taxes by British firms, the richest in Shanghai; moreover, when protection was needed for the settlement, the British were the most numerous among the men under arms, whether they were Shanghai Volunteers or regulars sent out to meet the crisis.

Until that critical year of 1940, when the Japanese and the British manoeuvred against each other to storm the election station with newly made voters, the cosmopolitan commonwealth of Shanghai was in fact less like a modern democracy than a mediaeval city state ruled by a patrician clique – in this case the British ratepayers. And, no matter how much show of democracy there might have been in those general meetings which each year voted on financial matters, in practice the wealthier merchants kept affairs in their hands from beginning to end of the settlement. Of the five British members elected to the council in 1936, all represented major business interests, and the current head of Jardine Matheson was among them, as his predecessor had been on the first council in 1854. The taipans ruled Shanghai as they had never succeeded in ruling Hong Kong, and this was why, to businessmen all over the China Seas, Shanghai seemed a merchant's Utopia. It was probably the last of the world's cities that could be regarded, in the tradition of Genoa and Venice and the great Hansa towns, as a republic living and dominated by the trader.

In the other treaty port concessions, in Japan as well as in China, the foreign merchants followed the example of Shanghai and set up their municipal councils, which policed and taxed the areas under their control, laid out the streets and sustained small groups of Volunteers. In the Shameen concession at Canton, in Tientsin and to a less extent in Hankow, they succeeded in creating pleasant but vulnerable European suburbs. In Yokohama and Kobe they established the nuclei of modern communities which the Japanese later built up into major westernized cities. In Japan the foreign concessions were handed over to the host country in 1899, the European-dominated municipal councils ceased to operate, and, while the British merchants remained until 1940, and returned before the decade ended, they ceased to exist as a legally constituted community with extra-territorial rights. The settlements in China, except for Hong Kong, became precarious in the stormy years before the rise to power of the Kuomintang. Hankow and Kiukiang, far up the Yangtse, were particularly vulnerable, and in 1927, faced with riots and threats of military action, the British abandoned the concessions at these ports, though their gunboats continued as far as possible to protect the traders who remained on the Yangtse. Concessions where troops could be landed easily, like

Shameen Island and Tientsin, were retained. But in none of the other treaty ports did such a powerful mercantile commonwealth arise as in Shanghai. This was due largely to the fact that all these other places were really subsidiary to Shanghai – their most important firms were branches of the great houses of the city at the mouth of the Yangtse, and even their courts and consulates were subject to its rule. They were the outposts, parts of a network centred on Shanghai and dependent on it. In the year when Hankow was quietly surrendered, fifteen thousand British troops were poured into Shanghai; the moral of this difference in reaction was that any single treaty port on the China coast was dispensable (particularly if it lay at the end of long communication lines) except Shanghai, which was the key to the trade of China, as Hong Kong was the key to Shanghai, and Singapore was the key to the whole of the eastern seas.

I 2

PRIVATE HOUSES

'To give a correct idea of the everyday life of the European,' wrote J. N. Cameron in 1865, 'it is necessary rather to distinguish between the unmarried and the married than between the man of narrow and the man of extended means.' He was talking of Europeans in Singapore, but his remark could as easily apply to the white inhabitants of Hong Kong or Shanghai, of the new settlements on the coast of Japan or of the tiny British beach-heads of Sarawak and Labuan, and it could apply as easily in the 1930s as seventy years before. The coming of the white women brought a gradual change in the living pattern of the Far East. It set a fashion for the individual household detached from the place of trade or service. Except among young unmarried men, it broke up the collegiate existence that had been followed by the men of the East India Company and which was retained in the factories of Canton and the hongs of early Shanghai. It made association between European men and Asian women seem morally reprehensible, so that it became furtive, and thus the gap was widened between the Englishman and the people over whom he ruled and from whose labour he grew rich.

Chinese officials, even in the eighteenth century, had come to the con-clusion that, undesirable as the foreign devil might be, the foreign she-devil was even more to be avoided. Accordingly, though the interests of trade and of corrupt mandarins demanded that English merchants should be allowed to reside for periods in Canton, their women were strictly forbid-den to enter even the restricted ghetto of the eighteenth-century factory area. At the time of the Opium Wars, when some of the mandarins did encounter European women in the households of 'barbarian' envoys at Macao, they were shocked by the impropriety of their low-cut dresses and even more by the pertness with which they would make an appearance 'to pay their respects'.

The mandarins' instincts were mainly correct. Much that was individual, adventurous and attractive in the lives of those Europeans who first entered the Far East dwindled as English women became more numerous and a life more closely modelled on that of the Home Counties evolved in the Straits Settlements and the treaty ports, and even in distant places like Kuching and Jesselton.

Yet it can be argued that the arrival of the Englishwomen in the Far East was a consequence rather than a cause; that as markets were stabilized and cities replaced factories, the inevitable result was the creation of a secure environment in which a man could cease adventuring, settle down to create a family, and live at the steady pace of humdrum respectability.

The steady pace became the approved gait of British Far Eastern society as soon as its pioneer period began to wane, which meant the 1860s in Singapore, the 1880s on the China coast, and the 1900s in Borneo and the Malayan hinterland. A rigidity and a formalism developed even tighter than those that bound contemporary England. From 1900 onwards, racial distinctions, as well as class distinctions within the British community, became more sharply defined; the social rituals became more important; the routines more mechanical and closer to those of the temporarily lost homeland.

As early as the 1850s Alfred Russel Wallace |had noticed the difference in this respect between the British and the Dutch. The Dutch, he remarked, 'have adopted customs far more in accordance with the climate than we have done in our tropical possessions. Almost all business is transacted in the morning between the hours of seven and twelve, the afternoon being given up to repose and the evening to visiting.' The routines of the British became, as the nineteenth century advanced, steadily less appropriate to anything but a temperate climate. The Singapore merchant of 1865 arranged his day on the model of his City of London counterpart. At nine he breakfasted briskly, taking no more than half an hour. Then he set off for work in Commercial Square, driving his carriage from a new residential suburb over bridges crowded with his colleagues. Before ten he was in town, walking around the square to pick up the news of the morning and sense the state of the market. Half an hour later he was in his office, where he worked until one. Then tiffin, and at two o'clock the Exchange, and then the office again until half-past four or five.

Sixty years later the Singapore routine had hardly changed, except that hours in the 1920s were even longer than in the 1860s, extending from eight-thirty or nine to five or half-past, with particular pressure – in those days before regular air services – on the weekly mail day. All this, one must remember, took place in an extremely humid atmosphere with a temperature between 80° and 90°. Singapore was typical; everywhere in the east where the British founded their commercial centres, the City of London working day, like the English Sunday, was faithfully observed.

Other members of the colonial society were as bound by routine as the office worker. The planter was tied to the rhythm of a kind of arboriculture as monotonous as the work of any factory; the timberman in the teak forests was bound by the needs of the seasons; the civil servants and the officials of the Chinese Customs followed, from the beginning of their training as cadets, to their retirement to Surrey villas, working lives as regular as those the commercial merchants and his underlings. Even rajas, if they were British, had their routines, and, if James Brooke tended to play a little cavalierly with time, his successor Charles followed a strict and monotonous daily pattern of supervising the offices and law courts of his little kingdom.

It was in this life, conventional, stratified, and, except in occasional crises, far more predictable than life in Europe, that the majority of Englishwomen found a contented place. All its qualities they exemplified more faithfully than their menfolk, who on their own had found ways to soften and humanize it. It was almost a century after the East India Company arrived that English women reached the Far East, the Company in its earlier days having much the same view of their presence as the Chinese officials in Canton. By the end of the seventeenth century Company servants' wives had reached Madras and Calcutta with official permission. Presumably without permission, some of the interlopers had also brought their wives on the long voyage which ended at the Siamese port of Mergui; three of them, wives of mercenary captains serving the king of Siam, are known by name, and one at least, Mary Leslie, stayed on in Mergui after her husband died in the massacre of the English in 1687, and left a line of descendants. According to Maurice Collis, they still live in Mergui (now a Burmese port) and bear the name of Leslie. Mary Leslie and her fellows were probably the first English women to travel east of India, and their children almost certainly the first English children to be exposed to the humid heat and the endemic sicknesses of the eastern shores of the Bay of Bengal.

But for many decades English women and their children were only occasionally to be met in the Far East. There were rarely more than three or four European women at any one time in eighteenth-century Bencoolen. Raffles took his first wife Olivia to Penang and to Java; and his second wife Sophia to Bencoolen. Both were exceptional women, of independent mind and character, but their fates demonstrate why, in those days when English settlement had hardly begun east of Bengal, few men cared to take their womenfolk into the East Indies. Olivia died from the fevers of Java in 1814; three out of Sophia's four children died within a few months at Bencoolen. Penang, Batavia, Bencoolen, were all, in the Napoleonic age, singularly unhealthy settlements, and it was only the woman of exceptional devotion or exceptional poverty who followed her husband there. Macao, farther north, had the reputation of being more salubrious, and there, in the 1830s, the wives of the Company's supercargoes and of the country traders would go more often with their children.

Yet it was long, even after British domination became established in Malaya and on the China coast, before European women became really numerous in the English settlements. By 1845 there were ninety European women and fifty children in Hong Kong, but many of these were Portuguese. As late as 1863 there were only seventy-four foreign women in Shanghai, and at a ball held in the following year there were ten men to every one woman. During the same decade, for a ball in Yokohama only twenty women could be assembled, half of them wives of the officers of the British garrison. Even in 1887, only five British women attended a party in Kuching which the Raja Charles Brooke gave for their benefit. One of the reasons for this shortage of women was that most of the large commercial houses laid it down as a condition of their contracts that the young griffins who came out from England should not marry within their first five-year term of service. But the unhealthiness of cities like Shanghai and Hong Kong during their early years must also have had an important influence. Singapore, which was so well known for its healthy climate that it became a resort for convalescent India Hands during the 1850s, attracted many more European women during the early days than the settlements of the China coast. In 1871, there were already 299, and thirty years later the census of 1901 showed 1,124, as against 1,737 men. As almost two-thirds of the European residents were British, the same proportion would mean about 750 British women. And 750 British women meant that the married mono-racial household became the standard pattern among the tuans.

It also meant the virtual end of an institution that was by no means intrinsically evil, though its consequences were sometimes rendered unfortunate by prejudice. From the days when the East India traders first came to the Far East, Englishmen had found Asian girls attractive. Nor were the peoples among whom they came to live always averse to their girls becoming the mistresses of white men. 'Even the great men of Tonquin,' William Dampier noted in 1688, 'will offer their daughters to the merchants and officers, though their stay is not likely to be above five or six months in the country: neither are they afraid to be with child by white men, for their children will be much fairer than their mothers, and consequently of greater repute, when they grow up, if they be girls.' And Wallace, writing of the 1850s, claims that it was considered honourable by men of good family in Bali for their women to live with white merchants, and he quotes the case of a raja who went to the extent of – as he thought – protecting the honour of an English trader by ordering the stabbing to death of his native concubine because she had accepted a flower from another man. Many of these unions were as close and lasting as the most faithful conventional marriage. Will Adams, in the seventeenth century, cheerfully forgetting his English wife in Gillingham, lived happily to his death with the Japanese woman he had married according to the style of the country, and Francis Light, even when superintendent of Penang, lived openly and faithfully with his Eurasian mistress, Martina Rozells. Often the attraction of the native woman would overcome any urge which the Englishman might have to marry a woman of his own race. Somerset Maugham in his *Notebooks* records the case of one man who had lived with a Malay woman and had four children by her; he went home and became engaged to an English girl, but the thought of the woman in Sarawak haunted him and he broke off the engagement to return to her.

It is true of course that very often relationships between English men and native girls were characterized by callousness and even contempt. In the treaty ports, and particularly the smaller ones, it was the custom for merchants and consular officials to take Chinese girls as temporary mistresses, and there was a famous scandal when the vice-consul at Ningpo picked a concubine from the Church of England missionary school, and set up house with her and her family in Foochow. It certainly was not a case of 'all for love', for as soon as the bishop of Hong Kong denounced him publicly, the vice-consul abandoned the girl. Some of the merchants on the China coast eventually married their Chinese mistresses, but other relationships of the kind ended quite differently, and as early as the 1850s Sir George Bowring in Hong Kong was complaining about the 'large population of children of native mothers by foreigners of all classes' who 'seemed wholly uncared for' and were 'beginning to ripen into a dangerous element out of the dunghill of neglect'.

There was a great deal of probably unavoidable hypocrisy in British life in the Far East during the nineteenth century, which began with opium selling and evangelical religion going hand in hand, and it is interesting to observe how attitudes towards concubinage changed during that era. At Bencoolen mixed unions were widely practised, and no stigma seems to have attached to any of the parties involved, including the children, who usually suffer most in such situations. The same tolerant attitude applied in early Penang. But the missionaries had not yet appeared in strength and it was the missionaries who raised the first public cry against such relationships, and the English women, as soon as they arrived, added to pastoral denunciation the pressure of social ostracism. It hurt their feelings to realize that they were not always preferred to women with coloured skins. (Later, in twentieth-century Shanghai, they had to fight on more equal ground, when it was Russian women, white both politically and cutaneously, who alienated the affections of their menfolk.) Most Victorian Englishmen had a guilty fear of clergymen which their descendants have lost, and a dread of moralistic women which has proved more durable.

When the Church and the memsahibs were united, there were very few even among the most powerful men in the east who were willing openly to defy them. Raja Charles Brooke was a rare and refreshing exception when he took advantage of his regal status to advocate openly mixed marriages, which he believed would bring into being a race both mentally and physically capable of creating a vigorous society in a tropical climate, and who dealt very forthrightly with bishops criticizing the amatory lives of his European officers. More typical was the action of the Colonial Office which, round about 1910, bowed to the nonconformist conscience of England and issued an order specifically forbidding officers of the Malay civil service to keep native mistresses. The practice continued, clandestinely particularly in stations away from the larger British communities and in outlying territories like Sarawak and North Borneo. Among the planters, also, unmarried managers and assistants frequently carried on relationships with Malay women or, less frequently because it was considered imprudent, with Tamil women from their coolie lines. But the days when men could live openly with their Eurasian or Asian concubines and, like Light and James Scott, suffer no social stigma, were passing already by the 1860s.

As the white women arrived, the old form of merchant's establishment, where taipans and griffins lived in the same house and messed at the same tables, gradually passed away, though it survived in a different form in the various kinds of communal housekeeping which were provided for young men during their first terms of service in the east. Cadets in the Malay civil service lived together in bungalows provided by the government, and the Chinese Maritime Customs provided extensive communal residences for its younger European employees. These were situated around Quinsan Gardens in the former American part of the International Settlement of Shanghai and consisted of about a hundred bed-sitting rooms with baths,

situated in red-brick terrace houses around the square. In a special building there was a common dining room as well as a bar, card-rooms, bil-
liard-rooms and a dance-hall. On a more modest scale, many of the large
commercial houses in Shanghai provided quarters on the same basis for
their junior staff brought out on contract from England, and the same
custom survives to this day in Hong Kong.

Such collegiate patterns were the last survival of the system developed
in the old East India Company factories. For many of their inhabitants
they provided an environment reassuringly similar to the boarding schools
they had only recently left in England. For others they were bases from
which the unfamiliar world of the east could be explored, and in such
establishments at least a flavour of the old free and adventurous spirit of
the China Seas survived, untrammelled by the domestic anxieties which
older men took upon them when they set up their separate establishments.

The earliest individual homes of Europeans in the Far East were those
of the interlopers of the seventeenth and eighteenth century, in places like
Mergui and Junk Ceylon. They were very much like the houses built by
Siamese and Malays – wooden structures, raised above the ground and
thatched with attap; the space beneath the floors was used as a godown or
warehouse. Such houses Alfred Russel Wallace still encountered in the
1850s when he visited English merchants who had settled in distant
regions of the Dutch East Indies, like Lombock and Bali. Attap houses
had the virtue of being quickly raised, and for this reason the first dwellings in the early British settlements in Malaya were of this type, including
even the large governor's mansion which Raffles had built on a hill
overlooking the site of Singapore.

I have built a very comfortable house [he told the Duchess of Somerset] . . . and I
only wish you were here but for half an hour, to enjoy the unequalled beauty and
interest of the scene. My house, which is one hundred feet front, and fifty deep,
was finished in a fortnight from its commencement.

'The sides are rough planks and venetian windows, the roof is attaps', said
a less enthusiastic observer. 'It is withal so insubstantial that after a
Sumatra squall inquiring glances are cast up to discover whether the
house is still there or in the valley behind it.'

A few years after foundation, in both Penang and Singapore, houses
became substantial and even took on a touch of orientalized Regency
elegance. When Penang was declared a presidency, and Philip Dundas
landed in 1805 with his train of officials, the colony – less than twenty
years old – was so poorly equipped with houses that those who owned
them could charge what then seemed astronomical prices; Raffles, a mere

assistant secretary, had to pay £330 a year for a house for his family and the two sisters he had brought out to find husbands. But the arrival of so many well paid tuans began a spate of building in Penang, in which the merchants competed with the officials. Raffles built 'Runnymede', Scott built a great two-storied mansion named 'Scotland House' in which the Malayan style of large airy rooms and spreading eaves was captured in stone and tile instead of wood and attap, and W. E. Phillips, acting governor after Dundas's quick death from malaria, built Suffolk House, which Lord Minto described as one of the handsomest houses he had seen in 'India'. Suffolk House was designed 'in a mixed style of English and Indian architecture', and John Crawfurd, who was entertained there in 1821 during his mission to Siam and Cochin-China, declared that:

the taste of Mr Phillips has rendered it the most beautiful spot of the kind in India, after Barrackpore, the country residence of the governor-general: it is, in short, an English gentleman's mansion and park, where clove and nutmeg trees (in full bearing during our visit) are substituted for oaks, elms and ashes. The grounds contain from two to three hundred spotted deer.

If the high officials of the East India Company tried to transplant to the Far East the style of life and dwelling of the country gentry of southern England, the traders continued the old mercantile custom, familiar in the great commercial cities of Europe, of combining their places of dwelling with their places of business. A mere decade after Singapore was founded only the poor people living in the outskirts of the city still made do with attap houses. The warehouses and dwellings were now built of brick and lime, roofed with tiles, and the whiteness of their walls was varied by green venetian blinds. Most of the merchants' establishments were built around Commercial Square and the traders lived above their offices. But already by the 1830s, as prosperity came to Singapore and the first memsahibs appeared, a few of the richer merchants began to move into the great houses with high ceilings and finely arched loggias which Coleman built for them. They fronted the beach to the east of Commercial Square, divided from it by the Singapore River. By the time J. N. Cameron knew them in the 1860s the tide of fashion had already swept into the country the merchants and government officials who built them, and Singapore's first hotels had been created in these pioneer patrician mansions. But Cameron still found them admirable.

They are all large buildings, generally kept snowy white, with pillared porticoes and balconies, and green-painted latticed doors and windows; to each also is attached a compound or garden of fair dimensions, tastefully laid out with trees and shrubs. . . . It is a very fine sight from the beach to see these houses lit up at night, the brilliant argand lamps in use shedding a flood of light round the lofty white pillars and colonnades of the upper stories, while the lower parts of the buildings are hid by the shrubbery of the gardens in front.

In Shanghai, once the settlement had shaken itself into shape, the buildings of the hongs were even larger, if not more handsome, than the merchant houses of Singapore. Shanghai had no Coleman, and for a long time its structures were put up without benefit of architects, by Chinese master builders combining memories of the Portuguese buildings of Macao with the utilitarian requirements of the British taipans. The result became known as the Comprador style. The houses were square buildings, with compounds behind them enclosing sheds and godowns; the ground floor was divided into four great office rooms, the upper floor into four other rooms which served as messes and dormitories. Around both floors, verandahs were built, and used freely for evening relaxation, while broad windows looked out over the forest of masts on the river below. It was the double row of columns supporting the verandahs which gave the white-painted buildings a dramatic air as one first saw the long line of them facing outward from the Bund, like an Asian echo of Canaletto's Venice. Of the mercantile buildings that arose a little later in Yokohama and Tokyo, a Japanese writer saw the prospect somewhat differently, likening the line of new buildings to 'the teeth of a comb in closeness and orderliness'. A quieter, remoter world, was represented in the miniature palace which Malayan craftsmen built at about the same time in Kuching for James Brooke after he had taken over the rule of Sarawak.

It is an edifice 54 feet square [he recounted], mounted on numerous posts of the Nibong palm, with nine windows in each front. The roof is of Nipa leaves and the floor and partitions are all of plank. Furnished with couches, tables, chairs, books, etc., the whole is as comfortable as man could wish for in this out-of-the-way country; and we have besides a bathing-house, cook-house, and servants' apartments detached. The view from the house to the eastward comprises a reach of the river, and to the westward looks towards the blue mountains of Matang; the north fronts to the river, and the south the jungle. Our abode, however, though spacious, cool and comfortable, can only be considered a temporary residence, for the best of all reasons, that in the course of a year it will tumble down, from the weight of the super-structure being placed on weak posts.

Some of the early Victorians in the east were, like Brooke, late Romantics who sited their dwellings for the view; others were moved rather by the advantage of living near to the waterfront, which was the centre of commerce. It was when the white women arrived in numbers and the married merchant became the norm that fashion began to dictate that houses should be detached from offices and that suburban living was as desirable in Singapore or Shanghai or Hong Kong as in contemporary London. In Penang and Singapore the process of suburbanization began. In Penang it was linked with the passion for growing spices which made every merchant become a planter, and which dotted the hillsides with large white houses capped with great roofs of red tiles. In Singapore it was a matter of taste rather than profit, for by the time the merchants moved out of the city the possibilities of plantation on the island had already been exhausted.

In gaining its earliest suburbs, Singapore retained its compactness. The city of the 1860s ended sharply about a mile from the beach. There was another mile of almost uninhabited green belt, and then the houses began, at first rather close together, each on an acre or two of rising ground, and then thinning out and standing mainly on the summits or slopes of the low hills that surround the city of Singapore. They were all built on roughly the same plan and constructed by Chinese builders. Most of them were bungalows, about ninety feet long by seventy feet deep, raised on arches five feet from the ground. They were surrounded by pillared ver-andahs, eight to ten feet wide, on to which doors from all the rooms opened; these doors served also as windows being 'in two halves, opening down the centre like cottage doors at home, with the lower panels plain and the two upper ones fitted with venetians to open or close at pleasure'. Inside the house the doors between the rooms were usually kept open, privacy being assured by hinged silk screens. The rooms were lofty, at least fifteen feet high. The bedrooms were small suites in themselves, each with a dressing room and, beyond it, a bathroom with a brick tiled floor, on which stood an enormous Chinese jar containing sixty or seventy gallons of water. One bathed by standing on a small wooden grating beside the jar and splashing water with a small bucket over one's body. 'The successive shocks to the system which are obtained by the discharge of each bucketful of water,' remarks one contemporary, 'seem to have a much more bracing effect than that of one sudden and continued immersion.' From the front of each bungalow a portico projected about thirty feet, to cover the carriage way and the flight of stone steps leading to the verandah. At the back a covered way led to the kitchens, stables and servants' quar-ters which were always built outside the house. All the buildings were stuc-coed white, and the doors painted light green, while with age the tiled roof, with its deeply overhanging leaves, would turn a deep brown. Some of the suburban houses were of two stories; but their construction was very similar to that of the bungalows.

These Singapore houses were lighted with argand lamps, and the dining rooms were kept cool with the swinging punkahs which Indian servants operated from the verandah, though the Singapore nights, unlike those in most of India, were cool enough to make this unnecessary in the bedrooms. Apart from the punkahs and the bathing arrangements, the most novel aspect of these houses would be the arrangement of the kitchen, which was adapted – as Asian kitchens still are – to the intense conservatism of Indian or Chinese cooks.

There is no fireplace [J. N. Cameron tells us] but in the centre of the room a table of solid brickwork is built with slabs of stone or brick tiles laid on the top; at one end of this a small circular chamber is built to serve as an oven; a strong fire is placed inside, and when the brickwork is thoroughly heated, the fire is raked out, and whatever dish is required to be baked placed inside and the aperture closed in, the heat given out from the bricks being sufficient to cook it in a short time. The rest of the table is divided into a series of little fireplaces, over which proceed the ordinary processes of cooking. Wood or charcoal only is used as fuel.

'Colonial' houses of this type, light and roomy, with their oriental touches in appearance and arrangement, formed the basic model for a century of suburban housing, as Shanghai spread landward towards Bubbling Well Road and Hong Kong climbed more scenically up the slopes of the Peak. Modern inventions replaced the argand lamp and the punkah with electric light and the ceiling fan, baths with running water supplanted the great bathing jar, and before the Second World War refrigeration and even air conditioning had added conveniences and comforts unimagined by the early members of British Far Eastern communities. But the kitchens remained enclaves of Asian conservatism, their wood and charcoal fires surviving all western man's inventiveness.

In the cities, overcrowding finally forced a change in the pattern of commodious suburban houses in great gardens of palms, magnolias and exotic fruit trees. Many such houses survive in the cities the British founded, but – except on the China coast where they have been 'socialized' – they belong only to the rich, who need not now be English. By the end of the First World War housing accommodation was becoming scanty in most of the cities of Malaya and the China coast, and Shanghai pioneered in the construction of ten or fifteen storey apartment blocks, put up during the 1920s by speculative combines in which some of the great taipans of Shanghai, like Sir Victor Sassoon, played a leading part. In the Malayan towns and Hong Kong, where space was still more freely available than in Shanghai, flat-dwelling was slower to appear. Instead villas or bungalows, often in excruciating imitation of London suburban styles, were built on small lots in the outskirts of Singapore and also of the new rubber towns of the Malay states, Kuala Lumpur and Taiping and

Ipoh. They were designed for the man in a junior position, on a modest contract, and their very look emphasized the difference between the lower-middle-class elements which the tin and rubber trades brought into the country and the old merchant patricians. Hong Kong, before the Second World War, tended to spread out laterally over its hills and valleys, kept from imitating the upward rising of rival Shanghai by an ordinance which until 1955 forbade the construction of buildings over five floors high.

The planters' bungalows, which began to appear in the interior of Malaya as rubber became an important industry after 1900, varied according to the tastes and means of their proprietors. The companies usually started by building crude wooden bungalows, meant as temporary dwellings until the plantations were established, and either thatched with attap or roofed with corrugated iron. Elevated on piles and surrounded by verandahs, they were little more than boxes for living. Later they were replaced by more substantial houses, often of concrete, but rarely with the spacious elegance of the houses on the earlier plantations at Penang. On the rare occasions when the planter was also the owner of the estate and was therefore inclined to regard himself as a permanent resident, he would spend more thought and money on his house and often built the Malayan equivalent of a country grange, two storied and spacious. The British imported their styles in furniture, like their styles in dress, from England. The will of Francis Light, bequeathing his land, his house and its contents to the faithful Martina Rozells, gives a list which probably represents the typical furniture of an early European house in Malaya; it consisted of 'one set of Mahogany Tables, two Card Tables, two Couches, two bedsteads large and two small, a dressing table and eighteen chairs, two silver candlesticks, one Silver teapot, two sugar dishes . . .'. Later settlers would go to the Chinese cabinet makers, who were adept imitators, and get them to make furniture in the current English style, but the indispensable piano would be imported from England; in that humid climate it was rarely in tune. Indeed, the visitor who entered a Singapore or a Shanghai drawing room in the 1860s or the 1870s would find very little that was unfamiliar in its contents, once he had become accustomed to the punkahs. Perhaps the most important difference would be the presence of mats from Bengal or China instead of carpets; these mats were sometimes watered to help keep the air cool. On the verandah the visitor would find one feature common to India and the Far East alike; the reclining chair with elongated arms over which the legs could be cocked for ease and coolness. There would also be a profusion of strange flowers in the vases of the drawing room, which were often stuffed with the orchids he had only seen at home – if at all – as rare hothouse plants. Also, if his hosts were more inclined than the average Englishman abroad to flirt with the strangeness of the world in which they lived, he might see some blue and white Chinese ware used for ornamentation, or even a few native weapons and other artifacts, displayed as curiosities rather than as objects of art. It was in the bedroom that he would find the most unfamiliar furnishings. Some Malay and China Hands had picked up the habit of sleeping on a Chinese wooden bed, with only a thin mat covering its boards, and a wooden pillow shaped to support the head and neck. Though no cover, except a sheet laid over the mattress or mat, was necessary, it was customary to drape something light over the waist (this was superstitiously supposed to prevent fever). Every eastern sleeper went to bed with that strange companion, the Dutch Wife, a tightly packed cylindrical bolster over which one laid a leg to provide greater coolness. The Dutch Wife is almost extinct, but the same is not true of that nightmare producing enclosure, the mosquito net. Mosquito coils, made from some pungent Asian herb, were burnt in Far Eastern houses, but they were rarely effective in keeping the insects completely away, so nets of many kinds were devised. Some were enormous, like rooms within rooms, and their owners set up desks inside them where they could work at night, but these were generally less effective than the standard net hung from a frame above the bed and tucked carefully under the mattress.

Privacy was limited throughout the east by the fact that every house, whether its owner were married or single, carried like a ship its crew of servants, numerous and extraordinarily specialized in their functions. The more servants a householder kept, the higher his standing among both whites and natives. Servants were cheap and government officials in particular went to extraordinary lengths to establish 'face'. Even the enlightened Raffles, when he was lieutenant-governor of Java, kept a hundred and eleven house servants, not counting the three hundred and forty-seven overseers and coolies who were employed tending the country estates he maintained. A junior official of the Chinese Customs in the 1860s would recruit on first arrival, as Edward Bowra did, a staff of five, and this did not include a cook, since Bowra messed with his colleagues; it did include a teacher of Chinese, a 'body servant', a groom and two coolies to sweep the yard, fill Bowra's bath, and carry him around in a sedan chair.

The average merchant or official, with no great pretensions, would find himself employing from five to seven servants, and this number was fairly constant whether one lived in Malaya, on the China coast or in the treaty ports of Japan. Only the young bachelor, living in an assistant manager's bungalow on some remote plantation, or trailing through the jungle on forest officer's duty, or perhaps sharing a house with his civil service colleagues, could make do with a single personal servant.

In the eighteenth century, at Bencoolen, the servants had been either Malay slaves or Bengalis whom the Company's officers had brought with them from India. When the presidency was established in Penang, many of the higher officials arrived with European servants and three Englishmen headed the great establishment which Raffles gathered around him on Java. But most of the domestic servants in the early Straits Settlements were Bengalis, either free men or convicts distinguished by a small iron ring on the leg; the tales told by sensationally minded Victorian ladies of being awakened to morning tea by men carrying on their brows the words '*Doomga* – Murder' are probably apocryphal, though such branded killers were certainly among the coolie gangs used for public works. Indians also performed outside services, acting especially as dhobis or washermen. According to one visitor to Bencoolen in 1812, they charged the exorbitant price of 6 dollars for a hundred pieces of linen. In Malaya, at least, washing remained their province.

In the second half of the nineteenth century, and especially after the last of the convicts left the Straits for the Andaman Islands in 1873, the Chinese took over household work everywhere in the Far East, until they were to be found in almost every European house from Penang to the treaty ports of Japan. 'When good they are about the best class of household servants,' said J. R. Logan in 1851, 'but when bad they are clever and dangerous rogues.' A few officials and planters had Malay personal servants, but these were rare. Generally speaking, even in Shanghai, the Chinese servants came from Canton; they were considered better cooks and generally more reliable than northern Chinese.

The essential nucleus of indoor servants consisted of the houseboy, cook, and water-carrier, but most households also employed an under-houseboy. Since the Cantonese had developed a code of division of labours as rigid as that of a modern trade union, this pattern existed throughout the Far East. Very often there would also be a sweeper – an Indian untouchable. If there were children an English nurse might be employed, but usually they were looked after – and in most cases very well indeed – by a Chinese amah, in her white coat and her wide trousers of glistening black cotton. Whoever could afford it, sent his children home to England for education when they had reached preparatory school age, so that the governess rarely appeared in European households, though she might – like the famous Anna Leonowens – find a place in the houses of Asian princes.

Each house would add to its minimum establishment a gardener and a groom, and sometimes a coachman. In the treaty ports they would be Chinese ; in Malaya they were usually Malays, and so after the introduction of the automobile in the early Edwardian age, were the chauffeurs. Each house would also have its tailor (usually a Chinese), its Indian barber who shaved the master each morning, and its dhobi, but their services would usually be supplied on contract and shared with a number of other households. The cost of such an establishment rose considerably from the nineteenth to the twentieth century. In 1841 it was estimated that a staff of *fourteen* servants could be got in Singapore for 70 dollars; in 1928 a staff of *five* servants, with the part-time services of a dhobi, would cost 170 dollars a month, roughly £20. This was about one-third of the average expenditure of a married government official or commercial employee.

Relations between the mistress of the house and her servants were conducted according to a delicate protocol. The white clad, polite Cantonese who padded silently about the house in their cloth shoes, were determined in guarding their rights – the right to shop in the bazaar with the consequent squeeze on household expenses, and a free hand to run the house in their own way provided they produced satisfactory results. The wise woman kept out of the kitchen as much as possible and enjoyed the freedom from domestic work which the system was devised to guarantee her. She might take a discreet hand in the garden, at least to the extent of cutting her own flowers, she might devise her own menus, and there were always the European shops where her servants would be as unwelcome customers as they would be guests in the local clubs.

As the British began to move into the Far East, enterprizing retailers soon followed the wholesale merchants who were the aristocrats of trade, and in 1822 George Armstrong opened in Singapore what was probably the first shop designed specifically for the convenience of the English residents and the transient ships' officers. Other shops followed. In 1833 a London tailor and a European hairdresser established themselves. But even in 1840 Major Low was complaining that 'European shops, as they are termed, are not numerous, nor, although respectable, are they in keeping with such a mart'; apparently their deficiencies were made up by the regular merchants, who displayed European goods in their godowns and, despite their pretensions, do not appear to have been above a little retail trading on occasion. By 1860, however, the European population of Singapore had grown large enough to justify the establishment of the first Far Eastern department store, Robinson and Co., on Commercial Square, which opened with boasts of 'a carefully selected stock of mantles, ribbons, bonnets, Lyons and Spitalfields silks, Organdie and Chantilly muslins, barege robes, balserine ditto, opera cloaks ...'. In Shanghai there were five European shops by 1848, and in 1859 the first ladies' dress shop opened. During the later years of the nineteenth century appeared those Far Eastern chain stores whose branches were found in every important coastal city from Penang to Bangkok and from Hong Kong to Yokohama; Whiteway Laidlaws, who specialized in tropical outfitting, and Kelly and Walsh, the ubiquitous booksellers, are names which still stir the memories of Old Asia Hands. There had been European bakers in the Far East since the first appeared in Penang in the 1790s. European chemists, confectioners, butchers, even undertakers advertising patent iron coffins that would withstand tropical insects, set themselves up in Singapore and Shanghai and Yokohama during the 1860s and 1870s. Somewhat later, after the First World War, the Cold Storage Company's establishments began to appear in the principal towns of Malaya. In addition to providing frozen meats, fish and dairy products, the Cold Storage ran grocery departments with many foreign products and made it possible for nostalgic housewives to reproduce ever more faithfully the meals of England. Nor was it long before the enterprizing Chinese began to edge into this profitable carriage trade. By reason of their imitativeness they were better tailors than the Bengalis and cheaper than the London tailors, to whom they soon became formidable competitors, providing for the services as well as for civilians, like the Mr Cock Eye who in the 1870s advertised himself as the leading naval and military tailor in Yokohama.

What the tailors made for their European customers we shall discover shortly. Meanwhile, let us peer into some of the houses of the Far East to see what the Bengali convicts or Cantonese cooks who presided over their kitchens provided for the tuans and taipans.

The cuisine was basically English, interpreted by native cooks and embellished with a few oriental touches which reflected past Indian connections rather more than present Chinese ones. The Chinese culinary tradition is the best in Asia and in the whole world is rivalled for versatility and subtlety only by the French. From the days of the Canton factories, Englishmen were entertained by Chinese merchants and certainly, if we can judge from William Hickey's account, they thoroughly enjoyed the great meals of birds' nest soup, roasted snails, plovers' eggs and sharks' fins which they were offered, but such experiences had little effect on the meals they ate at home, even though they were prepared by Chinese cooks.

The East Indiamen in the seventeenth century ate a slight breakfast, and an enormous dinner at noon, with wine, large quantities of tea, and, often, a potent punch of brandy and rosewater. The evening meal was lighter. By the eighteenth century the pattern was already being elaborated, and at Bencoolen an extra meal was added, the light breakfast being followed by tiffin, a snack meal with punch; dinner, with four or five dishes, followed in the afternoon, and then in the evening there would be supper. In 1824 in Singapore dinner was still at 4 in the afternoon and supper at 9.30, but already it was the custom for ceremonial dinners to take place at 7.30, and by 1840 this had become the regular hour for those who had any pretensions to gentility.

At that period, John Turnbull Thomson, government surveyor in Singapore, paid a visit to Penang and was entertained by one of its merchants on his plantation outside Georgetown. That evening Thomson ate a dinner of true Victorian amplitude. After the gentlemen had taken sherry and bitters, the party sat down to a table on which the family silver was prominently displayed. Several kinds of soup appeared first. After soup, wine was drunk, and the fish followed. After the fish had been cleared away, the table was loaded with meat and poultry dishes which exemplified the complex trading network of which Malaya was already the centre: the mutton was from Bengal, the capons came from China, the fowls and ducks from mainland Malaya, the ham from England and the potatoes from Java. A round of healths was taken, and then came the one oriental item of the meal – curry and rice, with Bombay duck, sambals, salted turtle eggs and omelettes. Again, there was a taking of wine, and next came the shapes and custards and the macaroni pudding. Champagne followed, and a great cheese was placed on the table, to be despatched with pale ale, the meal ending with fruit and more wine.

Such meals continued to be typical of European society in the Far East for many years. A doctor in the Shanghai of the early taipans remarked that the frequency of liver trouble was hardly surprising, given the kind of meals his patients insisted on eating:

They begin dinner with rich soup and a glass of sherry; *then* they partake of one or two side dishes, with champagne; then some beef, mutton or fowls and bacon, with *more* champagne, or beer; *then* rice and curry and ham; *afterwards* game; *then* pudding, jelly, custard, or blancmange, and *more* champagne; *then* cheese and salad, and bread and butter, and a glass of port wine; *then* in many cases oranges, figs, raisins and walnuts are eaten *with* two or three glasses of claret or some other wine; and this *awful* repast is finished at last with a cup of strong coffee and cigars!

At the same time, eating during the hot hours of the day had declined. The huge midday meals of the seventeenth century had vanished. In Cameron's Singapore of the 1860s, tiffin had become a light meal – 'a plate of curry and rice and some fruit, or it may be a simple biscuit with a glass of beer or claret'. But who would need more, after consuming the breakfast which, Cameron will have us believe, was customary among the gentlemen of Singapore? 'A little fish, some curry and rice, and perhaps a couple of eggs, washed down with a tumbler or so of good claret, does not take long to get through and yet forms a very fair foundation on which to begin the labours of the day.'

There were variations within this general pattern of feeding, depending on the kind of materials that were locally available. In Malaya the beef was tough and fit only for use in soup, but poultry was abundant and cheap, and mutton usually excellent; in Shanghai frogs found their way into the diet, usually curried, for they were so common in the ditches around the settlement, and so prized by the Chinese, that the taotai had insisted on including them in the list of protected animals when local sportsmen had requested the establishment of a close season on the game which formed another important part of the Shanghai diet. In Malaya it was tropical fruits that gave an individual touch to every menu; they included plantains, ducoos, mangoes, rambutans, pomeloes and mangosteens, a local fruit not unlike the custard apple. The great prickly fruit called durian was also available, but, though some Europeans acquired the Malay's passion for durian, it was hardly suitable for a polite dinner table, since it smelt ripely of dung. In Shanghai there were strawberries from the local gardens and peaches and grapes which the junks brought down from the north. With fruit and vegetables a particular care was needed; for the sicknesses which early doctors attributed to overeating were often due to the Chinese gardeners' methods of fertilizing with human urine and night-soil. One surprising amenity appeared on Far Eastern tables well over a hundred years ago. Modern visitors in Hong Kong are often struck by the name of Ice House Street. It was here that in 1847 a building was constructed to hold lake ice brought by ship from the United States. The ice business flourished in Hong Kong, but in Singapore a similar enterprize established by the Chinese merchant Whampoa failed surprisingly for lack of custom; later, in 1861 an ice-making machine was imported into Singapore, but it failed to work and for many years afterwards liquids had to be cooled by the tedious method of turning the bottles in buckets of saltpetre.

There were of course thousands of Europeans, particularly in Malaya and Borneo, who rarely ate meals of the kind that populated the nostalgic memories of writers of memoirs. Planters living on their own with a single servant to do all the household tasks, administrators in distant posts, teak men in Thailand, visitors arriving at government rest houses in the backlands, became used to a kind of sub-cuisine whose menus were scanty and monotonous and whose products were, at best, parodies of English meals. A weak, rancid soup would be followed by bony fish, and the main course would be tough local chicken, the meal ending with caramel cream. The main variation was that chicken curry sometimes replaced roast chicken, and bananas all too often unripe would excuse the cook from making even so modest a dessert as caramel cream.

And what of the man who sat down to his modest or elaborate meal in the Far East? How was he clad to do honour to the food? In broadcloth and a wig at Bencoolen during the eighteenth century, and in very much the same garb, minus the wig, at Penang and Singapore when they were founded in 1786 and 1819. It was, then, the sign of European superiority to dress as one did in London, to sweat and bear it. Light was regarded with distrust, not because he kept a Eurasian mistress, but because in his home at ease he would relax in the native sarong. As late as the 1930s young men in respectable merchant houses were warned against wearing sarongs even at night, instead of pyjamas, since this was one of the acts that betokened a break in European solidarity. The changes that did take place in British Far Eastern garb during the century after Raffles founded Singapore were in fact aimed at devising a comfortable tropical garb which would make no compromise with native dress.

Wallace, visiting Malacca as late as the 1850s, complained of the extreme conservatism which the English still maintained in their dress, preserving 'the tight-fitting coat, waistcoat, and trousers, and the abominable hat and cravat'. However, even by this time there had been some relaxations as compared with the previous century. In the mornings, before going to the office, it had become customary for the European to lounge in pyjamas, often made splendidly of Chinese silk. When he went down to do business and when he went to church on a Sunday, the merchant was still expected to dress as he might have done in England, and some, even in the 1840s, still wore beaver hats in the streets of Singapore, but in the evening he might adopt a lighter garb of white jacket and trousers, with canvas shoes; the black jacket was expected only on ceremonial occasions, at least until the 1870s, when it became required dress for dinner everywhere. In his office a man might take off his coat and work in his shirt sleeves; in his club, anywhere from Kobe to Penang, he was expected to keep it on.

Later in the century – after the lessons of the Indian Mutiny had sunk in and even the army had begun to adopt more sensible tropical dress – the age of the solar topee and white garments made of light washable materials arrived. For a surprising number of years the solar topee (now used only by a few elderly Eurasians and Chinese) was regarded – as an official guide to the Federated Malay States described it in the 1920s – as 'the most important article of dress for white men or white women in the tropics'. In this era suits of white drill, made up by a Chinese tailor, were considered the necessary basis for a man's wardrobe in the tropics – a newly laundered suit to be worn each day. Even this garb the English often contrived to make surprisingly uncomfortable, for the jacket was often in the style known locally as *tutup* (meaning 'closed' in Malay); it was starched and close fitting and had a high neckband rather like a Nehru jacket. One gains a fair idea of an average wardrobe of this period from the instructions which the British North Borneo Company issued to its young officers first going to the east. They were instructed to buy six stiff shirts and collars and six cricket shirts, four white drill suits, three mess jackets, a light suit, riding breeches and a dress uniform with helmet. The arrival of the planters created something of a revolution in clothing, and by the 1920s sartorial liberation had come to the backlands with the adoption of shorts and the eventual demotion of the solar toppee in favour of the wide-brimmed planter's hat. Finally, in the 1930s, the arrival of cheap ready-made light clothes from Europe ended the period when the Chinese tailor and his limited styles reigned supreme, and prepared the way for the present situation, in which white garb has been left to house-boys and dark suits in light synthetic cloths have become the customary wear among Europeans in the Far East.

Women's garb in the east was always a little more sensible than that of the men, largely because the women, even in the early Victorian era, took advantage of the gauzes and muslins which were similar to the materials worn by Asian women; they also developed, early on, a sensible predilection for white. In general, however stiff they may have been socially, their dress was at least less rigidly formal than that of the men. There is an entertaining paragraph on this point in a book called *The Chersonese with the Gilding Off*, written by a lady named Emily Innes who raced through Malaya in the 1880s.

Perhaps I should mention, lest English ladies should be shocked at my speaking to the cook in my sleeping costume, that it was much more elaborate than what is worn in England under similar circumstances. In Malaya no one gets into bed, as they do in colder climates; the heat of the sheets, blankets and counterpanes would be unendurable; therefore most people only lie on the bed (which consists of a mattress or mat, covered with a single sheet) with no covering over them, but their nightdress. This custom makes it necessary that the nightdress should be a presentable costume. Luxurious bachelors usually had magnificent suits of Chinese silk for sleeping in; but I contented myself with, first, a toilette of thin flannel

14—TBITFE * *

as a protection against rheumatism, and over that a chintz dressing-gown, or 'morning robe', to quote the language of the shops; so that in any emergency, such as a mailboat leaving, or a murder, or a fire, I was ready dressed. In fact, in Malacca and Singapore, I have seen ladies go to church on Sundays in much the same garb.

For a later age, the author of the guidebook to the Federated Malay States rather archly remarks that 'the delicate question of clothing for ladies resolves itself into the question: How much can you discard and still appear in public?' He warns ladies that they should not consider Malaya a place for wearing out their old frocks. 'Light washing dresses of muslin and similar materials are chiefly worn.' And he adds a series of recommendations which complete our portrait of the English lady in Malaya before the Second World War.

A light coat for motoring in the evenings is always useful. Boots are a better protection against mosquitoes than shoes, but shoes are preferred as lighter and cooler. Doeskin or chamois gloves are generally worn in the day time as a protection against the sun. A white sun umbrella is almost essential, a scarlet lining to it being, according to scientific authority, the best colour to ward off sunstroke. It is also more becoming than green.

When, garbed in their changing fashions, the gentlemen and ladies of the Far East left the private worlds of their houses and entered that social world which will be described in the next chapter, they travelled in a variety of private and public conveyances. In Penang by 1810 little buggies or phaetons were already being driven on the roads which Light had built, drawn by Sumatra ponies which Minto described as 'the smallest fairy-like horses you ever saw'. Those who had no carriage of their own could hire a palankeen carriage, such as Captain Welsh took at the time for a trip up Penang Hill; 'an ill-made and not very comfortable litter on four wheels', it cost him three Spanish dollars a day.

In Singapore carriages were imported soon after the first roads had been laid out; by 1840 there were 140 four-wheeled and 44 two-wheeled carriages on the island, and their numbers increased rapidly. They varied greatly, from the chari – a jolting box on four wheels, through the merchant's elegant little phaeton, with the groom running beside it, to the four-horsed carriage in which Governor Butterworth would drive to receptions, with lantern-bearing lackeys trotting by the wheels. Palankeen carriages were made in Singapore, but those who wished to ride comfortably imported their carriages from England. Later, in Selangor, a local and more comfortable form of gharry was developed which became a favourite form of transport in Kuala Lumpur. It was a light and well sprung two-wheeled pony carriage.

In the cities of the China coast it was some time before the streets were long or solid enough for carriages, and the earliest form of transport in both Shanghai and Hong Kong was the sedan chair, which has continued in Hong Kong until the present day, when a few chair coolies still make a wretched living carrying people up the stepped streets from one steep level of the city to the next. Until the 1880s chairs were still the customary way of ascending to the houses built high on the slopes of the Peak, but in 1888 the funicular known as the Peak Tramway was completed and the chair coolies became a fast declining class.

The earliest wheeled conveyance in the treaty ports was the wheel barrow, which was often used for passengers who did not wish to travel quickly; it needed only one man to propel it and was therefore cheaper than a chair. But it was an undignified vehicle which the Europeans avoided, though the members of the China Inland Mission apparently had a predilection for this uncomfortable kind of travel as part of their policy of reaching the Chinese by trying to live Chinese lives.

Both the sedan chair and the wheelbarrow suffered from the appearance in the 1870s of the man-drawn carriage known as the rickshaw. The history of the rickshaw – or jinricksha – is rather curious, since it appears to have been a western contrivance adopted by Asians with such zest that it has passed for a Japanese invention. An American Baptist missionary named Jonathan Goble designed the first jinricksha in 1871 and had it made by a Japanese carpenter so that his invalid wife might have long rides in the open air. The idea immediately caught on among the Japanese, who imitated Goble's vehicle, and by 1874 rickshaws, as they were eventually called by contraction of the original Japanese name (itself meaning *man-power vehicle*), had spread to Shanghai. Very shortly afterwards the rickshaw reached Hong Kong and the fashion spread through the cities of Indonesia and Malaya until eventually it reached Calcutta. Until the pedicab appeared in Shanghai in 1924, the rickshaw was probably the vehicle most used by Europeans as well as by the more prosperous Chinese and Japanese. Today it has largely vanished from its country of origin, Japan, where it is now used only by geishas, and it is almost certainly extinct in Shanghai, but in Hong Kong, as in Calcutta, it is still a familiar sight in the streets.

By 1850 horse carriages were common in the streets of Shanghai and Hong Kong, where the few ladies languidly took the air in them at evening, and in the following decade stage coaches linked the treaty ports of Japan. In 1878 steam tramways appeared in Singapore. The turn of the century saw the appearance of the first motor cars. A pioneer Benz was imported into Singapore as early as 1898, and in 1902 the first two Olds-mobiles appeared in Shanghai, but it was not until after the First World War that motor buses began to run in Far Eastern cities, modelled on the London buses, as they are in Hong Kong to this day. Already, by 1928, there were seven thousand cars in Shanghai, but until the 1950s other types of transport were in the aggregate more important in the Far East than the automobile. Manpower was cheap, as the great staffs of servants demonstrated, and if the British rulers took to cars, it was partly for the convenience they provided, but even more for the prestige they conferred in a social world where 'face' was all-important.

13

THE SOCIAL WORLD

The symbolic sanctuaries of British society in the colonies and protectorates of the Far East were – as elsewhere in the empire – Government House (or the Residency) and the Club. On the China coast, where the empire was commercial rather than political, the Club reigned supreme. These institutions crowned the pyramid of society. Government House, whose occupant wielded a great deal more actual power than the British monarch for whom he deputized, was not merely the pivot of administration; it was also the centre of the imperial cult. The Club on the other hand dictated who should belong to accepted society, and what that meant was stated with naive frankness in Cameron's survey of the Singapore of his mid-Victorian day. 'Society may be said to be composed of the chief government officials, the merchants and bankers with their assistants and clerks – the lawyers, the doctors, and the military – at least, any of those positions *prima facie* give the necessary social status.'

Even members of these groups, as Cameron was careful to point out, might be excluded for various reasons, the most important being any detectable portion of Asian ancestry. A Chinese merchant, a Eurasian doctor, emphatically did not belong to society. Whole categories of the purest blooded Europeans were also excluded: shopkeepers, for instance. 'To an American,' grumbled William T. Hornaday in the 1880s, 'it seems extremely silly for wholesale merchants and their clerks to hold themselves, socially, above the retail merchants and their clerks, regardless of the amount of business they do, and their moral and intellectual standing.' Ships' chandlers, though they often became rich men, were among the outcasts, which was why Lord Jim (and his real life original in Singapore) was able to find refuge from shame in such a business. Sailors, soldiers, policemen – all such humble Atlases who held the weight of empire on their shoulders – lived in the limbo of unrecognition;

in the British society of the Far East they had neither place nor power.

Distance from Britain, far from loosening the ties that bound Britons into a rigid world of class distinctions, tended to tighten them. Other ruling elites, like the Manchus in China, may have become lax with time, sinking into the great sea of native life that surrounded them, but the British, who in Asia made no permanent home in the lands they dominated, feared and avoided the onset of such laxness. East of Suez they became even more conscious of their nationality than they would have been at home. Imperial festivals took on, for them, a preternatural importance. The King's Birthday, and after 1918, Armistice Day, were observed with the greatest possible official pomp, even if the place were only some outpost in a Malay native state and the participants a couple of administrators, a handful of planters and a file of Sikh policemen. Organizations like the St George's and the St Andrew's Society, which existed in all the major cities around the China Seas, sustained the level of patriotic sentiment, and the balls held on the days of the English and Scottish patron saints were among the most splendid social occasions of the year.

The East India Company, with its obsessive Elizabethan concern for degree and ceremonial, had already established elaborate systems of protocol and precedence with an appropriate mercantile slant. Civil officers in the Penang presidency of 1805 who held the rank of senior merchant were, at ceremonial gatherings, regarded as the equivalent of lieutenant-colonels, junior merchants of majors, factors of captains, and writers of subalterns. At the top of the hierarchy, above merchants and officers alike, stood the august figure of the governor-general, who was stationed away in Calcutta, but would make rare visits to the outlying regions under the Company's control and would then strike fear into the hearts of his subordinates. 'And all the great men who were there to welcome him stood a great way off,' said Raffles' observant Malay secretary Abdullah when Lord Minto arrived in Penang, 'and not one of them dared to offer his hand; they only raised their hats and perspired.'

When the Company ceased to control the trade with Canton, and, later, to govern the Straits Settlements, its precarious unity of the mercantile and the political came to an end. Under the colonial service, merchants, as such, no longer had any special position in the tables of precedence. What counted now was whether one had a title and, if not, one's civil, military or naval rank. When the governor or the resident held an official dinner, everyone sat down strictly in the order published in the Government Gazette. The discriminations of the Club could not be followed openly in Government House, and so among the men in their tail coats and uniforms and the women in filmy evening dress, one would see Malay sultans and important Chinese merchants in their silk and brocade native garb, and sometimes a turbanned Indian. One might even find oneself sitting at table below one of the titled Asians, as the gallant chatter rose around the table and the band of the local regiment played Gilbert and Sullivan on the verandah outside. In that particular setting everyone accepted a little racial mingling and the pretensions of the native princelings were regarded with indulgence. This, after all, was a question of government. One mixed on such occasions with Malays and Chinese as one might mix with them on the legislative council. This did not mean that one wished to see them in one's club.

The Club; capitalized, the word ceases to mean any one of the hundreds of clubs devoted to various interests and to various groups which have arisen over the decades in colonial cities and treaty ports in the Far East. It means, rather, the complex of attitudes embodied in those special and quintessential clubs which towered over their rivals by representing the most powerful elements in the British population. The Shanghai Club, the Penang Club, the Kobe Club, the Hong Kong Club, the Selangor in Kuala Lumpur, the Tanglin in Singapore, the Sarawak in Kuching; these and a few like them represented the peak of clubdom; the lesser clubs could only aspire to imitate. To such clubs belonged the principal government officers, the leading merchants of the great import and export houses, the bankers, lawyers and doctors; army and navy officers, who had their own United Service Club, were also eligible for the Club. So too were the griffins – the junior members of the merchant houses; indeed, membership of the Club was for them almost a condition of employment. But it was long before even the richest of retail shopkeepers could be voted into membership of one of the more august clubs. Women also, in the classic days, were excluded. So, in the vast majority of cases, were natives of any rank or kind. The Selangor Club was a qualified exception. Situated in the capital city of a native principality, it could hardly avoid granting membership to a few carefully chosen Malay aristocrats, who were usually tactful enough to appear rarely. For this reason it was derisively called the Spotted Dog. But there were plenty of planters' clubs with tiny memberships in remote rubber-growing areas even of the native states which were strictly confined to Europeans.

In the past the exclusiveness of European clubs aroused a varying amount of bitterness among Asians and even in recent years the reluctance of the Tanglin Club to open its membership became a political issue in Singapore. Probably no one in Malaya or on the China coast felt so strongly about clubs as the Indians, who waited impatiently until they could take them over when India became independent in 1947 and devise their own forms of exclusivism. Comparatively little was heard of the question in either Malaya or Hong Kong or in the treaty ports before the Second World War, and even in the more nationalistically conscious 1940s and 1950s the Malays and Chinese were motivated less by a desire to join than a resentment at the thought of being kept out. To be excluded meant a loss of face.

The arguments used to justify exclusion are familiar and rather plausible. Asians themselves, it is urged, have many kinds of social organizations which are restricted racially, regionally and in various other ways; these a European would not be allowed to join, even if he expressed a desire to do so, which he would not, since he would have no wish to mingle in the special affairs of other people. Why, therefore, should he be denied a place where, after work, he could meet his compatriots and settle down to drink a few stengahs, play billiards or bridge, read the newspapers from home, or merely chat about the day and its troubles and triumphs? In such a simple form the argument is hard to dismiss. The real dilemma only becomes evident when one remembers that the clubs were not only the meeting places of people of a particular race or of particular shared interests. They were also, inevitably, gathering points for the ruling elite, and this applied as much to the smallest planters' club as it did to the august precincts of the Shanghai Club, from whose windows facing on to the Bund the members looked out at the shipping which daily added to their wealth and – for many years – to their power.

The clubs are rarely much more than a century old. They did not come into being until after the collegiate system of the Company's factories and of the early merchant hongs had died away. The men who lived together in the factories of Canton needed no club, and in early Singapore, the Exchange, which was opened by the shopkeeper George Armstrong in 1831 as a kind of coffee house, served as an adequate meeting place for the small number of merchants trading there at the time.

The first actual club to be founded in Singapore, and probably anywhere in the Far East, had no pretensions to being the arbiter of local society. It was a billiards club, which charged a 50 dollars admission fee to keep out the undesirable; its premises remained open from six in the morning until ten at night; all record of it vanished a year after its founding. The Hong Kong Club was the first of the great clubs of the Far East to come into existence; it was founded in 1846. But it was not until the 1860s that the merchants and officials in most of the British communities began to find such organizations necessary. To that decade belong the Shanghai Club, the Singapore Tanglin Club and the Kobe Club. The

Selangor Club was not founded until the 1880s, the clubs in Bornean towns like Kuching and Jesselton came into existence even later, and most of the planters' clubs in the hinterland of Malaya date from before or shortly after the First World War.

The clubs were egalitarian in the same way as army messes, at least in their avowed intentions. Once one had been accepted as coming out of the right social drawer, questions of rank were unimportant; the griffin was the equal of the taipan. There was even a rough kind of equality between large clubs and little clubs. Not merely were they all as exclusive as they could contrive, but they provided roughly the same facilities for their members.

The bar of the Shanghai Club might claim to be the longest in the world, the Kobe Club might boast nine billiard tables, the Hong Kong Club might have an excellent dining room, but basically what all the clubs offered fell into the same pattern. Cards, billiards, a reading room, sometimes a dining room, conversation of sorts and, above all, a well-stocked bar. (The Shanghai Club in 1870 spent 16,724 dollars on drinks as against 72 dollars on its reading room.) The atmosphere in the larger clubs, where it was *de rigueur* to wear a coat and tie in the bar, was certainly more strictly formal than that in the planters' clubs, whose members would appear in shorts and open-necked shirts, but planters were mostly of lower-middle-class origin and occupied a somewhat insecure position in the Far Eastern social hierarchy.

What none of the smaller clubs provided, of course, was that intercourse of the powerful which went on in settings like the Shanghai Club, the Selangor Club and the Tanglin Club. In spite of the pretence of equality among members, there was an end of every long bar that was tacitly reserved for taipans and tuans, and here the exchanges of views and the veiled negotiations which affected the commercial and political policies governing colonies and concessions would often be transacted.

In every Malayan city and every treaty port, the Club would stand like a great tree crowded by saplings, for the desire of the exile to mingle with his own kind led to the creation of scores of minor clubs that represented various kinds of limited interests. Most people, even if they had been admitted to the club, would also belong to several of these lesser fellowships. A list compiled as early as 1920 showed no less than sixty-two clubs and societies founded by the British colony in Shanghai. Some, like the United Services Club, and the Merchant Service Club, represented special groups; occasionally these groups, like the naval ratings of the Union

Jack Club, belonged to the socially excluded classes. Others represented special interests, like horticulture, philately, chess, photography, chamber music, amateur dramatics. Yet others nostalgically celebrated the local origins of their members, like the St David's Society and the Association of Lancastrians. But by far the greatest number, led by the Race Club (founded in 1850) and the Cricket Club (founded in 1860), were devoted to sports of many kinds.

Sport was a veritable cult in the Far East, even more than in nine-teenth- and early twentieth-century England. It was considered physically necessary because of the prevailing superstition that to be healthy in a tropical climate one must take plenty of exercize. Even more, it was considered socially desirable, as an expression of the British power to astonish and excel. The young griffin, if he did not arrive showing a demonstrative eagerness to indulge in as many sports as possible, would be called before his taipan and instructed in the obligations of his position. Newly recruited government cadets were advised to provide themselves with cricket and football boots, golf clubs, and squash and tennis rackets, and were expected to find a use for them.

The enthusiasm for sports, which in later years acquired such formid-able social overtones, began as a means of avoiding boredom on the part of energetic and not particularly intellectual men trapped in the early isola-tion of the Straits Settlements and the treaty ports. Perhaps because life was exciting in other ways, with Dutchmen and death always around the corner, there is little to show that the young men who manned the East India factories of the seventeenth century were greatly addicted to sports of any kind and there was scanty room for such activity in the confined spaces round the factories at Canton. But the merchants there, once the season for buying tea and selling opium was over, retired for their months of relaxation in Macao, where, being nineteenth-century Englishmen, they entered enthusiastically into the local horse-racing and astonished the lethargic Portuguese by their devotion to cricket.

Anywhere during the Victorian age, as soon as a few British merchants or officials were gathered together, one of their first concerns would be to start up outdoor games. In Singapore the process began in the 1830s, and the first game to be organized was fives, which was introduced in 1836 by Dr Montgomerie and for many years remained popular there; doctors regarded the heavy perspiration it produced as one of the reasons for the high standard of health among Europeans on the island. Shortly after-wards the evening games of cricket began on the greens of the Esplanade.

There has always been a touch of the missionary in the English sports-men and in the 1830s the British residents of Singapore also set about encouraging the competitive sporting spirit among the native population by introducing what was to become one of the regular events of the year – the New Year's Day Sports, for non-Europeans only; for once the English were content to be amused spectators. The report on the event in the *Singapore Free Press* at New Year 1839 provides an unconscious commentary on the different attitudes of Asians and Englishmen to organized athletics.

The European Gentlemen of the Settlement have for some time back observed the laudable practice of ushering in the New Year with sports and pastimes among the native population, in which suitable rewards are appropriated to those who compete. Boat-racing is the most favourite and most attractive of these diversions. Indeed it is remarked how very few games or exercises of an active and athletic nature the Malays have; even boat-racing, as sport, is an exotic: and the only games peculiar to them appear to be a sort of foot-ball and kite-flying, the latter being an exercize practised in various ways in many parts of the civilized world, in a manner of which the poor Malays have not the smallest idea. In their sampans, however, whether pulling or sailing, they beat in their own waters every competitor. The first race was a pulling match, the reward for the winner 15 dollars. The next was a sailing match between Malay sampans, about ten of them mustering for the race. They made a beautiful start of it; their long, light, sharp hulls cutting through the water under a fresh breeze in the best style –

> 'So shoots through the morning sky the lark,
> Or the swan through the summer sea.'

The run was about four miles, which was accomplished in a very short space of time, the first boat being rewarded with a prize of twenty, and the second with one of ten dollars. A race of common Malay sampans, manned with Kling boatmen, was then well contested and excited a considerable degree of interest.

After these were over, the Sports on shore commenced with a pony race mounting native riders. A very grotesque congregation of men and horses assembled at the starting post, very few of whom reached the winning post. Some wrestling then ensued, in which the only competitors were Klings, who made far better work of it than we ever saw done by the more lusty Chinamen, whom we have sometimes seen vying with each other in the same contest. A great deal of foot-racing, etc. etc., then became the order of the day, and continued until four o'clock, when the ground began to get clear of its various multitudes, all of whom seemed equally delighted with the Sports, not the least interesting or important of which were the scrambles for copper pice which some lively young gentlemen were ever and anon projecting into the air.

The New Year Gymkhana – as it was later called – became one of the regular events of the Singapore season, taking place on the padang in front of the Cricket Club, on whose verandah would sit the governor, the sultan of Johore, the state just over the channel from Singapore, and Raja

Charles Brooke, who made a point of visiting Singapore for the occasion. By this time the original sports had been mingled with the buffoonery of a mid-Victorian English fair. There were rickshaw races, sack races, pig-catching and climbing the greasy pole. Native boys engaged in eating contests, swallowing piles of hard ship's biscuits, and timed by the governor's aide-de-camp in all his finery. At the climax of the entertainment, the guests laughed uproariously as Chinese and Malay boys plunged their heads into tubs of molasses to fish for silver coins with their teeth. It all ended with imperial splendour, the trooping of the colour, the march past of the troops, fireworks, the booming of guns from the fort, and a ball at Government House, to which, needless to say, the winners of the events were not invited.

Of all the sports which the English practised in the Far East those which aroused the most passionate interest and participation were horse racing and the hunt; the latter practised in unorthodox forms adapted to the peculiar circumstances of the east. In nineteenth-century England to hunt and to race horses were hallmarks of the nobility and the gentry, and it was only natural that the merchants, who on the China coast and in the Straits Settlements had largely supplanted the landed aristocrats, should fervently adopt pastimes which, apart from any intrinsic excitement, proclaimed their pretensions in status and at the same time reminded them vividly of home.

In Singapore the Sporting Club was founded in 1842, and held the first horse races in February 1843, the event culminating with a Race Ball at the house of the Recorder. The following year regular auctions of horses imported from Australia began in Commercial Square; the eleven animals sold in 1844 fetched prices varying from 100 to 350 dollars. With them came Australian jockeys, who from this time onwards competed on most of the race courses in the Far East.

In Shanghai it was difficult to establish racing immediately because of the rough, ditch-scored nature of the ground on which the settlement arose, and the early merchants had to content themselves with such simple sports as foot racing and – for hilarious variety – wheelbarrow racing. After the area of the settlement had been extended and it became possible to find level ground, the Shanghai Race Club was founded in 1850 and in that year the first race was run, with Australian horses. For many years conditions were rather primitive and the grandstand was so exposed to the winds that the few ladies in the settlement would not attend the meetings. But as the settlement developed, the prestige attached to horse racing grew rapidly, and the great trading houses would compete with horses sporting their colours and on some occasions ridden by the taipans themselves.

Luck and training decided who should win these races, for very soon Mongolian ponies of thirteen hands or less began to replace the larger Australian horses, and in 1870 it was decided that these alone should be allowed to compete in Shanghai. The ponies – called griffins because, like young clerks arriving in the east, they were yet unbroken – were imported by the Race Club in whole shipments from the north, and after being vetted they were disposed of by lot, at a fixed price, so that the clerk and the taipan had the same chance of buying a winner. Since the horses of taipans and of high customs officials so often carried away the cups, one can only assume that a certain amount of horse trading took place after the quality of the various ponies had been revealed. By the 1920s racing in Shanghai had reached its peak, and the famous mercenaries like One-Arm Sutton would bring their horses out of China for the spring and autumn meets, which took ten days, when the banks and the foreign merchant houses closed at eleven o'clock each morning so that their staffs need not miss the races. The racing mania spread to every treaty port in China and Japan where there were more than a handful of Englishmen. Amoy in particular was famous for its meets, which the local mandarins attended in full dress (the taotai even gave a cup each year). Even in Peking, in 1865, when there were only sixty Europeans in the newly founded legations, the British were able to organize annual races which became a leading event of the season for the non-missionary half of the foreign community. Horse racing also became intensely popular in Malaya and particularly in the Malay states after the plantations and the tin mines began to create a prosperous European community. Courses were established first at Taiping and very shortly afterwards at Kuala Lumpur, Seremban and Ipoh, whose race meets are still extremely popular with Malayan residents of all races. Even in North Borneo, despite the hot climate and the minuscule size of the British community, pony racing was passionately followed.

Hunting was more difficult to establish than racing, for a number of inconvenient reasons. Foxes were not common in any of the Asian countrysides where the British established themselves and the terrain was likely to be either jungle, difficult to penetrate on horseback, or, in the case of China and Japan, cultivated ground broken by irrigation ditches and the little mud walls of rice paddies. Usually the Chinese peasants whose land was ridden over could be placated by suitable payment, and after a time the mounted barbarians chasing through the countryside around Shanghai became so familiar that peasants would even accept chits for compensation and duly appear in the settlement to receive payment. In Malaya, plantation country was chosen, where the alleys between the trees were excellent for riding. But though foxhounds were imported they could not stand the pace of the hunt in the hot, humid Malay climate, so that the Hunt Clubs were eventually reduced to organizing mounted paper chases. Paper chases were also popular around Shanghai, where winners only were granted the right to wear pink coats, but hounds were also introduced successfully, and only the fox was lacking. Pariah dogs were tried, but did not run well enough, and in the end a horse-drawn, nauseatingly scented drag was substituted. For many years the Paper Hunt and the Drag Hunt rivalled each other in preserving at least a semblance of the most insular of all English sports.

If the hunt assumed such caricature forms, shooting enthusiasts encountered notable fields of slaughter in many parts of the Far East. The countryside around many of the treaty ports, and particularly around Shanghai and Osaka, was in the early days abundantly populated with pheasants, woodcock, snipe and wild duck. The earliest treaties only allowed foreigners to go for restricted distances outside the ports but even then it was possible and safe to make a day's shooting expedition out in the country around Shanghai, though at one period the taotai insisted that every hunting party should be accompanied by a Chinese constable; Canton, where the feeling against foreigners ran higher, was a much more dangerous region, and several wandering Englishmen were killed there by village mobs. Later on, in the 1860s after the Treaty of Nanking, longer expeditions were possible and the shooting parties would set out in a slow and clumsy houseboat called a Soochow Boat, up the creeks and channels of the hinterland, where excellent shooting was to be had among the reedbeds and in the open cottonfields. During the 1870s and the 1880s these expeditions shot phenomenal numbers of birds. Five men on one three week trip from Shanghai in 1889 bagged 2,049 birds. This, however, was nothing to the holocausts that went on in Malaya during the early days of the Federated Malay States, when on one occasion five men shot 609 snipe in a single day, and could have killed more in the remaining hour of daylight if their cartridges had not run out. Such overkill had its inevitable results; the game population of these areas diminished rapidly, and Victor Purcell describes one shooting trip into the Chinese hinterland during the 1920s on which he and a companion shot a single pigeon.

Other sports were pursued with almost equal zest. Polo was popular in Malaya, and even found a place in the restricted confines of Hong Kong. There, however, the most sacred game was cricket, held in such reverence that the Cricket Club, an exclusively British institution, has to this day been allowed to cling to its three-and-a-half acres of strictly segregated and extremely valuable land in the very heart of one of the world's most congested cities. The Singapore Yacht Club was founded and held its first regatta in 1834, with five boats racing on a six and a half mile course, and sailing continued to be a popular sport not only in Singapore and Penang, but also in Shanghai and Hong Kong, where a local refinement was introduced when European yachtsmen competed in specially built racing junks. Golf became an elite sport both in Hong Kong, where it was played on links in the New Territories, and in Malaya, particularly in the higher inland towns, where today it is reputed to provide the setting for deals among the sports conscious Malay politicians. Perhaps the most astonishing of successful imports was football, that cold-climate game which indefatigable Englishmen played even in the dense heat of Malaya and Borneo. More amazingly, it found devotees among the native inhabitants, and today one can walk out in Penang or Singapore when the temperature is in the 80s, and watch Chinese and Tamil boys playing vigorous games of soccer. In Hong Kong, where large stretches of level ground are scarce, a miniature football is played, with seven men to a side.

Except for tennis and swimming, the sporting world of the British community was mostly a masculine one; there were race courses in the Far East where women were not even allowed to bet. Yet the very presence of English women, once they began to arrive in considerable numbers, encouraged a whole series of more domestic and less organized pastimes. The cult of therapeutic exercize led to the popularity of both walking and casual riding. Cameron's portrait of Singapore in the 1860s shows the British starting from bed at the five o'clock gun from Fort Channing, and setting out by six for the morning walk or ride along the green and flowery lanes of the Tanglin hillsides.

Nor are these morning walks always given over to solitary commune with nature. At no other hour of the day are the roads out of the town so lively with Europeans. One can always depend upon picking up a companion and getting and giving all the little gossip of the night before; or more seriously discussing the last China or Europe mail news. During these walks, too, may be encountered pretty nearly the entire rising generation of European parentage – the heirs and heiresses, to be, of Singapore's merchants, who with their ayahs or native nurses are sent to 'maken angin' – literally, 'eat' the morning.

Two miles was the general length of the morning walk, though there were gluttons for exercise who would have done six miles before they returned home for the early cup of coffee or tea with biscuits or bread and butter, the far Eastern equivalent of the Indian *chota hazri*. The morning walk or ride was balanced by the evening drive, which would take place between five and the regular tropical nightfall at six-thirty, while the single men played their cricket or fives. The drive would always end with a few turns around the Esplanade, just as the evening drive in Shanghai would end with a few turns, to see and be seen, along the Bund. On those evenings in the easy Victorian days when the band played – and military, police or municipal bands played regularly everywhere the British settled in the Far East – the whole European community would gather, sitting in their carriages, to hear the popular music of the day.

Many evenings were taken up with dinner parties, for the merchants of the Far East were notably hospitable, usually entertaining at least once a week, and during the nineteenth century, while the British communities still remained relatively small, the newly arrived bachelor with the right social credentials had no difficulty in making his way from table to table until he was familiar with the relative merits of each house's entertainment and could make his choices. Inevitably the parties were overloaded with men; most women who arrived in the east were already married and even a plain girl could be the centre of attention where bachelors were twenty times more numerous than spinsters. After dinner the ladies would amuse themselves mildly by looking through albums of romantic views, but when the gentlemen joined them the floormats would often be rolled back for dancing, in the early days to the tune of fiddles but afterwards to the piano. Those who had no partners would settle down to playing loo or vingt-et-un, the favourite card game of the 1840s. Later the fashion would change to whist, and then, irrevocably, to bridge, which in the twentieth century became an obsessive addiction in almost every British home and club in the Far East; not to play bridge became one of the failings that helped to make a man socially suspect.

The gentle outdoor game of croquet, admirable for languid, humid afternoons on the coarse-grassed lawns of Malaya and China, arrived by the 1870s. So did the taste for garden parties, which ranged downward in splendour from the august occasions, with brass bands and colourful native notables in attendance, that were held in the manicured gounds of Government House. In Malaya, picnics on the seashore or at picturesque spots like the waterfall on Penang Island were popular, and in Japan they were often combined with a trip to some Buddhist temple or Shinto shrine which satisfied the Victorian taste for the curious.

The fashion for balls began when the first yearnings for social elegance appeared with the officials who arrived at Penang in 1805 to establish the presidency there, and the first recorded ball was held in 1807 on Lord Mayor's Day, an appropriate occasion to be celebrated by a company of merchants. 'The Honourable the Governor,' we are told in the *Prince of Wales' Island Gazette*, earliest of Far Eastern English newspapers,

The Social World

The scene as Chinese and Europeans went to the horse-races in Shanghai, 1879.

Sketches of actors at Turon Bay, by Alexander.

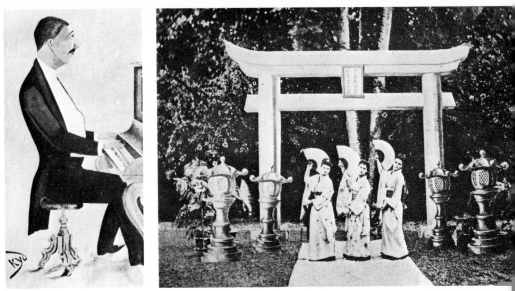

(*left*) Caricature by R. W. Bradell of J. M. Fabris, who organized so many amateur theatricals in Singapore in the late nineteenth century, that he was known as 'the George Grossmith of the Far East'.

(*right*) Scene from a performance of Gilbert and Sullivan's *Mikado*, performed by members of the British community in Singapore in 1893.

(*left*) Caricature by R. W. Bradell of A. Y. Gahagan, who was a leading comedian in the amateur theatricals performed in Singapore in the last years of the nineteenth century.

(*right*) Members of the Singapore Amateur Dramatic and Musical Society in a performance of Gilbert and Sullivan's *The Yeomen of the Guard*, put on in 1903.

(*above*) The clothes and stance of these Chinese men, photographed in 1913, would seem to owe much to (*below*) the formal group portraits so popular with the English at the turn of the century.

Sketches published in *The Graphic*, 1881, of scenes from life in China: (*top*) two Englishmen are rowed in a sampan and (*below*) an Englishman enjoys a languid canoe on a lotus lake.

Humorous sketches of incidents during a trip in a Chinese house-boat, 1889.

(*above*) The marble palace of Charlie Wun Ho, the 'gambling king' of Macao. Surrounded by a lily pond, the building is in marked contrast to the street of gambling houses (*below*), many of which were owned by Wun Ho.

The off-duty hours of the English communities in the Far East were often spent in jungle picnics (*above*) or rafting parties (*below*).

Malaya, 1913.

Formal portrait of a party at the Kuala Lumpur Races, 1913.

Another scene at the Kuala Lumpur Races.

(*above*) The February meeting at Kuala Lumpur race-course, 1923.

(*below*) Polo, learnt by the English in India, was another very popular sport in the Far East. Photographed at the Iskander Club Tournament, Easter, 1923.

The Committee of the
Selangor
St. Andrew's Ball
1913
request the pleasure of the company of

Miss Tyler

at the Ball to be held on the evening
of Friday 28th November, at the
Town Hall, Kuala Lumpur, at
9.15 o'clock.

R.S.V.P.

H. L. Snowie
Hon. Secy.

Balls were as important a part of the 'Season' in the Far East as they were in London.

Programme.

PIECE.	NAME.	COMPOSER.
1 March	"La Reine de Saba"	Gounod
2 Overture	"Phèdre"	Massenet
3 Selection	"Gondoliers"	Sullivan
4 Excerpt	"Angelus"	Massenet
5 Mazurka	"La Czarine"	Ganne
6 Selection	"Count of Luxembourg"	Lehar
7 Polonaise	"Life for the Czar"	Glinka
8		

GOD SAVE THE KING.

F. G. Moss
Bandmaster.

Band programme, Singapore Botanical Gardens, 1913.

Diary of Voyage
By S.S.

List of Passengers
PER TWIN S.S.

"WARWICKSHIRE,"

SAILING FROM

LIVERPOOL, 5th January, 1923.
MARSEILLES, 13th January, 1923.

"WARWICKSHIRE'S" OFFICERS, &c.

Commander			Captain H. PETERSON.
Chief Engineer			Mr. J. R. FARISH.
Surgeon			H. THORP, M.B. Ch.B., M.Sc.
Chief Steward			Mr. E. T. NAYLOR.
Chief Stewardess			Mrs. STONE.

BIBBY BROS. & CO.
LIVERPOOL and LONDON

The voyage diary and passenger list of the s.s. *Warwickshire* of the Bibby Line.

Scenes at balls held in Kuala Lumpur, 1913: (*above*) the Lake Club ball and (*below*) the St George's ball.

Cruise ships were becoming increasingly common in Far Eastern ports during the years immediately before the Second World War. Photograph of a tea party on board in 1937.

'Good-bye Yokohama', a streamer farewell as a cruise ship leaves port in 1937.

One of the most popular attractions for the more intrepid tourist was a visit to the Great Wall of China. Though the going may have been difficult, there was no transport problem.

On arrival at the Wall.

Hong Kong, a general view of the city and harbour with the Peak tramway in the foreground.

'together with the whole of the beauty and fashion of the island assembled at an early hour. The ball commenced between eight and nine. Mr Clubley had the honour of leading Mrs Raffles down the first dance to the tune of "Off she goes".' Music was provided by 'the musicians of the island' and by the band from Captain Harris's ship. 'One of the performers danced a hornpipe a la tamborina, which bore strong marks of his being a perfect adept in the art, and called forth loud and reiterated bursts of applause from his fair beholders.'

From that time onwards the calendar of the imperial year was marked by frequent balls, sometimes at Government House or the Residency, sometimes, when a naval squadron arrived, on the flagship in the harbour, sometimes under the auspices of a club or society, and very often given *con amore* by one of the local merchants or a higher official who possessed a sufficiently large house. In the later Victorian age these events became more formal, a change symbolized by the substitution of the black for the white jacket, which was insisted on by Governor Butterworth for official balls in Singapore as early as the 1850s. In one respect – the shortage of women – the occasions never changed, and to make it up by inviting even the most westernized of native women was, until after the Second World War, unthinkable. Today it is only in Hong Kong, last of the crown colonies in East Asia, that anything resembling the more splendid balls of the past takes place, when the Europeans in full evening dress flock over on the Star Ferry to the annual St Andrew's and St George's balls held in the imperial surroundings of the old Peninsula Hotel across the water at Kowloon.

A great deal of the entertainment that went on in the British communities was in fact self-made, amateur concerts and dramatic performances alternating with occasional visits from professional performers (to both of which subjects I shall return in the next chapter). But there were no regular and reputable entertainments until the cinema arrived after the First World War, and in social terms this tended to take the place of the professional theatre, with the rich merchants and officials appearing in full evening dress for the first performance of a noted film.

The adventurous and those who belonged below the level of accepted society were somewhat better provided for. In the French concession at Shanghai the lack of trade was compensated for at an early date by the growth of a vast entertainment industry, with dance halls, gambling houses, opium dens and brothels functioning quite openly and financed, in many cases, by otherwise respectable European merchants. On a smaller scale, the French concession at Canton provided similar entertainment. It was in the decades between the world wars that the meretricious gaiety

197

of the China coast ports reached its height, owing to the advent of the White Russian women who acted as taxi girls in the dance halls and provided an aristocracy for Shanghai's prostitute population, which was claimed – perhaps with an excess of local pride – to be proportionately higher than that of any other city in the world.

Even the Straits Settlements, with their British Sundays, recognized the different moral attitudes of the Chinese inhabitants by allowing opium shops and brothels to operate; there was an inspector of brothels in Singapore and during the 1880s this office was held by a certain Phillips who combined it with the post of superintendent of the sailors' home, where he was in the habit of giving temperance teas for seamen. There is no doubt that many of the seamen whom Mr Phillips entertained found their way to some of the establishments intended for the Chinese, while the efforts of the Temperance Societies, which were founded in both Singapore and Malacca in 1837, did little to change their drinking habits or to lessen the number of taverns and punch houses which catered to them. In 1853 the committee of the Singapore Sailors' Home denounced 'the low coffee shops and spirit houses in the outskirts of the town, where there is but too much reason to fear the unwary sailor is stupefied by deleterious spirits, and unscrupulously robbed . . .'. It was the old tradition of Hog Lane repeated, and through the nineteenth century little was done to change it. The sailors and soldiers drank and fought in the bars of Singapore and Hong Kong and Shanghai, but what happened in their poor white world was so distant from the concerns of the respectable that they were usually left to follow their pleasures without rescue or interference. In fact, despite the few temperance enthusiasts, the general attitude towards drinking was a permissive one, and climatic and therapeutic excuses were freely given.

The good folks of Singapore [says Cameron] are by no means inclined to place too narrow restrictions on their libations, and it has been found in the experience of older residents that a liberality in this respect conduces to good health and long life.

The American traveller William T. Hornaday went away in the 1880s with a less tolerant view of drinking habits in the Straits Settlements.

The extent to which intoxicating liquor of all kinds are drunk in the East Indies is simply appalling. The drinking habit is so universal that, as a general thing, when you go to call on an acquaintance in his house, or to visit a stranger in company with other friends, the greeting is 'What will you have to drink?' If you say you do not drink, or do not wish anything, you are urged most urgently to 'take something' until it becomes positively disagreeable; and really the easiest way is to compromise by taking a glass of their beastly lemonade or abominable soda. Furthermore, when your new acquaintances, or old ones either, for that matter, call upon you at your hotel for half an hour's chat, you are expected to order drinks for the crowd, until the crowd is full of whatever it likes best. To omit this feature is to give positive offence in some cases, and even at the best to send your visitors away saying that you are uncivil and not worthy of the acquaintance of gentlemen.

Hotels were a kind of neutral ground where passing travellers or those not yet accepted into the community could stay, and where gentlemen could gather with not-quite-gentlemen in a world less formal and defended than that of the club. Here the retail shopkeeper or the ship's mate was the equal of the taipan or the tuan besar. The first establishment that might be described as a hotel in the Far East was the tavern at Bencoolen where visitors who were not *persona grata* with the East India Company would stay; the American Dudley Leavett Pickman, who visited Bencoolen in 1808, remarked that 'the most extravagant charges' were made for 'very modest living'. During the early 1830s there was an English hotel at Macao, and after the East India Company's monopoly ran out in 1833, part of the Company's factory at Canton was turned into a hostelry for visitors.

The famous hotels of the Far East, like Raffles in Singapore, the Cathay in Shanghai, the E. and O. in Penang, the Peninsula in Hong Kong, and the Oriental in Bangkok, are quite recent creations, dating from the late nineteenth or early twentieth century, and the acceptance of the hotel as a social centre where the elect might hold their dinners and balls is equally recent. The real pioneer hotels of the China coast and the Straits Settlements have long vanished; they were much more modest establishments than their celebrated successors, largely because until the end of the nineteenth-century hospitality was still manageable enough to be dispensed in the home, and hotels remained conveniences for friendless travellers, ships' officers, and those residents who were inclined to a little mildly disreputable amusement.

In 1832 a hotel, whose name has not survived, was opened in Commercial Square, Singapore, by John Francis, who advertised a billiard room and 'refreshment Hall'. In 1839 an itinerant French painter named Gaston Dutronquoy arrived in Singapore and opened the London Hotel; later he moved into one of the old mansions of Coleman's day on the Esplanade, and eventually his establishment, under the management of another Frenchman, Casteleyns, became the Hotel de L'Europe, and remained until the end of the century the leading hotel in Singapore. Its main rivals – the Royalist and the Adelphi – were established soon afterwards. Similar hotels sprang up throughout the Far East – Shanghai's first was opened in 1848 – and the kind of service they offered is suggested in the advertisement of the Hotel du Louvre, which flourished in Yokohama during the 1870s.

This new and magnificent hotel, situate in one of the finest quarters of the town and in the Centre of its Business Portion, close to the Banks and Chamber of Commerce and opposite to the Catholic Church, by its Elegance and its Cuisine – the only one of this description here – and the care bestowed on the general Superintendence, offers to Travellers unusual convenience such as Billiards, Dinners, either private or à la carte ...

Most of the hotels also ran livery stables to provide horses and carriages for their guests. One hotel in Singapore during the 1880s included a kind of dance hall, popularly called the 'Tingel-Tangel', with an orchestra of Austrian and Polish girls, dressed in blue muslin frocks with blue sashes; the girls also drank beer with the customers and danced with them for fifty cents a dance. Later on, as the European population increased, the hotels, which originally had a monopoly of providing meals, had to compete with establishments like Emmerson's Tiffin Rooms, which was set up in the 1870s opposite the Harbour Office in Singapore and which became 'a regular haunt of all and sundry, from the Tuan Besar down to the seafaring class'. In Shanghai the many 'tables d'hôtes' which appeared towards the end of the century fulfilled a similar function.

During the early years of English presence in the Far East, when terms of duty were long, the sense of isolation was often intense. Even in the 1860s it was considered reasonable for a man to remain at least six or seven years in Singapore; after that he was thought to need a year at home to recover his health and to tint the cheeks of his wife, which tropical life had sallowed. With the opening of the Suez Canal, the five year cycle, with four years of duty and one of leave, became customary; though even now there were exceptions, particularly among missionaries, who would sometimes stay as many as twenty years at their posts before accepting furlough.

Furthermore, as communications improved and as travel in China, Japan and Malaya became safer and less arduous, the British Far Easterners began to break up the long periods between leaves with trips and vacations. Shortly after the occupation of Penang the advantages of its mountain slopes over the unhealthy lowlands around Georgetown were recognized, and trips by pony and palankeen were made up the narrow tracks that were cut through the jungle. Early in the nineteenth century the governor built a large bungalow there, at a level of 2,200 feet, which was soon surrounded by the holiday homes of civil and military officers looking at the splendid view of the strait, the green jungles of Province Wellesley beyond it and the blue mountains of Kedah in the middle distance. In the 1880s a resort hotel was built half-way up, with bath-houses 'so planned as to collect the waters of the falls before they have become heated by a long exposure to the sun'. Government Hill, as the mountain was called, became the first and for long the only hill resort in Malaya. Only after the Second World War was the example of the Himalayas followed at all extensively, when hill resorts were opened up in mountain jungles that had formerly been the preserve of the abori-gines. The best known were Maxwell's Hill, Fraser's Hill and, above all, Cameron Highlands, in whose equable climate Malaya's first tea planta-tions were started. Here, after the area had been opened out by the government and roads had been built, those British who had decided to become 'White Malayans' bought land and built houses for retirement. Hotels sprang up, some of them in deep jungle settings, and by the time of the Japanese invasion in 1942 a series of typical British-Asian hill stations had come into being – more modern than Darjeeling and Mus-soorie and Simla, but in their way of life essentially similar – where it became fashionable for the wealthier British residents of the Straits Settle-ments and Kuala Lumpur to spend at least a part of the hot season.

Around Singapore the wide island beaches were attractive and as early as the 1850s the government began to build seaside bungalows intended for the use of officials on tour but also available to any European who cared to use them. Shortly afterwards merchants clubbed together to build their own cooperative bungalows, where it was the custom from the 1860s to go for two or three weeks at a time and enjoy the air and the sea bathing. Since the waters were infested by sharks, protection had to be given by driving barriers of stakes into the seabed. Much later, after the foundation of the Federated Malay States, a seaside resort with many bungalows and bathing enclosures along palm-shaded beaches was built at Port Dickson, north of Malacca in the state of Negri Sembilan, and here many of the British stationed in the Malay states would spend their holidays.

For those who wished to travel farther in Malaya, the government not only created the best road system in east Asia, but also established a series of rest houses, usually rather more substantial than the Indian dak bun-galows. They were often built in spectacular situations, and served a number of purposes – as halting places for officials, as miniature resorts to which people would often drive from the town or the plantation for a weekend of relaxation, and, in thinly planted areas, as evening gathering places for remotely stationed Englishmen who were too scattered to be able to support a club. A stay at the rest-house could be pleasant or the reverse, depending on the talents of the cook for making imitation western food. 'People who are wise enough to be particular about their bedding,' warns an official guide book of the 1920s, 'will never regret bringing with them a roll containing a couple of sheets, a couple of pillow cases, a mosquito net and their favourite size and shape in pillows.' Perhaps the only reliable feature of the rest-houses was the presence of an ample supply of beer and whisky, but even the worst of them represented an extraordinary advance on the conditions of travel which the first officials had encountered on entering the native states in the 1870s. In China the custom of spending the hottest months of the year away from the treaty ports was already well established by the end of the nineteenth century. Hong Kong, of course, had its Peak, where many of the taipans had separate holiday houses, though the fogs created problems, and until the advent of air conditioning it was hard, on the higher slopes, to build a mildew-proof house. Later a beach resort sprang up at Repulse Bay. From Shanghai and from the legation quarter of Peking, the taipans and diplomats with their families would travel hundreds of miles each summer, in the 1880s and afterwards, to the little northern ports of Chefoo, Weihaiwei and Peitaiho, where the climate was healthy, the beaches broad; there, for a month or two each year, there would be balls and dinners and picnics and band concerts – a gayer version of life in one's own Chinese station, with the ocean bathing added. Those isolated in Peking might also go, during the height of summer, into the Western Hills, where the decay of Chinese Buddhism was evidenced in the number of temples available to be converted into villas.

Japan had not only a developed system of highways, but also an abundance of native inns and its own tradition of seasonal tours to picturesque locations. At first, ordinary Europeans were supposed to travel no more than twenty-five miles from the treaty ports and were strictly forbidden to visit Kyoto, where the emperor still lived. Foreign representatives, however, were allowed by the treaties to travel all over Japan; the native authorities put what obstacles they could in the way of fulfilling this aim but the British representative with whom they had to deal was the redoubtable Rutherford Alcock, who in 1860 defied obstruction by organizing an expedition to Fujiyama, which he was the first European to climb. When the regulations were relaxed merchants from Osaka and Yokohama would make trips to Hakone and Fujiyama by litter and horse-carriage, and to Kyoto on moonlit nights by flat-bottomed river boat. Europeans even became used to the Japanese inn, which was in those days extraordinarily inexpensive (about a shilling a day per person for bed and board), but which was liable to have its own disadvantages. 'Buy an ichigu's worth of powdered crude camphor,' recommended the *Yokohama Guide* in 1874, 'and sprinkle abundantly on and under the bed and on the floor of hotels for a foot or so around the bedding. Sound sleep is assured as a result.'

In the end the British made their own contribution to the list of picturesque resorts when towards the end of the nineteenth century the English missionary, Walter Weston, who happened to be a mountaineer, set out to explore the neglected Japanese Alps and to sing their praises to his fellow missionaries, who followed his example and turned Karuizawa, once a desolate way-station on the mountain road to Edo, into a summer retreat. Those days are long past and Karuizawa is now typically Japanese in its combination of the conventionally traditional and the stridently modern. But its origin, and the love of the mountains that inspired its creator, remind one that the British in the Far East were by no means exclusively concerned with the pursuit of power and profit; though there may have been the motives that drew most of them originally to the Orient, there was also a place in the world they created for the life of the mind.

14

THE LIFE OF THE MIND

The British communities in the Far East have often been represented as philistine in taste, reactionary in opinion, and artistically and intellectually uncreative. There is substance in the accusation, particularly as applied to the settlements of the China coast, but before we enter too deeply into a discussion of the life of the mind as it was lived in those distant regions, it is as well to recollect a few salient facts. First, as I have shown, the British population was always small; except when large numbers of troops appeared in Malaya during the Second World War it can hardly at any one time have exceeded seventy-five thousand; moreover, it was divided into widely spread local communities which varied in numbers from round about ten thousand (Shanghai, Singapore and Hong Kong at their peak) down to a few hundred, or even a few dozen in the case of places like Chinkiang, Labuan and Christmas Island. To find a suitable analogy one has to think of southern English towns mainly populated by the class of people who went to work in the Far East. How many middle-class towns in the Home Counties with populations of ten thousand or less have made significant contributions to intellectual or artistic life? The answer of course is that such communities occasionally do produce important individual artists or intellectuals, but rarely provide the mental nutriment which keeps them at home.

Most of the British who found their way to the Far East before the Second World War were men, already formed in their attitudes, who had been selected carefully by governmental examinations or by the London offices of private corporations. The likelihood of the artist or the philosophic radical ever reaching Malaya or the China coast was thus very small, unless he travelled at his own expense, which a few writers did. On the China coast and in the Japanese concessions the main qualifications for employment were personal influence in the business world and an interest in making money. Most of the amateur scholars who arose in the Far East during the nineteenth century appeared in Malaya, where the local British community was leavened – both in the Company's time and later – by civil servants with a classical education and often with scientific interests.

Then we must take into account the education they brought with them. Here we reach the final reason for the intellectual poverty of the British communities before the Second World War. In Malaya there were no universities at all until 1949, nor did institutions of higher learning exist in Shanghai or the other treaty port concessions. Hong Kong University was indeed established in 1911, but it was poorly endowed and for long was mainly a professional school, with engineering and medicine dominant and arts a poor third among the faculties; the faculty of science was not added until 1939, and until the 1950s honours courses were offered only in engineering. It was, in fact, a glorified technical school for the local Chinese population, and only after 1950 did it attract European creative scholars of a type likely to affect the climate of thought in the surrounding communities. The settlements of Malaya and the China coast, in other words, lacked any nuclei of professional scholarship which might have acted as centres of intellectual growth, just as they lacked anything resembling a true artistic or literary world.

The limitations of what did exist are shown clearly in the field of local education. Most of the government-supported schools in Malaya, Borneo and Hong Kong were provided with the intention of imparting the English language and the elements of western knowledge to children of the Malay, Chinese and Eurasian middle classes. For the prototype to these institutions we have to return again to Stamford Raffles, and the Singapore Institution (later to be known as the Raffles Institution) which he founded in 1823 as his last important public act before leaving Asia for good. In the three aims which Raffles set forward for the Institution his humanism was mingled, as always, with an administrator's eye to the future. Partly he wished his creation to be a research institution where the literature and traditions of the Malays could be collected and studied. Partly he wished it to be a kind of college for Europeans, where servants of the Company and any others who wished to do so could study the native languages of the peninsula. But the aim which he placed first was that of educating the sons 'of the higher order of natives and others'. In practice, the Institution was viewed with disfavour by the Company's directors in London and was allowed to languish during Crawfurd's rule in Singapore, so that in the end – though a library and a museum were developed – the main practical function of the Institution was in fact to educate Malay, Chinese and a few Siamese children; the 'others', meaning presumably British children, did not avail themselves in large numbers of the Institution's facilities. In Penang the Free School, which antedated the Singapore Institution, fulfilled the same function; so did the Victoria Institution, founded in Kuala Lumpur after the British penetration of the Malay states. They – and similar schools in Hong Kong – were the Far Eastern manifestation of that movement which, beginning in India, envisaged the eventual solution of strife between British and Asian man in the triumph of European culture and the appearance of a native middle class which would accept the mores of its conquerors and, incidentally, provide a convenient reservoir of potential employees for the lower ranks of the civil service. This type of education in institutions closely imitating English grammar schools resulted in the importation of British pedagogues; in Malaya alone by the 1920s the educational services employed almost a hundred European administrators and teachers. Their intellectual calibre was not generally high (what Englishman over fifty does not carry in his memory an incompetent schoolmaster who went out to teach 'the blacks'?) and for the most part they fitted very well into the conventionalities of Far Eastern British society.

Before the Second World War British children were almost invariably educated separately from native children. Those who attended schools of any kind usually belonged to the lower ranks of the community; anybody who could afford it sent his children home, partly because it was healthier and partly because no school in the east enjoyed a social prestige equivalent even to that of a very minor English public school.

In 1805, when Philip Dundas arrived to take over the presidency of Penang, the humblest man in his train was the schoolmaster Thomas Callum, who was engaged to teach the children of the Company's officials. Callum founded the first British school east of India, but unfortunately no record remains of the training he imparted. By 1829 an 'English school' existed in Singapore, but the description seems to have been intended merely to define the language of instruction, since there were three native assistants to the one English master, and we are told that the fees for English children were 15 dollars and those for native children only 4 dollars. It is likely that Mrs Whittle made a greater appeal when in 1837 she established her Boarding and Day School, for European girls only; the charge was 5 dollars for day scholars, and 12 dollars for boarders, providing a service for families isolated in the out-stations. In 1845 the Rev. Vincent Stanton, colonial chaplain at Hong Kong, established a school for English children, the first of its kind on the China coast, and in 1864 the Catholic missionaries in Shanghai founded the Francis Xavier School for foreign boys, while St Joseph's Convent offered a school for foreign girls. Later, in 1886, the Freemasons – anxious not to leave the field entirely to the Catholics – founded their own school and in 1892 this was taken over by the Shanghai Municipal Council, which also paid a subsidy to the Francis Xavier School. An interesting indication of considerations which determined European parents to send their children to schools in the east rather than at home is given by the fact that more than one-third of the British and American boys attending the Francis Xavier School were charity boys, sometimes receiving clothes as well as instruction. It was largely the poorer whites who sent their children to these schools because they had no alternative.

The best of these English schools was probably the Central School in Hong Kong, which developed out of a decision in 1902 to segregate the teaching of Europeans under governmental auspices. It began as the Kowloon British School, ironically situated in a building given by a distinguished Chinese citizen, Sir Robert Ho Tung, for inter-racial teaching in English. Joseph Chamberlain, then Colonial Secretary, was opposed to segregation, but gave in to the united demands of British parents. During the 1920s the education of all European children over nine years old was concentrated in the Central School, and it was not until the late 1940s that non-Europeans were eventually admitted, a few years before segregation was legally ended in the United States. The record of the Central School is a reasonable true reflection of British opinions in the Far East, which remained firmly against any close intermingling of the races until the empire had ceased to be politically viable, and then trimmed to the wind of necessity.

Creative scholarship, during the long age of the British ascendancy, was almost entirely divorced from educational institutions. Apart from a few wandering professional scientists, it was mainly the work of administrators. The tradition began in the Bencoolen days with William Marsden, whose *History of Sumatra* (1783) was marred by the Europe-centred view of history current at the time; he had little to reveal of Far Eastern history before the arrival of the Portuguese. To a less degree the same criticism applies to Raffles' *History of Java* (1817) and to the *History of the Indian Archipelago*, published three years afterwards by his rival and successor, John Crawfurd. Raffles' close friend and subordinate, John Leyden, helped to fill the gap by his translation of the important Malay chronicle, the *Sejarah Malayu* (*Malay Annals*, 1821), and there seems no doubt that Raffles intended to do further work on the native sources of Malayan history, for in Java he made a great collection of manuscripts which was lost when all his possessions were burnt in 1824 in the fire that destroyed the *Fame*, on which he was returning to England. Among those officials who in later years followed the tradition of Raffles, Crawfurd and Leyden were Sir Frank Swettenham, whose *British Malaya* (1906) was the pioneer work on its subject, Sir Richard Winstedt, whose *History of Malaya* (1935) is still probably the best of its kind, and Victor Purcell, who utilized his experience as protector of the Chinese in Malaya to write the first authoritative accounts of the Overseas Chinese, *The Chinese in Malaya* (1948) and *The Chinese in Southeast Asia* (1951). These officials, writing in leisure time or in retirement, were the most systematic of the historians of the region until after the Second World War, when professional scholars turned their belated attention towards south-east Asia. When a leading local journalist, Charles B. Buckley, produced *An Anecdotal History of Old Times in Singapore*, (1902) he uncovered a mine of information relating to the first fifty years of his city, but presented it without system or discrimination. J. N. Cameron, an earlier newspaper man, produced a better organized and more vivid (though perhaps less informative) book in *Our Tropical Possessions in Malayan India* (1865), which all historians of the region use (as I have done) as an indispensable sourcebook on mid-Victorian Malaya. The small scholarly community in this region, which consisted mainly of officials, journalists, lawyers and doctors (the merchants were little interested) was supported by a tenuous succession of journals in which they could publish their discoveries, beginning with James Richardson Logan's *Journal of the Indian Archipelago and Eastern Asia*, which lasted from 1847 to 1859, and continuing with the *Journal of the Straits Branch of the Royal Asiatic Society*, established at the same time as the society in 1878, and still appearing today as the *Journal of the Malayan Branch of the Royal Asiatic Society*.

Chinese studies among the British of the Far East really began with the first interpreters to the East India Company, who learnt the language under great difficulty because native 'linguists' were forbidden to teach them under pain of death. Nevertheless, as early as the 1730s, Company employees such as Andrew Reid and James Flint had mastered the rudiments of the language. They put their knowledge to little scholastic use, and it was left to the missionaries, and especially to Robert Morrison in Canton, and his associate William Milne in Malacca, to begin serious Chinese studies. Later, a distinguished Chinese scholar, Sir John Bowring, became one of the early governors of Hong Kong. But considering the extent to which they depended on China for their livelihood, the inhabitants of the treaty ports were surprisingly little interested in either the language or the civilization of the Chinese. Pidgin sufficed for most everyday needs and the Chinese compradors cushioned the taipans from much direct contact with native merchants. The tide of scholarship, which had paused at Canton in Morrison's day, swept on to the European universities and, later, to the universities within China itself. Unlike the administrators of Malaya, the consular officials of the treaty ports and the colonial service cadets in Hong Kong produced little in the way of substantial scholarship.

Though Einstein made a fleeting visit to Shanghai in 1923 and lectured to a puzzled audience on relativity, scientific studies by the British in the Far East before 1941 were mainly in the biological sciences, and for excellent reasons. Trade depended on vegetable products, survival depended on the conquest of sickness, and natural history was the queen of the nineteenth-century scientific world. The preoccupation went far back. In the mid-eighteenth century Alexander Hamilton reported that an East India Company factory on the coast of Borneo was badly run because the chief factor, a certain Cunningham, was interested only in zoology. But the Company itself was alive to the importance of natural history, and in 1792, when Lord Macartney went on his embassy to the Chinese court, he was accompanied by two botanists who assiduously collected plants as the expedition wended its way to Peking and on to Jehol. Raffles comes forward in this context also. The great collection he lost on the *Fame* also included many natural history specimens and live animals, and, besides playing a leading part in the foundation of the London Zoo, he established the Singapore Botanical Gardens in 1822, under the superintendence of Dr Wallich from Calcutta.

But it was later in the nineteenth century, with men like Wallace, Fortune and 'Rubber' Ridley, that the pursuit of natural history reached its peak and, by taking tea plants to India and rubber to Malaya, affected profoundly the economy of the British empire in Asia. Equally important was the practical application by Sir Malcolm Watson of the discoveries of Sir Ronald Ross regarding the causes of malaria. Port Swettenham had been opened in 1901 to assist the shipping of tin and rubber from the Malay states, but it was so infested by fever that after a few months the government decided to close it down. Watson, however, applied Ross's discoveries so capably that the spread of the disease was halted and Port Swettenham remained open; thus he initiated the process by which Malaya in our century lost its reputation as one of the white man's graves.

In the arts one looks in vain for achievements comparable to Watson's work on malaria or Wallace's intuitions regarding the nature of evolution. The talents, where they appear, are small, the minor masters dominate every field.

If in architecture there was no one of real importance except Coleman of Singapore, in painting the one name that is likely to stir more than a passing interest is that of George Chinnery, a member of the Royal Hibernian Academy who found his way to the China coast at the very beginning of the nineteenth century and lived there, mostly in Macao, for fifty years until his death in 1852. No other artist who went to the east rivalled Chinnery in his perception of the nuances of Asian life and scenes; he was sensitive to the art of the country and allowed it to influence his own increasingly calligraphic style of painting and drawing.

A number of lesser artists, trained in the topographical techniques of the early nineteenth century, such as J. Wathen, J. T. Thomson, William Alexander and R. N. Beechey, made appealing drawings and water-colours of Malayan and Chinese scenes, but the style in which they worked died out by the mid-century, and after that time little of real interest was produced. Itinerant miniaturists, portrait painters and landscapists wandered through the various British settlements during the mid-Victorian period and appear to have done rather well on commissions from well-to-do merchants, but already by the 1850s their popularity was waning before that of a new invention introduced to Malaya by one of their own company. This was the painter G. Dutronquay, who founded the London Hotel in Singapore. In 1843 Dutronquay added to his interests by setting up in Singapore the first Daguerrotype studio in the Far East. Dutronquay ended a victim of his own multiple acquisitiveness, on a gold mining expedition to the Muay River in Johore, where there is reason to suppose he was murdered, but the photography he introduced became a far more popular and profitable trade than painting, and twenty years later in Shanghai Edward Bowra encountered a former tide-waiter (a junior customs man) who had turned photographer and had earned £15,000 in three years from the free spenders of the China coast. The decline of professional painting was followed by the rise of amateur painting. The first Arts Club held its opening exhibition in Singapore in 1882, and others followed in the larger British communities. Their productions were universally mediocre.

Music was for many years a matter of unsophisticated entertainment, and always of performance rather than creation. Touring entertainers made an early appearance; Signor Masoni gave a violin recital to the elite of Singapore in 1831. But mostly, apart from the military and naval bands, it was amateur music, at first made rather informally when people met in each other's homes. The leader of musical activity in early Singapore was Dr Jose d'Almeida, the Portuguese ship's surgeon who set up a pharmacy in the settlement shortly after its foundation and in 1825 founded a successful import and export business. For many years d'Almeida held regular concerts at his home, to which all were welcome, and his sons were later active in the public organization of music in the Straits Settlements. The pioneer association in this field was the Liedertafel, founded by the German Teutonia Club early in the 1860s, but shortly afterwards, in 1865, the d'Almeidas founded the Amateur Musical Society with a mainly British membership. Its first concert was held on 28 December; the programme illustrates the musical taste of mid-Victorian Singapore. A tiny orchestra of six members played the overture to the *Caliph of Bagdad* and a Hadyn quintet. The glee singers followed, with *The Larboard Watch*, *The Village Blacksmith*, a negro melody and, to end, 'Locke's old music to *Macbeth*'.

In later years musical taste became more sophisticated, and in the Edwardian era Singapore had its Philharmonic Society, with a full-scale orchestra consisting largely of Germans. Shanghai, which by this time was already the most wealthy of the settlements in the Far East, employed a Municipal Orchestra which would play Mozart on clear nights in Jesselton Park, and after the First World War the settlement became part of the international concert circuit, visited by Kreisler, Heifetz, Moseivich and Galli-Curci.

But of all the arts the favourite among the British exiles was the drama, and that for social rather than artistic regions. It suited the extroverts who formed so great a part of Far Eastern communities, it passed the time and brought people together, and it enabled performers and audience to create a little world of illusion, shut off from Asia and Asiatics, in which for a time they could forget their exile. Everywhere, from Singapore and Shanghai, down to the small treaty ports like Ningpo and Chefoo, the amateur theatre flourished. Fourteen years after Singapore was founded, the first dramatic performance was given there in 1833, with tickets at 1 and 2 dollars for a performance that started at 7 o'clock. The players were ambitious and generous. They performed 'Dr Young's celebrated and much admired tragedy of The Revenge', followed it up with a farce called *The Mock Doctor* and a series of comic and sentimental songs, and ended with a recitation from Campbell's *Pleasures of Hope*. The *Singapore Chronicle*, itself pioneering in Eastern theatrical criticism, was damning.

Instead of lachrymose effect as is proper, the acting produced a very contrary one on the risible nerves of the audience, and, excepting the tedium produced in listening to a continued series of unintelligible dialogues the piece altogether afforded some amusement from the burlesque character of the performance.

By 1850 Shanghai had its first play, when the Amateur Dramatic Club acted in a godown loaned by one of the merchants. In 1860 the Osaka

Amateur Corps Dramatique performed *Cool as a Cucumber* and *Ticket of Leave*, and in 1869 the merchants and customs officers and their wives in Ningpo were rendering *Ill-treated Il Trovatore* and *Ici on parle français*.

Singapore pioneered not merely with performances but also with a theatre. Early plays were performed in the London Hotel, but in 1845 the Assembly Rooms were opened, a large lath-and-plaster building, roofed with attap; they contained, as well as a ball room, a Theatre Royal equipped with a well for the orchestra and scenes painted by a brother of the Academician William Dyce. This sufficed until the Assembly Rooms were pulled down in 1856. Then, in 1861, when the Town Hall was built, it contained another theatre, the occupation of which was a cause of dispute between the two groups now performing, the Savage Club and the Corps Dramatique; the Corps Dramatique, by superior intrigue, succeeded in keeping the Savage Club out of the new theatre, and the latter soon expired for lack of a place to perform. In Shanghai the first wooden theatre was built in 1867; it burned down in 1871 and was succeeded by the Lyceum, the largest and most elaborate theatre of its day in the Far East. Hong Kong, on the other hand, was no better provided than the smaller settlements, since it did not acquire a theatre until as late as 1962.

As the titles I have quoted will suggest, the nineteenth-century British, when they turned actor, were inclined to express themselves through the most ephemeral of domestic comedies and light farces. Reading through an account of the plays performed by amateurs in Singapore over thirty years, I found, after the ill-fated *Revenge*, not a single tragedy, and only two other plays whose names would mean anything to readers today – *She Stoops to Conquer* and *The Critic*. For the rest, it was with trivialities like *Damp Beds*, *The Spectre Bridegroom*, *Miss in her Teens* and *My Young Wife and Old Umbrella* that the Malay and China Hands entertained themselves and each other. Anything more serious was left to the rare professionals who arrived, either singly or in companies. The difference which even one professional could make was shown with the arrival of Mrs Deacle of the Theatre Royal, Dover, who came in May 1844 with two officers of the Bengal Army who had been acting in Calcutta. She built an attap theatre called Sans Souci for her performances, gathered and galvanized the local amateurs, and, during the few months she stayed, produced *Macbeth*, *Venice Preserved*, *The Merchant of Venice* and several other plays in the classical repertory. A local Anglican clergyman took the opportunity to make himself more unpopular than usual by preaching a sermon against Mrs Deacle, declaring that no modest woman could appear in the character of Portia.

One good resulted from the sermon on Sunday [commented a local paper], although not the one exactly intended by the Revd gentleman, viz., persons who never visited a theatre before, went on Monday, and the house was crowded.

The theatre, it is clear, not only gave the mid-Victorian colonial British a fine means of self expression; it also served, on occasion, to crystallize their antagonisms.

Even in conditions when men had largely to make their own amusements, literature probably played a lesser part than drama and music, dancing and dining, in the lives of such active and materialistic people as the inhabitants of the Far Eastern settlements. One finds in letters and memoirs here and there the names of books that exceptional people read. We encounter Raffles reading omnivorously between Gargantuan tasks and James Brooke keeping up with the times in his distant principality, reading *David Copperfield* and *Vestiges of Creation* on publication, following the polemics of the Tractarians and the first steps of the evolutionary controversy; we look over the shoulder of Edward Bowra translating *The Red Chamber Dream* and lecturing the Ningpo Book Club on Ignatius Loyola; we catch a surprising glimpse of Spenser St John, sitting with Lieutenant Everest in the jungle before an attack on a pirate stronghold in Borneo, and reading to each other *Paradise Lost* and Thomson's *Seasons* – a 'very pretty and appropriate amusement during a warlike expedition' as Raja Brooke commented when he came upon them; we watch Patrick Noone setting off to end his short life among the aborigines of Malaya with a mandolin in his hand and a Collected Shakespeare and Arnold's *Light of Asia* in his pack. And we find Somerset Maugham noting that an official he meets has a collection of modern French novels – and noting it with surprise, as something exceptional.

So indeed might we note it if we were transported to the Far East of the 1920s or the 1890s or the 1860s. People undoubtedly read a great deal, but the calibre of what they read can probably be judged by the titles of the favourite magazines in the reading rooms of the clubs – *Country Life* and the *Bystander*, the *Royal* and the *Strand*, the *Illustrated London News* and *Blackwoods*, with back copies of *The Times* and the *Morning Post* where taipans gathered and of the *Mail* and the *Mirror* in the planters' backwoods. The general attitude towards literature – apart from the exceptional people who force themselves into the limelight of any history – is indicated by the difficulties which attended the foundation of a library in Singapore. The first effort was made by a private individual, the shopkeeper George Armstrong, who in 1831 established a circulating library in connection with his Exchange Rooms; it was mainly visiting captains and

213

ships' mates who came to borrow his books. An attempt was made in 1837 to found a public library, but it foundered, and it was not until 1845 that thirty-two of the inhabitants, including a Parsee and a Portuguese, by subscribing 30 dollars each, founded the Singapore Library. This was twenty-six years after the settlement was established, and in spite of the fact that the general standard of literacy and education among British residents was far higher than the standard in England itself during the 1840s, since the illiterate – even if they went to the east as seamen – rarely settled there. Light literature, like light drama, was most in favour, and a great deal of time was spent reading the newspapers from England (news first, and then – assiduously – the advertisements which indicated the changing fashions and fads at home) and the surprisingly numerous productions of the local press.

The local newspapers consumed most of the rather weak literary impulses of the Malayan and Chinese settlements. There was surprisingly little creative authorship, and that mainly among the historians already described, none of whom could be regarded as a paragon of literary style. It is surprising that Burma, where there were even fewer British, produced out of its colonial service at least two writers of high distinction, George Orwell and Maurice Collis. The only writer of comparable distinction who lived in the British Far East long enough to become part of the European community was actually a Frenchman, Henri Fauconnier, whose *Malayisie* was the best novel on the planter's life to emerge before the Second World War.

The two writers whose names are popularly associated with the region were both visitors. Somerset Maugham was in Malaya and Borneo for comparatively short periods in the 1920s keeping a sharply observant notebook and drawing from his observations the material for a number of stories which offended local sensitivities. Joseph Conrad first reached the east in March 1883 as mate on the ill-fated *Palestine*, which burnt off Sumatra. He spent on this occasion about six weeks in Singapore. He returned there in September 1885 on the *Tilkhurst*, and left for Calcutta and Dundee a month later. In July 1887 he reached Java on his third and longest Asian trip; in August he signed on as mate of the *Vidar* and until January 1888 sailed with her to the coasts and inlets of Dutch Borneo. He then went almost immediately from Singapore to Bangkok, which he left on 9 February as master of the *Otago*, bound for Sydney. On this occasion he was about seven months and in all less than ten months in the Far East. But out of these relatively brief visits he abstracted the material for *Lord Jim*, *Almayer's Folly*, *The Outcast of the Islands*, and a number of fine stories which demonstrate how a great artist can give lasting and splendid form to what other men would regard as the most fleeting of experiences. In the days before the Japanese swept British power temporarily from the China Seas, one finds no one else to compare with Fauconnier, Maugham and Conrad. There were a few men who wrote nostalgic fiction about native life, and of these Hugh Clifford, another civil servant, was probably the best, with slight but often charming sketches of a passing Malay culture. But in that period no writer produced a novel like *Passage to India* or *Burmese Days* to portray in memorable terms the British societies of the Far East.

Newspapers, like education, arrived as soon as the settlements began to emerge from their most primitive pioneer origins. *The Prince of Wales Island Gazette* was the first of them, appearing in Penang during 1805, shortly after the settlement became a presidency. *The Singapore Chronicle* published its first number, of four pages, in 1824, and in 1826, two years after the Dutch occupation ended, the *Malacca Observer* commenced publication. These early papers appeared either fortnightly or weekly. Since their potential circulations were very small, they tended to become government sheets. In fact, for a long time anything but subservience was difficult in Singapore, since Crawfurd as Resident established a censorship law which lasted from 1824 to 1835. For a while Crawfurd himself contributed to the *Singapore Chronicle*, and then all went well, but afterwards there were differences of opinion between him and the editor, and the paper had to appear with many blank spaces where articles had been censored. By the time this restrictive law was repealed, the *Chronicle* was dying of its wounds; it expired in 1837 because of the competition of the *Free Press* whose name celebrated the fact that it was founded immediately after the censorship law was repealed. The *Free Press* prospered, to become eventually a daily, as it still continues. So does another and more famous early Singapore paper, the *Straits Times*, which was founded in 1845. In 1850 there were 198 Europeans in Singapore, but they supported two newspapers. The situation on the China coast was no less curious, for, in the 1830s, as events were building up to the Opium Wars, the small British community in Canton published three papers. All were subsidized, and represented definate interests. The *Chinese Repository*, edited by Dr Morrison, was a missionary sheet, the *Canton Press* was run by Jardine Matheson and the *Canton Gazette* by the rival opium trading firm of Dent.

As new settlements were opened around the China Seas, papers were needed to impart news of commercial importance and also to provide an organ for mercantile opinion. The *China Mail* started publication in Hong Kong in 1845, though its famous rival, the *South China Post*, did not appear until 1903. In Shanghai the *North China Herald* began in 1850, and the *North China Daily News* in 1864. 1864 also saw the birth of the first European paper in Bangkok, the *Siam Times*, but this had a short existence, and it was not until 1887 that the prestigious *Bangkok Times* appeared. The *Japan Herald* and the *Japan Times Overland Mail*, both published in Yokohama, served the European settlements there from the early 1860s. Finally, when British interests penetrated the Malay states, the *Malay Mail* began in 1896 to appear in Kuala Lumpur, where it is still published.

All these papers must be observed within the narrow perspectives of the world they served. For subscriptions, for advertisements, often for the subsidies that kept them alive, they depended on men whose interests were essentially commercial. They therefore gave great prominence to shipping and market news and any other information that might affect trading interests. They stressed news from China, which interested even those in Malaya, and paid that exaggerated attention to the deeds of their own readers which one finds in all small communities conscious of their isolation; the activities of the local amateur theatre would be treated with a solemnity appropriate to a Covent Garden opera. After the early days in the Straits Settlements, papers that might be called government organs were rare. Generally speaking, they represented the merchants rather than the officials, and when they disagreed with the government it was invariably to give expression to the sentiments of their commercial constituents. Singapore newspapers supported the agitation for liberation from Indian rule. Hong Kong newspapers supported the merchant-led campaign for a greater share in local government. Papers in both Hong Kong and Shanghai consistently demanded with varying degrees of emphasis a tougher policy towards China. The most extreme in this respect was the *Shanghai Recorder*, dominated by Jardine Matheson, but other China coast papers joined in the recurrent criticism of the Foreign Office for what the merchants regarded as its weakness in failing to open China more widely to British trade. Another favourite target was the Imperial Maritime Customs, which was often represented as unnecessarily officious in its impositions. The tone of these papers varied from the rhetorically descriptive to the vituperatively denunciatory; it is hard to find anywhere a kind of abuse more eloquent than that which the *China Mail* would heap on any attempt to conciliate the Chinese government, towards which it felt the only possible policy was one of unmitigated aggressiveness.

Free trade was perhaps the banner under which all these papers were most surely united, and the kind of Tory respect for traditional diplomacy which often inspired British officials was anathema to them. On the other hand, they were the reverse of radical. Any left-wing attack on the British imperial position that might be made in England united them in angry refutation; in the Far East, of course, no one even thought of making such an attack. The newspapers had no concern for the rights of the native peoples of Asia; their agitations, even when most extreme, were aimed merely at expanding the ruling oligarchy to include all people of British race.

Malaya and Hong Kong, if not Shanghai, were ruled by authoritarian systems which would certainly not have tolerated papers daring enough to propose radical changes in the imperial system. But the pressure they could have exerted went unused. The newspapers were conscious of representing the British community and they believed that the solidarity of that community must remain unbroken. The white man, if his rule were to survive, must maintain his collective face against the native masses.

That was the unspoken law. Any man who in speech or action seemed to break it was likely to find himself under pressure to depart. This applied not only to political but also to moral breaches of front. Adultery, provided it were discreet and between socially accepted people, could be tolerated and often happened. Sexual relations with other races had to be carefully concealed, and the young man who went out openly with a Chinese girl in Singapore or Shanghai or Hong Kong would find his career suddenly melting away. Homosexuality was the worst sin because British imperialists regarded it as a fatal flaw in past empires; it was, least of all, to be tolerated. When a homosexual scandal did break in Singapore during the 1930s, the press was instructed to keep it secret and those involved were quickly deported, without trial; the only two who remained had committed suicide.

It was this insistence on maintaining a tight social cohesion while at the same time defending the right of individuals to make as much money in any way they wished that shaped the newspapers of the Far East, as it shaped also the men who opened them on those bright mornings under a hostile sun. Undoubtedly the inhibitions which their situation forced upon them explain at least in part why the British communities of the Far East were so intellectually and artistically sterile. Only their trade was free to grow.

PART III

Imperial
Twilight

15

THE CATASTROPHE

To many a young Englishman who went east in 1930 it seemed as though the empire would never end, as though the lordly relation in which his race stood to the native peoples of the Far East would continue into the indefinite vagueness of the future. Some historians, like Northcote Parkinson, claim now, with hindsight, that British influence began to ebb in the early twentieth century, that the crucial date was 1905, when Britain signed the treaty of alliance with Japan and withdrew her Far Eastern fleet, leaving her interests to be guarded by small craft and small garrisons in the face of the growing power of the empire of the Rising Sun and the burgeoning of Chinese nationalism. To others the key date was 1927, when, faced by militant nationalist mobs, the British withdrew from their advanced inland posts in China, the concessions in Hankow and Kiukiang on the Yangtse. Certainly by 1932 it needed a willing blindness to fail to read the signs, for that was the year when the Japanese threat began to loom darkly.

Much that happened from 1932 onwards in the Far East belongs to military and political rather than social history, and I shall be content to sketch lightly the pattern of events and observe somewhat more closely their effects on the British communities. For almost a decade the cloud gathered most heavily over Shanghai. In 1931 the Japanese had already overrun Manchuria. In January 1932 a group of Japanese monks in Shanghai was attacked by a Chinese mob, and one was killed. The Japanese submitted an ultimatum to the local Chinese authorities, and when their terms were not accepted landed troops at Hongkew in the International Settlement and marched through it to the Chinese suburb of Chapei. The International Settlement was now threatened by a battle between the Japanese and the Chinese armies of warring factions which were stationed in the vicinity. The municipal council declared a state of emergency, the 2,300 Volunteers were mobilized, British regulars were sent from India, and for the first time in the history of Shanghai many of the merchants decided to send their families away to safer places. Those who remained were appalled to see their racecourse used as a battlefield by warring Asians, and shook with apprehension when a sampan loaded with explosives, which amateur Chinese terrorists sailed into the river in the hope of destroying a Japanese warship, blew up accidentally and rattled the windows of the Shanghai Club. Rather like the blimps of England who cheered Hitler on in the mid-1930s, the taipans were inclined to be sympathetic to the Japanese who, they felt, were treating the irritating Chinese in the way Britain should have treated them if a succession of political ninnies had not reigned in Whitehall.

Eventually, British diplomats mediated a truce between Chinese and Japanese, and a demilitarized zone twenty kilometres wide was established around the International Settlement and the French concession. The British emergency forces departed and, since the treaty ports were by now the only coastal points in China immune from threats of foreign and civil war, trade flourished more than ever. But it was significant that about this time the flow of new foreigners into the International Settlement began to diminish, and of those who came many were Jewish refugees from Hitler's Germany, driven by necessity to seek refuge in one of the few places in the world with an open frontier.

The next Shanghai incident took place in 1937, when a shooting affray between Japanese and Chinese on the perimeter of the demilitarized zone led to another confrontation. Once again the Volunteers mobilized, and Chinese refugees streamed into what they imagined would be the safety of the city. Their own planes, bombing inaccurately, killed almost two thousand of them in the centre of the International Settlement, and the foreign residents felt the terror closing around them. The European shops closed, the Country Club was turned into a hospital, and the august Shanghai Club, whose threshold women's feet had defiled only once a year, for the annual ball, became a reception centre for foreign families wishing to evacuate. The taipans watched their women and children boarding launches and destroyers to be taken down river to the liner *Rajputana*. No ships now came up to moor opposite the Bund, and the naval authorities even argued that the International Settlement should be completely abandoned. The merchants refused to go and lived in partial siege, with shortages building up and some of their number, who had gone north for the summer, stranded in the beach resorts of Peitaiho and Weihaiwei. Many of them still saw the Japanese as saviours, fighting the battle of international trade against the upstart Chinese nationalists. The fighting ended in

November, and people who had left or been kept away began to filter back into the settlement, but conditions did not approach normal until early in 1938, when the Paper Hunt went out for the first time since the crisis began and a hundred and twenty people showed the British spirit by riding over a veritable obstacle course, dotted with barbed wire entanglements and hidden trenches.

But even normality had changed, for now the Japanese held the military power in Shanghai and celebrated it with a Victory Parade through the city. They had brought in 200,000 troops, while this time the British had sent a mere 2,500 to protect their interests, no more than the Americans and fewer than the French, who guarded their concession with 4,000 Annamites. The shift in power began to show in other ways. The Japanese puppet government of the region made difficulties with the municipal council. The Japanese challenged the British control of the Chinese Maritime Customs, and gained an important point when its deposits were shifted from the Hong Kong and Shanghai Banking Corporation to the Yokohama Specie Bank. These ominous changes did not for the time being lessen the flow of trade or profit, so that most merchants accepted the situation philosophically, and the city's night life became more extravagant than ever.

When the Second World War began, its first perceptible effect on life in the International Settlement was the expulsion of the Germans from British clubs. Shortly afterwards the younger men began to depart for service in England and in August 1940 all British land forces were withdrawn; the volunteers and a detachment of American marines were the only protection which the Settlement retained in a situation already becoming ominous. In January 1940 unidentified terrorists had tried unsuccessfully to kill the secretary of the Shanghai Municipal Council. Shortly afterwards, by a cunning expansion of the ratepayers' list, the British had defeated a Japanese attempt to swamp the elections for the council, but the victory was a hollow one. It bred a resentment which almost ended in tragedy at the next general meeting of ratepayers, held in the Shanghai racecourse, where the president of the Japanese Ratepayers' Association shot at and wounded the Jardine taipan, J. H. Keswick, who was presiding as chairman of the municipal council. Concessions were at last made, and a provisional council was set up in which British, Japanese and Americans each had three representatives, the Chinese four, and three other places were reserved for less numerous foreign nationalities. The atmosphere in the Settlement grew tense. Respectable women began to leave and the graveyard gaiety of the night-clubs reached new heights, like a little Rome awaiting the barbarians. It did not long await them. In

November the American marines – the last regular soldiers – departed, and on the day of Pearl Harbour the Japanese sank the only British gunboat that remained and occupied the Settlement.

Immediately the status of British residents was changed and the dismantling of their political-social domination began. The consular staff was placed under hotel arrest. British members of the council were forced to resign, as were British police officers, while the Volunteer Corps was disarmed and suspended. All British subjects were obliged to register with the Japanese police and to wear red armbands. The Kempetei, the Japanese equivalent of the Gestapo, moved into the Settlement, and almost from the beginning of the occupation individual foreigners were interned on suspicion or taken to the interrogation unit which the Japanese had established in one of the smaller hotels, where they were kept in primitive, crowded circumstances and examined under torture. Such practices seemed intended more to terrorize and humiliate the European population than to gain any information that might be of conceivable use to the torturers.

Surprisingly, however, most of the British were at large in Shanghai for more than a year after the Japanese occupation. For many it was already a time of hardship. Bank assets had been frozen and only small sums could be drawn each month, which many people found inadequate to maintain their families. Others lost their employment. The British Ratepayers' Association, which had been founded in the 1920s, played an important role administering relief funds guaranteed by the British government and buying foods wholesale which it sold cheaply in a cooperative store organized in the grounds of the Anglican cathedral. Though most of the merchants were still at liberty, the traditional trading activities of the Settlement had ground to a temporary halt. Some people were actually fortunate enough to leave, with the concurrence of the Japanese, when the *Kamakura Maru* sailed in August 1942 with a full load of passengers, including the consular staff and some seven hundred other people, selected according to a priority list compiled by the British government, which favoured technicians and ships' officers, who would be useful in the war effort at home.

Those who had no skills were left for the duration of the war, awaiting the pleasure of the Japanese, who in November 1942 took their first major steps against the British community by arresting some hundreds of its leading members and interning them in a bare cramped mansion formerly used by the American marines. There were few conveniences and the Korean guards were often brutal, but the lot of the internees was mitigated in the beginning by the fact that the uninterned majority were able to help them considerably by providing food and other assistance through the Ratepayers' Association.

At first it seemed as though the Japanese might be content merely to decapitate the British community by isolating its most important citizens, but in January 1943 general internment was announced. The British were called in batches, with as much luggage as they could carry in their own hands, and were marched through the streets – as an object lesson of the downfall of the white conquerors – to the seven buildings (schools, camps and clubs) which had been selected for their reception. Families were allowed to stay together in special camps, and sometimes in these unlikely circumstances, they even managed to increase. After the early, most difficult days, conditions improved a little, partly due to the arrival of Red Cross parcels and of small cash allowances made through the Swiss consul, and partly to the efforts of the internees themselves, who developed their powers of improvization and not only started up again the familiar amateur dramatic groups but also set up schools to improve their minds and cultivated kitchen gardens to improve their diet. Outside, in the International Settlement, a parody of the old life went on, with the night clubs still open and filled with White Russian girls, the race-course turned over to the new amusement – the public decapitation of so-called criminals, and many of the British warehouses open again, but only to be plundered of their contents, which were shipped to Japan.

Elsewhere in China the British were either interned, if they happened to be in Japanese held territory and could not escape, or made their way into western China. Thence, in December 1944, those who still remained and had not been absorbed into any war activity, were evacuated to India. In this way most of the uninterned British missionaries left China until after the end of hostilities.

The British in Shanghai were more fortunate than their brethren elsewhere in the Far East, since the very defencelessness of the International Settlement saved it and its inhabitants from the horrors of war and the rigours which afflict the defeated after a victory in battle.

The quick and easy Japanese conquest of Hong Kong, of Malaya and of the British territories in Borneo is the subject of an immense literature, analyzing from various points of view the causes of the humiliating collapse of British power in these regions. With the military aspect of this series of calamities we are not concerned. But the attitudes of the British communities who suffered the effects of defeat are part of our subject. The military unpreparedness evident in both Malaya and Hong Kong was due largely to the fatal longevity of illusions about the power of Britain and the weakness of its potential Asian enemies which were shared by

British governments on the one hand and Far Eastern Hands on the other – shared until it was too late for the neglect they had engendered to be remedied.

Pride of race, contempt for other races, and an enervating century of security lay at the basis of these illusions. Despite all the evidence from the Russo-Japanese war of 1905 onwards, the British still regarded Asians as inferiors, at once amusing and exasperating, and until 1940 few of them realized how strong Japan had become and how intent on establishing an Asian empire which it did not propose to share with others. If the British had been forced to fight for their empire in the Far East as they fought to keep and consolidate their empire in India, the situation might have been very different. But, except for a few jungle skirmishes, Malaya and the Bornean territories had been won without a struggle and had been defended for a century by a handful of men. Even Hong Kong had never been seriously threatened. This feeling of security, created and sustained by sea power, left most of the British who lived in the Far East with the feeling that all they had built up so peacefully would be endlessly and effortlessly retained. When that great bubble of illusion burst, some reacted with fortitude and some with panic; the imperturbable, unconquerable British showed themselves to be men like others.

Hong Kong's agony was the first and the shortest. On the day after Pearl Harbour, 8 December 1941, the Japanese attack on the New Territories began. The British there faced the struggle with an ill-founded sense of security, partly based on the fact that only a few weeks before the garrison had been strengthened by two battalions of Canadian troops. That the Canadians were category C troops who had received little training and came without transport or full equipment was not evident to the men in the counting houses of Victoria or the women in the villas of the Peak. They saw the event as a proof of imperial solidarity, as an earnest that the government in London thought their island defensible and meant to defend it. In fact, without planes and with insufficient anti-aircraft guns, it could not have held out for more than a short time against the Japanese. It took the Japanese four days to take the New Territories and Kowloon. On 18 December, after two demands for surrender had been rejected by the Governor, Sir Mark Young, the Japanese attacked the island. On Christmas Day their victory was complete; the British had surrendered.

Those who fought included regular British soldiers, wartime recruits like the Canadians, and the volunteers, mainly British, of the Hong Kong Defence Force. According to all the accounts, the volunteers – griffins, junior officials, shopkeepers, engineers – fought as well as most of the regulars and better than some of them; some of their units suffered very heavy casualties. A tradition exists among those who survive that the Volunteers and the governor were willing to fight on, and that they and other civilians were betrayed by the military who could have held out much longer.

The price of defeat was harsher in Hong Kong than in Shanghai. Some prisoners were slaughtered and some European women were raped by the victorious soldiery. But the vast majority were marched off immediately into internment. There was no period of respite and no repatriation. The British residents were divided into a number of groups. A few were left free for the time being so that the administration of the island would not completely collapse. These included Sir Vandeleur Grayburn of the Hong Kong and Shanghai Banking Corporation, and Dr Selwyn Clarke, the director of the medical services, who not only carried on his appointed tasks for more than two years but also helped the internees as far as it lay in his power. For this the Japanese, after he had served their purpose of preventing the health services from falling into immediate chaos, arrested and tortured him and finally sentenced him to four years' imprisonment. Sir Vandeleur was also arrested and died in prison. The governor, Sir Mark Young, was kept in the Peninsula Hotel, which was the Japanese headquarters, for the duration of the war. Those who had been enrolled in the Volunteers were treated as prisoners of war and interned with the soldiers in a deserted and derelict British barracks at Shamshuipo on the Kowloon side of the harbour. Many of them were later taken to Japan to work as dock labourers or as the lowest of menials in the factories, cleaning the latrines and the baths used by the workers.

The civilians, of all ages and sexes, were interned at Stanley Prison and those who survived malnutrition and sporadic ill-treatment remained on the island until the war was ended. Their situation was different from that of the internees in Shanghai, since the European community was not split up in various camps, nor was it divided from its leaders. 'The Bag', as Stanley Prison was called, contained most of the higher administrators and the important merchants and bankers. The result was that though it was temporarily deprived of property, the Hong Kong British community continued to exist as a unit and to maintain its hierarchical structure even in defeat. The taipans still remained the taipans, the colonial secretary, in the absence of the governor, became the leader of that society of prisoners, and a solidarity developed in confinement which was to survive among those who experienced it long into the years after the war.

In Borneo, where rule was divided between a white raja and a commercial company neither of whom had more than the necessary complement of armed police to maintain internal order, the collapse of the fabric of empire was even more rapid and complete than in Hong Kong. The Japanese invading force landed on 17 December at Miri, near the borders of Sarawak and Brunei; the place had a certain economic importance because of its oil installations. The Japanese, facing little resistance, systematically absorbed the British territories. On Christmas Day Kuching, the capital of Sarawak, was in their hands; by 8 January they had occupied Jesselton, the capital of North Borneo.

Raja Vyner Brooke was in Australia when the invasion took place. Most of the administrative officers in both North Borneo and Sarawak stayed at their posts. They were interned in a compound on the edge of Kuching. There too were brought the women and children who had been evacuated up country when the invasion began and who were later captured by the Japanese. A few made their way into Dutch Borneo and were rescued by aeroplane before the Japanese arrived. For those who stayed in the prison camp conditions were increasingly difficult. Women and children were segregated from the men. Food became steadily shorter and many people died of malnutrition or of untreated diseases. Some, like the raja's representative, Captain Le Gros Clark, who had assumed the position of spokesman for the prisoners, were killed by the Japanese. It was one of the worst civilian camps.

Malaya was the last of the British strongholds in the Far East to fall completely under Japanese domination, partly because of its area, and partly because of the resistance put up by the 85,000 British troops who before the end had been poured into the peninsula and into the island of Singapore, an army far larger than any that had sailed in the past to the Far East and far more tragically ineffective. Again, although the military history of the struggle in Malaya does not concern us directly we are concerned with the attitude of the British community, which was probably more complacent than anywhere else in the Far East. Shanghai and Hong Kong had always lived on the edges of the volcano of a changing China; the error of the China Hands had been to assume that the Japanese, unlike the Chinese, were friends of the white men. People in Malaya, on the other hand, believed that their very remoteness was a guarantee, in spite of the fact that as early as 1937 the general officer commanding in Malaya had warned that an attack on the peninsula was both feasible, and, in the event of a war, likely. But, more than anything else, they put their faith in the great naval base which had been built in Singapore during the 1920s at a cost of £63,000,000. The base was a citadel on its own, where a whole staff of naval personnel lived in a special town within the dockyard walls on the north-western shore of the island, provided with shops, churches, playing fields and clubs, and enjoying their own social life apart from that of the resident community in Singapore City. The great fifteen-inch guns of the base looked out over the water to the west of Singapore, and no battleship approaching from that side would have got past their fire. But it was only from the ocean that Singapore was defended. There were fortifications on the southern beaches of the island, but none on the northern side, facing the narrow strait that lay between the island and the peninsular state of Johore. Moreover, the naval base had never been provided with a fleet and when the war began in 1939 Singapore and the rest of Malaya were defended by five battalions of regular troops plus the Volunteers of the Straits Settlements and of the Federated Malay States. The great base and the peacetime garrison were in fact no defence at all, but Europeans in Malaya believed they were, which explains both their curious lack of concern before the Japanese arrived and the panic into which many of them fell when what had seemed impossible actually happened.

The first Japanese attacks took place on Pearl Harbour Day, 7 December, in the remote north-eastern state of Kelantan, where there were comparatively few British residents, and early reports convinced people that the British forces, reinforced since 1939, were holding their own. Even in Penang, dangerously near to the scene of fighting, a false security prevailed and the bar of the Eastern and Oriental Hotel was crowded every day until 11 December, when Japanese planes swept down unchecked over the town, bombing and machine gunning. The raids continued for several days, chaos ensued and orders were given for evacuation. What the actual orders were, and even whence they emanated is still a mystery, but it is certain that they were interpreted to mean that all Europeans – and Europeans only – were to leave the island. They did leave, abandoning the possessions they could not carry and crowding on to the ferry boats in such haste that young children snatched hurriedly from their beds were often clad only in their nightclothes. The women and children, the European members of the Volunteer Corps, the shopkeepers and police officers and civil officials, all departed except four men who determined to stay – the British doctor in charge of the General Hospital, two clergymen and a Salvation Army officer.

This highly selective evacuation of Penang did incalculable damage to the prestige of the white men, whose courage seemed as hollow as their claims to stand like parents protecting their Malayan and Chinese and Tamil subjects. It was followed by similar scenes as the British order in Malaya folded up before the rapid and irresistible advance of the better armed, better trained and more resourceful Japanese. British officials were

229

ordered to withdraw and their Malay subordinates were left to welcome the Japanese and make whatever terms they could for themselves. British doctors and nurses were hurried away, leaving Indian doctors in charge of the hospitals. Those who stayed, like the British doctor and superintendent of the leper colony near Kuala Lumpur, did so because they felt their Hippocratic oath obliged them to disobey orders that conflicted with it, but there were few such men and by 10 January the British were in full retreat from Kuala Lumpur and the heartland of the Malay states, the roads packed with military vehicles, estate lorries and private cars, and the refugee-filled trains manned by scratch crews of English, Scots and Australians, replacing the ill-paid Indian drivers who had deserted the footplates. Soldiers destroyed the bridges after they passed over them. Planters set fire to their factories and engineers dynamited their mining dredges before they headed south or slipped into the jungle to start the guerilla activity which some of them sustained until the end of the war. In Kuala Lumpur the poor Chinese and Malays surged out of the slums and looted the European shops; the British houses which they did not gut were taken over by the Japanese for the duration. What the British had created was not merely being deserted; it was also being physically destroyed.

There was only one way for the fleeing tuans to go and that was south to Singapore, the city which still felt secure under the illusory protection of the vast guns which pointed only out to sea. In Singapore women were unwilling to sail on the early evacuation ships which left for Batavia, because they felt it would never be really necessary to leave their husbands who had to stay to run their businesses or serve in the Volunteers. Even after the first landing in Kelantan, and even after the first air raid on Singapore on 8 December, people still planned to attend the Penang races, to spend Christmas at Cameron Highlands, or at the very least to see the New Year in with a dinner and dance at Raffles, the Adelphi or the newer, more fashionable Seaview Hotel. Even when Penang fell, and later when the redoubtable Mrs Rattray, proprietress of the Green Cow Tavern in Cameron Highlands, came breathing indignation at Japanese soldiers and British officials alike for being ejected from 'the highest hotel in Malaya', they still thought the interruption was temporary and that next year if not this they would revisit their habitual holiday places. They flocked to Raffles to dance to Dan Hopkins and his band, and to the Adelphi where the Reller Band performed nightly, and to the Alhambra to see Greta Garbo enact in *Mata Hari* the role of the fifth columnist which Japanese agents in their own city were assuming at that very moment.

Meanwhile the city became steadily more crowded, as refugees of all races crowded in from the peninsula, until its population was almost doubled. Many of the refugees had arrived with a suitcase and almost no money, and they often found it hard to rent a place to live until they could get on a boat to India or the temporary safety of Java. Many of them encountered racketeering landlords who even at this time of crisis were intent only on making profit. The agony columns of the newspapers carried the advertisements of men or women who had lost touch with their families in the flight.

As the fighting drew nearer, as doubts of the impregnability of Singapore began to dawn upon its inhabitants, the mood changed somewhat, though the actions did not. People still flocked to the cinemas, but now it was to take their minds away from the realities of their situation. They still danced in the blacked-out hotels, but now it was in defiance rather than complacency. As long as the ships could safely make their way into harbour with troops and supplies, they loaded up with refugees. The personnel of the naval base left early; their skills were needed in England. The reluctant women sent their children away and then decided to leave themselves, trailing out to the office which the P. & O. had set up to allocate ship space; it was situated in the suburbs where there was less risk of the queues being bombed than down in the city where the air raids were becoming frequent.

On the last day of January the British troops abandoned the peninsula and retreated over the causeway from Johore to Singapore Island. But for those who remained, Singapore still offered many comforts that were not usual in a city under siege. There was plenty of food; Singapore could have lasted several months without being starved out. Thanks to the Chinese habit of keeping many pigs, there was even an abundance of fresh meat, and boys still delivered Cold Storage milk by tricycle to the Tanglin houses that were occupied. The clubs continued to function, and there was no shortage of drink; a million and a half bottles of liquor were to be destroyed at the end of the siege to keep it from the throats of the Japanese soldiers. The shops – Robinsons, the British Pharmacy, Kelly and Walsh, the Cold Storage – carried on to the end, and their European staffs stood fact, maintaining the creed of business-as-usual which had always sustained the commercial British of the Far East. The boats still came in and left with their cargoes of women, of children, and, now that even the authorities did not believe the island could be held, of military and civilian personnel considered essential. Armed deserters forced their way on to ships. Business men drove down in their cars and abandoned them as they argued or bought their way aboard. The cars were later tipped into the water to deprive the Japanese of their use.

Meanwhile the strait of Johore had proved an illusory moat, and despite the destruction of the causeway the Japanese landed on the island, and relentlessly, day after day, the fighting moved nearer the city, its circle engulfing the cottages on holiday beaches and then the great bungalows in the outer suburbs. The civilians who remained were driven towards the centre of the city. Some of them put on uniforms and fought in the Straits Settlements Volunteers. Others stayed to make the last bit of money (outboard motors still sold well to the desperate optimists who had left departure till the end), and others because of a sense of responsibility to businesses that in a week would be the prey of looters. Some remained out of pride. There were still women among them. On 15 February Singapore surrendered. The civilians were interned in Changi Gaol, where their experiences were similar to those of the British interned anywhere else in the Japanese-occupied world. For more than three years they waited, a shadow guard for the empire that in the end would return to play its last act across the Far Eastern stage.

16

THE FINAL PHASE

During these years of defeat when time ran slowly, from the beginning of 1942 to the autumn of 1945, the only British in the Far East were the prisoners in their camps and the soldiers and planters who, in increasing numbers from 1943 onwards, penetrated Japanese-held Malaya and Borneo and established contact with the bands of guerillas which had sprung up in these regions, Chinese in race and usually Communist in political orientation. After the surrender of Germany in May 1945, it was evident that the final defeat of Japan was only a matter of time and during that summer rumours of peace began to stir the dead leaves of hope in the internment compounds.

On 14 August 1945 the Japanese finally surrendered. Two days later, in Hong Kong, the British empire in the Far East came back to life when the colonial secretary, F. C. Gimson, emerged with the surviving civil servants from the shadows of Stanley and set up a temporary administration to start public services again. Not until 30 August did the British forces under Rear-Admiral Harcourt arrive to impose law and order and halt the looting that had followed the Japanese laying down of arms. At about the same time the British and American forces arrived in Shanghai; on 5 September the British landed in Singapore and hauled down the Japanese flag from the town hall; the formal liberation of Borneo waited until 11 September.

To Hong Kong, to Malaya, to Borneo, the British returned as rulers. Unlike India and Burma, which were to achieve independence in 1947, none of these colonies by the 1940s had developed any political movement that might provide an alternative to British government and it was more than a decade before Malaya and Borneo achieved the political independence which for Hong Kong is still in the future.

The situation in Shanghai, on the other hand, had changed completely owing to political events which had taken place outside the city during the Japanese occupation. By an agreement signed on 11 January 1943, the British and American governments agreed to abandon all extra-territorial rights and all concessions in the treaty ports of the China coast. After a hundred years of active life, the International Settlement no longer existed, and when the allies returned in 1945 a Chinese administration was set up to rule the city. The Municipal Council and the Volunteer Corps, vital organs of the former cosmopolitan commonwealth of Shanghai, were abolished, and the British inspectorate-general of the Chinese Maritime Customs, that most extraordinary of all impositions upon a sovereign government, at last came to an end.

But the taipans returned, property rights of foreigners were guaranteed by the Chinese government, and the merchants were represented on an advisory council set up to assist the native local authorities. The warehouses and offices of foreign companies, the factories and wharves of Hongkew, resumed their old activity, and by 1949 the British investment in Shanghai had reached the astonishing total of £300,000,000. Though representation on the advisory council was the last thin vestige of political influence, it seemed as though the British commercial empire in China had risen in all its former strength and for four profitable years Shanghai became its old busy and meretriciously gay self. Many of the men who had suffered in the internment camps emerged to direct their old businesses and thousands of others came out from England to fill the higher posts in the offices. European shops and hotels flourished as never before, for Shanghai was now not merely the largest port in China; it served as a vast funnel through which 80 per cent of the country's trade now passed. The clubs were reopened and a social life centred upon sports and entertainments started up again. Prices were higher than ever before and the companies had to pay high wages and generous cost-of-living allowances to keep their foreign employees who, now that fast air travel had become a commonplace of Far Eastern life, were much less inclined than in the past to stay out the term of an unsatisfactory contract.

At the same time, the missionaries returned to reap their post-war harvest of converts. They came literally in boat loads. One former American military transport ship made several voyages from San Francisco in 1946 and 1947 carrying cargoes of British and American missionaries, sleeping in improvized canvas bunks in the holds, women and children segregated from the men. By 1949 the China Inland Mission alone had almost a thousand missionaries back in the field in various parts of China, in addition to their wives and children, and for a brief period they appeared to be having unprecedented success in gaining converts.

But the rich harvests of these years were not long vouchsafed either to missionaries or to merchants. Like the great conversions, Shanghai's post-war commercial prosperity was built on foundations of political sand. It depended on the survival of the Kuomintang government, and by the end of 1948, when the Chinese Communists had secured Manchuria with Russian connivance, the future of Kuomintang power on the Chinese mainland was already problematical. In January 1949 Peking and the old taipan sea resort of Tientsin had already fallen to the Communists; by April they reached Nanking and gained control of the Yangtse Valley, which meant that they had cut Shanghai's vital line of communication with the Chinese hinterland. On 25 May they entered Shanghai itself and by the end of the year Canton and Chungking had fallen and China was under virtually complete Communist control, with the foreign commercial enterprizes and missions at the Party's mercy.

The British communities in Shanghai and Hong Kong, looking back over a century of successful trading, in spite of passing difficulties with Chinese Imperialist and Nationalist regimes, failed to understand that the national hatred of foreigners which had found impotent expression under earlier rulers was now about to be exploited by a militarily strong government whose nationalist aspirations were reinforced by an ideological hatred for the system of unbridled free enterprize which the Shanghai taipans represented. The taipans for their parts believed that the Communists would create a stronger, more orderly and less corrupt administration than the Kuomintang, in which they were correct. They also believed, less correctly, that with this administration they could still do business, and it was largely the arguments of the China Hands, led by such firms as Jardine Matheson, that persuaded Britain to give early recognition to Mao Tse-tung's government.

In 1950 animosities between the Communists and the west were intensified by the Korean War, which, as a side effect, drastically reduced the amount of trade passing through Shanghai. In any case, the Communists had no intention of leaving the wharf and factory installations of their greatest port and industrial centre in foreign hands, and once the native industrialists and compradors had been squeezed dry, they turned their attention to the foreign houses, among which the British were still the richest and most active. The method followed was a gradual building up of intolerable impositions. The state controlled and limited imports and exports as well as the movement of money. Foreigners could no longer enter Shanghai without special entry visas or leave without exit permits. Even though trade declined the Communists insisted that foreign offices and factories should continue to operate without discharging any of their native employees. This averted threatened unemployment and at the same time gave the Communists a way of forcing the foreign owners to abandon their assets without actual expropriation. The inflated wage bills soon exceeded the incomes of the factories and trading houses. The home offices had to subsidize them and continued subvention was assured by refusing exit visas to the foreign employees, who became virtual hostages. When at last the firms decided that it was useless to continue their enter-prizes in China, the Communists would offer to buy them out, and would then present exorbitant claims for outstanding taxes, wages and other charges until in the end very little was left in the way of compensation; the negligible bill would be settled by payment partly in foreign exchange and partly in promises of Chinese export goods. The process of liquidating the British firms took almost a decade. By 1960 the vast British enterprizes in Shanghai were virtually surrendered, the taipans had departed, and the European population of the city was reduced to a few individuals. The great commercial buildings along the Bund had become Communist Party offices, the Shanghai Club a seamen's hostel, the Country Club a school, and the race-course a public park; the Cathay Hotel was renamed the Peace Hotel, dedicated to earning hard currency from the foreign visitors who came out of curiosity to see the New China. The factories and wharves constructed with British and other foreign capital were incorporated into the state system.

The spread of Communist power over China brought persecution and imprisonment to some missionaries and death to others, but in spite of the hatred preached against them as agents of imperialism they probably suffered less in the aggregate than their predecessors during the Boxer Rebellion. The main attack was indirectly delivered. In May 1950 Chou En-lai called a number of leading Chinese Christians to a meeting in Peking and forced them to agree that the Church would accept Com-munist leadership and divest itself of 'imperialist influences'. Mounting pressure was exerted on Chinese Christians to dissociate themselves from foreign missionaries and by the end of 1950 all organizations but the Catholics had decided to withdraw their European workers. Most of the missionaries left without hindrance, abandoning their possessions, and crowding into Hong Kong, where at one time six hundred missionaries and their families were packed into a disused army camp, awaiting the ships to take them to their next field of work. By the end of 1951 only a small handful of missionaries were left in China, capriciously selected for persecution, and they lived in poverty, maltreated and often imprisoned. By the end of 1953 almost all those who survived had been allowed to depart and the missionary had become an extinct type in China.

Imperial Noon and Twilight

Family group.

Shanghai, the Garden Bridge and Soochow Creek.

Shanghai; the public gardens and bandstand with a view across the river to the factories.

Ipoh, Perak; the Railway and Hotel building.

The visit of the Prince of Wales, later Edward VIII, to North Borneo in 1922.

The Prince, Lord Louis Mountbatten and Raja Brooke of Sarawak, pictured at the reception given by the Raja in honour of the Prince's visit.

Raffles Hotel, Singapore.

Singapore, a view across Queen Elizabeth Walk, with the Cathedral of St Andrew in the background.

The waterfront at Singapore in 1953, showing the contrast between the Malay and Chinese buildings in the foreground, and the modern European office blocks being erected in the distance.

The surrender ceremony at the end of the war, Admiral Rui Tako Fugeta handing over the sword to Rear Admiral Harcourt.

Flats for artisans in Malacca, a visible sign of a growing awareness of social needs and responsibilities.

The most distinctive of all the missionary organizations in the Far East, the China Inland Mission, had also – as such – ceased to exist. It abandoned all hopes of continuing to work in the country for which it had been specially designed, and even changed its name to the Overseas Missionary Fellowship, which by 1953 had already 370 missionaries based on a new centre at Singapore and operating in Malaya, Thailand, Indonesia and the Philippines. Other organizations similarly changed the direction of their efforts, so that the missionary remains an important figure in the surviving British communities in the Far East.

To Hong Kong came not only the missionaries but also the taipans. Those companies which possessed enough resources outside Shanghai to survive the Communist takeover of their business there, shifted headquarters to the British colony, which from 1950 became the centre of a China trade that began to revive as the Chinese understood that – under the veil of propaganda – they had to sustain certain necessary links with the capitalist world.

At the end of the war the fate of Hong Kong had been doubtful, since the Chinese Nationalists felt that they had a claim on it under the agreement abandoning the treaty port concessions and the Americans were inclined to support their point of view. Undoubtedly the prompt action of Colonial Secretary Gimson in setting up a provisional administration by officials released from internment and the arrival of Admiral Harcourt shortly afterwards helped to re-establish the British claim. Gimson's *ad hoc* administration lasted only three weeks, and from 7 September 1945 for almost eight months, the island and its territories were ruled by a military administration. On 1 May 1946 the former governor, Sir Mark Young, returned, and re-established the civil administration. It resembled a Bourbon restoration; to critics at the time it seemed to forget nothing of the past and to learn little from it. The old system of government by executive and legislative council was re-established. Once again all the members of the legislative council were nominated by the governor, except for two, elected, as before, by the justices of the peace and the chamber of commerce. The head of Jardine Matheson was a member of both executive and legislative councils. The three Chinese representatives (again all of them sat on both councils) were men who had become absorbed into the British trading community. It was estimated in the 1950s that a solid group of twenty men controlled government, public utilities and foreign trade in Hong Kong. The masses of the colony's vast Chinese population, which reached 1,600,000 in 1945 and is now more than double that number, had no representation at all, though eventually, those who were ratepayers had the minor privilege of electing some members to the urban council. The amazing fact is that this antiquated crown colony machinery has continued to work with relatively little disturbance for more than twenty years after its restoration. Present signs suggest that it may well continue to work so long as Hong Kong maintains its curious position as Britain's last remaining colony in the Far East and China's only open gate to the world outside.

Not only was the old system re-established. The old people came back to operate it. The former governor, Sir Mark Young, ruled for only a year after his return, but the officials who emerged from internment at Stanley became a tight clique, consolidated by shared sufferings, which for a long time formed the most powerful group in the administration. Now, nearly a quarter of a century afterwards, their numbers have been greatly reduced through retirement and they have been largely replaced by cadets who have come out to join the Hong Kong colonial service since the end of the war, and by the specialists of many kinds who have been introduced as social services spread under the influence of welfare state attitudes developed in the imperial centre of Britain.

The returning officials, and the businessmen who began operating once again after private trade and exchange facilities were re-established in 1946, attempted to recreate not only the political structure of old Hong Kong but also its characteristic social life. In this they were less successful. It is true that the clubs were opened again, and the Hong Kong Club, looking out from its superb site by the waterfront, became its old self, hardly less exclusive than in the imperialist past, the haunt of high officials and prosperous British businessmen. The Cricket Club kept its greens free from the taint of Asian participation. But efforts to maintain segregated bathing places were unsuccessful and the Jockey Club, which had been opened to carefully selected Chinese members in the late 1920s, was now thoroughly infiltrated by native merchants and industrialists, whose inherited love of gambling was displayed in the unprecedented volume of the bets placed at every meet. The districts which formerly had contained only British houses were now occupied largely by Chinese millionaires and it was only in the blocks of apartments specially built for government officials and in the military cantonments that Europeans still lived apart among their own kind. Even the Central British School was desegregated and, transformed into the King George V School, accepted pupils of all nationalities and races.

But it was not merely the gradual breaking of old barriers between European and Asian that changed the post-war British community in Hong Kong; it was, equally, the expansion and diversification of the community itself. Including servicemen and their families, there are now about

33,000 Commonwealth citizens resident in Hong Kong, most of them British; this figure does not include the large number of transients who stay too long to be counted as mere travellers and who contribute in their own ways to the new Hong Kong. Among them are journalists who find Hong Kong the best listening point for China, orientalists who gravitate to the colony because they cannot gain access to China itself, and a considerable number of young people from Britain of both sexes who take temporary employment in Hong Kong on their way elsewhere; the London secretary who sees the world by working her way through Montreal and Vancouver to Hong Kong and thence, later, via Singapore and Bombay back to London, taking perhaps years on the way, is a post-war phenomenon which has now become familiar in the Far East. But even the resident population of Hong Kong is different from what it was thirty years ago. There are more officials and more kinds of officials because of the increase in both population and welfare facilities. Those of the great hongs which survived the Communist takeover in Shanghai have shifted their headquarters to Hong Kong, which means that they employ larger staffs in the colony than in the past; Jardine Matheson alone employs one hundred and fifty Europeans. The Hong Kong and Shanghai Banking Corporation is now entirely centred on Hong Kong. Changes in transport patterns have also affected the European population structure. Hong Kong is now one of the great junctions of the world's airways, and twenty different airlines use the airport and have their offices in Victoria or Kowloon; in addition, many Far Eastern shipping lines which formerly worked in and out of Shanghai now make Hong Kong their base. On another plane, the expansion of the university has brought internationally known scholars and writers to Hong Kong; among them the English poet Edmund Blunden spent many years in the colony. With a population so enlarged and so diversified it is not surprising that older residents lament that while before the war one knew everyone of importance in Hong Kong, now there are far too many people to know more than a fraction of them.

There are other ways in which the patterns of Hong Kong life have changed from those of the classic imperial era. Life is less ample, in a physical sense at least. Few of the British residents live in the great houses which their predecessors built. They must usually be content with apartments provided by the government or by private employers, though – like the salaries – these will probably be larger than they could expect at home. The large households of servants are reduced to a cook, a coolie and a wash-amah, and in many cases the houseboys are being entirely replaced by women servants, who are cheaper. Even so, living is now so expensive, since most food must be imported, that extravagant hospitality is almost a thing of the past. Three other important developments have greatly changed British life in Hong Kong. The old Far Eastern custom of signing a chit for any kind of purchase, for which the money would be collected once a month by a kind of dun called a shroff, has died out except in the clubs, since shopkeepers can no longer either recognize or rely on their customers. The employment of European women in offices has become widespread and often the wives of lower paid officials compete with the wandering London stenographers, so that Hong Kong commerce is no longer the entirely masculine world it was thirty years ago. And it is no longer considered socially obligatory for people in relatively high positions to send their children to England to be educated; some still do, but many are content with the King George V School, whose policy of enrolling children of all races has been widely accepted.

The post-war political history of Malaya and the British territories in Borneo has differed widely from that of Hong Kong. Today, after a dramatic series of changes of status, none of these territories is ruled by Britain, though all remain within the Commonwealth and are linked with the former imperial centre by important political, military and above all economic connections. The British returned in 1945 to establish a military administration which, like that in Hong Kong, lasted well into 1946. The British Labour Party, then in power, followed a deliberate policy of colonial liberation, and had every intention of speeding Malaya along the same road of independence as India and Burma. The first step was the creation of the Malayan Union in 1946, with predominantly Chinese Singapore as a separate colony. A measure of constitutional government was intended, but the Malayan Union failed to meet the satisfaction of the Malay population, which feared that it might result in Chinese domination, and in 1948 it was replaced by the Federation of Malaya, in which the former native states and the settlements of Malacca and Penang were allowed a degree of autonomy under a fairly strong central government, with the sultans becoming constitutional rulers in their various territories. Meanwhile, in Borneo, the raja of Sarawak and the North Borneo Company had abdicated their sovereign rights and in 1946 the territories formerly under their rule became the Crown Colonies of Sarawak and Sabah. In 1955 both Malaya and Singapore were given constitutions granting participation in the government by elected representatives of the people, and in 1957 Malaya finally gained independence, while Singapore acquired dominion status. In 1963 all the former British territories in the region came together to form the new country of Malaysia; Singapore, Sarawak and Sabah gaining complete independence from Britain as they entered the new federation. Brunei alone remained outside Malaysia, and today this tiny state is the last remaining British protectorate in the Far East. In the event, Singapore did not agree well with the Malay-dominated states of the peninsula and after a little more than two years it seceded and became an independent city state, reliant for its survival on its classic role as the commercial entrepôt of south-east Asia.

During these many political changes, the British community, losing its political power and much of its social ascendancy, has retained other forms of power and influence, and has actually increased numerically since the days of colonial rule. The post-war history of the British in these regions can be divided into three periods – that of the return, from 1945 to 1948, that of the so-called Emergency, from 1948 to 1960, and that of developing independence, from 1960 to the present.

In Hong Kong few of the British escaped the Japanese invaders, so that those who came back into normal life had almost all served their times in prison camps. In Malaya there was a sharp division between those who had stayed, and in 1945 emerged half-broken from the frightful conditions of Changi Gaol, and those who fled and returned, often with army rank, to play their part in the military administration. An enduring bitterness developed between these two groups, one of whom felt it had been betrayed by the other, so that, as Lord Mancroft remarked at the time, 'the unholy influence of Changi seems to crop up at every turn amongst the European population'. A third discordant element was added by the fact that officials who had died in Japanese prison camps had to be replaced by men with no training in Malayan conditions. The tripartite feud between these three mutually resentful groups split the Malayan administration until after the granting of independence, and spilt into the social and commercial worlds. Equally disturbing was the adjustment which had to be made through the Malayanization of the government service. With independence not far ahead, British officials were being replaced as quickly as possible by Malayans; between 1947 and 1954 the number of Asians in higher administrative positions more than doubled, so that already, three years before independence, there were two native officers to every three British, and in some areas a majority of the district officers were Malays.

As soon as the military administration got essential services going in Singapore, Penang and Kuala Lumpur, the prewar export houses, management companies, and European retail stores returned to resume operations, and the clubs opened their doors, re-establishing continuity so thoroughly that returning members were presented with the chits they had signed for drinks during the last days before the fall of Malaya. The planters set about clearing the undergrowth of seedlings which clogged their groves and getting their factories back into production, and the tin companies installed new equipment to start the mines working. Communications were difficult at first; many rail and road bridges had been destroyed during the war and the Japanese had torn up a great deal of the railway lines in eastern Malaya to build the notorious Railroad of Death in Siam, on whose construction many of the prisoners captured in Singapore had died. But a good start had already been made in re-establishing the old economic and social patterns when the emergency began in 1948 with the rising of the Chinese Communists.

These were the same underground bands with whom British infiltrators had worked in Malaya during the Japanese occupation. When they realized that political developments in Malaya, with the tendency towards control by Malay traditionalists, were running contrary to their aims of a political takeover, they started a guerilla war. It began, significantly, with the killing of three British planters at Sungei Siput in the state of Perak. It lasted for twelve years of bitter jungle fighting.

During this time a dramatic division appeared between life in the larger towns, where danger rarely appeared and social life blossomed, and the rural areas, where danger was constant, and 356 British civilians, mostly planters and miners, had died violently by the time the emergency ended. Those who survived had lived in a state of embattled alertness in their estates and mines, turning their houses into little fortresses defended by barbed wire and searchlights, and commanding their own contingents of special constables (Malays, Tamils, sometimes even Chinese) whom they had usually to train in such elementary matters as firing a rifle before they could be of much defensive use. The planters' cars were turned into miniature tanks, the windows and the engines covered with armour plating, and they moved about armed and usually with guards. Many of their wives shared their besieged lives; indeed, during the emergency there was a great deal of dogged courage in evidence, which suggested that the British who had returned were trying to wipe out the impression of cowardice left in Asian minds by the headlong flight to Singapore in 1941. The situation of the planters was somewhat eased by the recruitment of several hundred British police sergeants who had served against terrorists in Palestine. Among other tasks they helped to organize the defence of the estates and the mines. But their presence was a mixed blessing, for many of them were adventurers of the kind bred by civil wars, and their treatment of the Asians with whom they had to deal, whether guilty or otherwise, often showed a brutality and a crude arrogance that had not before entered into the pattern of British control in Malaya.

Independence left the British a notable presence in Malaysia and Singapore commercially and even militarily. The famous naval base was reactivated and a fleet was actually established there. Air bases were built on Singapore island. A dwindling military force remained after the emergency ended; to dispel any feelings that the old imperial rule remained, its members dressed in civilian clothes when they were outside their depots, so that the British uniform ceased to be a familiar sight in the streets of Malayan towns. Present British policies, however, decree that by 1970 the military presence in Malaya and Borneo, and everywhere in the Far East except Hong Kong, will have virtually come to an end.

In comparison, the British civilian community has – like that in Hong Kong – increased since before the war, and is still increasing. In 1947 about one resident in three hundred was European. In 1961 the proportion had increased to one in two hundred and fifty, or approximately forty thousand, of whom the great majority are British, though a number of East Indian Dutchmen have settled in Singapore. The British include several familiar categories: the managers and assistant managers of the eight hundred British-controlled plantations, the staffs of 60 per cent of the tin mines, the higher officials in the British-owned commercial houses, which dominate more than half the import and export trade of the region. (In theory, no one not a citizen of Malaya or Singapore can take a post which a citizen can fill, but this makes little difference in practice, since almost from the beginning the subordinate clerical posts in Far Eastern commercial houses had been filled by Eurasians and Chinese.) Many British professional men still remain, and are likely to do so, since the first native lawyers and doctors are only just beginning to graduate from the local universities in Singapore and Kuala Lumpur, both of them post-war foundations. After independence many of the British civilian administrators remained to assist in the smooth transfer of responsibilities and the training of local successors, and British officers were seconded to the new Malayan forces. Most of these have now departed but their place has at least partly been taken by advisers and technicians sent out under foreign aid programmes. Closely related to these are a group whose existence was unimagined in the imperial age – the student volunteers who have come in considerable numbers from Britain, Canada, Australia and New Zealand; most of them have been teachers, but they have also included doctors, nurses and agriculturists.

Finally, and not least important, the new universities have attracted many British academics, some of them distinguished scholars and writers who have given the British community an intellectual quality unknown before. They include the historian, C. Northcote Parkinson, and the poets

D. J. Enright, James Kirkup and Patrick Anderson, while Anthony Burgess, whose trilogy, *The Long Day Wanes*, is the finest work of fiction yet written by an actual resident of Malaya, served for several years in the Malayan educational service. D. J. Enright was the hero of an incident in which the classic roles of Englishman and Asian were reversed, and in which academic freedom emerged triumphant from its first battle in the new Singapore. In a public lecture he criticized the official programme for a 'national culture' and was immediately threatened by the local government with expulsion; the students of all races surprised the Singapore authorities by rallying to Enright's support, and in an emergency meeting carried by 522 votes to 5 a resolution condemning a government attempt to 'strangle free discussion'. 'The Enright incident', as it is called, is remembered among all academics in south-east Asia as a major victory in their struggle to maintain objectivity in the passionate situations that arise in ex-colonial states newly come to nationhood.

The presence of such new elements as professors, writers and student volunteers has wrought considerable change in the British community in Malaya. Government House no longer heads that community and the authority of the Club is waning; I met professors in Singapore who had never been inside the Tanglin, an omission unthinkable in the past among Europeans of any standing. Such academics – and the student volunteers even more – have broken out of the tight circle of the tuans and tend to choose their associates among their colleagues, regardless of race. Some other classes of Englishmen still cling together, but the separation is rarely as obvious as that defiantly proclaimed by the few remaining exclusive clubs. It is practised most by those everlasting proletarians of the British community, the servicemen, who tend to gather where their kind meet, the men having their favoured bars and the women frequenting the top floor restaurants of Whiteway Laidlaws or the ice-cream bars of the Cold Storage. Seasoned Far Eastern Hands are now more inclined than in the past to patronize the excellent Chinese restaurants, where they mingle with the wealthier Chinese, now given to western dress and largely western manners. Even sexually the pattern is changing and opening. Young accountants in the commercial houses need no longer fear to lose their jobs if they go out with the attractive Chinese office girls of Singapore and Kuala Lumpur, which many of them do. Nor can one ignore the change in tastes which the presence of academics and intellectuals has wrought in Hong Kong, Singapore and Kuala Lumpur alike. The production of *Saint Joan* by a dramatic society in Hong Kong was an extraordinary and daring event during the 1920s; now amateur players vary domestic comedies with Greek tragedy and the Theatre of the Absurd, film societies show the most avant garde productions, and the presence of the British Council with its libraries and lectures has helped to raise the level of literary taste. There are still sections of the British communities where philistinism reigns and profit is the first consideration, but the shadow is no longer almost universal.

On the future of the British in the Far East one can only speculate. The political empire still exists in Hong Kong, but it can hardly survive beyond 1998, when the lease of the New Territories comes to an end and Hong Kong, across a narrow strait from a hostile China, will become virtually untenable. In the Malayan region there is still a strong British commercial and cultural presence; one can hardly call it an empire, since, unlike the old treaty ports, it is not defended by force and does not enjoy the privileges of extra-territoriality. How the military withdrawal in 1970 will affect it one cannot yet envisage, but unless strongly nationalist groups in Malaya and Singapore decide on a wholesale programme of expropriation (which at present does not seem probable), the British community is likely to remain an important element in the lives of these countries long after the British empire which created it has passed into memory.

Bibliography

Alcock, Sir Rutherford, *The Capital of the Tycoon; a Narrative of Three Years' Residence in Japan*, 2 vols, London, 1863

An Embassy to China: Lord Macartney's Journal, 1793–1794, ed. J. L. Cranmer-Byng, London, 1962

Attiwell, Kenneth, *The Singapore Story*, London, 1959

Baring-Gould, S. and C. A. Bamfylde, *A History of Sarawak under its Two White Rajahs*, London, 1909

Bartlett, Vernon, *Report from Malaya*, London, 1954

Bastin, John and Robert W. Winks, *Malaysia: Selected Historical Readings*, Kuala Lumpur, 1966

Bastin, John, *The British in West Sumatra (1685–1825)*, Kuala Lumpur, 1965
    The Native Policies of Sir Stamford Raffles in Java and Sumatra, Oxford, 1957

Beasley, W. G., *Great Britain and the Opening of Japan, 1834–1858*, London, 1951

Belcher, E., *Narrative of the Voyage of H.M.S. Samarang, during the years 1843–46*, 2 vols, London, 1851

Bertram, James, *Beneath the Sun*, New York, 1947

Boulger, Demetrius Charles, *The Life of Sir Stamford Raffles*, London, 1897

Bredon, Juliet, *Sir Robert Hart*, London, 1909

Brooke, Rajah Charles, *Ten Years in Sarawak*, 2 vols, London, 1866

Brooke, Rani Sylvia, *The Three White Rajahs*, London, 1939

Buckley, Charles Burton, *An Anecdotal History of Old Times in Singapore, 1819–1867*, Singapore, 1902

Cady, John F. *South-east Asia: Its Historical Development*, New York, 1964

Cameron, John, *Our Tropical Possessions in Malayan India*, London, 1865

Campbell, Arthur, *Jungle Green*, Boston, 1954

Campbell, Reginald, *Teak-Wallah*, London, 1935

Carse, Robert, *The Age of Piracy*, London, 1957

Chapman, F. Spencer, *The Jungle is Neutral*, London, 1949

Chesterton, E. Keble, *The East Indiaman*, London, 1933

246

Clodd, H. P., *Malaya's First British Pioneer: the Life of Francis Light*, London, 1948

Collis, Maurice, *British Merchant Adventurers*, London, 1946
 Foreign Mud, London, 1946
 Raffles, London, 1966
 Siamese White, London, 1936

Commonwealth Pen, The, ed. E. L. McLeod, Ithaca, NY, 1961

Crawford, Oliver, *The Door Marked Malaya*, London, 1958

Crawfurd, John, *History of the Indian Archipelago*, 3 vols, London, 1820
 Journal of an Embassy to the Courts of Siam and Cochin China, London, 1830

Curle, Richard, *Into the East: Notes on Burma and Malaya*, London, 1923

Dampier, William, *Voyages and Discoveries*, ed. Clennel Wilkinson, London, 1931

Darton, F. J. Harvey, *The Life and Times of Mrs Sherwood (1775–1851) from the diaries of Captain and Mrs Sherwood*, London, 1910

Davies, Donald, *More Old Singapore*, Singapore, 1956
 Old Penang, Singapore, 1956
 Old Singapore, Singapore, 1955

Derwent, Rev. C. E., *Shanghai: a Handbook for Travellers and Residents*, Shanghai, 1920

Divine, David, *Those Splendid Ships: The Story of the Peninsular and Oriental Line*, London, 1966

Drage, Charles, *Servants of the Dragon Throne*, London, 1966

Eames, J. B., *The Englishman in China*, London, 1909

Endacott, G. B., *A History of Hong Kong*, London, 1958
 An Eastern Entrepôt, London, 1964
 Government and People in Hong Kong, Hong Kong, 1964

Fairbank, J. K., *Trade and Diplomacy on the China Coast*, Cambridge, Mass., 1953

Fauconnier, Henri, *Malaysie*, Paris, 1930 (translated as *The Soul of Malaya*, London, 1931)

Fisher, Charles A., *South-east Asia*, London, 1964

Fleming, Peter, *One's Company*, London, 1934
 The Siege of Peking, London, 1959

Forrest, T., *A Voyage to New Guinea*, London, 1780

Foster, William, *Early Travels in India*, London, 1921
 John Company, London, 1926
 The East India House, London, 1924

Fox, Grace, *British Admirals and Chinese Pirates*, London, 1940

Gibbon, Ashley, *The Malay Peninsula and Archipelago*, London, 1928

Ginsburg, Morton and Chester F. Roberts, *Malaya*, Seattle, 1958

Gleason, Gene, *Tale of Hong Kong*, London, 1967

Gull, E. M., *British Economic Interests in the Far East*, New York, 1943

Gullick, J. M., *A History of Selangor*, Singapore, 1960
  The History of Early Kuala Lumpur, Singapore, 1956
  and Gerald Hawkins, *Malayan Pioneers*, Singapore, 1958

Hahn, Emily, *James Brooke of Sarawak*, London, 1953
  Raffles of Singapore, London, 1948

Hall, D. G. E., *The History of South East Asia*, London, 1955

Hall, W. H., *Narratives of the Voyages and Service of the Nemesis, from 1834 to 1840*, London, 1844

Hamilton, Captain Alexander, *New Account of East Asia*, Edinburgh, 1727

Hauser, Ernest O. *Shanghai: City for Sale*, New York, 1940

Hickey, William, *Memoirs*, ed. Peter Quennell, London, 1960

Historiography of the British Empire-Commonwealth, ed. Robin W. Winks, Durham, North Carolina

Holman, Dennis, *Noone of the Ulu*, London, 1959

Holt, Edgar, *The Opium Wars in China*, London, 1964

Hornaday, W. T., *Two Years in the Jungle*, London, 1885

Houston, J. V. Davidson, *Yellow Creek*, London, 1962

Illustrated Guide to the Federated Malay States, ed. Cuthbert Woodside Harrison, London, n.d.

Ingrams, H., *Hong Kong*, London, 1952

Innes, Emily, *The Chersonese with the Gilding Off*, London, 1885

Keppel, H. *The Expedition to Borneo of H.M.S. Dido*, 2 vols, London, 1846

Kirkup, James, *Tropic Temper*, London, 1963

Lyall, Leslie T., *A Passion for the Impossible: The China Inland Mission, 1865–1965*, London, 1965

MacGregor, David R., *The Tea Clippers*, London, 1952

Makepeace, William, *One Hundred Years of Singapore*, 2 vols, London, 1921

Marsden, William, *History of Sumatra*, London, 1811

McKie, Ronald, *Malaysia in Focus*, Sydney, 1963

Michie, A., *The Englishman in China during the Victorian Era as illustrated in the Career of Sir Rutherford Alcock*, 2 vols, Edinburgh, 1900

Moffat, Abbot Low, *Mongkut the King of Siam*, Ithaca, NY, 1961

Moorhead, F. J., *A History of Malaya*, Kuala Lumpur, 1963

Morse, H. B., *The International Relations of the Chinese Empire*, 3 vols, London, 1910
  and Harley Farnsworth, *Far Eastern International Relations*, Boston, 1931

Morrison, Ian, *Malayan Postscript*, London, 1942

O'Donovon, Patrick, *For Fear of Weeping*, London, 1950

Owen, Frank, *The Fall of Singapore*, London, 1960

Pal, John, *Shanghai Saga*, London, 1963

Parkinson, C. Northcote, *Trade in the Eastern Seas, 1793–1813*, London, 1937
  War in the Eastern Seas, 1793–1815, London, 1954
Pearson, H. F., *Singapore: A Popular History*, Singapore, 1961
Pelcovits, Nathan A., *Old China Hands and the Foreign Office*, New York, 1948
Philips, C. H., *The East India Company, 1784–1834*, Manchester, 1940
Poot, F. L. Hawkes, *A Short History of Shanghai*, Shanghai, 1928
Purcell, Victor, *The Memoirs of a Malayan Official*, London, 1965

Raffles, Lady Sophia, *Memoirs of the Life and Public Services of Sir Thomas
  Stamford Raffles*, 2 vols, London, 1830, 1835
Raffles, Sir Thomas Stamford, *History of Java*, London, 1817
Rand, Christopher, *Hong Kong, the Island Between*, New York, 1952
Robinson, J. B. Derry, *Transformation in Malaya*, London, 1956
Robinson, P. F., *The Trade of the East India Company from 1709 to 1813*,
  Cambridge, 1912
Rogers, P. R., *The First Englishman in Japan: The Story of Will Adams*, London,
  1956
Rose, Sauk, *Britain and South-East Asia*, Baltimore, 1962
Runciman, Steven, *The White Rajahs*, London, 1960
Russell, S. M., *The Story of the Siege of Peking*, London, 1901

Scott, J. M., *The Tea Story*, London, 1964
Sherry, Norman, *Conrad's Eastern World*, Cambridge, 1966
Sidney, Richard C. H., *In British Malaya Today*, London, n.d. (*c.* 1926)
Slimming, John, *Temiar Jungle*, London, 1958
Soothill, W. E., *China and England*, London, 1928
  China and the West, London, 1925
Stacey, Tom, *The Hostile Sun*, London, 1953
St. John, Spenser, *Life in the Forests of the Far East*, 2 vols, London, 1863
  Life of Sir James Brooke, Rajah of Sarawak, Edinburgh, 1879
Swettenham, Sir Frank, *British Malaya*, London, rev. ed., 1948
  Stories and Sketches, ed. William R. Roff, Kuala Lumpur, 1967

Tarling, Nicholas, *Piracy and Politics in the Malay World*, Melbourne, 1963
Thomson, John Turnbull, *Translations from Hikayat Abdullah*, London, 1874
Thomson, Virginia, *Thailand, the New Siam*, New York, 1941
Thorn, William, *R. R. Gillespie, a Memoir*, London, 1816
  The Conquest of Java, London, 1816
Tregonning, K. C., *History of Modern Sabah, 1881–1963*, Singapore, 1965
  The British in Malaya, 1786–1826, Tucson, 1965
Twining, Thomas, *Travels in India a hundred years ago, being notes and remin-
  iscences of Thomas Twining*, ed. William H. C. Twining, London, 1893

Vella, Walter F., *Siam under Rama III, 1824–1851*, Locust Valley, NY, 1957
  The Impact of the West on Government in Thailand, Berkeley, 1955
Vincent, Frank, *The Land of the White Elephant*, New York, 1874

Wallace, Alfred Russel, *My Life*, 2 vols, London, 1905
 The Malay Archipelago, London, 1869
Wathen, James, *Journal of a Voyage in 1811 and 1812, to Madras and China*,
 London, 1814
Webb, Derek S., *Hong Kong*, Singapore, 1961
Wilbur, Marguerite Evans, *The East India Company and the British Empire in
 the Far East*, Stanford, 1945
Williams-Ellis, Amabel, *Darwin's Moon: A Biography of Alfred Russel Wallace*,
 London, 1966

Index

Abdullah, 186
Aberdeen, 27
Abyssinia, 82
Acheen, xx, 6, 81–82
Adams, Will, xx, 6, 71–2, 114, 166
Alcock, J. Rutherford, 45, 60–1, 153, 155, 202
Aleppo, xix
Alexander, William, 210
Alexandria, 20, 117–9
Almayer's Folly, 214
Amboyna, xxi, 5, 8, 22
American Trading Company, 80
Amherst, Lord, xxiii, 59, 121
Amoy, xxii, xxiv, 27, 41, 60
Andaman Islands, 141, 175
Anderson, Patrick, 244
Annam, xvi, xxvii, 223
Antheunis, Lucas, 4
Appenzell, 145
Armstrong, George, 176, 188, 213
Army in the Far East, 34–45
Arrow War, xxiv
Asiatic Journal, 116
Assam, 87
Athenaeum, 77
Auchmuchty, Sir Samuel, 39–40
Austen, Admiral Sir Francis, 24
Austen, Jane, 24
Australia and Australians, xx, 29, 83, 88, 119, 125, 192–3, 228, 230, 243
Ayuthia, xxi, 5, 81–2, 120–1

Babylon, xx
Balfour, Capt. George, 152–3
Bali, 166, 168

Banda, xx, 8
Bandjermesin, 74–5
Bangkok, 95, 177, 199, 214, 216
Bangkok Times, 216
Banking, 17–8
Bantal, 9, 34
Bantam, xx, xxi, 4–6, 8, 23
Baptist Missionary Society, 100–1
Barnaby George, 81–2
Basra, xix, 20
Batavia, 10, 40, 54, 75–6, 120
Beauchamp, Montagu, 107
Beechey, R. N., 210
Belilios, E. R., 132
Bencoolen, xxi, xxiii, 5–11, 23, 33–4, 37, 51, 55, 89, 101, 117, 120, 127, 164–6, 175, 178, 180, 199, 207
Bengal, 34, 39, 66, 77, 89, 127, 140, 145, 165, 173, 178
Bengal, Bay of, 52–3, 72, 81, 121, 164
Bengal Fusiliers, 45
Bengal Light Infantry, 37
Bengalis, 9–10, 34, 135, 175, 177
Birch, James, 38
Blake, William, 105
Blue Funnel Line, 30
Blunden, Edmund, 239
Bombay, 7, 25–6, 35, 48, 52, 57, 117–8, 239
Bonham, Sir George, 131
Borneo, xvii–xviii, xxi, xxiv, xxvii, 23, 50, 74–5, 78–81, 88, 104, 122, 124, 128–9, 163, 179, 189, 195, 205, 214, 225–8, 233, 240, 243
Bowen, Sir George, 147–8
Bowra, Edward, 44, 174, 210, 213

Bowring, Sir John, 61–2, 68, 142–3, 166, 208
Bridges, Dr. W. T., 58
Bridgman, Elijah, 104
British and Foreign Bible Society, 100–1
British Council, 245
British India Steam Navigation Company, 124
British Malaya, 122
British North Borneo Company, xxiv, xxvi, 65, 76, 78, 80–1,
Brooke, Sir Charles, 65, 78–9, 81, 108, 164–5, 167, 192
Brooke, Sir James, xxiv, xxvi, 49, 65, 74–80, 99, 164, 170, 213
Brooke, Sir Vyner, 66, 79, 80, 228
Brown, David, 90
Brunei, xxiv, 75–6, 78–80, 228, 240
Buckley, Charles B., 208
Bugis, 9, 34, 135
Burgess, Anthony, xviii, 244
Burma and the Burmese, xix, xxi, xxvii, 43, 62, 77, 95, 127, 135, 146, 214, 240
Burmese Days, 215
Butterfield & Swire, 21

Cabot, John, xv
Cairo, 118–9
Calcutta, 9, 14, 25–7, 35, 39, 51, 118–9, 124, 146, 164, 183, 186, 209, 214
Caldwell, D. L., 58
California, xix, 32
Callum, Thomas, 206
Cambodia, xiv, xxi, xxvii, 33, 71–2
Campbell, Reginald, 96
Cameron, James, 121
Cameron, J. N., 134–5, 162, 169–70, 172, 178–9, 185, 195, 198, 208
Cameron Highlands, 201, 230
Canada, xviii–xix, 88, 94, 125, 130–1, 226, 243
Canaletto, 170
Canton, xxii, xxiv, 11–16, 19, 23, 25–7, 29, 31, 34, 41–2, 48, 51–2, 59, 62, 85, 100–3, 114, 116–7, 120, 136, 142, 144, 151–2, 160, 162, 164, 175, 177, 186, 188, 190, 197, 199, 208–9, 215
Canton Gazette, 215
Canton Press, 215

Cape Horn, xix–xx
Cape of Good Hope, xix, 20, 29, 113, 117, 119
Catherine of Braganza, xxii
Cavendish, Thomas, xix–xx
Celebes, 9, 86
Ceylon, 29, 90–1
Chamberlain, Joseph, 148, 207
Chang Tso-lin, 85
Chapei, 221
Charles I, xxii
Charles II, xxii
Chefoo, 27
Chiang kai-shek, 46
Chiengmai, xix–xxi, xxviii, 95
China and the Chinese, xv–xxvi, 5, 10, 12–20, 23, 25–7, 29–30, 34, 36, 39, 41–6, 50, 52–3, 56–65, 68–70, 72–3, 78, 80, 83–8, 90, 93–4, 96, 101, 104–8, 113, 119–21, 124, 128–32, 135, 139, 141–7, 150–61, 163, 165–6, 171–4, 176–7, 179, 181, 183, 185–8, 191–7, 199–200, 202, 204–5, 208–10, 215–6, 221–3, 225, 228–9, 231, 233–40, 242, 245
China Association, 107, 132
China Inland Mission, 104–7, 109, 119, 121, 183, 234, 237
China Mail, 215–6
China Merchants Steam Navigation Company, 30
China Seas, xv–xvi, xviii–xx, xxii, xxv, xxvii, 3, 5, 11, 20–1, 24–5, 27, 29, 33, 47–51, 56, 77, 98–9, 125, 160, 168, 215
China Steam Navigation Company, 21
Chinese Maritime Customs, xxiv, xxvi–xxvii, 68–9, 73, 150, 164, 167, 216, 223, 234
Chinese Repository, 102, 215
Chinkiang, 73, 150, 204
Chinnery, George, 210
Chou-En-lai, 236
Christmas Island, 76, 204
Chulalongkorn, xxviii, 68
Chungking, 85
Church Missionary Society, 100
Churches, 98–110, 166–7
Chusan, 41
Clark, Captain Le Gros, 228
Clarke, Sir Andrew, 63
Clarke, Dr. Selwyn, 227

Class Distinctions, 5, 31–2, 43–5, 127, 185–6, 244
Clifford, Hugh, 215
Clubs, 180, 185–90, 222, 231, 238, 241, 244
Clunies-Ross, John, 75–6
Coates, Captain, 82
Cochin-China, 8, 72, 169
Cocks, Richard, 6–7
Cocos Islands, 76
Cohen, Two-Gun, xxvii, 83, 85
Coleman, George Drumgold, 140–1, 170, 209
Collet, Joseph, 9–10, 100
Collis, Maurice, xxviii, 102–3, 164, 214
Colonial Civil Service, 56–8, 62–7
Columbus, Christopher, xv
Communists in China, 83, 85, 235–6
Communists in Malaya, 233, 235, 242
Conrad, Joseph, xviii, 18, 29, 141, 214–5
Constantinople, 20
Consular Service, 56, 57, 59–62, 68, 152–9, 161, 166
Convicts, 88, 175
Cornwallis, Lord, 52, 89
Courteenes, Sir William, xxii
Cowie, W. C., 81
Crawfurd, John, 37, 55, 72, 139, 169, 205, 207–8, 215
Cricket, 194–6
Crimean War, 45
Cutty Sark, 27

Dale, Sir Thomas, 22
D'Almeida, Dr. José, 210–11
Dampier, William, 6, 26, 81–2, 165–6
Darjeeling, 30, 87, 151, 201
Darwin, Charles, 86–7
Davis, John, xviii, 22
Davis, Sir John, 57–8
Dent & Co., 15–6, 27, 80, 142, 215
Dickens, John, 52, 66
Diplomats and Diplomacy, xxiii, 59–60, 101
Drake, Sir Francis, xix–xx, 3, 72
Dress, 48, 98, 179–82
Dryden, John, xxi
Dutch, xv, xx–xxiii, 4–5, 7–8, 10–12, 22, 26, 31, 33, 37, 39–40, 54–6, 74–5, 77, 82, 89, 100, 110, 114, 130, 134–5, 190, 215, 243
Dundas, Philip, 53, 168, 206
Durham, Lord, 126

Dutronquoy, Gaston, 199, 210
Dwellings, 5–6, 17, 167–76, 239
Dyaks, 19, 29, 78–9, 108, 128
Dyce, William, 212

East India Company, xvii, xx–xxiv, xxvi, 3–5, 7–17, 20, 22–3, 25, 29, 34, 37, 41, 47, 51–2, 54–5, 57, 59, 63, 66, 72, 75, 77, 81, 87, 89–90, 99–100, 102–3, 108, 113–14, 127, 145–7, 151–2, 162, 164–5, 168–9, 186, 190, 199, 208–9
East Indiamen, 23–6, 28, 47, 51
Edo, 122, 203
Education, 53, 79, 205–7, 238–40
Egypt, 29, 118–9
Egyptian Transit Company, 118
Einstein, Albert, 209
Elgin, Lord, xxv
Elizabeth I, xx, 3, 6, 71
Elliott, Captain Charles, 57, 141–2
England, 25, 28, 52, 77, 84, 97, 113–4, 116, 119, 130, 163, 165, 169, 175, 178, 192, 223
Enright, D. J. 244
Eurasians, 10, 55–6, 63, 83, 88, 127, 132, 167, 180–1, 185, 205
Ever-Victorious Army, 84–5
Extra-territoriality, xxviii, 68, 156–7, 234

Farquhar, Major, 38, 55–6, 138
Fauconnier, Henri, 94, 214–5
Federated Malay States, xxv, 43, 65, 67, 129–30, 181–2, 194, 201, 229
Federation of Malaya, 240
Fendall, John, 75
Fitch, Robert, xix–xx
Flint, James, 208
Floris, Peter, 4
Foochow, xxiv, 27–8, 30, 60, 151
Food, 177–80, 196
Foreign Mud, 103
Forrest, Captain Thomas, xvii, 88
Fort Cornwallis, 53
Fort Marlborough, xxi, 5, 9–10, 33, 89, 100
Fortune, Robert, 87, 105, 121, 209
Francis, John, 199
French in the Far East, xxi, xxvii, 12, 23, 39, 47–8, 59, 61, 153–4, 197, 223
Frobisher, Martin, 21
Fujiyama, 202

Gama, Vasco da, xix
Genoa, 160
George III, xxiii, 14, 59
Georgetown (Penang), 89, 136–7, 141, 145–6, 178, 200
Gillespie, Colonel, 40–1
Gillingham, 166
Gimson, F. C., 233, 237
Gladstone, W. E., 80
Glasgow, 27
Goa, xx
Goble, Jonathan, 183
Gordon, Charles, xxvii, 83–5, 98–9
Gough, Sir Hugh, 42
Government, 9, 51–70, 126–33
Grayburn, Sir Vandeleur, 227
Greenock, 27
Gujeratis, 135
Gutzlaff, Carl, 102–4

Hakone, 202
Hamilton, Alexander, 72, 74, 209
Hankow, xxv, 27, 30, 105, 151, 160–1, 221
Harcourt, Rear-Admiral, 233, 237
Hare, Alexander, 74–76
Hastings, Warren, 72
Hatch, Arthur, 100
Havelock, Henry, 98
Haydn, Josef, 211
Hayne, Benjamin, 10–11
Health, 7–8, 41, 44, 48, 93, 164–5
Henessey, Sir John Pope, 144
Hickey, William, 14–5, 114–5, 177
Hirado, xxi, 4, 6–7, 22, 31, 101
Holland, 39
Hong Kong, xv, xxiv, xxvi–xxviii, 16–18, 20–1, 29–30, 32, 36–8, 42–7, 56–8, 62, 69, 73, 76, 79–80, 83–4, 104, 107–9, 113, 119–120, 125, 128–33, 136–7, 141–5, 147–53, 155, 158, 160–2, 165–6, 171–3, 177, 179, 183, 187–9, 194–5, 197–9, 202, 204–9, 212, 216–7, 225–8, 233, 235–41, 243–5
Hong Kong and Shanghai Banking Corporation, 18, 223, 227, 239
Hong Kong Volunteer Corps, 46, 226–27
Hope, Admiral Sir James, 84
Hornaday, W. T., 185, 198
Hotels, 197, 199–202, 227, 229–30
Hunting, 190–4, 223

Hyogo, xxv

Ibans, 78, 128
Ieyasu, 123
Imperial Airways, 125
India, xv, xvii, xix, 3, 7, 10–12, 25, 29, 34–8, 41, 43, 51–4, 58, 77, 87, 96, 98–9, 108, 117–8, 129, 152, 172–3, 209, 225, 231, 240
Indian Mutiny, xxvi, 37, 137, 140, 180
Indian Ocean, xvi, 11
Indians in Malaya, 9–10, 34, 65, 88, 92, 94, 128, 172, 176, 187, 195, 230 (See also Bengalis, Gujeratis, Tamils.)
Indo-China, xxvii
Indo-China Steam Navigation Company, 21
Indonesian Archipelago, xv–xvi, xx, xxiii, 5, 18, 22, 29, 40, 49, 77, 86–7, 183, 237
Innes, Emily, 181–2
Innes, James, 103
International Settlement. See Shanghai.
Ipoh, 193
Ireland, 35, 127

Jacarta, xxi
James I, 5, 71
James II, 72
Japan, xvi–xvii, xx–xxi, xxv–xxvi, 4–8, 16–19, 21–2, 31, 33, 35, 43, 47, 71, 80, 85, 100–1, 104, 109, 119, 122–4, 128–9, 132, 151–2, 156, 158–60, 166, 174–5, 183, 193, 196, 200–4, 215, 221–34, 241–2
Japan Herald, 216
Japan Times Overland Mail, 216
Jardine, William, 13, 102–3, 131–2
Jardine Matheson, 13, 15–16, 21, 27, 143, 160, 215–6, 223, 235, 237, 239
Java, xv, xx, 5, 8, 25, 39–41, 48, 54–6, 74–5, 164–5, 175, 234
Jehol, 59, 209
Jesselton, 163, 189, 228
Johore, xxv, 65, 72, 74, 90, 101, 210, 229, 231–2
Jourdain, John, 22
Junk Ceylon, 11, 127, 168
Justice, 61, 66–7, 156–8, 161

Kanagawa, xxv
Karuizawa, 203

Kedah, xxiii, xxv, 65, 201
Keeling, Captain, 5, 22, 76
Kelantan, xxv, 65, 229–30
Kennedy, Sir Arthur, 143
Keswick, J. H., 223
Kiangsi, 87
Kirkup, James, 244
Kiukiang, xxv, 151, 160, 221
Kiungchow, 150
Klang, 90, 93
Kobe, xvii, xxv, 17, 128, 160, 180, 187–9
Kongmoon, 150
Kowloon, xxiv, 31, 43, 197, 226–7
Kuala Kangsar, 121–2
Kuala Lumpur, 35–6, 64, 90, 93, 124, 130, 136–7, 172, 183, 187, 193, 200, 206, 216, 230, 241, 243–4
Kuching, 78–9, 163, 165, 170, 187, 189, 228
Kuomintang, 83, 159–60, 235
Kyoto, 123, 202

Labuan, xxiv, xxvii, 79, 109, 162, 204
Labuan Trading Company, 19
Lancaster, James, xx, 3–4, 6, 21–2
Laos, xxvii
Lawrence, Sir Thomas, 14
Leith, Sir George, 52, 146
Leonowens, Anna, 67, 175
Leslie, Mary, 164
Leyden, John, 207–8
Light, Francis, 11–12, 31, 36–7, 39, 51–2, 66, 89, 127, 136–7, 140–1, 145–6, 166–7, 173, 180, 182
Lintin Island, 15, 26–7, 102
Lister, Charles, 71–2
Literature, 213–5
Liverpool, 27, 30
Lockhart, Dr, William, 104
Logan, J. R., 175, 208
Lombock, 168
London, xvii, xx, 6, 11, 17, 27, 30, 44, 52, 99, 113, 116, 118–20, 125, 132, 147, 163, 172,, 180, 205, 209, 226, 239
London Missionary Society, 100–1, 103, 105, 108
Lord Jim, 214
Low, Sir Hugh, 91

Macao, xv, xxii, 15, 17, 29, 59, 77, 102, 104, 120, 134–5, 137, 142, 144, 162, 165, 170, 190–1, 199

Macartney, Lord, xxiii, 59, 121, 209
Macassar, xxi, 82, 87
Macbeth, xix
Mackintosh, Captain William, 24
Madras, 3, 9, 14, 35, 37–9, 52, 117, 119, 164
Madeira, 116
Magellan, Ferdinand, xv, xix
Malabar, xix, 92
Malacca, xvi, xix–xxii, xxiii, xxvi, 23, 38–9, 49, 54, 74, 90–1, 101, 103, 120, 124, 130, 134–5, 139, 146–7, 180, 182, 198, 201, 208, 240
Malacca Observer, 215
Malaisie, 94, 214
Malay Archipelago, The, 87
Malay Regiment, 43
Malaya and the Malays, xv–xix, xxiii–xxiv, xxvi–viii, 3, 8–10, 20, 29–30, 33, 35, 37–8, 43–4, 47, 49, 53, 54–6, 58, 62–5, 67, 73, 74–8, 81–2, 88–94, 96–7, 100, 103–4, 109, 113, 118, 120, 121–2, 125, 127–36, 139, 165–70, 172–9, 182–3, 186, 188–9, 192–4, 196, 200–1, 204–5, 208–9, 216–17, 225–6, 228–33, 237, 240–5
Malaya Volunteer Corps, 47, 229
Malayan Union, 240
Malaysia, 240
Manchuria, 20, 85, 121, 221, 235
Manchu Emperors of China, xvii, 70, 73, 83, 85, 186
Manila, xv, 41
Mannington, Philip, 146
Mao Tse-tung, 235
Marine, East India Company's, 36–7, 49–50
Marsden, William, 207
Matheson, James, 13
Maugham, Somerset, xviii, 166, 213–5
Mauritius, 47
Maxwell, James Argyle, 140
Mayhew, Thomas, 44
Medhurst, W. D., 107
Melville, Viscount, 52–3
Mercenaries, 81–6
Mergui, xxi, 4, 72, 81–2, 121, 164, 168
Messageries Maritimes, 120
Michelbourne, Sir Edward, 5
Michie, Alexander, 17–18
Middleton, Henry, 3, 4, 6, 22–3

Military Policy and Activities, 33–50, 159–60, 225–32, 243
Milne, William, 101, 103, 208
Mindanac, 49–50, 79
Missionaries, 99–108, 166, 168, 203, 225, 234, 236–7
Molière, 117
Moluccas, xix–xx, 8, 48
Mongkut, 67–8
Mongolia, 121, 193
Monetecorvino, John of, xix
Montreal, 239
Moral Standards, 9–10, 40, 165–7, 197–9, 217, 244
Morrison, D. Robert, 100–3, 208–9
Moses, Charles Lee, 80
Mozart, 211
Mukden, 85
Municipal Government, 144–9, 153–61, 223, 234
Music, 210
Mysore, 38

Nagasaki, 17
Nanking, xxiv, 42, 57, 61, 85, 107, 154, 194, 235
Napier, Lord, 59, 102
Napoleon, xxi, 35, 54, 117
Nash, John, 137
Navy in the Far East, 36, 45, 47–50, 52–3, 161
Negri Sembilan, xxv, 64, 201
New Brunswick, 95
New England, 27
New Guinea, 87
New Zealand, 88, 119, 243
Newspapers, 215–7
Nias, 89
Nice, John, 101
Ningpo, xxii, xxiv, 41–2, 151, 166, 211–3
Noone, Patrick, 213
Nootka, 12
North Borneo, xxiv, xxvi–xii, 65, 76, 80–1, 167, 193, 228
North China Daily News, 216
North China Herald, 216
Nova Scotia, 27

Opium, xx–xxiv, 12, 15, 16, 26–7, 100
Opium Clippers, 27
Opium Wars, xvii, xxiv, 15–16, 35, 41–2, 59, 104, 151, 162

Oregon, 104
Orwell, George, 214
Osaka, 194, 202, 211–12
Ossian, 117
Ostend, 11, 114
Outcast of the Islands, 214
Overseas Missionary Fellowship, 237
Overland Route, 117–20

Pahang, xv, 64
Painting, 209–10
Palambangan, 39
Palestine, 242
Palmerston, Lord, 79, 141
Papineau, Jean Louis, 73
Parker, Peter, 104
Parkinson, C. Northcote, 24, 63, 100, 140, 221, 243
Passage to India, 215
Pearl Harbour, xvii, 224, 226, 229
Pearl River, xxii, 12, 136
Peitaiho, 202, 222
Pegu, xix–xx, 25
Peking, xxiii–xxiv, xxvii, 16, 35, 41–2, 59–60, 104, 121, 151, 154–5, 193, 202, 209, 235
Penang, xvii–xviii, xx, xxii–xxiii, xxvi, 12, 29, 31, 36–7, 39, 47–8, 50–4, 66, 89–90, 101–1, 113, 117, 124, 127–8, 132, 134, 136–7, 139–41, 143, 145–7, 164–9, 171, 173, 175, 177–8, 180, 182, 186–7, 195–7, 199–200, 206, 215, 229–30, 240–1
Peninsular and Oriental Line, 21, 27, 29, 113, 118–20, 231
Perak, xxv, 38, 63, 90–1, 96, 121, 124
Perlis, xxv, 65
Perry, Commodore, xxv
Persian Gulf, xix
Phaulkon, xxii, 68, 82
Philippines, xvi, xix, xxv, 19, 49, 237
Phillips, W. E., 169
Pickering, Walter, 62, 121
Pidgin English, 13
Piracy, 3, 32, 49–50, 63, 72, 78–9, 142
Pnom Penh, 71
Police, 156–60
Polo, Marco, xix
Pondicherry, 38
Population, 128
Port Dickson, 43, 201
Port Swettenham, 209

Portuguese, xv–xvi, xix–xxii, 5, 12, 15, 17, 25–6, 33–4, 101, 110, 130, 134–5, 165, 170, 190, 207, 211
Potianak, 75
Pottinger, Sir Henry, 57, 142, 147
Prince of Wales Island (see Penang).
Prince of Wales Island Gazette, 196–7, 215
Province Wellesley, 201
Purcell, Victor, 62, 67, 194, 208

Racing, 190–3, 195
Raffles, Olivia, 164–5, 197
Raffles, Sophia, 164–5
Raffles, Sir Stamford, xxiii, 9–10, 12, 37–41, 49, 53–6, 63, 74–5, 77, 88–9, 117–8, 136–41, 146, 164–5, 168–9, 174, 180, 186, 205, 207–9, 213
Railways, 64, 90, 124
Rainier, Admiral, 48
Rangoon, 124
Raymond, George, xx
Red Sea, 20, 117, 119–20
Reid, Andrew, 208
Repulse Bay, (Hong Kong), 202
Residents in the Malay States, 63, 65, 129
Resorts, 201–3
Richard, Timothy, 106
Rickshaw, 183
Ridley, H. N., 91, 209
Roads, 134–5
Robinson, Sir Hercules, 62
Robinson, Sir William, 148
Ross, Sir Ronald, 209
Royal Asiatic Society, 208
Royal Society, 7
Rozells, Martina, 166, 173
Rubber, 91–4, 173, 187, 209
Russia and Russians, xxii, 20, 46, 83, 85, 150 (See also White Russians)

Sabah, xxvi, 240
St Helena, xx, 23, 117
St John, Spenser, 213
Sarawak, xviii, xxiv–xxvii, 18, 49, 65, 74, 77–81, 109, 162, 166–7, 170, 228, 240
Saris, John, 4–5, 123
Sassoon, Frederick, 132
Sassoon, Sir Victor, 172
Scholars and Scholarship, 7, 102, 207–9

Science and Scientists, 77, 86–7, 91, 209
Scott, Sir Giles Gilbert, 109
Scott, James, 12, 39, 52, 90, 127, 145, 167
Scott, Sir Walter, 117
Selangor, xxv, 63–4, 82, 90, 96, 124, 136, 182
Seramban, 193
Shaftesbury, Lord, 103
Shakespeare, William, 117
Shameen, 62, 151, 160–1
Shamshuipo, 227
Shanghai, xvii, xxii–xxvi, 16–18, 21, 27, 29–30, 32, 35–6, 42–6, 57, 60, 68–9, 73, 83–6, 104–5, 107–9, 113, 119, 128–9, 132–3, 143–4, 149–62, 167–8, 170–3, 175, 177–9, 183–4, 187–9, 192–200, 202, 204–9, 211–12, 215–7, 221, 223–5, 227–8, 233–7, 239
Shanghai Defence Force, 35, 47
Shanghai Recorder, 216
Shanghai Volunteer Corps, 45–7, 83, 155, 158–60, 222, 225, 234,
Shansi, 106–7
Sherwood, Mrs., 115–6
Shimadzu, 123
Ships and Sailors, 3–4, 20–32, 45, 47–50, 113–21, 123–4
Shooting, 194
Shops, 176–7, 231
Siam, xvi, xix, xxi, xxv, xxvii–viii, 3–5, 8, 11, 23, 26, 30, 33, 67–8, 72, 79, 81–2, 85, 94–6, 104, 120–1, 124, 127–8, 164, 168–9, 179, 237, 242,
Siam Times, 216
Simla, 201
Singapore, xvii, xxiii, xxvi, 11–12, 17–21, 27, 29, 31, 36–8, 43–7, 52, 55–6, 62–3, 66, 73–4, 78–9, 90–1, 101, 103, 108, 113, 117–20, 123–5, 128, 131–2, 134–41, 143, 145–7, 161–4, 168–73, 176–80, 182–5, 187–8, 190–2, 195, 198–201, 204, 209–17, 228–33, 237, 239–45
Singapore Chronicle, 211, 215
Singapore Free Press, 119, 191, 215
Singapore Volunteer Corps, 46–7, 60
Sinkiang, 121
Slavery, 10, 89, 175
Social Activities, 14–15, 165, 185–203
South China Post, 215

Spain and Spanish, xix, xxv, 41, 101
Speedy, Captain T. C., 82, 122
Sports, 190–6
Srivijaya, 136
Stanley (Hong Kong), 57, 227, 233
Stanton, Rev. Vincent, 206
Starkey, William, 4
Straits Settlements, xxiii, xxvi–vii, 5, 29, 36–7, 58, 62–3, 65, 76, 90, 109, 118–9, 123–4, 130–2, 140–1, 144–7, 163, 175, 186, 190, 192, 198–9, 201, 211, 216, 229
Straits Settlements Volunteers, 229, 230, 232
Straits Times, 215
Studd, C. T., 107
Suez, 27, 117–9, 186
Suez Canal, xix, 18, 20, 22, 28, 30, 113, 117, 119–20, 200
Sulu, 49–50, 79
Sumatra, xv, xx–xxii, 11, 26, 76, 81, 89, 168, 182, 207, 214
Sun Yat-sen, 85, 102
Surrey, 164
Sutton, One-Arm, xxvii, 83, 85–6, 193
Swettenham, Sir Frank, 62–5, 121–2, 136–7
Swift, Jonathan, 127
Szechwan, 85

Taiping (Malaya), 43, 172, 193
Taiping Rebellion, xxvii, 45, 73, 83–6, 98, 154–5
Tamils, 65, 88, 92, 167, 195, 229, 242
Tanglin, 43–4, 139, 187–9, 195
Taylor, Hudson, 104–6, 120
Tea, xxii–xxiii, 13, 15, 27–30, 87, 151, 209
Tea Clippers, 27–9, 151
Teak Trade, 94–6
Teak Wallah, 96
Ternate, xix
Thailand (See Siam)
Thatched House Club, 132
Theatre, 211–13
Thompson, G. H., 103
Thomson, John Turnbull, 178, 210
Tibet, xvi
Tierra del Fuego, xix
Tientsin, 107, 124, 151, 160–1, 235
Times, 60
Timor, xx

Tin Mines and Miners, 63–4, 88–9, 96–7, 127, 241–3
Tinghai, 41–2
Tippu Sultan, 38
Tokyo, 109, 123–4, 170
Tomlin, Jacob, 104
Tonking, xvi, xxi, xxvii, 6, 23, 165
Torrey, Joseph W., 76, 80
Town Planning, 135–44, 151–2
Trade in the Eastern Seas, 24
Trade and Traders, xxii–xxiv, 3–21, 51, 71–2, 163–4, 169–70, 234, 236–7, 239
Transport, 17–18, 20–32, 114–25, 182–4
Trans-Siberian Railway, 20
Treaty Ports, 124, 128, 132, 150–61
Tregonning, K. C., 100
Trengganu, xv, 65
Tsiyanfu, 107
Turkey Company, xix
Turner, Cecil, 107
Twining, Thomas, 115–16

United States, xv, 61, 179
Urban Settlements, 134–61
Uri, 145

Vacations, 200–3
Vancouver, 239
Vancouver Island, 12
Venice, 160, 170
Victoria, Queen, 150
Victoria (Hong Kong), 43, 136, 143, 226
Volunteer Forces, 35, 45–8, (See also Hong Kong Volunteer Corps, Malaya Volunteer Corps, Shanghai Volunteer Corps, Singapore Volunteer Corps, Straits Settlements Volunteer Corps.)
Von Overbeck, Baron, 80

Waghorn, Thomas, 118
Wallace, Alfred Russel, xviii, 18, 77, 86–7, 163, 166, 168, 180, 209
Wanchai (Hong Kong) 143
Ward, Frederick T., 83–4
Wathen, J., 210
Watson, Sir Malcolm, 209
Weddell, Captain John, xxii
Weiheiwai, xxiv, 150, 202, 222
Wellington, Duke of, 52
Westminster, 41, 132, 143
Weston, Walter, 203

Whampoa, 15, 25, 51
Whampoa, H. A. K., 131, 179
White, Samuel, 3, 68, 72, 81–2
White Russians, 46, 159, 198, 225
Wickham, Henry, 91
Wilberforce, William, 10
Wilson, Adam, 76
Winstedt, Richard, 208
Women, 9–10, 19, 106, 162–7, 198, 240
Wuhu, 150

Xavier, St Francis, 110

Yangchow, 107
Yangtse, xxiv, xxvii, 28, 30, 50, 73, 124,
    150–2, 160–1, 221, 235,
Yokohama, xvii–xviii, xv, 17, 19, 31, 43
    50, 113, 120, 124, 128, 160, 165,
    170, 177, 200, 202, 216
Young, Sir Mark, 226–7, 237–8
Yu Hsien, 107

DATE DUE

5/24			

GAYLORD   PRINTED IN U.S.A.